In Pursuit of Right and Justice

In Pursuit of
Right and Justice

Edward Weinfeld as Lawyer and Judge

William E. Nelson

NEW YORK UNIVERSITY PRESS
New York and London

NEW YORK UNIVERSITY PRESS
New York and London
www.nyupress.org

Library of Congress Cataloging-in-Publication Data
Nelson, William Edward, 1940–
In pursuit of right and justice :
Edward Weinfeld as lawyer and judge / William E. Nelson.
p. cm.
Includes bibliographical references and index.
ISBN 0-8147-5828-2 (cloth : alk. paper)
1. Weinfeld, Edward, 1901–1988.   2. Judges—New York (State)—
New York—Biography.   3. United States. District Court (New York :
Southern District)—Biography.   I. Title.
KF373.W348N45   2004
347.73'14'092—dc22   2004007007

New York University Press books are printed on acid-free paper,
and their binding materials are chosen for strength and durability.

Manufactured in the United States of America

10 9 8 7 6 5 4 3 2 1

To John Sexton

Contents

Preface   ix

Introduction   1

1   Always a New Yorker   7

2   Youth   17

3   Getting Started   31

4   Family   58

5   Politics and Public Service   76

6   Friendship   97

7   The Making of a Judge   113

8   The Patriarch: Edward Weinfeld's Judicial Style   133

9   The Liberal: Edward Weinfeld's Judicial Values   156

10   Teacher and Mentor   174

11   The Judge as Societal Advisor   194

12   The Blessings and Tribulations of Age   207

13   And the Just Shall Bring Forth Wisdom   221

Notes   229

Index   285

About the Author   291

Preface

As a first-year law student in the autumn of 1962, I became fascinated by the question of how judges actually decide cases. In my second year of law school, I took the Legal Process course, in which Norman Dorsen taught the famous Hart and Sacks materials. Although I developed immense admiration for and a lifelong friendship with Norman and great respect for Professors Hart and Sacks, whom I later came to know, the course itself did not address my empirical concerns. Indeed, I received my lowest grade in law school in Legal Process and an implicit message that I was fascinated by the wrong question.

A little more than a year later, my clerkship with Judge Weinfeld gave me the answers I was seeking. As Weinfeld's law clerk, I enjoyed the privilege of observing how an outstanding jurist functioned at an extraordinary level of sophistication. I came to appreciate that the outcome of litigation was largely a product of effective fact-finding and analysis.

I tried to articulate my understanding of how Weinfeld decided cases in my article, "Judge Weinfeld and the Adjudicatory Process: A Law Finder in an Age of Judicial Lawmakers," 50 *N.Y.U.L. Rev.* 980, 982 (1975), which the judge told me accurately captured the essentials of his decisionmaking process. But the academy was largely unpersuaded. I distinctly remember a conversation in which Duncan Kennedy, after reading a draft of the article, expressed a view that no judge in the late twentieth century possibly could function as I claimed Weinfeld functioned. And, I remember a debate with Bob Gordon on the pages of the *Law and History Review*, where I defended, many would say implausibly, what I understood to be Weinfeld's faith that law has substantive meaning and content derived from fundamental principles of justice.

I owe a great deal to Norman Dorsen, Bob Gordon, Henry Hart, Duncan Kennedy, Al Sacks, and others like them who, however much they disagree with each other, all understand that substantive judicial judgments contain an important political ingredient. They have forced me to continue striving to articulate how law can be something other than politics, and what we can learn today from the legacy of Edward Weinfeld. They and, of course, Weinfeld himself are the intellectual grandparents of this book.

I am also indebted to many others. First and foremost are the members of the Weinfeld family. The judge's two daughters, Ann Schulman and Fern Cohen, have met with me, talked by telephone on many occasions, and thereby provided invaluable information about their father and their family. They also have read several drafts of the book, offered many useful suggestions and much helpful advice, and provided photographs for the book from their personal collections. Fern has also graciously shared with me her March 2000 manuscript, "Included Out (Excluded In) . . . Mostly about My Father, Tennis, Me, and Freud . . . ," which she has since revised for publication and on which I have relied extensively both for facts and for interpretation. Amy Schulman did invaluable work when she taped a series of oral interviews with her grandfather, and she generously permitted me to use the transcripts of those interviews.

I also placed considerable reliance on *Edward Weinfeld: A Judicious Life*, published in 1998 by the Federal Bar Foundation. I am grateful to the committee of P. Kevin Castel, Barry H. Garfinkel, John G. Koetl, Mitchell A. Lowenthal, Amy Schulman, and Whitney North Seymour, Jr., for its work in producing this book. Finally, I need to thank Judge Weinfeld's secretary, the late Marie Vollrath, who in addition to shepherding me and many others through the year of our clerkships, performed yeoman service in organizing and boxing Judge Weinfeld's papers following his death. Her work made it possible for me to do the research required for this biography in far less time than it might otherwise have taken. Barbara Wilcie Kern continued where Marie Vollrath left off by developing a catalogue for the judge's papers. Barbara also did outstanding work in cite checking the manuscript before it was sent to the printer.

Many people have read this biography and contributed valuable ideas. I presented drafts to a day-long conference of Weinfeld clerks and family members in June 2001, as well as to New York University's Legal History Colloquium. I also circulated a penultimate draft to all former Weinfeld law clerks. So many colleagues, law clerks, and participants in the Colloquium provided helpful feedback that I cannot name them all, but I must especially single out Alex Aleinikoff, Vicki Been, Barry Garfinkel, John

Goldberg, John Koetl, Bill LaPiana, Dan Levitt, Bob Litt, Mitch Lowenthal, Liam Murphy, Victoria Nourse, and Bruce Yannett. Martin Lipton has made himself available to help with the book in every way I have needed aid, and Bill Eskridge has continued to press me on my understanding of Weinfeld's jurisprudence.

Jonathan Martin was an unusually able and effective research assistant during the period I wrote most of the first draft of the book, while Lisa Mihajlovic performed with great ability and patience all the administrative and secretarial chores involved in the preparation of a book for publication. My thanks to both. The Filomen D'Agostino and Max E. Greenberg Faculty Research Fund of New York University School of Law provided major research support, and Dean Richard Revesz provided additional support toward the costs of publication, for which I am most grateful.

This book is dedicated to John Sexton, who has contributed more to my life than anyone except the members of my own immediate family. When I first came to know John in the early 1980s, I introduced him to Judge Weinfeld and, over the years, the three of us had several wonderful lunches together. While the judge was in his final illness, John became a candidate to be dean of NYU Law School. When I visited the judge two days before his death and he asked how the race for dean was proceeding, I reported my optimism that John ultimately would be selected. The judge smiled. I know how proud he would be of the work John did in transforming his alma mater from an excellent law school into an exciting center of legal intellectual activity unsurpassed anywhere in the world.

Finally there is my family, Elaine, Leila, and Greg, who have survived my writing of another book, and Judge Weinfeld himself. As I sit drafting these acknowledgments and gazing at his photograph, I worry that my biography of the judge is not good enough. I am convinced that Weinfeld's jurisprudence can contribute importantly to maintaining the rule of law in the twenty-first century, but I fear that I have failed to articulate adequately why this is so. I can only ask readers to look beyond my failings to one of the great figures to sit on the twentieth-century American bench.

William E. Nelson

Introduction

Edward Weinfeld was born in obscurity on Manhattan's Lower East Side. But he did not die in obscurity. An article-length obituary appeared the day after his death in the *New York Times*, followed by an editorial the next day, and he was buried from Temple Emanu-El, New York's preeminent Reform Jewish synagogue. His death also was noted in national media such as the *Washington Post*, the *Los Angeles Times*, and the *San Francisco Chronicle*.[1]

The *Times* obituary noted that Weinfeld was "one of the nation's most respected Federal judges" and had "attain[ed] a reputation that extended far beyond his own court." He "was known for dedication and fairness of such a high order that he became a legend in legal circles"; the article added that "[l]awyers felt compelled to raise their own performance when appearing in his courtroom because of his high standards." The article finally quoted Supreme Court Justice William Brennan to the effect that "'[t]here is general agreement on bench and bar throughout the nation that there is no better judge on any court.'"[2]

On the next day—that of his funeral—the *Times* entitled its lead editorial "The Devotion of Judge Weinfeld." It described Weinfeld as "the most admired judge on the Federal bench," with a "sense of fairness, earnestness and commitment to doing justice [that] were conspicuous," and quoted a lawyer's statement that "'[w]hen you're in his court . . . , you know you're before the bar of justice.'" It concluded that it would have been "'easier to salute him . . . if he had laid claim to some innovative legal philosophy or sought attention through "great" opinions or a monopoly of "important" cases.' Instead, Judge Weinfeld's career was distinguished by 'the purity of its devotion and its quiet dedication to the business of judging.'"[3]

Despite the praise lavished on him at his death, it remains unclear whether Edward Weinfeld's life and career will have lasting significance.

After all, he never rose above the rank of United States district judge. Throughout his career, he was thus only one of several hundred trial judges in the federal judicial system. Arguably, as he always maintained,[4] he sat on the most important federal trial court —the United States District Court for the Southern District of New York—but, even on this court, he was at any given time only one among some twenty judges, nearly all of whom have been or will be forgotten after their deaths.

Thus, Weinfeld will not enjoy lasting fame because he held some uniquely high office, such as justice of the Supreme Court of the United States, that few others attain. Nor will he be remembered because he used judicial office to generate new legal doctrines. Unlike his friend and colleague Judge Learned Hand, Weinfeld did not author opinions, such as *Masses Publishing Co. v. Patten*[5] and *United States v. Carroll Towing Co.*,[6] which gave rise to important legal doctrines in areas as diverse as the First Amendment and the law of negligence.[7] And, Weinfeld's decisions, at the time he handed them down, received no more publicity on average than cases decided by many other federal judges.

Some, accordingly, might think that a biography of Edward Weinfeld is unwarranted. One former law clerk, for example, is "pessimistic" about "Judge Weinfeld's place in history." This clerk comments,

> I fear he will be forgotten in a generation or so; indeed I doubt that many law students today have any idea who he is. The people who get the attention are those with agendas; it is the virtues of the polemicist that attract notice, not those of the careful and invariably correct lawyer. [Thus,] . . . Weinfeld . . . is [not] likely to survive. And that is, of course, far more of a negative reflection on our own culture than on the judge.[8]

There are three reasons, however, why such pessimism is unwarranted and why Weinfeld should enjoy a secure place in history.

First, the judge's climb from humble origins to distinction provides an excellent illustration of the way Catholics and Jews descended from turn-of-the-century immigrants were assimilated into the mainstream of New York and ultimately American life during the course of the twentieth century. Indeed, Weinfeld, at least at the margin, contributed to the process of assimilation by the way in which he trained a younger generation of law clerks, nearly all from immigrant backgrounds, to rise to the pinnacle of New York's legal profession. The narrative that follows tells the story of this climb and process of assimilation. It begins with the arrival of Abraham Weinfeld, Edward's father, as a pants presser working and living amid anti-Semitism on the impoverished Lower East Side; by the end of the story, Weinfeld's former law clerks will be ensconced in positions of power, prestige, and wealth as leaders of the New York bar, corporate entrepreneurs, and professors at leading law schools.

Weinfeld's climb, it is suggested, is not irrelevant to the many people of all colors, skins, faiths, and tongues who today are striving to improve their economic well-being and to live with their fellow Americans in harmony. His climb is not simply a tale of how culturally comparable, white Europeans coalesced into a new power structure better able than Anglo-Saxons alone to dominate the people of and from the Third World. On the contrary, the techniques of assimilation pursued by Weinfeld to advance his own and his acolytes' careers can still serve as paradigms for future upward mobility on the part of others.

A second reason to remember the life of Edward Weinfeld is that he left an unusually rich collection of personal papers that enable us to examine the compromises he had to make in order to attain professional advancement. In part, his story tells us that the descendants of turn-of-the-century immigrants did not achieve success without significant sacrifice. In particular, forthcoming chapters will show that, in order to find time to pursue his career, Weinfeld disciplined himself to ignore many of the ordinary diversions of life; popular culture and spectator sports other than tennis, for instance, were totally outside his field of vision. More significantly, Weinfeld sacrificed some, though not all, aspects of family relationships.

Perhaps, the study of Weinfeld's life can even help people who are trying to balance their own personal and professional lives. Weinfeld may not have achieved the right balance and may not even have been conscious of the choices he made to reach his balance. Obviously, there is no one right balance. Nonetheless, a reader who is now pondering how much of life to forego in order to gain professional acclaim can gain understanding by looking back on the arguably excessive sacrifices Weinfeld made.

Weinfeld's life is not unique, however, in providing a vehicle for studying the roads to upward mobility and success, or the tolls that are exacted for traveling them. We could just as readily study innumerable other people who have achieved success and paid a high personal price for doing so. It is for a third reason that Weinfeld's life and career were significant, and it is this third reason that made him unique.

Judge Edward Weinfeld was special because the singular style of judging he adopted permeated every aspect of his work from the bench. It made him the preeminent trial judge in twentieth-century America. Although practicing lawyers had the highest respect for his judicial style, Weinfeld never systematized it into an innovative legal philosophy that would bring him public acclaim; on the contrary, his approach always remained closely tied to his own personal values and to the historical contexts in which cases came to his court. But he did follow a distinctive jurisprudential approach. My main goal in the pages that follow will be to explicate his approach more clearly than he, as a workaday lawyer and judge, ever found it necessary to do.

Politically, Weinfeld was a fairly typical mid-twentieth-century New Dealer, and not surprisingly his jurisprudence had a liberal or progressive cast. Weinfeld was an egalitarian who was comfortable with the social welfare state and believed in government action designed to improve the lot of the disadvantaged. His belief in equality extended even to women long before today's feminism had become a fashionable cause. He also was a champion of civil liberties and individual autonomy.[9] On the surface, Weinfeld's jurisprudence appears similar to that of leading members of the Warren Court, such as Justice William J. Brennan, whose judicial career overlapped Weinfeld's, and to the jurisprudence of other progressives of their era.

But, in fact, Weinfeld's jurisprudence was markedly different. For the Warren Court and those inspired by its example, law is an instrument used to steer the course of progressive social reform.[10] Cases are seen as providing judges with opportunities to reconfigure law in a way that ultimately will lead to the reshaping of society. Indeed, the idea that judges decide cases and write opinions for the purpose of influencing social reality so permeated late-twentieth-century thought that the biographer of Learned Hand, not a notably liberal judge, saw even Hand as pursuing promotion from the Southern District to the Second Circuit Court of Appeals in order to escape the burdensome routines of fact finding that characterized the work of a trial judge. Hand, according to his biographer, wished instead to devote his time and intelligence to deciding legal issues of consequence that would influence the direction of society.[11]

Weinfeld, in contrast, found fact finding and the routine duties of a trial judge fulfilling. Unlike Hand, Weinfeld always strove to avoid making new law. Whenever he could, he tried to base decisions on preexisting rules or bedrock legal principles; he achieved just results by searching for and finding facts that called those rules and principles into play. Unlike the judges on whom late-twentieth-century academic thinkers focused their attention, Weinfeld never approached a case as a vehicle for creating legal doctrine that would change the way the world worked. His goal in every case was only to do justice between the parties. Nonetheless, his conception of justice routinely led to liberal, progressive results.

It may be tempting to pigeonhole Weinfeld as a judicially restrained liberal, rather than a liberal judicial activist such as Justice Brennan. But it would be wrong. The concept of judicial restraint, at least as it was developed by the legal process theorists of his time,[12] does not account for Weinfeld's style of decision making. The idea of deference to other branches of government, whether legislative or executive, simply did not enter his mind. He never worried about the countermajoritarian difficulty. The wishes of political majorities carried little weight in Weinfeld's courtroom; he always sought to achieve justice under law, whether others liked it or not. Weinfeld, as we shall see, often was an activist in trumping the ambitions of political actors in other branches of government when his vision of justice required.

The point is that Weinfeld's vision of justice was simultaneously a progressive one that enabled him to develop the law in a fashion that reflected societal change and an apolitical one that did not rest on contested policy judgments. In Edward Weinfeld's courtroom, fidelity to law produced just results that others can achieve only by politicizing the law. Understanding Weinfeld's approach thus might provide a means for achieving social justice in individual cases without the political divisiveness that increasingly characterizes the judiciary today.

The next twelve chapters will strive to portray Edward Weinfeld's life with attention to his personal growth as well as to his efforts at socioeconomic mobility. Most of all, the chapters will focus on Judge Weinfeld's jurisprudence, especially on its roots in his early legal practice and private life. Then, a concluding chapter can again consider the significance that should be accorded to Weinfeld and his jurisprudence in the future. The concluding chapter will summarize how enormously the world has changed in the century since Edward Weinfeld was born, grew up, and climbed out of obscurity on New York's Lower East Side. Then, it will ask whether the changes have been so great that Judge Weinfeld and his jurisprudence are no longer relevant. If so, is their irrelevance a reflection on him or on us? If we keep these questions in mind, perhaps this biography of Edward Weinfeld can teach us as much about ourselves as it can about the judge.

1

Always a New Yorker

Edward Weinfeld worked and dwelled his entire life within walking distance of the tenement on the Lower East Side in which he was born. Admittedly, Weinfeld enjoyed long walks; nonetheless, the apartment on East Sixty-sixth Street in Manhattan, to which he moved in his late sixties and in which he died only four months short of his eighty-seventh birthday, was only about three miles north of that Lower East Side tenement. And his offices, as a practicing attorney, a state government official, and, later, a federal judge were only about a mile south of his birthplace—on lower Broadway, Centre Street, and Foley Square. Except for commuting trips to Albany as a state official, Weinfeld never lived or worked north of Sixty-sixth Street or west of Broadway; indeed, until he was nearly seventy, he never lived or worked north of East Third Street. New York, or more specifically lower Manhattan, and especially Manhattan's Lower East Side, was in Weinfeld's blood.

Weinfeld related to Manhattan differently than do most people who today work or reside on the "glitzy"[1] island south of Ninety-sixth Street. Many twenty-first-century New Yorkers were born and educated elsewhere, came to the city for a job that would further their career, and ended up staying. Even those who were born in New York often attended prestigious schools and colleges outside the city and ultimately returned mainly for employment; others who work on Manhattan spend significant interludes residing in its suburbs or summering at its vacation haunts. Manhattan is a magnet whose unrivaled resources exert a forceful, cosmopolitan pull on its workers and residents. Their commitment is to the island's economic or professional opportunities, to its intellectual or artistic endeavors, to the varied sensual pleasures it offers—to "the unrivaled opportunities for working, eating, and spending that New Yorkers revel in."[2] One senses most contemporary residents would flee Manhattan if it lost the particular magnetic attraction that binds them to it.

Weinfeld's ties were different. They were of an Old World sort—they were ties, almost agrarian in nature, to the land of his youth and to its people. Although Weinfeld, of course, was not a farmer, he related to the Manhattan landscape much as his forebears had related to their ancestral landscapes in the Austro-Hungarian empire. He had both the security and the limitation of vision that come from living an entire life in one place. Every street he walked, every corner he turned held memories—memories of youth, of groups to which he had belonged, of people he had helped, of conversations he had held, of successes, and sometimes of failures. His life was completely intertwined with the streets, buildings, and people that surrounded him. He lived and worked in what one recent author has christened "working-class New York," where people who were "generous; open-minded but skeptical; idealistic but deflating of pretension; bursting with energy and a commitment to doing" sought "to revolutionize society in the name of justice and equality."[3]

Weinfeld's relationship to lower Manhattan was like his father's relation to the Galacian town of Gorlice, then in the Austrian empire and now in southeastern Poland, where he was born in the early 1860s, or his mother's relation to the Hungarian farm village of Lelesz, now in eastern Slovakia, where she was born in the mid-1870s.[4] Although lower Manhattan was far more densely populated than Gorlice, which had fewer than three thousand Jewish inhabitants, and Lelesz, with a population under two hundred Jews, its geographic dimensions were similar. From his birthplace, Weinfeld could walk two miles south to Battery Park at the southern tip of Manhattan, three miles north to Central Park in mid-Manhattan, four miles northwest to DeWitt Clinton High School, on Tenth Avenue and Fifty-ninth Street,[5] from which he was graduated in 1918, and a mile northwest to New York University, located at Fourth Street three blocks west of Broadway, where he attended law school from 1918 to 1922. The trial courts that he frequented, both state and federal, were located a mile south of his birthplace, as was the federal court of appeals; the state appellate division had its courthouse a mile to the north. And, when Weinfeld married and moved into his own apartment, it was located merely a half-block away from his birthplace, next door to which his parents still resided.

During his youth and early years of practice, Weinfeld never considered leaving the dependable confines of lower Manhattan. Everything he could possibly need—family, shelter, education, employment, food, entertainment—was within short walking distance. Like his European forebears, he would leave his birthplace only for the most special of reasons— to argue his first case in the Court of Appeals at the capital city of Albany and to marry a woman who had grown up (although he had met her in Manhattan) in the neighboring municipality of Brooklyn. What made New York different from Gorlice and Lelesz was that unlike the European towns, it offered a young man a future: merely by working hard within the boundaries of a few square miles of Manhattan, the young Weinfeld could become a great lawyer and ultimately a judge of national repute. No such opportunity had awaited his father, Abraham Weinfeld, within the confines of Gorlice. Accordingly, Abraham first left the town of his birth at the age of thirteen.[6]

Nothing certain is known about Abraham during the decade or more between his initial departure from Gorlice and his permanent settlement in New York. It is possible that he came to New York as early as 1879[7] and stayed for some undetermined amount of time before returning to Austria. It seems likely that he returned to Gorlice at some point during the 1880s because we know that, when he came to America in 1888, he left a wife and two or three children behind in Gorlice.[8] Whatever his wanderings, it seems clear that Abraham was torn during the 1870s and 1880s between his need for the security of a home in Gorlice and a competing need to earn a livelihood. He needed economic opportunity, but he yearned just as much for stability. His son Edward's relationship to lower Manhattan needs to be understood as the same quest for opportunity conjoined to stability that his father had pursued.

When Abraham Weinfeld left his wife and children in 1888 and came to New York, the immediate cause of his departure was to escape service in the Austrian army; he and two other young men fled Austria together and arrived shortly thereafter in New York.[9] Perhaps Abraham intended, as did many immigrants of that era, to have his family join him after he had established his ability to support them.[10] Or, his plan from the beginning may have been to desert his wife and leave her abandoned with their children in Europe. This too was a common phenomenon in the late nineteenth century,[11] and it is, in fact, what Abraham ultimately did.[12]

The Lower East Side to which Abraham Weinfeld came in 1888 was victimized by stark poverty and ferocious discrimination. It would remain that way for another half-century, during which his son Edward grew up and attained his early successes. During most of the half-century, the Lower East Side was probably the most densely populated place on earth.[13] It also was one of the more squalid. In his classic muckraking work, *How the Other Half Lives*, Jacob A. Riis described the Lower East Side as a place where "[d]irt and desolation reign[ed]" and "danger lurk[ed]"; where "hundreds of men, women, and children [were] every day slowly starving to death"; and where "the instinct of motherhood even was smothered by poverty and want" as the "poor abandon[ed] their children," leaving only little notes such as one Riis had read "in a woman's trembling hand: 'Take care of Johnny, for God's sake, I cannot.'"[14]

Those who controlled New York's economy and society, and for much of the time its politics, displayed little tolerance toward the poor. Recipients of public assistance, for example, were seen as people "'without habits of industry or thrift, improvident, usually physically or mentally deficient, who [were] unable through efforts of their own to gain a livelihood.'" It was "'common knowledge'" that such poor persons were "'constantly seeking, and generally receive[d] at somewhat regular intervals, public charity or assistance; they ha[d] a practically constant status as 'poor persons'; they [were] not able to maintain themselves for any long period of time even under ordinary conditions.'"[15]

Similar contempt was reserved for the working poor. Only a "very few men in every hundred or thousand," it was said, had sufficient "industry, brains and thrift" to get ahead. Wage workers, according to the same writer, remained employees of others because they had "not initiative enough to be employers themselves"; they remained "poor" because of "lack of brains, lack of wit to earn, thrift to save, and knowledge to use [their] savings." "No man who ha[d] endeavored to carry out an enterprise," according to a turn-of-the-century sermon, could avoid being "well-nigh appalled at times by the imbecility of the average man—the inability or unwillingness to concentrate on a thing and do it." Indeed, the "nature of man" was thought to be such that "the superior few and the inferior many scarcely appear[ed] to belong to the same species."[16]

This contempt for the poor typically rested on a foundation of religious and ethnic prejudice. The young Edward Weinfeld could not have avoided knowing of virulent anti-Semitism on the part of prominent people such as Henry James, who expressed shock at the "'Hebrew conquest of New York'" that was transforming the city into a "'new Jerusalem,'" and Henry Ford, who as late as the 1920s issued repeated warnings against the "'Jewish menace'" and in 1938 even accepted the Grand Cross of the German Eagle from the Nazi regime.[17] Nor was anti-Semitism confined to elites; many Americans in and out of New York

City saw Jews as "inflamed radical[s] responsible for Communist revolution in eastern Europe . . . [and] a vast conspiracy designed to enslave America."[18]

For Jewish immigrants like Abraham Weinfeld, anti-Semitism was not new; they had known it back home in Europe. They had also endured poverty as bad as, if not worse than, what they would encounter on the Lower East Side. More significant for them was the Lower East Side's hominess. With a cacophony of Yiddish voices and signs in Yiddish as well as English, the immigrants could feel that they were living and working just as they had in the old country, within a "small compass, meeting only people of their own nationality." As one immigrant observed, it was as though "we were still in our village" in Europe.[19] Thus, it was easy on the Lower East Side to "create community"—a new community in many respects like what the immigrants had left behind in Europe, but in one respect remarkably different. The vital difference was that energies that had been pent up in the old country were "unleashed in this new land of apparent boundlessness."[20]

It was in this familiar world of class, ethnic, and religious conflict, anti-Semitism, and hatred of the poor—but also a world of opportunity—that Abraham Weinfeld arrived in 1888. He began at the very bottom—as a pants presser. But soon he was rising up. By 1898, he had the ability to support a family, but instead of bringing his wife and children from Austria he married another woman, Fanny Singer, who had migrated to New York from Lelesz, Hungary, in the early 1890s. They had four children—Morris, the eldest, Edward, Bertha, and Isadore.[21]

Meanwhile, Abraham and Fanny prospered. By the time Edward was born on May 14, 1901, at 233 East Third Street, Abraham was the keeper of a saloon in the building next door, at 231 East Third Street, which in addition to the saloon contained a big kitchen and a room in the back, known as National Hall, which was large enough to accommodate sixty to eighty people. The room contained four or five pool tables serving the saloon, except on Saturday and Sunday nights, when the room was typically emptied and rented out for weddings. As Weinfeld later observed, "[i]t was a good business, and my parents had some money." As Edward was growing up, the Weinfeld family lived in a spacious apartment immediately above the saloon, which contained four bedrooms, a living room, a music room with a piano, a dining room, and a kitchen.[22] The dream that had led Abraham Weinfeld to leave Gorlice and come to New York—the dream of opportunity in conjunction with security—thus had materialized as Abraham and his family had become among the more prosperous immigrants living on the Lower East Side.

It must be emphasized, however, that Abraham Weinfeld's New York was not the New York of today. Abraham's New York was not a cosmopolitan world capital from which lives around the globe were controlled. The Lower East Side was a still small community, or group of communities, in which one's life and standing depended on the immediately surrounding group of people whom one knew. It was not today's Wall Street and Upper East Side; on the contrary, it was Gorlice transposed and writ large. It was in such a traditional European setting, not in the New York we know, that Edward Weinfeld grew up, walked, and lived much of his life.

Indeed, Edward Weinfeld walked everywhere and knew lower Manhattan in a way in which only people who walk all its streets can ever come to know it. As already noted, he walked to high school and he walked to law school; he walked to work first as a lawyer and later as a judge. He also walked for recreation. On Sundays, Weinfeld walked along an accustomed East Side route from his apartment on East Third Street to Fifth Avenue and Fifty-ninth Street and back,[23] while on workdays, if time was available, he hiked across the Brooklyn Bridge and back, typically with one of his law clerks; he would walk "as far as the stairwell at the Brooklyn side, whose railing he touched just before turning around, much like a racer in a school yard would touch a distant wall before returning."[24]

Indeed, Weinfeld walked around Manhattan whenever he could find an excuse. Frank Tuerkheimer, his clerk during the 1963–64 year, relates the following:

Walking, to the judge, however, was not as one ordinarily construed the term. The analogy to the racer was apt. One . . . afternoon, shortly before 6:00, the Judge said he was leaving and would be walking to a dinner engagement on the Upper East Side. I had a sense he was not averse to company and so I asked if I could join him on the walk. He smiled and said, "Sure."

The Federal Courthouse is located just north of Chambers Street. The destination in the upper 60's was perhaps five miles away, a fairly long distance to cover through city traffic in the hour and a quarter the judge had allowed. Keeping pace with the judge, I noticed quickly that this was not a leisurely stroll—by Canal Street it was evident that this was a

Edward Weinfeld and his eldest Granddaughter,
Amy Schulman, crossing the Brooklyn Bridge,
1964.

workout. By 14th Street, it was more of a workout than I had anticipated. Around 23rd Street I began to experience acute pain in the shins,
a pain that kept getting worse except during infrequent stops at intersections—stops compelled by red lights. As we continued, it dawned on me
that hope for relief from the increasingly painful shins depended on red
lights at intersections. In the meantime, I was trying to concentrate on
our conversation in which the judge was talking about some factual nu-
ance in an admiralty case he was in the midst of. This was not easy, pain
aside, since it was hard to hear what he said because of the street noise
and the fact that he was invariably a foot or two in front of me.

As we approached 34th Street, the light facing us was red. Thirty-
fourth Street is a major cross street and the possibility of a 30 to 60 second period of relief suddenly seemed like an awaiting paradise. I, the

law clerk in his mid-20's, wished with all my might that the light remain red. Simultaneously the Judge, in his mid-60's, said: "Frank, I hope that light changes before we get there; we have to keep moving."[25]

Two decades later, with Weinfeld in his mideighties, his walking habits remained unchanged. One hot, early summer day, after he had attended a New York University graduation function on the Upper West Side, the dean of the law school insisted that a car service be summoned to return Weinfeld, who at that time was chairman of the school's board of trustees, to his chambers. Despite his age, Weinfeld refused. He was willing to compromise with the dean and agreed to ride the subway part of the way, but the idea of passing up a walk on a summer day was more than he could accept.[26] And, a car service—well, it was beyond the pale of thought; such things simply had not existed on the Lower East Side where Weinfeld had grown up.

Weinfeld's taste in restaurants was similarly modest. One evening, the judge and Mrs. Weinfeld were invited to a restaurant by close friends. As Weinfeld subsequently explained,

> [W]e went to a place one night. I came home and I said, "I don't think I'm going to accept an invitation to go there again." I think these restaurants should serve menus where only the host has the price. I was absolutely shocked at some of the charges for entree items. I said, "You know, a family lives on that—a family of four for a week—in its food supply for what was charged for one item." I said, "I don't care how much money a man has. It isn't important; you get good, simple, wholesome food, and that's sufficient."[27]

Weinfeld's tastes were decidedly not those of wealthy New York lawyers at the outset of the twenty-first century; they were the tastes of the quintessential Lower East Sider at the beginning of the twentieth—fresh blueberry muffins from the Municipal Cafeteria for breakfast,[28] lunch at the Horn and Hardart Cafeteria[29] (a famous self-service, New York chain in which different choices were available behind glass doors, which a patron could open by inserting the proper coins to pay for the food), and a somewhat more elegant dinner at Longchamps (another old New York chain serving cocktails and modest American, never ethnic, cuisine) or Manny Wolf's (a steakhouse).[30] Despite their proximity, Weinfeld, unlike today's elite New Yorkers, never frequented the ethnic restaurants of Chinatown,

Little Italy, or Greenwich Village, or even the great Jewish restaurants of the Lower East Side, such as Ratner's and Sammy's Roumanian Steak House.

Edward Weinfeld had a deep and abiding love for his New York, such that when he left it for more than "seven, eight, or nine days" he "g[o]t kind of restless, . . . ready to return."[31] He missed the city where people knew their neighbors, helped their neighbors, and joined with their neighbors in a community in which they worked and lived their lives and through which they collectively negotiated their place in the larger nation of America.

Two incidents, which occurred when Weinfeld lost small but valuable items on the street, exemplify how he experienced New York. The first occurred in May 1967, when he lost a cufflink while paying a taxi driver. He called the lost property bureau at the police department for a week to see if it had been turned in. The second occurred in May 1975, when he lost a gold Cross pen on the subway. Again, Weinfeld's response was to write the transit authority to see if the pen had been turned in.[32]

Neither incident reflects the instincts of a jaded, twenty-first-century New Yorker. Weinfeld appears genuinely to have thought, or at least to have found it reasonable to hope, that someone would find the items he lost and then return them. His thought, or at least hope, offers insight into his New York mentality; his New York was a small community, whose inhabitants helped each other and where cufflinks and gold pens lost on street corners would eventually be returned to their rightful owner.

The tight, cohesive New York communities that Weinfeld knew, which had given the city much of its character in the first half of the twentieth century, tended to disappear during the 1950s and 1960s, as the children of the immigrants who had created the communities dispersed in New York's many suburbs and ultimately even in distant states like California and Florida.[33] But Weinfeld, whose life had gained its meaning in the immigrant, Jewish community of the Lower East Side, remained. It was only after nearly all Jews had left the neighborhood and only Ratner's, Sammy's, and the matzoh bakers of Rivington Street remained that the Weinfelds finally abandoned their East Third Street apartment and made a bold move uptown to East Sixty-sixth Street. But the move did not alter Edward Weinfeld's understanding of what it meant to be a New Yorker. Even after the Municipal Cafeteria, Horn and Hardart, Longchamps, and Manny Wolf's had closed their doors, Weinfeld continued to live a plain, simple life with his neighbors—that is, the people with whom he came into contact, now largely through his judicial work. Unlike many New Yorkers of today, he did not try to dominate or rule those within his network. Instead, he continued to try to empathize with them and help them, as his father and mother had been taught to do as children in Gorlice and Lelesz and as he had been taught to do as a young man on the Lower East Side.

2

Youth

Edward Weinfeld enjoyed a secure childhood within what he recalled as a "close family." According to Weinfeld, his mother ran "a typical Jewish household"; all day Friday "the kitchen would be going with all kinds of goods that were traditional for Friday night and for Saturday." But the Sabbath was not the only special day for the Weinfeld family. Every Wednesday afternoon was another. Because of his father's business, Weinfeld's family could not always have meals together, except on Wednesday afternoon. Then, the family would always "have a big dinner, and usually it was broiled poultry of some kind; it was a very full dinner from beginning to end, including a little wine."[1]

Weinfeld also had fond memories of "bucolic" weekends with his aunt—his mother's sister—at her home in Newark, New Jersey, when he was about nine years old. He remembered the Newark of his youth as "sort of countrified" with "trees and grass in the streets." Weinfeld and his brother, Morris, and sometimes his sister would go out to his aunt's house every two or three weeks and spend the weekend; it was "sort of a holiday weekend," and "the families were very close."[2]

As was true with many upward-aspiring, immigrant households, music was important to the Weinfeld family. There was a music room containing a piano in the family apartment, and Edward himself received violin lessons over a period of perhaps five years, between the ages of about eight and thirteen. The lessons, however, were "fleeting" and were eventually "discontinued" because the young Edward "lacked the ability or coordination" required for serious musical attainment.[3]

The young Weinfeld was much more serious about work. Before he went to high school, he worked in his father's saloon, which was located in the same building as his apartment on the floor immediately below. Edward "was the hat check boy and got tips."[4] "[T]here was little time for play," which could occur only "in moments stolen away from family obligations and chores"; "as a dutiful son," Weinfeld simply "did not steal away to hitch rides on trolleys or play at stick ball or stoop ball as many of his contemporaries did."[5]

The most important work Weinfeld did was at school—something for which he had been well prepared by his parents, who, unlike many immigrants, "only spoke English at home." He attended P.S. 188 on the Lower East Side, which was the largest public elementary school in the world. But it also was part of New York City's "extraordinary public school system," and Weinfeld found his years at P.S. 188 to be "one of the richest experiences of [his] life."[6]

Central to his education were his "very dedicated" teachers, especially one named Margaret Bradley. Bradley "was a spinster" who traveled "about an hour and a half . . . by trolley" each way between her home in the Bronx and Weinfeld's grade school on the Lower East Side. She maintained a close relationship with her students and their families; "[a]ll on her own time, she'd visit students' families after school, had tea with them." She also remembered her students and kept in touch with them after they had moved on. In fact, Weinfeld last saw Miss Bradley in 1954—approximately forty-five years after she had taught him—when he visited her in a hospital during her final illness, shortly before she died in a convent. During that hospital visit, she introduced him to the other patients in her room by saying, "'This is my boy, Eddie, whom I talked about.'" As he well knew, he had always been one of "her favorites."[7]

"Miss Margaret," as Weinfeld called her, was a truly "extraordinary person,"[8] whose very presence in Weinfeld's life implanted a set of important values. Here was an Irish Catholic spinster bringing the upper-class, English culture of afternoon tea into the homes of Jewish immigrants on New York's Lower East Side. By doing so, she not only taught those immigrants and their children how to perform a particular cultural ceremony; she also identified for them the culture central to becoming an American. In today's multicultural New York, no teacher has anything resembling such power.

In large part, Margaret Bradley's cultural power rested on the fact that her efforts epitomized the New York City school system's policy of acculturating immigrants and promoting their assimilation into the American mainstream. Her taking afternoon tea was merely one small segment of a larger, coherent cultural agenda to "convert . . . the children of the immigrants of all races and languages into sturdy, independent American citizens." As part of this goal, teachers "[b]y virtue of their speech, their attitude, their manners, their dress, . . . set a model." Although teachers never said, "'Emulate us because we're Americans,'" they "sort of breathed Americanism all over you, [and] you absorbed it."⁹

Indeed, the entire curriculum was focused on promoting the assimilation of immigrants into what educators understood as a superior American culture. Central to the curriculum, for both practical and cultural reasons, was the teaching of English; in the words of President Theodore Roosevelt,

> We have room for but one language here, and that is the English language; for we intend to see that the crucible turns our people out as Americans, of American nationality, and not as dwellers in a polyglot boardinghouse; and we have room for but one sole loyalty, and that is loyalty to the American people.¹⁰

As the leading historian of the immigrant experience in New York City's public schools has observed, "Linguistic transformation was central to making Americans out of immigrants."¹¹

Like most children of Jewish immigrants of his era, Weinfeld appears to have been eager to absorb the school system's message of assimilation.¹² Like other children, he also may have paid a price for being assimilated. One child of immigrants, perhaps more sensitive than most, was "appall[ed]," for example, "to think what an immense transformation I had to work on myself in order to become what I have become"— a transformation involving "a kind of treason in it: treason toward my family."¹³ Here, it might be worth noting that, while Weinfeld always remained a dutiful son toward his parents, he became quite distant after their death from his brother, Morris, and other more distant relatives, and he was never close to his wife's family. We can only speculate whether his own process of assimilation, focusing, as we shall see, on intense work, drove a wedge between him and his extended family.

We can be certain, though, that Margaret Bradley and the New York City public schools taught Weinfeld many important lessons. The lesson that was most important, and the lesson he learned best, was how to read, speak, and write English. During his educational career in the New York City public school system, Weinfeld learned key skills of central importance in his subsequent career as judge and lawyer. He became a voracious reader who read thoroughly and thoughtfully; at his death, he left a library of over twelve hundred books, most with his handwritten comments and ideas scrawled on the frontispiece pages and other key pages throughout.

Sometime before he entered upon the practice of law, Weinfeld also learned how to write: his first briefs, written in his early twenties, show that he had already become a master of clear and persuasive prose. It seems unlikely that he learned how to write as part of his legal education; in the early twentieth century, the law school curriculum offered students few, if any, opportunities to practice writing, and NYU, the school Weinfeld attended, did not even have a law review during his period of study. On the contrary, it appears that he learned his writing skills in public school.

The public schools also taught the importance of dedication to and co-operation with others. In the words of William H. Maxwell, the superintendent of the city's schools at the turn of the century, the goal of the schools was to "bring . . . all social classes together in a common effort for improvement."[14] "The ethical purpose of the teaching of geography," for example, was to proclaim "the moral lesson that all men must work and that each man should so work that his labor will benefit not only himself, but the whole community."[15]

Finally there was the lesson of promptness. "[T]he Judge prided himself on promptness," and he gave Miss Bradley credit for teaching him its value. He told how she had wanted to attend the ceremony at which he took his oath of office as a federal judge, but how, at 9:30 on the morning of the ceremony, she had "telephoned. She was very upset; she was ill and she couldn't come down. We talked quite at length, and finally she said, 'If I keep on talking much longer I'll violate one of the rules that I tried to teach you: always be on time.'"[16]

According to Weinfeld, his teachers "exercised great discipline and instilled discipline in children." If a pupil "failed to do . . . homework or hand in a paper," he or she was "kept after school for perhaps an hour." And, when "a teacher kept a student back for disciplinary purposes, when the child got home an hour late, the mother knew why. There was no question you got a slap, that what you did was wrong."[17] Weinfeld undoubtedly disciplined himself effectively and worked hard in school, as well as at his after-school work in his father's saloon. Nonetheless, at the age of nine, he still had sufficient energy left to develop what would become one of the abiding intellectual passions of his life.

The passion developed out of his trips to the home of his aunt in Newark, New Jersey, in 1910, during Woodrow Wilson's campaign to be governor of the state. Weinfeld became fascinated with the political placards posted on telephone poles along the highways. He began reading the placards and then turned to newspaper articles about the gubernatorial campaign, which featured Wilson's strong speeches against New Jersey's political corruption. Two years later, Wilson ran for and was elected president. Weinfeld "vividly remember[ed] the 1912 campaign," and "that, basically was how [he] got interested and learned about Wilson." He subsequently "followed the Wilson career with tremendous interest" and ultimately acquired "almost every outstanding book by or about him."[18]

We need to pause to examine how a Jewish boy from the Lower East Side—the son of a saloonkeeper—could develop between the ages of nine and eleven a passionate, lifelong interest in a political figure as southern, racist, and cerebral as Woodrow Wilson. Wilson simply was not the kind of charismatic sports or entertainment hero to whom children become attracted today. But neither was 1910 today. In 1910, there were no video games, television, or radio. Movies and recordings were primitive; D. W. Griffith's *Birth of a Nation*, arguably the first full-length motion picture offered to the public as entertainment, would be issued only in 1915. Newspapers were the main connection to the outside world that people possessed, and the contests, political and otherwise, reported in those newspapers constituted one of their main forms of entertainment. Thus, it was not surprising that an English-speaking family like the Weinfelds paid attention to the New Jersey gubernatorial election of 1910 and even closer attention to the presidential race of 1912 and that the young Edward found himself interested in the same subjects as his family.

Abraham Weinfeld's occupation of saloonkeeper also may have contributed to Edward's interest in Wilson. Saloons were a major center of political activity on the Lower East Side early in the twentieth century,[19] and the speed with which Edward Weinfeld and his older brother Morris became Democratic Party regulars as soon as they began to practice law suggests that the Weinfeld saloon may have been a Democratic center. If so, young Edward's attraction to Wilson is not surprising. The national Democratic party had few heroes in 1910, and almost no figures perceived as capable of winning the presidency. As soon as Wilson was elected governor of New Jersey, many Democrats began touting him as a potential 1912 presidential nominee.[20] And with his electoral victories in 1912 and 1916, Wilson became one of only two Democrats to serve in the nation's highest office in the seventy-two-year period between 1861 and 1933. For a young Democrat starved for heroes, Woodrow Wilson was an obvious man to worship.

Then there was Wilson's appointment of Louis D. Brandeis as the first Jewish member of the Supreme Court of the United States. Weinfeld, who was a politically aware fifteen-year-old at the time of the appointment, left no record of his precise reaction to it, but he could not possibly have been ignorant of it. The Senate confirmation hearings featured vicious displays of anti-Semitism. In the end, though, Wilson stuck by his nominee, the anti-Semites lost, and Woodrow Wilson emerged as a hero.[21]

We can speculate that Weinfeld's attachment to Wilson affected his subsequent life and career in significant ways, even though Weinfeld himself never could articulate why Wilson was important to him. When asked whether "it was chiefly Wilson's intellect that drew you to him," his initial response was, "Some people think he was too intellectual; that was a criticism of him." But he was, Weinfeld added, "truly a scholarly man." When pressed further as to "why he was so appealing to you,"[22] Weinfeld had no answer and launched into a factual summary of Wilson's teaching career. Weinfeld simply was not an introspective person or one who engaged in "self-exploration," preferring to leave matters "primarily cloaked in silence or fact." In what would become a century "of baring one's soul and letting it all hang out," Weinfeld, like his hero Wilson, "remained the essence of modesty . . . [,] decorum," and "reserve." He took "seeming pride on never having read Freud nor been interested in any of his contributions" and was "not in touch with the complications of ambivalence."[23]

If Wilson helped set the parameters of Weinfeld's personal style, he may have been even more important in helping Weinfeld formulate his political values. Woodrow Wilson above all was a man of ideas, a man with sweeping policy visions. Building coalitions, winning elections, and acquiring political power was never an end in itself, but only a means to furthering ideas and policies. Enacting a reform program, not becoming governor, was the issue Wilson posed in the 1910 New Jersey election.[24] A decade later, Wilson was more than willing to sacrifice his own well-being in return for American entry into the League of Nations, the reorientation of American foreign policy toward internationalism, and his vision of how to maintain future world peace.[25] And Weinfeld's fondest memory in connection with Wilson was the peroration of the eulogy that Rabbi Steven Wise delivered in 1924, when Weinfeld was still a young man of twenty-three. Speaking of Wilson's efforts on behalf of the League of Nations, Wise declared, "Wilson was a failure, Wilson was a failure they say. . . . Low and contemptible is he who fails to dare; great and powerful is he who dares to fail."[26] At key moments in his future career, Weinfeld, remembering Wilson and Wise, always dared, as we shall see, to do the great things he believed right.

Weinfeld's scholarly labors and intellectual growth during his grammar school years appear in retrospect to have had the most important impact on his subsequent life. But three other aspects of his youth also are noteworthy. The first was tragic—the death of his younger brother, Isadore, from meningitis;[27] years later Weinfeld still remembered his mother's vigil at Izzy's bedside and her cradling him in her arms as he died.[28] The second was joyful—his election as president of his eighth-grade class;[29] here was an accomplishment demonstrating how much the young Edward Weinfeld, in his early teens, was liked and respected by his peers.

The final important development of Weinfeld's youth was his decision to become a lawyer when he grew up. Although he "had no true concept of a lawyer's basic function: representing people," he "never had difficulty" formulating his "future plans." As Weinfeld put it, "From the time I was old enough to formulate an idea or think about a future, I knew I wanted to be a lawyer." Perhaps, what impressed him so much about lawyers was their "gift with language,"[30] as well as the obvious respect they enjoyed in his community. Lawyers, when Weinfeld was young, were the "great men of our neighborhood," who "awed us little ones— and the big ones too." The "opening of the doors of the professions to us meant . . . new avenues, new opportunities" and "a new way of life—a status of respect and esteem in the community."[31]

Thus, by the time Edward Weinfeld graduated from eighth grade in the summer of 1914 and moved on in the fall to DeWitt Clinton High School, which had been founded in 1897 as the first public high school for boys in Manhattan,[32] the patterns of his future life and career already had largely been set. He would be a hard-working lawyer dedicated to helping others. His greatest respect would go toward those who displayed facility with words and ideas, and he would try to develop that facility in himself. Above all, Weinfeld would be a lawyer who dared to fail rather than one who failed to dare.

Perhaps the most striking fact about his high school years was the workload. While he was going to high school, he took his first job as a law clerk with an attorney named Henry C. Neuwirth, whose offices were

were at 120 Broadway. Weinfeld "worked three afternoons a week after school hours and a full day Saturday."[33] This was on top of heavy homework assignments. Weinfeld would do his homework for about three hours and then take a break and walk around Tompkins Square Park twice. This walk would leave him "refreshed physically and mentally" and enable him to "start all over" doing more homework.[34] Of course, he also walked to and from school and work. When the walks, the school day, the job, and the homework are added together, it appears that Weinfeld had already begun working on a 6:30 A.M. to midnight schedule similar to the schedules he would follow in later life.

Weinfeld had excelled in grammer school, where he had both been a favorite of teachers and been elected president of his graduating class. There is no evidence that he similarly rose to the top at DeWitt Clinton High. We can only speculate why. Perhaps his workload as student and afternoon law clerk was too heavy for him to handle. Or, perhaps the pond had become too large. When asked to identify his contemporaries in grammar school who went on to success, Weinfeld named Henry Mayer, who, he noted, "later became a distinguished labor lawyer."[35] In contrast, DeWitt Clinton's famous alumni included James Baldwin, Burt Lancaster, Charles B. Rangel, Neil Simon, and Lionel Trilling, as well as some forty state and federal judges who, along with Weinfeld, were invited to a reunion in 1976.[36] Or, maybe there were undefined limits on how high the son of Jewish immigrants to the Lower East Side could rise in Manhattan's early-twentieth-century high school.

Whatever the reason, it appears that Weinfeld lost a competitive edge—an urge to best his peers—that he may have possessed in grammar school. He gave up trying to compete against others and began to develop a lifelong habit of accepting his lot in life with modesty, of "denying the importance of winning," and of "compet[ing] primarily with himself and against . . . internal standards of excellence."[37]

Weinfeld was scheduled to graduate from DeWitt Clinton High School in June 1918, but, in competition with himself, he completed the curriculum in less than four years and graduated in January, six months early.[38] He planned to enroll in a six-year program of combined college and law courses at Columbia University and, at the time of his high school graduation, had already been admitted. But he faced a hiatus of several months between the end of high school and the beginning of college and took a job as a clerk for a lawyer, Ben Hartstein, to fill the gap.

Weinfeld "did very well," and Hartstein, knowing of Weinfeld's "intense desire to become a lawyer as quickly as possible," "persuaded" him "not to spend time going to college before taking law courses." Weinfeld "listened" to Hartstein "and became an evening law student" at New York University in the fall of 1918.[39]

In later years, Weinfeld would express "mild regret . . . about not having gone to college."[40] At the time, he "recognized that [he] would be losing something by not going . . . but thought [he] would compensate by [his] own reading." Accordingly, he began "a practice, apart from other times he had available for outside reading," of "spend[ing] every Tuesday night at home religiously reading different books in different areas." His years in law school, however, were such "hard work" that he was unable to keep up the practice, although he periodically reverted to it in later years. He worked for Hartstein five days a week, plus "a full day on Saturday"; classes lasted "two nights a week from 8:00 to 10:00 and three nights a week from 7:00 to 10:00. After classes, if [he] went directly home," Weinfeld "would study till about 1:00 in the morning and get ready for the next day's work."[41]

As he pursued the night course for his LL.B. degree, Weinfeld accumulated a passable but surely not outstanding academic record. In his first year, Weinfeld took a total of seven required courses, including such standbys as Contract, Property I, Torts, and Crimes;[42] he received five grades of D and two grades of C. His second year was not much better, perhaps even worse. He received one F on his first-semester exam in Procedure—a subject for which his alma mater now gives the Edward Weinfeld Prize at graduation to a student "for distinguished scholarship in the area of federal courts, civil procedure and practice, evidence and/or trial practice."[43] In the second semester, Weinfeld received a grade of D. His remaining grades in his second year were six C's and two D's. He received his one and only grade of A in Code Procedure in the first semester of his third year. Otherwise, in his third year, he received seven C's, two B's, and two D's. With this essentially C average, Weinfeld was awarded his LL.B. in June 1921.[44]

When Weinfeld received his degree, however, he was only twenty years old and hence too young to take the bar examination, for which the minimum age was twenty-one. As a result, he went back to New York University School of Law for a degree of LL.M.[45] His academic record in connection with this degree was only slightly better than his LL.B. record; in his five courses, he received two grades of pass, two grades of C, and one grade of B.[46] He attained a master's degree in June 1922, shortly after his twenty-first birthday, and so was eligible to sit for the bar.[47]

While Weinfeld's academic record in law school was merely passable, his social life, like that of many young collegians, blossomed, and he achieved outstanding success in student politics.

When he began law school, Weinfeld admittedly was concerned about "not wanting to appear as a 'square-head.'" He had good reason for his concern. He was not from an "'upper-crust'" background; even among the Jewish students at New York University, "there weren't too many from [his] area of the city." Although Weinfeld would claim six decades later that his "not wanting to appear as a 'square-head' had nothing to do with [his] living on the Lower East Side,"[48] other contextual evidence belies his claim. As we have seen, Weinfeld, as the son of Lower East Side immigrant Jews, probably had faced discrimination during his years in high school—discrimination that undoubtedly hampered the growth of "upper-crust" social skills and even may have tempered his academic achievements. Moreover, although his family was not poor, Weinfeld did not have great wealth to lavish on his social life; an even greater obstacle to extensive socializing was his full-time job, which gave him little free time during the course of any day.

Nonetheless, Weinfeld did become an active member of the law school and university community. One of his stylistic moves in his effort to avoid seeming "square" was to hold a cigarette in his mouth as if he were smoking it, without, however, lighting it.[49] Like so many other young men of his time, as well as earlier and later times, he began to engage in social drinking with friends; one of those friends, some fifteen years later, recalled their "boyhood binges."[50] Although Weinfeld's Lower East Side background and probable social naivete kept him from being extensively rushed by NYU's fraternities, one fraternity—Phi Sigma Delta—did extend him a bid. He accepted, "became very active in fraternity affairs," and "had a very great experience in" the fraternity.[51]

Weinfeld joined the Delta chapter of Phi Sigma Delta, a national Jewish fraternity, the first chapter of which, Alpha, had been founded at Columbia University in 1909. The Delta chapter was engaged in a "battle for supremacy at New York University" and was in the process of "becom[ing] very active on the campus." Its "men," who were "enter[ing] in every activity the school offer[ed]," included "scholars, athletes, and school and class officers." By the time Weinfeld graduated, the Delta chapter of Phi Sigma Delta "rank[ed] among the three best Jewish fraternities at N.Y.U."[52]

Weinfeld proved to be immensely popular among his fraternity brothers. During his third year of law school, they elected him Master Frater, the equivalent of president, of the Delta chapter. When Weinfeld stayed on at NYU for a fourth year to receive his LL.M., the chapter reelected him Master Frater for a second year.[53]

Upon graduation, Weinfeld moved into national fraternity affairs. His initial task was to serve as chairman of the national fraternity's Internal Expansion Committee[54]—a post in which he traveled to chapters of Phi Sigma Delta across the country. He visited five midwestern chapters, for example, on one eight-day trip in the spring of 1924.[55] While holding this chair for two years, from 1922 to 1924, Weinfeld also held office as executive secretary of the fraternity's Central Council in 1922 and 1924 and as vice-president of the Central Council in 1923. In December 1924, he was elected vice-president of the national fraternity, and in 1925, he was elected national president of Phi Sigma Delta for a two-year term from 1926 to 1928.[56]

The high regard in which his fraternity brothers held Weinfeld rested on his "reputation for DEPENDABILITY," which he had established "[a]t a sacrifice of time, effort and money." According to a tribute written at the time of his election as national president of the fraternity,

> Besides Law, Eddie's other vocation, avocation and invocation has been the Phi Sigma Delta Fraternity. He talks it, breathes it, dreams of it and works for it. . . . "Ed, I'll appoint you," meant that a committee was sure to function. "Frater Weinfeld, will you visit this chapter?" meant that not only was the chapter visited, but that a splendid, intelligent report was rendered. "Ed, will you take care of this?" meant that it was taken care of properly.[57]

Weinfeld, in the words of one friend who congratulated him on his election, was simply "a conscientious wretch."[58]

Dedication and dependability—two characteristics that Weinfeld would display again and again in the future—were only part of the persona that the young Weinfeld had developed by the time he finished his education. A third quality, probably developed, as we have seen, in high school, was lack of competitiveness. In a setting in which fraternities were engaged in "battle[s] for supremacy," Weinfeld was more concerned with maintaining "the flame of idealism of our founders," with "bring[ing] about a unity of thought and purpose," and with "the awakening of a fraternity consciousness on the part" of former fraternity members who had since graduated from college and moved on to their careers. He did not treat his election to the national presidency as "a triumphant moment" for "exultation and pride"; indeed, he had "begged not to be considered for the Presidency."[59]

The final quality that Weinfeld displayed in his years of service to Phi Sigma Delta—again, a quality that he would display repeatedly in years to come—was capacity for friendship. According to the tribute at the time of his election,

> You need meet Eddie but once to like him. He has a saturnine countenance upon which plays a ravishing smile that melts away all opposition. He has jet black hair with a natural wave in it that is the envy and despair of every frater's wife or sweetheart. He has a heart that is as big as he is. He has a frank and engaging way that does not permit of subterfuge. He has the knack of making friends and what is more important, of keeping them.[60]

Weinfeld made and kept friends because he cared about people as individuals and wanted to help them solve their problems and improve their lives. He listened well, responded graciously, and was compassionate, as one friend, Henry Waldman, recorded.

In a 1924 letter following his admission to the bar, Waldman—a fellow student at New York University and fraternity brother in the Delta chapter of Phi Sigma Delta—wrote Weinfeld "recall[ing] how depressed and heartbroken" he had been "several years ago upon my failure to reach the passing grade at law school." Indeed, he "was ready to give up the study of law." Weinfeld had listened to Waldman's plight, had "manifested" "great interest" in Waldman, and had offered "words of counsel and of inspiration [that] completely bolstered [his] spirit." From that moment, Waldman had "determined to reach greater heights . . . [and] always [to] bless . . . [Weinfeld's] memory."[61] Waldman, of course, returned to school, passed both his law school and his bar exams, and ultimately enjoyed a successful career.

At the end of his youth, Weinfeld likewise embarked on a successful—indeed, a remarkable—career. By the time he had reached his midtwenties, his intimate knowledge of much of New York, his employment experience, his possibly negative social experiences in high school and his more positive ones in law school and in his fraternity, and his formal education from grammar school through high school and law school had prepared him well for success. Weinfeld had cultivated valuable public speaking and writing skills that enabled him to communicate his thoughts clearly, precisely, and often eloquently. He also had become an unusually able listener and observer, who responded with empathy to the human situations he encountered. Finally, he had learned to be an indefatigable worker who could be relied upon to complete tasks thoroughly and intelligently.

At the same time, Weinfeld had developed and adhered to a strong sense of ethical bounds. Perhaps the most important was his loyalty to friends and community. Another, surely, was his lack of competitiveness; although not without ambition, Weinfeld did not chase after honors, and he avoided personal rivalries as a means toward his ends. Finally, there was his Wilsonian view of politics and public affairs—a view that made him suspicious of machine politics and supportive of an inchoate vision of rational debate as a vehicle for achieving beneficial social reform.

It seems clear that by the end of his youth Weinfeld also had developed the formal, austere demeanor that would characterize him throughout life. "He lacked the light touch and was so grounded in his beliefs about how a person should behave and conduct himself" that he could not "imagine alternative ways to be." Even more, he exhibited an "inhibition regarding play in almost any of its forms . . . [and] could not talk about movies . . . , sports or music, a contemporary novel, nothing out of the realm of history, politics or the law." His lack of "spontaneity," his "extreme caution," and his "inability to play" except at an occasional game of poker and later gin rummy, must, at least in the eyes of some, have made him "a dull boy."[62]

Nonetheless, even if he played little, Weinfeld had learned to relax. He had learned an important form of relaxation—lengthy walks—as early as high school, and in his early twenties he learned his one sport—tennis—from his younger sister and a fraternity brother. His most important form of relaxation, however, probably was his social drinking; throughout his life he required "a before-dinner drink after a long day's work"[63] and, on special occasions, continued his "boyhood binges." Thus, at one party in Weinfeld's home, his godson, then about five, kicked Weinfeld in his shin, to his father's great consternation; when asked by his father why he had done so, the boy responded, "You said Uncle Eddie had a wooden leg."[64]

Similarly, as Mrs. Weinfeld noted many years later on the day after the judge's fiftieth birthday party, "As usual, Weinfeld drank his dinner & the next morning wanted to know . . . [how] his birthday cake ha[d] tasted."[65]

None of this interfered with Weinfeld's ability to work and help others or with the joy he received from doing so. He was never "conflicted or in pain about who he was," and his behavior from his youth onward suggested that he was never, in his view, "miss[ing] out on much of anything at all." Although "consumed by his work," Weinfeld had learned in his youth to be "gratified" by it, to "function . . . well and . . . [to be] fulfilled."[66] Perhaps the most important thing he had gained from his education was psychological togetherness and toughness; by the time his youth had ended, he had learned to know himself and to have confidence in who and what he was.

3

Getting Started

Edward Weinfeld was graduated from New York University School of Law in June 1921 and learned in August 1922 that he had passed the bar examination.[1] During law school and the interval between graduation and admission to practice, Weinfeld had been working as a law clerk to a well-established attorney, Ben Hartstein, with whom he planned to begin practice. We can guess at the level of excellence that Weinfeld, merely twenty-one years old, had already attained by the fact that he was able to negotiate a partnership with Hartstein in which he, Weinfeld, without putting in any capital, would receive 20 percent of the new firm's annual income and have his name on the door of the firm of Hartstein & Weinfeld.[2] But the partnership was not to be. Weinfeld's parents wanted him to enter into a partnership with his elder brother, Morris, who also was a lawyer, and Edward Weinfeld, always a dutiful son, obeyed.[3] He sent out an announcement concerning his entry into general private practice in January 1923, presumably in partnership with his brother.[4]

Eighteen months later, the first published decision in an appeal argued by Edward Weinfeld was handed down. *J. Pratt Carroll, Inc. v. Murphy Fruit Co.*[5] arose when a potential buyer of apples sued Murphy Fruit, the client of Weinfeld & Weinfeld, for fraudulently offering to sell apples and for breach of a contract to sell the apples. Plaintiff, however, failed to draft its complaint in a fashion that separately identified and numbered what appeared to be its two separate causes of action, and defendant moved in the trial court for an order requiring that plaintiff do so. When the motion was denied, the defendant appealed, and the then twenty-three-year-old Edward Weinfeld argued the narrow procedural issue that the appeal raised.

Weinfeld's submission to the court is no longer extant, but it is possible to deduce its nature from the opinion that the appellate court wrote when it decided the case in his favor. The submission, as so reconstituted, appears to reflect what would be hallmarks of Weinfeld's later legal work. First, it contained a precise analysis of the facts, albeit in this case, only the plaintiff's pleading. It appears that Weinfeld dissected the complaint in detail in order to demonstrate that it contained two causes of action rather than merely one. Second, Weinfeld cited a line of controlling cases on point. That is, he did not cite only one case as the basis for his request for reversal of the judgment below; perhaps, the other side would have been able to distinguish merely one case. Instead, he placed the controlling case in the context of a long line of cases favoring his position and thus put his opponent in the position of needing to distinguish the entire line of authority, not merely a single case. Third, he brought to the appellate court's attention not only the governing rule but also the reasons for that rule. He explained,

> As there are two causes of action set forth, they should be separately stated and numbered, that the defendants may plead or move as they may be advised with regard to each. . . . [T]he defendants may have defenses to one that they have not to the other, or they may have relief as to one which would not be applicable to the other. In the present form of the complaint, the defendants cannot avail themselves of these different pleadings or motions.[6]

Weinfeld's submission to the court also displayed a sophisticated lawyer's understanding of litigation strategy. It is unclear whether Weinfeld had different defenses or wished to make different motions in respect to plaintiff's two distinct causes of action, but he nonetheless made his motion for their separate statement because the motion brought him two strategic advantages. First, his motion required plaintiff's counsel to redraft the complaint and serve it within six days; perhaps, Weinfeld had reason to hope that the brevity of time would induce plaintiff's counsel to make additional mistakes. More significantly, Weinfeld's appeal of a purely procedural issue signaled to the opposing side his own and his client's willingness to resist vigorously the lawsuit that had been commenced. Vigorous resistance, in turn, meant that plaintiff's counsel might need to spend vastly more time pursuing the case to final judgment than the damages sought by the plaintiff—four hundred dollars—would have justified.[7]

By challenging opposing counsel to devote more time to the case than the amount in controversy would have warranted, Weinfeld made an important statement concerning his understanding of the nature of the practice of law. Weinfeld did not treat law as a business; his goal was not to make as much money as he possibly could. On the contrary, his goal was to help his clients by providing them with the most effective possible representation. It appears that he was willing to devote extra hours to clients' cases, even if he could not bill them for the time, and this willingness gave him a strategic advantage over many opposing lawyers—an advantage of which he was aware and that he was willing to exploit.

Perhaps Edward Weinfeld's willingness to work long hours for minimal compensation was one reason why his partnership with his brother Morris did not last. In Weinfeld's words, "my brother and I had too many differences to work together," and, as a result, they "separated" and "terminated the partnership."[8] But the dissolution of the partnership was neither sudden nor contentious; in one case, for example, that began in 1925 and continued into 1926, Edward Weinfeld at one point used his brother Morris's stationery, at another point crossed off his brother's name and typed his own above it, and only at the end of the case used stationery on which his own name was printed. Throughout the case, moreover, it appears that they still shared the same office.[9]

The file papers make it clear, however, that the case—*Gellert v. Gellert*[10]—was Edward Weinfeld's case. His client, Helen R. Gellert, had brought suit for a separation from her husband, Leo L. Gellert, a dentist, on grounds of cruelty. The case was one in which social and legal patterns that would become increasingly commonplace during the course of the twentieth century appeared at a somewhat early date. One such pattern was that the suit for separation was commenced after Dr. Gellert had already moved out of the marital home; the legal issue the court needed to resolve was not whether the parties would live separately but who would receive custody of their child and how much alimony Dr. Gellert would be required to pay. The case also reflected the emergence of new cultural patterns. Helen Gellert was a woman of the new century, who used cosmetics to enhance her beauty. Leo Gellert, in contrast, "was ashamed to go out with his wife because of the cosmetics she used" and "would force her to wash this off when they went out." In addition, "he declared that she dyed her hair," although "she denied having 'dyed' her hair, saying it was 'rinsed.'" From Leo's point of view, Helen's modernist attitude was even worse than her makeup. When asked, "Do you make up to please your husband?" she responded, "I make up to please myself." The "big thing at stake" was that Mrs. Gellert "denie[d] the right of her husband to tell her how much rouge she shall use." Indeed, she testified that, whenever her husband forced her to wash off her makeup, "she would replace it in the dressing room of the first public place they reached."[11] Helen Gellert's attitudes simply were not those of a nineteenth- or early twentieth-century wife who had taken a vow to obey her husband, and it undoubtedly required courage on Weinfeld's part to agree to represent such a nonconformist.

On balance, his representation of Helen Gellert was successful. Mrs. Gellert was granted full custody of her child, with visitation rights to Dr. Gellert only on Sunday afternoons, plus thirty-five dollars per week in alimony and child support[12]—not a princely sum for the 1920s, but "enough to support the child and herself."[13] In addition, when Mrs. Gellert's child became seriously ill and she incurred out-of-the-ordinary medical expenses, Weinfeld was able to recover those expenses from Dr. Gellert through a special motion. He wrote a succinct memorandum of law in support of his motion, in which he carefully analyzed the facts in order to delineate the issue and then cited two controlling Appellate Division precedents in support of his position.[14] The trial court awarded payment of the medical expenses in a brief opinion that summarized Weinfeld's memorandum and cited the same two cases.[15]

Weinfeld also succeeded in obtaining publicity for the *Gellert* case[16]— a not insubstantial feat for a lawyer only twenty-five years of age. The Gellerts, of course, might have been happier without the publicity, but the two articles that Weinfeld was able to place in New York City newspapers probably contributed to his building a practice in matrimonial cases, which became one of his staples over the course of the next decade. In any event, Helen Gellert remained sufficiently satisfied with Weinfeld's representation to retain him in continuing litigation with her husband over the years. The final entry about the Gellerts in Weinfeld's files occurred in Leo Gellert's suit against his wife for divorce. Dr. Gellert moved to amend his complaint to name the correspondent with whom Mrs. Gellert had allegedly committed adultery, and Weinfeld opposed the motion, but the court granted it.[17]

Probably the least successful facet of Weinfeld's efforts on behalf of Helen Gellert was the fee that the court directed Dr. Gellert to pay Weinfeld—$250 for his work on the main part of the case plus an added fifty dollars for his work on the motion to recover medical expenses and $150 for a memorandum of law in opposition to the motion to name the correspondent.[18] Although no record remains, Weinfeld also must have received a fee for representing Helen Gellert in the main divorce action.

Fees like those that Weinfeld received in the *Gellert* case appear to have been standard ones that attorneys, who typically performed little work, received for representing clients in similar types of matters. A lawyer could earn a passable living by sprinting through many such cases. But in Weinfeld's case the fees were not of a nature that would enable him to become wealthy because he put in many hours to earn them: in the end, it appears that he earned well under one thousand dollars for a case that continued for nine years and involved the preparation of two sets of pleadings and motion papers, along with two memoranda of law.

Over the course of the next decade Weinfeld continued addressing matrimonial matters, some of which he resolved through separation agreements[19] but many of which ended up in litigation. In another highly publicized case in which he respresented, as he almost invariably did,[20] a wife seeking to escape from her husband, one Lena Grosberg sought a separation from Dr. Max W. Grosberg, plus two hundred dollars in weekly alimony and fifteen hundred dollars in counsel fees. Mrs. Grosberg claimed that her husband associated with "girls" who "were about 16 or 17 years old" and that he "felt that he had the right to go out at any time with any girl he wished to see." He left home when she questioned him one night about his arriving home late and "he announced that he was going off with 'his girlfriend.'" When Mrs. Grosberg later sought a reconciliation, Dr. Grosberg told her that "he liked his freedom and intended to keep it."[21]

Weinfeld left no record of the fee he earned in the *Grosberg* matter, but in other cases in which there remains evidence of his earnings, his fees were as modest as they had been in the *Gellert* case. For example, in *Franklin v. Franklin*, in which he wrote a twelve-page memorandum of law in opposition to a motion by a divorced husband to reduce alimony and support payments and to alter a child custody decree, he sought a fee of only $150.[22]

For small fees of this sort, Weinfeld often did a great deal of high-quality legal work. A relatively easy case was *Weinstein v. Weinstein*, in which the female plaintiff whom Weinfeld represented sought an annulment of a marriage for the defendant's fraud in failing to honor his representation that, upon completion of a civil ceremony, he would marry her in an Orthodox Jewish ceremony; Weinfeld wrote a five-page memorandum of law in support of her annulment claim.[23] A more difficult case, involving a question of law "never . . . passed upon squarely before,"[24] was *Udko v. Udko*.

There the plaintiff wife, whom Weinfeld represented, after obtaining a divorce in Arkansas, brought suit in New York for a divorce for her husband's adultery. The husband moved to dismiss on the ground that wife's procurement of the Arkansas divorce, which, he alleged, had been granted without jurisdiction over him and was therefore void in New York, nonetheless estopped her from seeking a new divorce in New York. Weinfeld responded to the motion with a thirty-four-page brief that cited and analyzed eighteen cases in detail. But he did not argue the novel question of law in the abstract. Instead, he urged that "the facts, the equities of the situation, and public policy" all required that the plaintiff be permitted to maintain her suit.[25] In particular, Weinfeld wrote,

> Admittedly, the plaintiff in this action was ill-advised by her Arkansas attorneys in instituting and procuring the entry of an invalid decree of divorce. In consequence, the position of the parties never having been changed, is the mistake of judgment and legal opinion to condemn her for all time and leave her drifting in society without any definite status? Is she truly neither maid, widow nor wife?[26]

Could the defendant husband, Weinfeld inquired, treat her divorce as valid if he wished to remarry or otherwise become involved with another woman, but at the same time treat it as void and invoke estoppel to prevent her from obtaining a new divorce if she sought to remarry or otherwise became involved with another man?

> Is her husband, the defendant, to be permitted to commit adultery . . . and openly flaunt such misconduct before the plaintiff and his child, with the wife standing by powerless to take any action because of her mistake and error of judgment? More important, is the public policy of the State to be carried to the point where, the wife is prevented from asserting the invalidity of the Arkansas decree (as contended for by defendant), and . . . the husband is given a weapon with which to accomplish the very purposes which are expressly prohibited by that . . . [policy]? Is the marriage one in name only, with the husband free to violate the marital vows and no redress to the wife? Such a situation is unjust, inequitable and shocking to the conscience.[27]

On this basis, the court agreed with Weinfeld and allowed Mrs. Udko's suit to go forward. Ultimately, Mrs. Udko obtained her divorce in New York on the ground of her husband's adultery.[28]

Weinfeld wrote an even more extensive and impressive set of briefs in a case in which he became involved only at the appellate level—*Lowenstein v. Lowenstein*.[29] By the time Weinfeld entered the case, Ralphina Lowenstein had walked out of her husband Louis Lowenstein's home, Louis had obtained a judgment granting a separation in his favor on account of her abandonment, and, pursuant to the judgment, he had received sole custody of their three sons. Ralphina's claim that she was justified in leaving her husband's home because of his "brutal, cruel and inhuman treatment" and failure to provide support[30] had been rejected by the trial court on the facts, and Weinfeld thus faced the daunting task of persuading an appellate court to reverse a trial court's fact findings. He succeeded in this task by drafting a remarkable brief that examined the facts in careful, thorough detail and presented an eloquent, mesmerizing narrative of Ralphina's victimization.

Weinfeld began by framing his argument: he stated his brief would "rely largely upon the findings of fact made by the Trial Court" in Mrs. Lowenstein's favor "and upon other undisputed evidence, either conceded or uncontradicted." Weinfeld also addressed immediately why the trial judge decided against Ralphina "despite his own findings of fact in her favor and such of the evidence as was conceded." "A clue," Weinfeld wrote, lay "in the Trial Court's erroneous conception of the measure of proof": according to the trial judge, "the law [did] not permit or justify a woman leaving her home unless it be shown *beyond peradventure* that the conduct of the husband amounted to cruel and inhuman treatment." Weinfeld found this "unusual test," which was "even more rigid than that laid down in criminal cases," "clearly incorrect for no rule is better settled than that in civil cases, a party is never required to prove his case by more than a fair preponderance of the evidence."[31]

Arguably, Weinfeld purposefully misread what the trial court had held; the court probably meant to declare not a burden of proof standard but a substantive rule of law prohibiting a wife from leaving her husband's home in the absence of extreme cruelty and inhumanity. The trial judge, however, had not learned to use language as precisely as Weinfeld used it. Turning the judge's imprecision of thought to his client's advantage, Weinfeld drove the point home:

[S]uch a mistaken rule as was here enunciated by the Trial Court cannot be condoned and must of necessity result in a reversal of this judgment. Were it not that the Court's opinion expressly declares the rule which he understood should be applied to the facts in the instant case, it would be incredible to believe that such a rule could be advanced. It is a baseless proposition which can find no support either in precedent or reason.[32]

Especially in light of the minuscule fees that they earned representing women in divorce cases, most lawyers probably would have quit after showing so strongly that the court below had applied an incorrect legal standard. But Weinfeld did not. Perhaps, he sensed that the Appellate Division might see him—still in his twenties when he argued the case—as a young upstart needing to learn respect for his elders and betters on the bench. In any event, he did not quit, but wrote a forty-six-page brief and a forty-four-page reply brief.

Weinfeld began by using the husband's own testimony that for the first ten years of their marriage, Mrs. Lowenstein "ran her home like a wife and mother should," had "exclusive control of the household and its affairs, and of the children," and received "allowances of approximately $40 per week to take care of the household needs and of her own necessities," as well as "the use of his credit with department stores and tradespeople." Then, on July 25, 1927, he gave her the sum of $135, and "from that time on, he never gave her a single penny," testifying that he "didn't *intend* that she should have any money." He also "cut off her credit with department stores and tradespeople," and, when she opened accounts with local grocers, butchers, and others "for the purpose of supplying the necessities of the household," he closed them, notifying everyone that "they were not to allow his wife to make any purchases whatever on his credit."[33]

Mr. Lowenstein's next move, as narrated by Weinfeld, was to deprive Ralphina of management of household affairs, when he directed one of the maids to take charge of the home and the children and to make all necessary purchases. Next, he hired private detectives to keep his wife under surveillance. When the detectives found no immorality on her part, he suggested that she sign a separation agreement and warned her "that if she did not sign the separation papers, he would make it so miserable for her that she would wish she had."[34]

Matters came to a head during the days following June 4, 1928, when the maid and the nurse left. Mrs. Lowenstein asked her mother to move in to help her with the children and with household chores, while Mr. Lowenstein "installed his spinster sister . . . in the apartment." On June 9, Mr. Lowenstein "forcibly removed" Ralphina's mother from the apartment. Ralphina left with her, only to return several hours later with a nurse, who stayed with her overnight.[35]

The events of June 10, the date on which Ralphina left the apartment, were hotly disputed. Here Weinfeld turned to the testimony of Ralphina and her supporters. According to this testimony, her husband "called her a 'dirty pig' and a 'beast' and struck her on the chest and on the head," causing her to fall backwards over a kitchen stool. When Ralphina tried to escape, her husband sought to shut the door, but her two eldest sons came to her assistance and enabled her to escape into a neighbor's apartment. She then returned with a policeman, who asked the two sons whether they wished to remain with their father or leave with their mother; when they stated their preference for their mother, she left with them and also picked up the youngest son, then only three years old, and carried him out.[36]

Having narrated the facts, Weinfeld made a significant strategic choice—he offered no explanation for the husband's behavior. It remains a mystery. But various random facts that he did report suggest three possible explanations. Weinfeld's problem was that two of the explanations tended to make the husband appear in a somewhat better light, while the third could not be proved.

The first explanation is that Mr. Lowenstein had suffered serious financial reverses and that Mrs. Lowenstein would not cut back her living standards or otherwise help him address the reverses. At approximately the same time that he gave his wife a total of $135 in lieu of her former forty-dollar weekly allowance, he requested a real estate agent to sublet their apartment—a move that his wife apparently vetoed.[37] May she also have squandered the $135 faster than Mr. Lowenstein had directed or spent the money on items he felt were unnecessary? We know that she subsequently was uncooperative in connection with finances when she refused during the course of reconciliation negotiations to give him "certain building loan shares in New Jersey standing in her name . . . so that he might be able to retrieve his position in the [stock] market." We also know that Mr. Lowenstein failed to return his wife's jewelry to her, perhaps because he had had to sell or pawn it.[38] Of course, a refusal on Mrs. Lowenstein's part to obey her husband's directions for resolving his financial difficulties may have been justified, but a narrative setting forth the justification would have had to be more complex than the story Weinfeld chose to tell.

The second possible explanation for Mr. Lowenstein's behavior was the one adopted by the trial court—that Mrs. Lowenstein's "restlessness, induced by the supposed banality of her daily life, . . . caused her to desire and engage in teaching school against her husband's wishes and to seek other pursuits designed to relieve the boredom of domesticity, which are claimed to be the prerogative of the so-called modern woman." "[T]his modern so-called independence," according to the court below, "satisfied her that she was right in seeking an independent income of her own, free from her husband and free from the care of his home."[39] Mrs. Lowenstein did, in fact, return to teaching school—her occupation before marriage—during the course of her dispute with her husband, but Weinfeld constructed a detailed chronological argument showing that she returned only *after* her husband had cut off her allowance and closed all her charge accounts and she was in desperate need of money.[40] He thereby avoided the issue of whether a wife had a right to engage in employment outside marriage without her husband's consent, an issue on which it probably would have been difficult in 1931 to get the Appellate Division to decide in the wife's favor.

Weinfeld also avoided any mention of a combination of the two explanations—that Mr. Lowenstein suffered financial reverses, that Mrs. Lowenstein insisted on addressing the resulting need for money by returning to work, but that Mr. Lowenstein insisted that they cut living standards instead. One piece of testimony by Mrs. Lowenstein is suggestive of this explanation; in her words, "First I spoke to him about the way we were living and that it was so embarrassing . . . *and I said, out of self-respect, if he doesn't help me to live the way I did before, I will have to earn some money by teaching.*"[41] Weinfeld stayed far away, however, from any explanation that the Lowensteins' marital discord sprang from a disagreement about how to solve their financial problems, since it would have been difficult in 1931 to get the Appellate Division to rule that such a disagreement would have justified her leaving the family home.

There was also a third explanation—namely, "the two revolting attempts at degenerate practices made by" Mr. Lowenstein upon Ralphina—the first occurring two weeks after he had given her the lump sum $135 payment and the second occurring only two days before she left his home.[42] Mr. Lowenstein, of course, denied the two attempts, and thus

Weinfeld could not prove them. Moreover, the fact of the attempt merely two days before the Lowensteins' marriage disintegrated suggests that husband and wife were continuing to engage in sexual relations until their marriage ended and raises doubts that Mr. Lowenstein was engaged in a purposive effort to drive his wife out of the house.

Thus, Weinfeld wrote a narrative that preserved the mystery surrounding the ruin of the Lowensteins' marriage; his brief observed that "there is not a single word in the record in justification of the plaintiff [husband] taking the position he did." He also focused on the fact that the decision of the judge below was "inconsistent with the findings of fact made by him in favor of the defendant [wife]."[43] The attorneys for the husband were not clever enough to construct the explanations Weinfeld avoided, which might have been helpful to their client, and thus they left the Appellate Division with little choice but to decide the case in favor of Weinfeld's client—on the grounds that the trial judge's "findings are so inconsistent that we may not follow him in his conclusions" and that the wife "showed her right to leave the plaintiff [husband] by reason of misconduct of his which appears established by the proof and which plaintiff failed to convincingly controvert."[44]

By the time of the two *Lowenstein* briefs, as well as the other matrimonial cases we have been examining, the mature Weinfeld had emerged. After graduating from law school with an at best mediocre academic record, he had transformed himself in a decade of practice into a highly effective advocate. The talents that he would exhibit throughout his career had become apparent.

The first was his ability to write clear, organized, and often eloquent prose—an ability that guarantees success in the practice of law and that few lawyers in any generation possess. The second was Weinfeld's facility in scrutinizing the facts and synthesizing them into persuasive narratives. Third was his remarkable strategic sense—his uncanny judgment about the lines of argument he should put forward and the lines of argument he should ignore.

Other qualities had also emerged. Weinfeld worked long and hard. For example, he mentioned to a friend that during one trial he "averaged about five hours sleep a night, including Sundays," while during another trial he "went to the Law Library where I remained until one-thirty in the morning preparing a memorandum of law."[45] Weinfeld found these long hours necessary because he did not work quickly; his mediocre grades in law school, for instance, probably resulted from a lack of speed in responding to exam questions. He never viewed himself as a genius and regarded hard work rather than genius as the key to success in law.[46] Indeed, on a sheet of paper headed "Advice to Lawyers," he had copied the following excerpt:

> There is no short cut to results. Everybody who wants to achieve has to sit down and be a man of detail. We sometimes talk about genius, but there isn't any genius in the world except the genius of getting ready.[47]

Moreover, Weinfeld did not tailor the amount of work he was prepared to perform to the fee that he would obtain for performing it. He worked as hard as was required by the legal matter in which he was engaged without regard to the client's ability to pay. As we have seen, this willingness to work without regard to payment often gave him an advantage over adversaries: sometimes it left him better prepared, while at other times the threat that he would be better prepared induced his opponents to settle.

Another Weinfeld trait was his empathy for underdogs and for various sorts of people who rejected dominant societal values. As we have seen, he represented mainly women in matrimonial cases, and at least some of those women had displayed a modern tendency toward independence from their husbands and toward demanding equal treatment. In part, his representation of women in divorce cases simply reflected his willingness to take on cases without regard to a client's capacity to pay; perhaps, he took on cases only to develop his reputation and thereby build a practice. Nonetheless, in advancing the cause of clients with discordant social views, he had to learn how to imagine and then to portray the world in divergent ways.

Above all, Weinfeld by the end of his first decade in practice had developed the habit of caring. He cared for the law, and he cared for his clients. As one of his clients for whom he had done a real estate closing recalled, he went above and beyond his lawyer's calling in serving her by going to her new home with her after the closing and, when she couldn't find the keys, crawling in the basement window and opening the front door.[48] Those who dealt with Weinfeld developed enormous affection and respect for him. Ralphina Lowenstein, for example, became a friend of Weinfeld and his family; both of Weinfeld's daughters report that Ralphina and her three sons were guests at the Weinfeld home at least annually and often more frequently, as were the Weinfelds at the Lowenstein

Edward Weinfeld as a young lawyer, circa 1925.

home. Weinfeld's older daughter even dated the youngest of Ralphina Lowenstein's sons when they both were young adults.[49]

The patterns that characterized Weinfeld's matrimonial practice also carried over into a second area of practice in which he engaged—criminal law. As in the matrimonial cases, Weinfeld often was able to obtain publicity for the cases he tried, and to do so at an early stage of his career when publicity would help build his practice. Two cases, both from the month of April 1928, exemplify Weinfeld's deftness as a publicist.

One was *People v. Goldberg*, in which Joseph Goldberg, a twenty-five-year-old paper box manufacturer, was accused of shooting in the back and killing twenty-two-year-old Abraham Hirsch. The only evidence against Goldberg was a statement that Hirsch made from his hospital bed; unable to sign the statement, Hirsch marked his "X" on it with a pen that he held in his mouth. Hirsch then died. But, immediately before his death, when "Detective William J. Nammack . . . asked him, as a matter of form, if he believed he would die, Hirsch, with almost his last conscious breath, declared on the contrary that he believed he would live."[50] When this evidence was presented to the court at Goldberg's preliminary hearing, Weinfeld pointed out that, according to the Court of Appeals,[51] a dying declaration is admissible as an exception to the hearsay rule only if made by a declarant who expects to die, and the examining magistrate accordingly rejected Hirsch's statement and released Goldberg.[52]

What is most remarkable about the publicity Weinfeld obtained for the *Goldberg* case is that the newspapers publishing the story never even hinted at the possibility that Detective Nammack may have testified as he did because he may have been bribed. Of course, Nammack may have been an honest detective who simply recognized that his testimony would result in Goldberg's release. But detectives normally do not give testimony like Nammack's that will clinch a defense case, and for some reason, Nammack did. One would guess that Weinfeld was astounded when he heard the detective's testimony.[53]

Two weeks later the newspapers reported on a second Weinfeld case, *People v. Printz*, although this time without mentioning Weinfeld himself by name. In *Printz*, Weinfeld had obtained a jury verdict acquitting a motorist who had run down an eight-year-old pedestrian. The issue in the case concerned the speed at which the defendant Printz was driving and whether his speed made him criminally negligent; the jury believed the defendant's rather than the district attorney's account and found him not negligent. Since the trial judge vehemently expressed his view to the jurors that they had freed a guilty man who had deserved punishment, Weinfeld was probably just as pleased that he had managed to keep his own name out of the article.[54]

In both *Goldberg* and *Printz* Weinfeld achieved striking successes, for the same reasons that he had often attained success in his matrimonial practice. In *Printz*, for example, he undoubtedly had scrutinized the facts closely and synthesized them into a narrative that proved persuasive to the jury.

Even when drafting a document designed to serve formalistic ends rather than sway a fact finder, Weinfeld dealt with facts impressively. Thus, when Guiseppe Filangeri sued the state for failing to protect his son Joseph from being killed by fellow prisoners in Sing Sing Prison, Weinfeld drafted a complaint with considerable flair. He painted a portrait of a young man ambushed by codefendants who bore him "ill will" because he had pled guilty, apparently after testifying against them; the state, according to Weinfeld's complaint, was aware of these facts but did nothing to provide young Joseph with the added protection he needed.[55] In marshalling these facts, Weinfeld wrote in clear, organized, and often eloquent prose, just as he had in his matrimonial cases.

The same was true in *People v. Lutterman*, in which Weinfeld filed a motion for a trial by jury on behalf of a defendant charged with usury as a misdemeanor. His claim was that if Lutterman had brought a civil action to recover the money he had lent, he would have received a jury trial; it followed as "a matter of simple justice that the defendants should similarly be entitled to a trial by jury where not only is their property involved, but also their liberty."[56] Likewise, in his requests to charge in *United States v. Weinberger*, Weinfeld sought to gain an edge for his client with precise use of language: for instance, he asked the court to instruct the jury "that if any one of the jury, after having consulted with his fellow-jurymen, entertains a reasonable doubt of the defendants' guilt, the jury cannot convict."[57] Weinfeld's requested instruction was technically correct—a jury in a criminal case could not convict if one juror, entertaining a reasonable doubt, voted to acquit. But the implication that the jury should acquit if one juror entertained a reasonable doubt clearly was incorrect.

Weinfeld's requested instruction in the *Weinberger* case, which he probably offered in other cases as well, also revealed his uncanny strategic sense about the impact that different lines of argument might have on different participants in the legal process. He understood, that is, how to achieve more for his clients than the law permitted while still acting in a technically correct fashion. He displayed this astute strategic judgment in the *Goldberg* case, for example, where he relied upon a technical rule of evidence and the testimony of a police officer to free his client from a gangland-style murder charge of which, for all we know, his client may have been guilty.

Of course, Weinfeld worked long and hard on cases in his criminal practice, just as he did on matrimonial cases. In *People v. Kestenbaum*, for example, he took the unusual step of citing cases in support of his jury instruction requests.[58] The most compelling illustration of his hard work was his sixty-two-page brief for the Court of Appeals in *People v. Leik*, in which the court did not even write an opinion;[59] the brief contained a typical, detailed, Weinfeldian analysis of the facts plus citations to over fifty different cases.[60] Although Weinfeld probably received a respectable fee from Robert Leik, who was a middle-class man with two children in college and a summer home on Long Island,[61] the comprehensivenes of his brief makes it likely that he was not compensated in full for all the hours he invested. Thus, the *Leik* brief again shows that Weinfeld did not treat law as a business. His goal was not to make as much money as he possibly could, but to provide clients with the most effective possible representation, even if that required him to devote extra hours to their cases without billing them in full.

The *Leik* case also emphasizes Weinfeld's compassion for underdogs and willingness to represent those who were unpopular—Robert Leik was a local politico under investigation by the Seabury Commission. The *Printz* case, in which Weinfeld obtained the acquittal for a motorist who had killed an eight-year-old pedestrian, and the *Goodman* case, in which he was involved in representing owners of theaters accused "of presenting . . . obscene, indecent, immoral or impure performance[s],"[62] further illustrate his willingness to work for clients of whom the public disapproved. Most significantly, his work even for these clients was never perfunctory. Although Weinfeld himself adhered to the most rigid of traditional standards in regard to professional, business, and sexual mores, his habit of caring enabled him to empathize with those who held different values.

As noted earlier, Weinfeld cared for the law, and he cared for his clients. Indeed, he became his clients' friend. This was true not only of Ralphina Lowenstein and her three sons but even of criminal convicts. One reason he disliked criminal defense work was that he often developed intense personal relationships with those he represented; he grieved when he lost their cases and they went off to jail.[63] But even then, he did not abandon them. Thus, there is one instance in which one of his clients, who had been convicted of acts involving organized crime for which he had done time in state prison, came to Weinfeld after his release. The man, who happened to be Jewish, had fallen in love with a woman who was not Jewish and wanted to marry her, but he was afraid to ask his mother for permission. Weinfeld, undoubtedly without asking for any fee, spoke to the mother on the convict's behalf, and persuaded the mother to permit her son to marry the gentile woman. The marriage was performed, a son was subsequently born, and eventually that son became a lawyer.[64]

As already suggested, Weinfeld's criminal and matrimonial practice was not a lucrative one. In one criminal case, for instance, in which he served as associate counsel for a prominent attorney in a federal criminal jury trial that lasted for six weeks, he received a fee of only $350; he took the case only because the defendant "was a very dear friend of dear friends of mine" and because his prominence created a "likelihood of future business from that source."[65] Undoubtedly, Weinfeld was somewhat better compensated when he represented parties in business matters or other matters involving money. Even in these sorts of cases, however, Weinfeld's practice was not about maximizing his income but about meeting the highest of professional standards and serving his clients well.

A large part of Weinfeld's commercial litigation practice involved arguing what many lawyers would have regarded as routine procedural issues having little direct relationship to the merits of cases. One very common set of issues, in particular, leaps out from the legal papers he has left—namely, issues about pretrial discovery. Weinfeld, however, treated these matters as anything but routine.

Consider, for example, *Artloom Corp. v. Robbins Bros., Inc.*, where the plaintiff had served a notice to examine the defendant, Weinfeld's client, before trial. Weinfeld served a motion to vacate or otherwise modify the notice, which he labeled "surely, a fishing expedition."[66] But he also addressed in detail the specific requests of the plaintiff; for instance, Weinfeld observed,

> Item 16 seeks to examine defendant on "Whether defendant gave shipping instructions for the merchandise referred to in Schedule E * * * ". Defendant in its answer (paragraph 8) admits "that the defendant has

given no shipping instructions with relation thereto." Still on Schedule E in item 17 of the notice, plaintiff wants to examine defendant as to whether plaintiff "was ready, willing and able" to ship the merchandise set forth in Schedule E. Clearly, plaintiff itself can best testify to that and there is no necessity for an examination of the defendant on that score.[67]

It must also be noted that, in support of this and similar observations, Weinfeld cited and analyzed six precedents.

Weinfeld's attention to detail typically gave him a significant edge over opposing counsel, who were not prepared as Weinfeld was to put in the time to master detail when their clients were unprepared to pay for that time. Thus, in *Bernstein v. Fan & Bill's, Inc.*, where Weinfeld had served a notice to examine the plaintiff and the plaintiff had moved to vacate the notice, Weinfeld focused on detail at a level that his opponent failed to address. He wrote,

> The application to vacate the notice of examination is based upon the affidavit of the plaintiff's attorney, but no affidavit is interposed by the plaintiff himself. The affidavit of said attorney merely argues matters of law and not of fact.[68]

Weinfeld thereupon proceeded to examine the facts and cited nine cases in a six-page brief in support of his right to take the plaintiff's deposition, which the court authorized him to take.[69]

At the same time, Weinfeld moved to vacate a notice of examination against Fan & Bill's by another plaintiff whose "failure to specify or itemize the matters upon which the examination is sought can be construed only as an attempt to gain the benefits of a fishing expedition." After analyzing in depth two precedents declaring generalized notices of examination defective because they "impose . . . upon both court and counsel the task of comparing the complaint and the answers paragraph by paragraph and endeavoring to ascertain therefrom what conclusions the examining party has in mind,"[70] Weinfeld ended up writing a thirty-page memo seeking to ascertain the matters on which the plaintiff wished to conduct the examination—a memo that even Weinfeld understood was unusually long, as is indicated by his concluding apologia/argument:

> The foregoing detailed memorandum has been made necessary by virtue of the length of the pleadings herein and the failure of the plaintiff to

enumerate and itemize the alleged matters upon which the examination is sought. Analysis, however, shows that there is no justification for the proposed examination, which seeks to wander far afield from the real issues in the case.[71]

Sometimes motions to vacate notices of examination before trial (e.b.t.) raised legal issues, such as whether an e.b.t. was appropriate if it might lead to questions that might incriminate a party or whether a particular party had the burden of proof on a particular issue and thus was entitled to take an e.b.t. in connection with that issue. In two cases involving Weinfeld in which such issues arose, he wrote memoranda in which he analyzed existing case law in detail, in both instances analyzing five precedents, once in a nine-page and once in an eight-page memorandum.[72]

Memoranda such as those we have been discussing demonstrate why Weinfeld during his first decade in practice had become an effective lawyer. In business as well as in divorce and criminal cases, Weinfeld was prepared to put in the time and to attend to detail in a way in which the lawyers who opposed him were not. When he sat down to write a brief, and undoubtedly when he walked into a courtroom to argue a case, he simply knew the material at hand better than anyone else. As a result, he enjoyed an enormous edge and provided his clients with superlative professional service.

Of course, he did not always win. In one case, for example, in which he submitted a twelve-page memorandum analyzing six controlling cases in opposition to a defendant's motion for a bill of particulars, the court still decided against him. Weinfeld had contended that granting the motion "in the manner and form requested by the defendant . . . would require the service of a bill of particulars consisting of seven or eight hundred pages" and that such a "request for unnecessary details . . . [was] palpably calculated to harass and annoy plaintiff."[73] The court ruled, however, that "the length of the list of items to be furnished or the difficulty of compiling such a list is not a valid reason for denying the bill."[74]

When we turn from procedure to the substance of Weinfeld's business practice, we see that many of the same patterns that characterized his criminal and matrimonial practice reappear. Perhaps the most notable is that, even in business cases, he typically represented underdogs—middle- and lower-middle-class people with relatively small claims or with claims that were not essentially about recovering money. A surprisingly large number of his clients, moreover, were women; one accordingly wonders whether Weinfeld's experience representing women in divorce cases had led him to develop a professional style that made him more comfortable dealing with women and women more comfortable dealing professionally with him than was true with most men.

In one case, for instance, Weinfeld brought suit on behalf of a woman who claimed that defendants had defamed her. At issue was the significance of a fifteen-hundred-dollar payment that the defendants had made to the plaintiff; the defendants had said that the payment was made as "hush money," "peace money," and "blackmail money," while the plaintiff claimed that the money had been paid in consideration of services she had rendered and that the defendants' statements were slanderous. In a memorandum in opposition to a motion to dismiss his client's complaint, which raised the issue whether the defamatory statements had been alleged with sufficient specificity, Weinfeld cited a published trial court opinion virtually on all fours with his own case.[75]

Weinfeld also represented a woman, Mary Raives, when she sued the United States unsuccessfully to enforce payment of an insurance policy issued on her son's life under the War Risk Insurance Act. The son had permitted the policy to lapse on two occasions for nonpayment of premiums, but had subsequently on both occasions reinstated it. In both reinstatement applications, he had stated falsely that he had not consulted a physician while the policy was lapsed, and the issue was whether his misstatements vitiated the policy. The policy itself stated that reinstated policies were incontestable except for nonpayment of premiums, but the statute under which reinstatement was made provided that policies could be contested for a second reason as well—namely, fraud.

After losing in the District Court on the ground that "the statute and not the policy governs, and since the statute expressly excepts fraud from the operation of the incontestability clause, the fraud of the insured vitiates the contract,"[76] Weinfeld wrote a thirty-four-page brief and a six-page reply brief, in which he collectively cited over forty cases, along with War Department regulations and opinions of the comptroller general. He addressed such issues as whether the insured's representations were truly fraudulent, as well as whether the language of the policy, the War Department's regulations, or the words of the statute should be controlling. He argued that, if the policy had been issued by a private insurer, the insured's misstatements would not have barred recovery and that, "when the Government enters the domain of private contract, courts have a right to exact from it the same standards of justice and fair dealing which they exact from private parties." Accordingly, when "the Government permit[ted] the insured to be lulled into a false sense of security by inserting . . . in the policy" an incontestability clause that did not protect the government against the insured's fraud, the government should be bound by its clause.[77] The Court of Appeals, however, unanimously rejected Weinfeld's contention, holding that the United States could be "bound only to the extent it has consented to be bound" and that "no agent had authority to waive the provisions of the statute."[78]

A third female client of Weinfeld was Fanny Smith, who had fallen down a flight of darkened stairs to which the defendant had directed her without warning. Smith had recovered a jury verdict of $250 to cover some $800 of lost wages and $21 of medical expenses. Obviously, the jury had reduced her damages for contributory negligence, and the defendant was arguing on appeal that the verdict should instead be reversed for contributory negligence. Citing seven cases, Weinfeld argued, however, that, since the question of contributory negligence had properly been submitted to the jury, its verdict should be affirmed.[79]

Defendant also argued that the verdict should be reversed because a witness had informed the jury that the defendant was insured. Analyzing ten cases in a brief that was somewhat extensive, given that only $250 was involved, Weinfeld responded that, when a "plaintiff's counsel . . . deliberately . . . convey[ed] to the jury the idea that the defendant is insured," a plaintiff's verdict would be set aside, but when the fact of insurance "c[a]me before the jury inadvertently or accidentally," then the verdict could be sustained. He then noted that the witness had spoken about insurance in a purely gratuitous response to a question by the trial judge.[80]

Weinfeld represented women like Fanny Smith in the same way that he represented men who were parties to cases involving small sums of money—thoroughly. Thus, when the Municipal Court rendered a judgment for $180 against Sam Mittman for converting eight suit coats from his partners, Max Grossinger and Joe Lieber, Weinfeld appealed and wrote a careful, though succinct, memorandum urging that damages were improperly assessed and that the Municipal Court lacked jurisdiction over a suit between members of an ongoing partnership.[81] He wrote a similarly short but careful memorandum in support of Morris Sadof's claim that four promissory notes upon which Lena Rosenstein had sued him for a total of one thousand dollars had been discharged in bankruptcy.[82]

Weinfeld's willingness to work on behalf of clients with relatively small claims is perhaps best illustrated, however, by the case of *Dubin v. Shander*. Morris Dubin had sued the defendant, a resident of Philadelphia, for $2,820 for breach of an employment contract. Since Dubin proceeded against the defendant by attaching accounts receivable in New York, he was required to post a bond, and he did so in the amount of $250. The defendant then moved to increase the bond to twenty-five hundred dollars, the trial judge denied the motion, and the defendant appealed. In a ten-page brief relying on five cases, Weinfeld effectively made the legal argument that the trial judge had not abused his discretion and hence ought to be affirmed. But he also did more. He went painstakingly through the facts then in the record and showed that the maximum costs that the defendant could possibly incur as a result of the attachment amounted to $172.15—for which a $250 bond was fully sufficient. Finally, he implied that the impact of requiring plaintiff "to give $2,500 security in a $2,820 case," when bonds typically were in a range of 10 percent of damages sought, would deter plaintiffs like Dubin from bringing relatively small claims.[83] Agreeing with Weinfeld, the Appellate Division affirmed.[84]

In addition to his briefs at the trial[85] and appellate levels on the defendant's motion to increase the security, Weinfeld also had to write a third memorandum in the case—in this instance, one in support of his own motion for a bill of particulars and in opposition to the defendant's motion for an examination of the plaintiff before trial. Needless to say, Weinfeld prepared his usual lucid and thorough memorandum;[86] the trial court granted the bill of particulars, refused defendant's request to examine plaintiff on two separate occasions, but did grant the request for an examination before trial.[87]

A significant area of litigation practice for Weinfeld in the late 1920s and 1930s—the years of the Great Depression—was bankruptcy and insolvency. Although bankruptcy and insolvency cases are capable of producing substantial legal fees, Weinfeld does not appear to have represented litigants who were capable of paying them. In one case, for example, he represented a coal company that was sued by the trustee in bankruptcy of another coal company on a check and eight promissory notes totaling $1,059.08—not a sum out of which he could receive any major fee. Weinfeld's memorandum did not even address the merits of the case—a matter on which he would need to expend further labor in the future—but simply sought to transfer the plaintiff's suit from the equity to the law side of the federal court.[88] And, in another case, he represented a wife to whom her husband had transferred the family home and other property several months before entering bankruptcy. Although the Second Circuit Court of Appeals, in a unanimous opinion by Augustus Hand, agreed with Weinfeld that the husband did not have an actual intent to defraud creditors, the court nonetheless held that the transfer was constructively fraudulent under New York law since the husband was insolvent at the time he made it.[89] It seems unlikely that a bankrupt without major assets or even a home would have been able to pay Weinfeld a substantial legal fee.

Of course, Weinfeld had occasional cases in which a prospect of earning a substantial fee existed. He lost some of these cases, however. He was unsuccessful in one case, for example, when he sought to compel the State Tax Commission to redeem $6,471.10 in stock transfer stamps that had been pledged to his client's decedent as security for a loan,[90] and in another, when he sought through a summary proceeding in New York to enforce a New Jersey judgment in favor of an automobile accident victim.[91]

On the other hand, Weinfeld did better in a case he tried involving a claim for four thousand dollars liquidated damages for breach of a contract to convey commercial property. In this case, he submitted an eighteen-page post-trial memorandum elaborating the facts and analyzing fourteen cases; his opponent's nine-page brief, in contrast, cited only six cases.[92] Weinfeld won, his client recovered the four thousand dollars,[93] and, assuming that the case was litigated under a standard contingency fee contract, Weinfeld received a fee in excess of one thousand dollars.

Weinfeld also may have earned a substantial fee in *Loder v. Alexander Hamilton Institute*, in which two women alleged that male employees of the defendant broke into the ladies' room of the defendant's building while the plaintiffs were present therein and slandered the plaintiffs by accusing them of "unchastity and moral turpitude and the commission of unnatural sexual acts." Again, Weinfeld, who in this case was representing the defendant on a motion to dismiss the complaint, outwrote his opponent. In connection with the entry into the ladies' room, Weinfeld found a controlling Appellate Division precedent, where an analogous claim had been dismissed; he searched out the record on appeal in that case, quoted the language of the complaint, and argued compellingly that the complaint in the instant case was weaker than the complaint in the precedent case.[94] In analyzing the slander allegation, Weinfeld zeroed in on the word "queer" as the one that "might possibly be construed . . . as conveying the suggestion of wrongdoing, moral turpitude or degeneracy"; he then quoted the dictionary definition of "queer" to show that the dictionary gave the word no such meaning and cited an Appellate Division precedent holding that, *"if the Plaintiff desired to extend the meaning of"* a word, *"he should have alleged as a fact the peculiar or slang meaning which he claimed the word had acquired."*[95] The plaintiffs' attorney, in contrast, wrote a much shorter brief with several citations to *Corpus Juris, Abbott's Forms of Pleading*, and the *Encyclopaedia of Pleading and Practice*; an effort to distinguish the main case Weinfeld had cited; and a general argument that "parlor definitions must yield to the reality of the innuendos."[96] Needless to say, the court granted Weinfeld's motion.[97]

During the first fifteen years of his practice, Weinfeld may have received his single largest fee in the case of *Field v. Rice*, in which he brought suit against the New York City health commissioner on behalf of licensed master plumbers. To obtain their licenses, the plumbers had been required to pass an examination administered pursuant to legislation that had been repealed and superseded by new legislation enacted in 1936. The health commissioner proposed to reexamine the plumbers under the new law and revoke the licenses of those who did not pass, and the plumbers retained Weinfeld for a fee of twenty-five hundred dollars, plus five hundred dollars in disbursements, to bring suit challenging the constitutionality of the commissioner's proposal.[98]

Finally, Weinfeld could hope for big fees in several corporate cases in which he was retained. In one of the smaller cases, *Mosberg v. Trattner*, he represented the owners of a restaurant corporation, Fan & Bill's Inc., which they had agreed to sell to the plaintiff and a partner for the sum of thirty thousand dollars. For reasons that were hotly disputed by the parties, the sale never was completed, the owners rescinded the contract, and they instead sold the restaurant to the plaintiff's original partner. On the plaintiff's motion for equitable relief aimed at preventing the sale to the partner, Weinfeld in a forty-four-page brief developed the defendant's factual claim that the plaintiff had failed to pay the money he owed at the time the contract of sale was to be performed and examined twenty-seven cases in support of his arguments that the defendant had a right to rescind and the plaintiff had no right to equitable relief.[99] A business worth thirty thousand dollars in the 1930s was a substantial one, and Weinfeld undoubtedly received a good fee for handling its legal difficulties.

In another case, Weinfeld represented dissident shareholders in a much larger entity, the Butterick Company, which, according to one of the two briefs he wrote in the case,

> owned and controlled The Butterick pattern business which extended throughout the entire world, and . . . engaged in printing, publishing and distributing women's magazines, such as the Delineator and others. However, its principal business was the manufacture and sale of patterns for women's clothes, and was the largest organization of its kind in the world.

The dissidents claimed that management was looting Butterick and sought the appointment of "independent trustees" who could "impartially administer the assets of the corporation, cancel such contracts as should be cancelled, and join in . . . suits against the malefactors who have brought the corporation to its present status."[100] Of course, if the dissidents obtained the relief they were seeking, Weinfeld would have received a very substantial fee. But it has been impossible to determine whether they did.

Weinfeld also was involved peripherally in one portion of a giant case, when he was retained by the Maryland-appointed receivers of the United Cigar Company, who were seeking to examine several New York residents about the disappearance of some $6 million of the company's assets. He might have earned a huge fee if he had gotten the opportunity to conduct the examinations he sought, but unfortunately he never received the chance since the Appellate Division ruled that the privilege of examination is available only to receivers appointed by a New York court,[101] which Weinfeld's clients were not.

A final corporate case, and one in which Weinfeld was centrally involved, was brought by him on behalf of shareholders of the American Woolen Company, which, he alleged, had wrongfully paid bonuses to various corporate officers in the sum of six hundred thousand dollars. Weinfeld wrote five extensive briefs on various pretrial matters in connection with this case,[102] as well as a lengthy, substantive letter to the federal judge who was hearing the case.[103]

Describing his corporate cases as "important and big," Weinfeld had high hopes that they would bring him "definite results in the way of compensation." But, as Weinfeld recognized, being owed large fees did not necessarily mean that he could collect them. In a case, for example, in which he represented two individuals associated with a New Jersey corporation, the corporation's entry into reorganization "greatly affected the payment of my fee," although he hoped, once the reorganization was completed, "that I may receive some small part of the fee that is due me."[104] He also had learned in part from his representation of a friend and frequent associate, Maxwell Shapiro, that lawyers often received only a small part of their fee—Shapiro had a contract with a client for a fee of $650, but when he sued on the contract he received a judgment from a trial court of only $204.[105]

As a result of difficulties of these sorts, Weinfeld's practice simply did not flourish financially. It appears that in the late 1930s his gross income from law practice, before making any deductions for office expenses, was perhaps about twelve thousand dollars per year[106]—an amount that did not suffice to cover all his expenses as a young husband and, by then, a father of two infant daughters. At one point, probably in the early 1930s, he had to borrow several thousand dollars from a friend and former fraternity brother, Joseph Eichler, and throughout the decade he was unable to repay. Of course, his inability to repay "disturbed" Weinfeld "quite a bit—in fact, more so than I am willing to admit." For example, when Eichler telegraphed in October 1935 that he needed one thousand to fifteen hundred dollars to help him purchase a new home, Weinfeld had to respond, "Terribly embarrassed[.] I cannot remit any amount now." As Weinfeld later explained,

> I was very anxious to do something to reduce the loan to you, but, unfortunately, despite an exceedingly busy year, I have found conditions to be such that have just about enabled me to meet all current expenses both at the office and at home.

After making three payments totaling nine hundred dollars during 1936 and 1937, Weinfeld still owed Eichler twenty-one hundred dollars at the end of the decade.[107]

But, as we have already seen, Weinfeld's early career in practice was not about making money; it was about fidelity to the law. On one occasion, for example, he was willing to spend a good deal of time working with the judges of the New York City Municipal Court in modifying the court's rules of practice. When the court proposed a new rule in connection with preclusion orders in cases involving bills of particulars, Weinfeld wrote to the presiding judge that "the wisdom of the rule and the power of the Board of Justices to make the same is, in my opinion, open to question"; in explaining his reasons for this conclusion, Weinfeld analyzed a section of the Municipal Court Code, as well as a Court of Appeals case, an Appellate Division case, and an Appellate Term case. When Weinfeld wrote a second letter following up his first, the chairman of the court's rules committee invited him to "drop in to see him to discuss the suggestions contained in your" first letter. Ultimately, the issue was addressed by the state legislature, and the court postponed taking any action.[108]

Weinfeld's fidelity to law also opened him to acknowledging and admitting the mistakes that he knew every lawyer must inevitably make. He did not let pride or even the interests of clients stand in the way. Thus, in one bankruptcy matter in which he learned after he had filed his complaint on the trustee's behalf of a precedent "not cited by the defendants," he brought the precedent to the court's attention and was "frank to state" that the precedent "seems to indicate that the action commenced herein should properly be on the law side of the courts instead of on the equity side." Thus, he accepted the contention of the defendants that "the bill of complaint on its face show[ed] no ground of equitable relief," but prayed that the court transfer the case to the law side rather than dismiss it.[109]

The first—indeed, the only—concern of Edward Weinfeld's professional career was "law and more law,"[110] and he always did whatever needed to be done as he strove to get the law right. His absolute fidelity to the law made him an unusual—indeed, a truly special—lawyer, just as in the future it would make him an unusual and truly special judge.

4

Family

We have seen how, as he neared the end of his first decade in practice, Edward Weinfeld had already developed most of the characteristics that those who knew him in his later years on the bench would identify as distinctively his. Growing up in "working-class New York,"[1] he had learned to accept with modesty a plain, simple life dedicated to helping others. He also had become an unusually able listener and observer, who responded with compassion to the human situations he encountered and with exceptional empathy to underdogs and others excluded from elite social networks. Finally, he had learned to be an indefatigable worker who could be relied upon to complete tasks thoroughly and intelligently, without regard to the profit, if any, that he would obtain by completing them.

He also had cultivated important professional skills of writing clear and often eloquent prose, of synthesizing facts into persuasive narratives, and of developing litigation strategies. Above all, Weinfeld by the end of his first decade in practice had developed the habit of caring for the law and for his clients.

But the wholly rounded Edward Weinfeld of later years was not yet present as the 1920s drew to their close. Some important experiences that would affect how he would think about the world as a judge had not yet occurred. Significant episodes that will be addressed in a future chapter were those in politics. This chapter will focus on family and on what Edward Weinfeld's experiences as a husband and father reveal about him in his later years on the bench.

The story of his family life began in 1923, the year in which Weinfeld commenced the practice of law in partnership with his brother Morris and hired a seventeen-year-old, recent high school graduate, Lillian Stoll, as his secretary. Lillian hoped to attend law school and thought that professional training in an attorney's office would help prepare her for the

the rigors of legal education. She planned to remain in the office only for one year, but ended up remaining for six.[2] Soon after she had begun working for Weinfeld, they began dating,[3] and nearly seven years later they would be married.

Theirs was a weird courtship, however, which must have put Lillian on notice that she was dating an unusual man. First of all, the courtship was a lengthy one. Once their relationship had become a romantic one, Lillian's father began "pressing for a marriage" and urging Weinfeld "to give up living in Manhattan and move to Brooklyn."[4] But Weinfeld resisted. For one thing, he did not feel ready, financially at least, to get married.[5] Then, there was his "implacability" about leaving the Lower East Side.[6] In his view, his "roots were in Manhattan: not only was [he] born and raised there, but [his] professional life was centered there."[7] Moreover, his parents lived there. In the end, if she wanted to marry Edward Weinfeld, Lillian Stoll would have to abandon the Brooklyn neighborhoods she knew, where her parents still lived, and relocate to the Lower East Side.

The courtship also must have been characterized by infrequent dates. According to Weinfeld, he "would see Lillian after hours."[8] The difficulty, of course, was that he kept such late hours. "Besides Law," on which, as we have just seen, Weinfeld worked intensely, his "other vocation, avocation and invocation" was "the Phi Sigma Delta Fraternity," which he "talk[ed] . . . , breathe[d] . . . , dream[ed] of . . . and work[ed] for."[9] There were also his friends. He was dedicated and dependable when it came to work, fraternity, and friends, and that left little time for Lillian. Thus, he "usually" had dates with her "on Saturdays," and even then, mainly on Saturdays during the summer.

Weinfeld left the following description of a typical date:

The office was very quiet on Saturdays, though in those days offices usually stayed open a full day. In the summer (presumably July and August), they closed at 1 o'clock. We would leave and go over to Whytes, a famous restaurant on Fulton Street. I remember exactly what I would have. I think Lillian did, too: the most delicious cold salmon you ever tasted, the finest blueberry pie just oozing with blueberries and juice— no gelatin or anything like that—and iced coffee. Then we would go to Manhattan Beach, where we rented lockers. Our group at that time included Bugsy (Belmont Freiwald), Joe Eichler, Al Cohen, and Sam Greenberg, who was later a state senator. There was a famous seafood restaurant, Villepigues (I think it still exists today), where we'd go for dinner. Then all of us would usually return [to Lillian's parents' home].[10]

Seventy-five years later, these trips to the beach with Weinfeld and four of his friends seem like odd dates from the perspective of Lillian Stoll. Even if Weinfeld's friends regularly attended the beach parties with steady dates of their own, the Saturday afternoons at the beach look more like a gathering of friends, which Weinfeld invited his secretary to join, than opportunities for a young couple to develop a romantic relationship.[11] One gets the sense from the length and nature of the courtship that marriage to Lillian Stoll was not the first thing on Edward Weinfeld's mind during the late 1920s. And one gets a further sense that Lillian had to know that, if she married Weinfeld, she would always be competing with and usually losing to others who made claims on her husband's attention.

Under these circumstances, Lillian's father insisted, after she had been dating Weinfeld for five years, that she break off the relationship with him and leave her job as his secretary.[12] It was only after Weinfeld paid a condolence call on Lillian following her father's death that their courtship resumed[13] and led several months later to their marriage, on December 22, 1929.[14] Following the wedding, the Weinfelds went to Cuba for a brief honeymoon,[15] and then they moved into a two-bedroom apartment in a newly constructed luxury building located on the northwest corner of Avenue A and East Third Street—half a block away from where Edward Weinfeld had grown up and where his parents still lived.[16]

Within four years of the wedding, as a result of births and deaths, profound changes had occurred in Weinfeld's family. The first occurrence was the death of Weinfeld's father on November 10, 1930.[17] His death was followed seven months later by the birth of Weinfeld's first child, a daughter, Ann, on June 14, 1931.[18] Eight months later, his mother died, on February 18, 1932,[19] and his younger sister, Bertha, who had been living with his parents, moved into the apartment of Edward and Lillian.[20] Two years later, a second daughter, Fern, was born on June 4, 1934.[21]

As the children were growing up, the Weinfeld marriage was a happy, "conventional"[22] one, in which Lillian Weinfeld took charge of the household and the children and otherwise subordinated herself to the career and concerns of her husband. Lillian was "likeable, practical and charming" and "ran the household with a smooth efficiency" that her husband "celebrated, calling her 'practical Lil.'"[23] Knowing how good a wife she was, Lillian recorded one entry in her diary describing how some

Edward Weinfeld, Lillian Weinfeld, daughter Ann (*standing*), and Fern (*seated on father's lap*), 1939.

"uncles had to tell EW what a wonderful 'wibele' [wife] he has—as if he didn't know."[24] As was true of many marriages of the time, Lillian Weinfeld made her husband's well-being "her primary focus" and seemed "content to live within his orbit" and provide "service and attendance to him."[25]

In return, he provided the necessary support. Although the Weinfelds were overcrowded in their two-bedroom apartment until 1940, when it became possible to rent the adjoining apartment, break through its walls, and combine the two into one large unit, the family otherwise led a comfortable, upper-middle-class existence. In particular, Lillian Weinfeld never needed to seek employment outside the home to earn income and always had household help to assist her with the apartment and with her two daughters.[26] Her sister-in-law, Bertha, also could provide some limited aid. As a result, Lillian was not tied to a workplace, to her apartment, or to the schedules of her children and was free to pursue her own interests.

One interest was entertaining. Lillian Weinfeld was a vivacious and gracious hostess who relished giving a dinner party. More significantly, she maintained an open-house policy: even though it was her husband's friends who typically showed up with little notice or even unannounced,[27] she always fed them, welcomed them, and talked with them. "Her knack for small talk and her interest in the extended family of clerks, fellow judges, lawyers, and friends were integral to the sense of home" she provided to her guests.[28]

Entertaining guests was an enjoyable and vital part of Lillian Weinfeld's life. In 1941, for example, her diary recorded that she hosted some thirty parties,[29] and over the years the diary showed that she clearly enjoyed the role of hostess. Some of her comments after parties were as follows: "'Twas a memorable evening," "wonderful stories told that night," "a 'swell' party," "the kids had a wonderful time," "very 'talky' evening, proud of our girls," "a very nice evening," "Tiny playing piano all evening," "nice evening—listened and saw Eisenhower on television," "good dinner—good talk," and "a good dinner party & evening."[30]

Of course, their friends reciprocated, inviting the Weinfelds to their homes with frequency. In addition, Edward and Lillian Weinfeld attended other functions together; many photographs show them dressed together in preparation for an evening out and display Lillian as a "beautiful" woman who was "vivacious" in relation to her husband. Occasionally, the entire Weinfeld family went to dinner together on Sunday nights—either at Longchamps or at Manny Wolf's restaurant on Third Avenue and Forty-ninth Street.[31]

In addition to her happy pursuit of an active social life, Lillian Weinfeld engaged energetically in charitable and other volunteer work. In doing so, she traded, as did other women of her era, on her husband's prestige as a lawyer, a government official, and eventually a judge—positions that made her one of the leading women residing on the Lower East Side. Nothing, however, pleased her husband more; it enabled him to see himself and his wife as a team serving the public good and helping individuals in need.

Lillian began her charitable work during World War II, when she became "active in Red Cross work and [was] a driver in the Motor Corps." She also engaged in other Red Cross work, "such as blood bank, some administrative work, [and] emergency duty at hospitals."[32] According to a note in her diary, she became "too busy to entertain," with "me in Motor Corps" and "EW in Housing."[33] Lillian's work as a Red Cross

Edward and Lillian Weinfeld, early 1940s.

ambulance driver was an "area . . . of competence"[34] in which her husband took pride. As he wrote to a friend, "her work and efforts in her unit" convinced him that the "Red Cross [was] really an outstanding organization" for which she was "doing a grand job."[35]

After the war, Lillian Weinfeld's activities continued. One involvement was with the Henry Street Settlement, the charitable institution founded by Lillian Wald to help the Lower East Side's poor. More important was her substantial role in Adlai Stevenson's 1952 presidential campaign: she served as cochair of the effort in New York County.[36]

Mrs. Weinfeld also became active for more than a decade in LENA, the Lower Eastside Neighborhoods Association, of which she was a cochairperson. She was also cochairperson, along with the New York City parks commissioner, of the Evenings-by-the-River committee, which under the auspices of LENA arranged free Tuesday and Thursday evening outdoor concerts during July and August at a twenty-five-hundred-seat amphitheater at Grand Street and Franklin D. Roosevelt Drive. One of her annual duties as cochair was to introduce Eleanor Roosevelt, who was the honorary chairperson for the concerts.[37]

When LENA gave Mrs. Weinfeld an award in 1966 for her service to the organization, she looked back on her thirty-six years of residence on the Lower East Side, "a good part" of which "was spent in communal activities in the city." In particular, she recalled that "[o]ne of the joys & honor[s]" of working on the Evenings-by-the-River concerts was her "association" with Mrs. Roosevelt—a "gracious lady [who] never missed the first concert of each series." She also told how she had become interested in the concerts when in the early 1950s she had learned that "the shell, the beautiful little ampitheatre on the river, was begging to be used" and that "all I had to do, I was told, was raise the money."[38]

It was a perfect job for the wife of a newly appointed federal judge. Today's ethical norms regard fund raising by a judge as inherently coercive and therefore prohibit it; of course, fund raising by a judge's wife would be equally coercive. We will never know whether Lillian Weinfeld was asked to take charge of the concert series because the people who controlled LENA were aiming to trade on Edward Weinfeld's judicial power or whether either of the Weinfelds even vaguely sensed that they were being used, albeit for a good cause. Nevertheless, it does seem clear that the joy and recognition that Mrs. Weinfeld obtained from her work with LENA grew out of her marriage to a judge and were an element of her happiness in that marriage. Other elements, of course, were the glory that her charitable labors cast on her husband and his appreciation of those labors—an appreciation that he expressed publicly by remarking on the "fidelity & devotion" of Mrs. Weinfeld's "efforts," which, he hoped, would "inspire others to serve."[39]

The portrait of familial happiness sketched so far becomes more ambiguous, however, when we examine the most difficult task that nearly every married couple faces—rearing their children. At the outset, it is essential to observe that Edward and Lillian Weinfeld performed this task for their daughters Ann and Fern with every outward sign of success. Both daughters flourished academically in high school and college;[40] later married and raised their own families; went on to receive professional degrees, Ann's a J.D. in law and Fern's a Ph.D. in psychology; and have enjoyed thriving professional careers. Although Fern did suffer an episode of anorexia and depression during her sophomore year in college, she understands the psychoanalysis she then underwent as a transformative event in her life that turned her in the direction of her later professional career.[41]

Even with the Weinfelds' outward success, however, some disquieting incidents still occurred as Ann and Fern matured. These incidents generated tensions that reveal a great deal about Edward Weinfeld as a person and ultimately as a judge.

The tensions were not between Edward and Lillian Weinfeld, who always presented a united front to their daughters. Rather, they were of two different sorts. The first sort was between, on the one hand, the moral and cultural norms by which Weinfeld lived and thought others should live and, on the other hand, his human empathy—his desire to give another person what he understood that person wanted. The second was between Weinfeld's love for his wife and daughters and his duty and fidelity to his work and the law.

Some of the incidents were trivial ones, but their triviality makes them no less revealing. They revolved around shopping trips for clothes that Mrs. Weinfeld took with her daughters. When the girls, who had gone out to buy one dress each, "fell in love with two," their mother, "[c]learly believing that we should limit ourselves," would never decide whether to let them have both but "would suggest that we take both home for my father to decide." "In his study after dinner," there would then occur a "ritual" in which "he would interrupt his reading or work while we would model each [dress] and without fail, he would admire us and say, 'Why don't you keep both?'"[42] The message conveyed by the ritual was always clear: even though the Weinfelds, who had to make do with a limited income, were committed to living a plain, simple life dedicated to helping others, Edward Weinfeld could not implement that commitment when the two daughters he loved wanted more. Faced with having to make a choice between realizing his virtuous beliefs or showing compassion for two human beings who had captured his attention, he opted for compassion.

As the the Weinfelds' two young daughters matured and boyfriends and eventually marriage entered their lives, analogous but graver family tensions arose. The tensions, on the whole, were generational: Edward and Lillian Weinfeld, in defense of the moral precepts of their generation, initially presented a united front against one of their daughters, even if it was not always clear which of the parents had been the author of the front. But, in the end, Edward Weinfeld would prove unable to maintain his generation's precepts and would find a way to yield to his daughter's wishes.

Their younger daughter Fern has written of the generational conflicts about sexual behavior over which she and her parents struggled once she went away to college. The issue first arose when Fern tried to explain to her mother why she "had felt compelled to break up with a boyfriend" while at the same time reassuring her that they "hadn't actually had sex." The explanation ended when her mother responded, "'I'm not going to tell your father that you had sex with your boyfriend; it would kill him.'"[43] We do not, in fact, know how Weinfeld reacted to news of the end of his daughter's relationship, perhaps because his wife never reported it, perhaps because she reported it as Fern told it, or perhaps because he was more tolerant of his daughter's choices.

During her college years and the years immediately following her graduation, Fern "dated considerably" and "had several serious relationships." As a result, when she finally met the man she ultimately would marry, her parents were dubious. Arriving for dinner at her parents' apartment before either her father or her future husband had appeared, she reported her marriage plans to her mother, who was "instantly skeptical and disapproving which . . . caused us both to end up in tears." When she told the same news to her father a little later, he greeted it "with a frown" followed by a "question, 'What makes you think that this one is any different from any of the others?'" Perhaps because Fern's answer was persuasive, Weinfeld succumbed, the dinner and the wedding plans proceeded, and the wedding ultimately came off.[44]

Something even more suggestive of Edward Weinfeld's value structure occurred when Fern and her husband-to-be began to live together before they were married—"unconventional for the late 50's and a secret to be kept." Although her parents knew and she and her future husband knew that they knew, "all of us maintained the fiction that none of us knew" despite the fact that to her "parents it bordered on immoral."[45] This acceptance of fiction shows again that Weinfeld did not meet behavior he found morally objectionable with condemnation; on the contrary, he allowed his human instincts of compassion and love to trump his moral scruples ultimately, even if not immediately.

Fern was not alone in presenting her parents with generational conflict. Some two deacdes later, Ann presented Weinfeld with a dilemma and crisis when she announced that she and her husband were being divorced. As an initial moral proposition, Weinfeld frowned upon divorce, except in cases where husbands were abusing their wives. As a young practitioner, he had represented a number of women in the throes of divorce, but he had not only portrayed but even more important understood the husbands he was opposing as abusive autocrats.[46] The difficulty was that Ann's case did not fit within Weinfeld's exception. Her husband was not abusive, and Weinfeld was quite close to him; indeed, Weinfeld and his son-in-law lunched together privately on innumerable occasions. Ann wanted a divorce merely because her marriage no longer was a fulfilling relationship for her.[47] Initially, Weinfeld "wondered aloud why two intelligent, good people could not work their problems out," but, as Ann had always anticipated, he acquiesced in the divorce once he confronted and came to understand the emotional needs of his daughter and son-in law. Moreover, he not only acceded to their wishes, but also remained close to both of them. His luncheon dates with his former son-in-law continued,[48] and, indeed, that son-in-law served as one of two family representatives at Weinfeld's funeral service.[49]

Ann talks of another occasion when she faced serious financial problems and found it extremely difficult to pay all her bills. Knowing her father's views about avoiding indebtedness, she did not tell him of her problems but solved them by herself. Only then did she tell him. He promptly scolded her, "You know you should have told me. I'm sure, after I spoke with her, that your mother and I would have given you whatever you needed."[50]

In short, when a crisis forced Weinfeld to confront a conflict between the moral values and precepts to which he adhered, on the one hand, and love, compassion, and faith in people he knew well, on the other, he opted for the latter. Moreover, he was prepared at the moment of crisis to listen to those involved in the crisis and to learn from what they had to say. In his family life, human values trumped abstract ones.

Weinfeld had not always adhered to this hierarchy of values in his practice of law, however. No practicing lawyer possibly can. At times, an attorney must advise a client that some abstract rule of law prohibits doing what the client, as a person, desperately wants to do. At other times, a lawyer can strive to obtain what his or her client wants, but someone other than the lawyer will make the ultimate decision whether the client gets it. In response to these realities, many lawyers develop a habit of ignoring human values and allowing themselves always to be governed by rules, even in contexts where they have the power to grant dispensations from the rules. Analysis of Weinfeld's family life is important because it shows that he did not become habituated, as so many lawyers do, to rigidly following rules. Where he had power as a parent to grant dispensations, he granted them. And, as we shall see in later chapters, he often adopted the same hierarchy of values as a judge.

But that was in moments of crisis. Absent crisis, Weinfeld's passion for moral structure and professional propriety often made him oblivious to ordinary human concerns. His daughter Fern, for example, has written that her father "could not grasp" her "sense of insignificance, of loss and distance" resulting from his inability to discuss seriously with her the work she has done as a psychologist. Although Fern recognizes that her "father was inordinately proud" of her, encouraged her "to each achievement and degree along with whatever hard work it might entail," and "loved [her] to the fullest extent of which he was capable," she craved more. She always wanted Weinfeld to engage intensely with her work just as he did with the work of lawyers and law clerks who surrounded him. But because she never "confronted [her] father with any of this"[51]—because she never created a crisis—she could never force him to engage.

Edward Weinfeld could be equally oblivious to Lillian Weinfeld's predicaments and concerns. A tale, famous within the Weinfeld family circle, will illustrate.

One Sunday morning when Ann was a college sophomore home for Christmas vacation, she learned that her roommate had just undergone emergency surgery, and she decided to visit her in upstate New York. Since the only train of the day was leaving within the hour, Ann, her mother (the family chauffeur), and her father jumped into the car and rushed off to Grand Central Station. Pressed for time, Mrs. Weinfeld decided to make a right turn on a red light—then and now, a violation of traffic regulations in New York City. At once, a police officer appeared, stopped the car, and asked, "'Lady, do you know you just went through a red light?'" Lillian explained that she was rushing her daughter to a train so that she could visit her sick roommate, but the officer was unimpressed. He now asked for license and registration, which Lillian, in the rush of leaving home, had forgotten. That prompted the officer to say, "'Lady . . . these are serious violations of the law; I will have to take you in.'"[52] Lillian protested that Ann had to catch the only train of the day to visit her gravely ill friend, but to no avail.

Meanwhile, Edward Weinfeld, who had ascended the federal bench only five months earlier, was sitting silently in the rear of the car, as "characteristically he leaned over backwards to avoid influencing anyone because of his position." But finally, under the pressure of time and the moment, he spoke: "Officer, you have to do your duty. My wife did break the law but my daughter will miss her train. I have a solution. Why don't you take my wife to the station and I will take my daughter to the train?" His words made his wife "stutteringly angry" and left the policeman "undone with laughter." As is true with most tales about Weinfeld, however, this one had a happy ending, as the policeman allowed all to proceed and Ann caught her train.[53]

Weinfeld was even more oblivious to popular culture than he was to his family's emotional needs. Thus, in 1956, when Mickey Mantle was scheduled to appear at a hearing and his lawyers requested a postponement so that Mantle's absence would not disrupt spring training, Weinfeld, who had never heard of Mantle, asked who he was and then refused; amid laughter in the courtroom, he ruled that other witnesses who also were busy had to appear on schedule and that Mantle would as well.[54] Three years later, when the football Giants were playing the NFL championship game at home and invoked an NFL rule prohibiting the telecasting of games within seventy-five miles of the site of play, Giant fans brought suit to compel the Giants to broadcast the game in New York City. The suit was assigned to Weinfeld, who never was able to understand why it brought more attention to him than any other case he ever tried during his thirty-seven years on the bench.[55]

Then there is another tale famous within the family circle. One weekend the Weinfelds went to a movie; it was a rare treat for Lillian because her husband usually worked if they did not have to attend some other social function at the time in question. The movie, however, was an extraordinarily popular musical that had been showing for months, and Lillian's wish to see it finally had prevailed. Unfortunately, midway through the movie they were nearly forced to leave, not because they disliked the movie but because Lillian had burst into uncontrollable laughter. It appears that during one of the songs, her husband leaned over and whispered to her that the fellow who was singing had a really nice voice and wondered who he was. She barely spoke the words "Bing Crosby" before exploding into near hysterical laughter about how out of touch Weinfeld was with matters of everyday life.[56]

Weinfeld simply had little interest in many matters outside his professional ken unless some crisis forced him to care, and Lillian Weinfeld was not one to create crises. Although the Weinfelds rarely went to movies, infrequently to theater or concerts, scarcely to museums, and rarely strolled together, Lillian for years tolerated the situation. Although she received little time or attention from her husband, she nonetheless had a full life while her daughters were growing up and she was active in charitable and community affairs on the Lower East Side. But as Ann and Fern grew up, married, and left home, Lillian Weinfeld's life became less full. The transformation of the Lower East Side into a crime-infested neighborhood, which initially forced Lillian to spend more time in her apartment and ultimately obliged the Weinfelds to move uptown to East Sixty-sixth Street, made her daily life even emptier.

At that point in her life, Mrs. Weinfeld's wish was to travel, and over the years she and her husband took a number of pleasant trips. In 1960, they took their first cruise—a twenty-one-day Mediterranean cruise on the Italian Line's *Christoforo Columbo*. They had arranged to travel with Jacob Potofsky, a prominent New York City labor leader, and his wife, who possessed detailed knowledge of the ship's ports of call. According to Weinfeld, "it was a marvelous voyage" in which they dined every evening with the Potofskys, including one evening at the captain's table, participated in a special meeting with the Seamen's Union, and toured with Mrs. Potofsky at the different ports, "looking around" and "doing shopping." Nonetheless Weinfeld became "restless on the return trip" and if he "could have hired an airplane, [he] would have returned back home."[57]

Some years later, the Weinfelds went on a second Mediterranean cruise and then visited Mrs. Lehman and her family for her eightieth birthday celebration at Gstaad, Switzerland. They spent about a week at Gstaad and "went up the mountains on different days" by "little trains." They "didn't go mountain-climbing, but there were gorgeous views," and for Weinfeld it "was a wonderful trip."[58] Then, there was "an enlightening and emotional" trip to Israel in 1977.[59]

A third trip to the Continent, this one by air, lasted three weeks. At the outset of the trip, the Weinfelds spent a week in London, and at the end, a week in Paris. The middle week was spent with friends who were vacationing at Forte di Marme, Italy, which Weinfeld described as "a waterfront place, . . . pretty much like Palm Beach." Although the Weinfelds were unable to obtain reservations in the same hotel as their friends, they were able to stay nearby and had "a very lovely week."[60]

Weinfeld's comparison of Forte di Marme to Palm Beach is, however, suggestive. As he explained on one occasion to his granddaughter, "[w]hen we go away . . . , we try to get to a warm climate."[61] Weinfeld, who was an avid swimmer, also enjoyed vacationing at waterfront locales. Thus, he took several summer vacations on eastern Long Island, and from the 1960s on, he took a number of week-long winter vacations in the Carribean.[62] His favorable reaction to the "gorgeous views"[63] of Switzerland suggests that he also cared about the natural settings of his vacation places, and he obviously enjoyed vacationing with friends. But reactions common to most other vacationers were noticeably absent from Weinfeld's recollections: he never said anything about the history, architecture, products and souvenirs, forms of entertainment, cuisine, or culture of the places he visited. These matters eluded him; he simply was not interested in them. Like other children of immigrants of his generation, he had invested so much psychic energy in becoming an American that he could not escape American culture and his American ways; in 1977 in Israel, for example, he spent the Fourth of July at the American Embassy.[64] While there is no evidence that Weinfeld, like many other Americans, found other cultures inferior, it is clear that he did not find them especially interesting.

But other cultures did excite Mrs. Weinfeld. As she grew older, she wished more and more to travel and to see the places in the world where she had never been, and she kept hoping that her husband would retire so they would have the necessary leisure. He, meanwhile, continued to be drawn to his work and his jealous mistress—the law. This growing divergence in their interests created significant tension between Edward and Lillian Weinfeld during the later years of their marriage.

Weinfeld was aware of the tension. As he acknowledged,

It does linger with me and raise the question whether or not I've been fair to Lillian—not taking time for vacation or for traveling and the rest. . . . I think most times, Lillian has been understanding about it and, more than that, very supportive. At other times, I have no doubt that in her mind she may have thought I was unfair.[65]

Weinfeld never responded, however, to the growing emptiness of his wife's life and to her growing need for his time and attention in order to obtain fulfillment. He never understood that his wife did not have a "love of work or life" "comparable" to his, which could substitute "as a recompense" for the fact that she "was sorely deprived of" his "attention and time" and that various elements in her social network were slowly collapsing.[66]

There was never any question that Edward Weinfeld loved Lillian. He "insisted that others recognize his wife's talents," he "treasured her beauty and competence,"[67] and he always acknowledged how her "devotion and encouragement through the many years ha[d] contributed" to his "achievements."[68] He continued writing her lover's notes, such as one on her sixty-fifth birthday:

> To Bubs,
> Upon becoming the youngest "Senior
> Citizen" in town with complete
> confidence she will always remain
> young in spirit.
> > With love,
> > Eddie

Ten years later, on her seventy-fifth birthday, he gave his usual gift of flowers, dinner at a restaurant of Lillian's choice, and a large sum of cash, which she acknowledged with "[m]any, many thanks for your love and devotion."[69] As Lillian had written some years earlier, "we know that love will never be at a loss for depth and sweetness."[70] Of course, Edward Weinfeld agreed.

Nonetheless, despite their love, Weinfeld never gave his wife his time and attention. As they aged, they spent fewer evenings out together at social events, with the result that Mrs. Weinfeld faced a decline in social interaction with friends. Although Weinfeld also spent fewer nights in chambers, he brought work home instead, and thus it is doubtful whether the added evenings he and Lillian spent at home together deepened their marriage.

Of course, Weinfeld also attended family functions, such as dinners for children and grandchildren. There were also special functions, such as a week-long vacation with the entire family on the occasion of his and Lillian's fiftieth wedding anniversary[71] and the wedding of his granddaughter, Amy, to David Nachman. Weinfeld took these events very seriously; as he said in presiding over Amy and David's wedding, nothing "has given me greater joy, shared by Grandma, than your request that I join you as husband and wife under the authority vested in me as a United States District Judge."[72]

But, in the end, Weinfeld could not give up devoting the essence of his being to his duties as a judge. As one granddaughter, during her years as a college undergraduate, wrote to Weinfeld, she was beginning to understand that without studying law she would "always miss out on the essential meaning of you: your talents . . . [,] your genius and your passion."[73] And, however much his wife wanted him to take senior status so that they could travel and spend more time together, Weinfeld never could bring himself to do it. "Keeping active status," as he saw it, constituted a statement that "'[t]his is my life's work; this is worth the challenge.'"[74] For Lillian Weinfeld, it ultimately became a statement that her husband's jealous mistress—the law—came before her.

As her isolation grew, it turned into depression. With nothing else to do, she joined her husband in his evening cocktail—a period in each day that became their best time together. Then, she began having a cocktail while she was waiting for him to come home, and eventually she began having too many cocktails. This loss of self-discipline with respect to alcohol only drove a further wedge, however, between her and her always disciplined husband, who became deeply upset, even angry, at Lillian's lack of care for herself.[75]

On his deathbed, Weinfeld expressed his love for his family, and undoubtedly that love was real. But his family was never at the center of his attentions. His very "identity was so embedded and entwined with his commitment to his work and striving toward excellence" that family was forced into the background, except at occasional moments of crisis. Even then, Weinfeld sometimes was absent, as he was when his daughter Fern faced a psychological crisis during her sophomore year at Radcliffe and Mrs. Weinfeld journeyed to Cambridge while the judge remained back in New York.[76]

Perhaps, his family suffered from his reserve, although they probably were also spurred to greater achievement. For Fern, "the distance between my father and me . . . left me with a hunger . . . to be worthy of inclusion among the best"—a hunger that proved to be both a troublesome pang and a foundation for achievement. And for Mrs. Weinfeld, "the sense of deprivation that accumulated over the years"[77] must have contributed to the isolation and depression of her old age, although it also may have driven her to her many achievements of middle age.

As for Weinfeld himself, he was never "conflicted or in pain" about his relationship with his wife and family and never felt that he was "miss[ing] out on much of anything at all" by placing his work and the law ahead of them. Although "consumed by his work," he was completely "gratified" and "fulfilled" by it.[78] Perhaps, his work also provided a crutch for avoiding family imbroglios with which he knew he could not deal. He may, for example, have avoided the intense engagement with his daughter Fern's work in Freudian psychology—engagement that Fern always wanted—because of what he labeled "the errant [*sic*] nonsense of Freud . . . in interpreting normalcy in family relationships to accord with [his] own analytical concepts";[79] maybe Weinfeld, whether fully conscious about his motivations or not, did not want to engage in conflict with his daughter to which he knew there could be no good ending. Similarly, he may not have given more time to his wife, who had become "depressed" and "hard to be with,"[80] because he knew he could not please her and that any attempt to do so would only make their relationship worse. Finally, he may have yielded to his daughters as they worked out their relationships with men not only out of compassionate understanding but also out of a desire to avoid conflict that could destroy his relationship with them.

About such matters, it is possible only to speculate. But the speculations are important because they may lead to deeper insight into the values of Edward Weinfeld as a judge. If they are correct, the speculations suggest a hypothesis—that Edward Weinfeld abhorred conflict. Litigation and debate, forms of ritualized combat with rules and procedures for bringing conflict to a resolution, were one thing. But pure, unstructured conflict could easily escalate, could lead to the destruction of relationships, and thus had to be avoided.

So understood, Weinfeld's family life adds to the overall portrait of him. In addition to his writing ability, his facility in synthesizing facts, his strategic sense, his work ethic, and his commitment to leading a modest life dedicated to helping others, we need to add two other elements—compassion and the avoidance of conflict. One more element—a belief in adherence to principle—still must be added. Then, it will be time to examine how Weinfeld obtained an appointment to the bench and how he combined the various elements of his persona into a coherent jurisprudence.

5

Politics and Public Service

Edward Weinfeld addressed the problem of his inability adequately to support his growing family by turning to politics. At the outset of the twenty-first century, when salaries of government officials are probably lower in relation to private-sector pay than at any time in American history, readers of this book may find it difficult to imagine that people would seek public employment in order to increase their income. Today, elite-trained lawyers seek office to do good, to obtain power, or to make connections they can exploit financially after their public service is completed. At earlier moments in the American past, however, talented lawyers like Weinfeld who could not make a living in private practice entered politics for its financial rewards.

For Weinfeld, the financial rewards from politics were not immediate. For several years during the 1930s, he served New York City's Tammany machine, which at the time was the only political organization with which a Manhattan Democrat without elite connections could associate, and got little or nothing in return. But ultimately, the ties of politics gave him and his family a comfortable living and brought him the little wealth he was able to accumulate during his life.

The first public evidence of Weinfeld's political activities occurred in December 1928, when he represented Irving Dolen, a Democrat[1] who had been defeated for assemblyman in the Sixth Assembly District by twelve votes out of a total of fifteen thousand cast. Dolen asked for a reexamination of the voting machines in three election districts in which discrepancies had been uncovered, but the Supreme Court denied relief. The Appellate Division, however, reversed on the ground that "where the closeness of the vote is coupled with proof of discrepancies, the discretion vested in the court" to order a recount "should be exercised, so that doubt and lack of confidence in the result may be removed."[2]

Weinfeld's role in the *Dolen* case appears to have been limited. He did not argue the case and is identified as merely one of the authors of the brief. There is no indication that Weinfeld was the brief's major author, and the case does not bear any of the hallmarks of Weinfeld's work—the opinion of the Appellate Division cites only one case and contains little detailed factual analysis; it merely emphasizes, as we have seen, the court's discretion.

Weinfeld played a greater role in a criminal case discussed in chapter 3, *People v. Leik*, in which he probably became involved as a result of his Tammany Hall connections. The case arose after two police officers of the New York City vice squad arrested Genevieve Potocki, and she, in turn, made a "charge against the officers . . . in the Seabury investigation." On March 23, 1931, she testified against the officers before the grand jury, and she later would testify against them at their trial in May 1931.[3]

However, before the trial could take place, Robert Leik, described by the judge who tried his case as "the general fixer of the neighborhood,"[4] met privately with Mrs. Potocki in her apartment. According to Potocki, Leik threatened that, if she testified against the police, she would not live long, and he told her that she had to leave the country so she could not testify. According to Leik, he met at Potocki's request and, in response to her pleas for help, offered to assist her in moving her business to a new location where she was not known.[5] The Seabury Commission believed Potocki's version and obtained Leik's indictment for uttering a threat designed to prevent a witness from testifying. Weinfeld, a Tammany loyalist at the time, represented this "general fixer of the neighborhood" against the Seabury charges both at trial and on appeal.

Weinfeld was also faithful to the Tammany machine in an October 1934 election case, in connection with his representation of Alexander Kraut, who was seeking the nomination of the Fusion Party for assemblyman in Brooklyn's Eighteenth Assembly District. The central committee of the Fusion Party had endorsed the Republican candidate, Arthur Franke, to run in the Eighteenth District against Irwin Steingut, the leader of the minority Democratic Party in the state assembly, who was seeking reelection. Kraut, on the other hand, claimed the right to the nomination on the basis of twelve thousand petition signatures that he had secured. Although Kraut had no chance of winning the election, his presence on the Fusion ballot would have taken votes away from Franke and thereby enabled Steingut to win with fewer votes. It was for this reason that the *New York Telegram* described Kraut as a "stalking horse" for Steingut and implied that Weinfeld's role in the case was to act on behalf of "Tammany Hall."[6]

Because of his uncanny ability to outwork any lawyer, the case, ultimately entitled *Peel v. Cohen*, was an ideal one for Weinfeld. The order of the trial court in favor of the Republican Franke and against Weinfeld's client, Kraut, was entered on October 24.[7] Weinfeld immediately appealed to the Appellate Division, which on October 26 by a three-to-two vote affirmed the judgment with slight modifications.[8] Again Weinfeld appealed, this time to the Court of Appeals, which on October 31 further modified the judgment, albeit without putting Kraut on the ballot.[9] Within this brief time frame, Weinfeld filed a sixteen-page typewritten brief in the Appellate Division and 129 pages of printed matter, including a thirty-six-page brief, in the Court of Appeals.[10] The Court of Appeals brief, to say the least, was meticulously prepared, with 120 specifically paginated references to the record below and citations to seven different prior cases. Weinfeld's brief to the Appellate Division, which must have been written overnight, was in substance the same as the Court of Appeals brief, although it was shorter and without the paginated references to the record.

Despite his efforts, Weinfeld lost the case on all three levels, and his client, Alexander Kraut, was not on the ballot to assist Irwin Steingut in his reelection effort. Nonetheless, Steingut won reelection, the Democrats won control of both houses of the state legislature for the first time since 1913, and Steingut became the new speaker of the assembly.[11]

No direct evidence remains about why Weinfeld was tapped to represent Kraut and thus to help Steingut's reelection campaign. That the chairman of Tammany Hall's "law committee" was the other attorney representing Kraut at the trial level[12] suggests, however, that New York City's Democratic organization regarded the Steingut campaign as a pivotal one in which it was necessary to deploy the best legal talent available—that is, Edward Weinfeld. Presumably, Weinfeld represented Kraut *pro bono*, but he received his compensation the next year after the Democrats took control of the state legislature.

When the new Democratic-controlled legislature met in 1935, it established, under the chairmanship of Manhattan Assemblyman Saul S. Streit, a Joint Legislative Committee to Investigate Bondholders and Shareholders Committees. These committees, typically formed when managers of large real estate trusts were unable to make full payment on their unsecured debt, were designed to protect the interests of investors who did not possess a large enough share of the real estate or other trust investment to protect their interests by themselves. The Streit Committee began hearings in August 1935,[13] with Edward Weinfeld as its chief counsel,[14] after he had received "approval as to . . . [his] political standing" from "the political organization with which" he was "connected."[15]

At least in terms of the volume of paper that it generated, Weinfeld's job as chief counsel to the Joint Legislative Committee was the biggest to date of his career. His papers contain five volumes of typewritten transcripts of committee hearings, which total approximately thirty-six-hundred pages, plus some seventy-five pages of printed committee reports and recommendations. Weinfeld's main public responsibility as chief counsel was to conduct the principal examination of witnesses during the committee's hearings, which comprised a total of forty-seven sessions between September 10 and December 19, 1935; Weinfeld conducted the examination during thirty-one of those sessions. He also played a substantial role in the sleuthing that provided him with the background on which to base his questions; in addition, he apparently drafted much of the Joint Committee's three reports and the legislative reform proposals that grew out of the committee's deliberations.

At times, the committee confronted difficulties as it tried to build a record. For example, when it sought to examine a Mr. Hitz and a Mr. Ford of the National Hotel Management Corporation, their attorney, H. S. Morse, reported that "both of those witnesses declined to answer the questions propoun[d]ed to them by counsel to the committee" apparently at an informal, prehearing examination. Morse promised to "produce Mr. Ford" "any time you want him," but Hitz, in the words of Assemblyman Streit, had "been evading service." Weinfeld then "interject[ed] . . . that I indicated that if he did not come down I would send State troopers after him, and then he came down voluntarily. The fact is that every time we tried to serve Mr. Hitz he made himself inaccessible to service." Observing that Hitz "goes to Texas and to Michigan and to other places, and to all over the country," Morse offered to "concede on the record that the corporation will refuse to answer, and Mr. Hitz will also refuse to answer on the advice of counsel" the questions previously put to him informally. Streit found this offer unacceptable, however, since "we want to propound other questions," at which point Morse asked, "Would you mind giving us a list of the questions that you wish to propound?" Weinfeld, sensing Morse's strategic ploy, answered, "Oh, no, I don't want to do that. I don't think you would want to give opposing counsel a list of questions a week before they are to be here."[16]

Weinfeld thereby kept the pressure on Hitz to compel him to testify on the committee's terms, and a week later Hitz in fact appeared before the committee and gave some forty pages of testimony. His testimony established that in 1932 he and several officers of Manufacturers Trust, with one thousand dollars of capital, founded the National Hotel Management Company, which was paid approximately $120,000 in fees over the next three and a half years to manage properties under Manufacturers' control; during that time, management expenses were approximately $47,000 and Hitz's salary was some $25,500—approximately two-thirds that of the president of the United States, with Manufacturers apparently receiving the remaining $47,500 as a return on its original $1,000 investment.[17] Clearly, Hitz received a good salary, and Manufacturers made a good investment during the nadir of the Great Depression.

The examination of other witnesses often was equally fruitful. For instance, one witness, a former Brooklyn borough president who chaired a bondholders' committee, could not remember why a prospective contract for sale of some of the bondholders' property contained a provision for the payment of forty-five thousand dollars to the members of the committee and their counsel;[18] he also did not know that the property's management company had permitted one tenant to run twenty-one thousand dollars into arrears on its rent and then given it a new lease at a lower rent or that two other tenants related to a management official were permitted to remain in apartments for over three years without paying any rent.[19] There also was testimony of an insider deal between a management company and a hotel, which was managed individually by the same man who headed the management company,[20] as well as evidence of a company that had "traded in its own defaulted securities at a time when investors did not know that the issues were in default."[21]

It is vital to emphasize, however, that Streit and Weinfeld did not run the Joint Legislative Committee in the fashion in which later congressional committees would be run: they did not seek to expose or shame people for the purpose of exposing or shaming them, but only to conduct an investigation in order to identify abuses in need of legislative reform and to build political support for that reform. Of course, Streit and Weinfeld needed publicity, and they were willing to spotlight scandals in order to obtain it. But the goal of their publicity was legislative reform, not the advancement of their own careers. Indeed, Streit left the assembly following the conclusion of the Joint Committee's work to become a judge of the Manhattan Court of General Sessions of the Peace,[22] and Weinfeld, as we shall see, ran for office only once in his life—in 1937, as a delegate from the Lower East Side to the 1938 state constitutional convention. For both of these posts, the nomination of Tammany Hall sufficed to insure election, and acclaim generated by exposing scandal was irrelevant.

Indeed, within less than three months of the commencement of its inquiry, the Joint Legislative Committee was recommending specific reforms. On December 11, 1935, Chairman Streit sent a letter to the heads of the two most prominent bondholders' committees; the letter listed nineteen abuses in which the committees had engaged and recommended the adoption of sixteen new procedures to avoid abuses in the future.[23] Both committee heads indicated their willingness to accept the suggestions contained in Streit's letter.[24] Nonetheless, Streit proposed legislation to end abuses,[25] and the legislature in June 1936 did enact five new laws to aid bondholders.[26] Following enactment of the legislation, Saul Streit left the assembly and was elected to the bench.[27] Weinfeld, however, remained on as associate counsel to the Joint Committee during the legislature's 1937 session, even after an upstate Republican had become the committee's chairman.[28] In that role, he managed to spend a total of three years in state employment, which paid "a fair remuneration," albeit "for a tremendous amount of effort."[29]

Throughout the three years, Weinfeld positioned himself as a reformer unafraid of using government power to regulate unscrupulous business practices. As Weinfeld's report on behalf of the Streit committee observed, bondholders' committees

received excessive fees for reorganization . . . [,] paid excessive fees to attorneys . . . [,] acquiesced in extragavant expenditures by trustees and management companies . . . [,] permitted unnecessary and prolonged delays in the reorganization of defaulted properties . . . [and] liquidated bonds without first submitting the fairness of the price at which they were sold to the court.[30]

He continued,

Not only did issuing houses often form their own protective committees, but they frequently formed "management companies" to run defaulted properties, collecting management in addition to committee fees.

In one case the Manufacturers Trust Company organized a management company which received $67,202 for managing property in default—and then Manufacturers Trust received $45,127 additional for managing its own wholly owned management company.

The issuing houses controlled the committees by refusing to give bondholders lists of fellow-bondholders. So profitable was the reorganization business that these lists were bought, sold and traded by "professional reorganizers."

In short,

When these bondholders' committees stepped into the picture, we find the "milking process" began anew. Each of the layers of administration in connection with the defaulted property received its share of the diminishing fund; the committee received its fees, its attorney obtained large allowances, the trustee paid itself, the trustee paid its attorneys, the management company received its fees, and attorneys for minority bondholders' committees often received fees.[31]

On the basis of this report, Weinfeld became the leading proponent of a proposal to create a state SEC[32] and even found his name appearing in headlines.[33] When a spokesman for the state attorney general opposed Weinfeld's plan and warned that "[i]f you overregulate the field of commercial financing, you will kill it" and New York would lose its place as "the financial capital of the world," Weinfeld responded,

When we proposed an enactment imposing active duties upon a trustee under trust indentures, . . . we were told no trust company would be willing to undertake trusteeship. But it is now in the statutes and the trust business is going on as usual, and the same people are undertaking trusteeships.

Weinfeld continued that, under existing law, the New York attorney general could step in "only after the damage is done"[34] and that "legislation before the fraud occurs, to prevent it, is just as necessary as that which seeks to punish after its discovery."[35]

After completing his three years with the Joint Legislative Committee, Weinfeld carried on his political career when Tammany Hall nominated him to what the *New York Mirror* labeled "the grueling, thankless task"[36] of serving as a delegate to the state constitutional convention from the Fourteenth Senatorial District. Unopposed for the Democratic nomination and with the additional backing of the Citizens Union,[37] Weinfeld had little difficulty winning the seat in the safe Democratic district. His victory provided some financial compensation—he earned twenty-five hundred dollars as a convention delegate,[38] and, of course, he continued to practice law while the convention was proceeding. But the main compensations for being a delegate were other than financial.

At the convention, which was required to be held periodically to determine whether the state constitution needed modification, Weinfeld continued, as he had on the Joint Committee, to serve as a skilled lawyer for his Democratic colleagues and to fight for liberal causes. When there was a need for case analysis during the convention's debates, Weinfeld typically was involved. On one occasion, for instance, he focused on a Louisiana decision to suggest how proposed language might be judicially construed.[39] On another occasion, he intervened in a debate on a proposed provision protecting the rights of labor. The debate had begun when an upstate Supreme Court justice, Gilbert V. Schenck, moved to strike the words "Labor of human beings is not a commodity nor article of commerce and shall never be so considered or construed" on the ground that there was "no authority to indicate that it is otherwise." Focusing on the hardships faced by workers in an industrialized economy, Frank E. Johnson supported the proposed language and maintained that it was "not as meaningless . . . as the Judge would have us think."[40] It was Weinfeld, however, who focused on "the direct question . . . asked by Judge Schenck as to whether or not there was any recorded case in which there was a reference to labor of human beings being considered a commodity." Weinfeld answered the question as follows:

> Well, there are such cases . . . going back through the years, as early as People v. Fisher,[41] reported in 14 Wendell 9, 103 years ago . . . [and] go[ing] down to recent years and as far down as the case of People v. Manners,[42] 293 App. Div. 548. . . . I know of no sound reason, in view of the history and the cases going back, it is true, over a century, why this particular provision should not be contained in our Constitution.[43]

On another occasion, the convention became embroiled in a dispute about the language it should use to enable the state to take property pursuant to a public purpose in excess of what would be devoted to a public use. Harold Riegelman proposed to amend language on which he and Weinfeld had agreed in committee because, in Riegelman's view, the agreed language was "unconstitutional as being in contravention of the Fourteenth Amendment." When Weinfeld asked him to identify "the decision that you refer to,"[44] Reigelman could not cite a Supreme Court case under which the agreed language would be void, although he did claim, and Weinfeld did not disagree, that his proposed alternative language would be acceptable under *Cincinnati v. Vester*.[45] Weinfeld thereby forced Riegelman to concede that, although his amended language would pass constitutional muster, the committee language he proposed to replace might do so as well.

Weinfeld's challenge to Riegelman entailed the drawing of a precise lawyer's distinction between the precedent Riegelman could not cite—that the language offered by the committee was unconstitutional—and the precedent he could cite—that his alternative language would pass muster. But Weinfeld's move also involved something else that was characteristic of his work as a lawyer—namely, thorough preparation. Weinfeld's response to Judge Schenck similarly involved superior preparation. In both instances, Weinfeld simply had researched and analyzed the case law more carefully than his opponent.

Indeed, Weinfeld quickly gained recognition as "a lawyer with a habit of knowing what he [was] talking about."[46] "It was said that he went home each weekend and spent his time studying the background of law and facts of the chief proposals slated for consideration in the ensuing week."[47] This thoroughness made him a potent ally for those with whom he agreed, helping them to "stifle . . . the best brains on the GOP side of the aisle," who could "not cope with his method of argument."[48] It meant that those with whom Weinfeld was likely to disagree often ran the risk that any proposition of law that they proclaimed would be proved false. In the end, however, Weinfeld's thoroughness earned him "the respect of delegates on both sides of the aisle."[49]

Weinfeld's lawyerly ability to make fine points surfaced on many occasions at the convention. Thus, in one debate concerning the date at which language proposed as a clause in the constitution had first appeared in political platforms, Weinfeld asserted, without contradiction, that "it [was] a fact" that the language initially had appeared some fifteen years later than a Republican opponent had guessed. On another occasion, when the Republicans suggested that a vote be taken on one "of the smaller matters that are before us" despite the absence of a quorum, Weinfeld interjected that the matter at issue was "just as important as any other matter" and hence that a vote would be inappropriate.[50] On many other occasions, Weinfeld engaged in procedural jockeying or asked detailed questions designed to pin opponents down on the precise import of language they were offering.[51]

On one such occasion, Weinfeld directly challenged former governor Alfred E. Smith, who was behind a proposal to prohibit municipalities from using real estate taxes to repay bonds issued to clear slums and construct public housing. Weinfeld began by observing that "the social and economic aspects of housing have been fully and ably discussed by distinguished delegates." He rose only to address the narrow claim that "the real estate owners" were "in no position to afford the burden or the expense" and "to clear away some of the brush which tends to confuse us upon this issue."[52]

Weinfeld began by stating that he "was a member . . . of the sub-committee which assisted in the drafting and preparation of the bill, and it was with deliberation and intention that . . . the exemption of real estate from taxation . . . was omitted from that bill." Indeed, "it was only after considerable debate and discussion between the members of the committee and the sub-committee that that purpose was accomplished." It "was accomplished," Weinfeld added, out of "a definite belief . . . that unless real estate might be called upon to contribute to the expense of housing," the state would "never get a real long range planned housing program." He also challenged Smith's claim that the real estate industry could "not stand the burden" of taxation for slum clearance and public housing because, as Weinfeld explained, the burden "is passed on to the tenants in the ultimate analysis, and they bear the burden of these improvements."[53]

Later in the debate on the housing clauses of the proposed constitution, Weinfeld challenged a key Republican leader, Abbot Low Moffat, and the chairman of his own committee, Joseph C. Baldwin, in reference to language offered by Moffat and accepted by Baldwin mandating that new public housing could only be constructed in replacement of preexisting slums. Baldwin's "agreeing with the stated purpose of this proposed amendment" was, according to Weinfeld, "an indication that the chairman of the committee did not really understand the purpose of that amendment." When he observed Baldwin rising from his seat, Weinfeld immediately responded, "Now, Joe, one minute please. . . . I want to say that as a member of the Housing Committee, and as a member of the subcommittee, I did not agree to this change, nor do I agree to the change." He then turned to Moffat, who had asserted that the legislature had unanimously passed his proposal during the preceding year, asking "was [it] not in fact defeated in the Senate . . . ?" When Moffat tried to wiggle out, the following colloquoy occurred:

> Mr. Weinfeld: I want to make an inquiry through the Chair: Referring to that particular bill, wasn't the substance of what now appears in the amendment and referred to in the memorandum submitted by Mr. Kuczwalski, contained in that bill?
>
> Mr. Moffat: That is true.
>
> Mr. Weinfeld: And wasn't that defeated in the Senate of this State?
>
> Mr. Moffat: The bill was but not for any reason which has to do with this section.
>
> Mr. Kuczwalski: Can the gentleman tell us why it was defeated? What were the objections?
>
> Mr. Moffat: I cannot tell you why the Democratic leadership in the Senate would not pass it.[54]

After Moffat's failure to establish his initial assertion that the state legislature had passed his proposal or his secondary assertion that the failure of passage was unrelated to issues under debate at the convention, Baldwin never even bothered to challenge Weinfeld's statement that he did not understand the meaning of the Moffat proposal.

Weinfeld then proceeded to his major point: that questions about the simultaneous clearance of slums and construction of new public housing were "much too hot for the Convention to handle. Such highly technical matters should be left for careful working out by the Legislature." He made the same point in connection with the proposal to prohibit municipalities from using real estate taxes to repay bonds issued to clear slums and construct public housing: namely, that the convention should "stand against any proposition being written into this Constitution which was legislative in character." It was impossible, he argued, for "any one individual . . . [to] tell with accuracy, with a fair degree of accuracy, the condition" of affairs "ten years from now, fifteen years from now, twenty years from now," and thus it was unwise to bind future legislatures to detailed rules that might preclude the taking of necessary actions.[55]

In addition to serving as a legal sharpshooter who made broad jurisprudential points about the difficulty of predicting the future, law and economics points about the passing on of costs, and narrow points about prior case law and legislative activity, Weinfeld did valuable work in the 1938 convention as a proponent of liberal causes. One of his liberal stands was against exempting railroads from contributing to the costs of grade crossing elimination. Another was in favor of protecting the right of workers to organize and strike.[56]

Weinfeld took his strongest liberal stands in favor of "the fundamental principle that human rights are superior to property rights." Indeed, he became quite passionate in support of that principle. He noted his concern, for example, that the proposed constitution did not protect the newly acquired statutory right of labor unions to jury trial in injunction cases. Similarly, he argued that criminal defendants ought not to be permitted to waive their right to trial by jury except after consulting with counsel; in Weinfeld's view, judges could not adequately protect the rights of defendants because "on occasion judges misunderstand their judicial function to the extent that they become part of the prosecution."[57] Weinfeld took his strongest stands, however, in favor of two other proposals—one, that the police promptly arraign those they arrest, and another, that the fruits of unlawful searches be excluded from evidence in criminal proceedings.

Weinfeld considered the issue of prompt arraignment "to be one of civil rights, not of persons charged with crime . . . , but . . . of the citizen who is charged with crime, and who may be innocent, but as a result of improper practice is subjected oftentimes to cruel punishment." He "believe[d] that there are innocent persons who are coerced into making confessions and who are convicted on the basis of those confessions" and also took note of two prisoners who had been beaten to death by police in the Nassau County jail. When Francis Martin, the presiding justice of the First Department of the Appellate Division, responded that the jail beating was "an isolated incident" and that it would be wrong to "cast aside the whole body of criminal law, because in one case, somebody was beaten up and died," Weinfeld retorted,

> It was more than being beaten up. . . . They did not die as a result of having been beaten slightly, they were beaten to death, and never afforded the opportunity of a trial or arraignment. Isn't that a reflection on the administration of criminal law by the police authorities because

they took the law in their own hands, depriving them of the right to trial
and they were never prosecuted for it.

For Weinfeld, prompt arraignment was "a basic fundamental right" that
"should be written into the Constitution."[58]

He likewise sought to exclude illegally obtained evidence from criminal prosecutions because "the preservation and maintenance of the fundamental guaranties today is . . . of paramount importance." In perhaps
the most forceful and inspiring speech of his life, Weinfeld continued by
discussing

the efforts that have been made against Democratic institutions. We
have heard very serious threats. . . . All these men are alive to the dan-
gers which are threatening our people throughout the entire world
today. . . . [W]e must go back to the glorious days of the early republic. . . . Let us not think of the Constitution as a cold parchment to be
venerated and reverenced only on great national holidays and then to be
forgotten throughout our daily lives and existence. Let us try to get the
spirit of true democracy. . . . With a proper appreciation of the early
struggles of the individual against aggressive government of over-zealous
public officials and mindful of present conditions, we should have no
difficulty in arriving at a conclusion as to our proper course.

What is important in these times is that we re-affirm our faith in
democracy; that we preserve the principles upon which that democracy
is found, and that in these days of dictatorship and destruction of individual liberties which all of us cherish, we must not only affirm, but
strengthen so far as we can, the basic principles of a free people. Let us,
as members in Convention assembled, as representatives of all the people, by our action and support of a real proposal, give notice to the
State, the Nation and the world that we still believe in and adhere to the
true principles of a democratic form of government.[59]

It was natural for Weinfeld, who represented a poor district, who had
years of experience as a criminal defense lawyer, and who, as a Jew, was
sensitive to the launching of the Holocaust in Germany, to argue for "the
fundamental principle that human rights are superior to property rights"
and to interpret human rights as including not only the opportunity to
obtain a decent standard of living but also protection against "aggressive
government of over-zealous public officials" and the consequent "de-

struction of individual liberties."[60] It is important, however, to appreciate that in 1938 his arguments and interpretations were well in advance of what most Americans and even some New Yorkers were yet prepared to embrace. Until that year, the New Deal had been about protecting the poor from exploitation by the rich; indeed, Weinfeld himself had begun his public career by working to shield bondholders from depredations by their protective committees. For classic New Dealers, government was the entity that would bring decency to the lives of the vast majority of Americans. It was only in 1938, at events like the New York constitutional convention, that new ideas about protecting individual rights against government encroachment began to emerge as a liberal cause, with delegates like Edward Weinfeld playing an important part in their emergence.[61]

The one remaining political issue on which Weinfeld had to take a stand—whether the New York City Council should be elected on the basis of proportional representation—had little to do either with older progressive ideas about uplifting the poor or with newer liberal ideas about protecting individual rights. But his position on the issue had a greater impact on his future career than any other stand he took during the convention's proceedings.

The issue was whether the New York City Council should be elected pursuant to a scheme of proportional representation that had recently been approved by the city's voters. The Tammany Hall machine, which, it will be recalled, had obtained Weinfeld's seat for him at the convention, had the power to win a plurality for its candidates in nearly every single-member district in the city and thus was guaranteed control of the council if council members were elected from single-member districts. The administration of Mayor Fiorello LaGuardia, on the other hand, was convinced that various opposition parties could each gain a number of seats under proportional representation and collectively might coalesce to control a majority of the council or least to provide effective opposition to Tammany.

The issue came before the constitutional convention when Tammany formed an alliance with upstate Republicans to insert a ban on proportional representation into the new state constitution. Weinfeld was torn. He did not himself favor proportional representation, and he did not want to disappoint the Tammany leaders who had advanced his career. But, as he explained when he ultimately voted against the ban on proportional representation, he was "a firm believer in the democratic principle that whatever the people in their considered judgment want, they should have," and the people of New York City had voted to have proportional representation.[62]

There were those who thought, as one friend wrote Weinfeld, that "your vote on the P.R. amendment killed your political future."[63] Another hoped that "the organization will take no measure against you in retaliation," but nonetheless recognized that it might.[64] Nearly a year later the *New York Post* was still urging Tammany leaders to "be broad-minded once in a while" and not retaliate against Weinfeld even though he had been "one of the few who had the sense to vote against the P.R. ripper amendment."[65] It was this threat of retaliation and the possible end to Weinfeld's budding political career that made his vote on proportional representation "so troublesome and significant a decision."[66]

It would be easy to interpret Weinfeld's vote as a brave and principled act reflecting his adherence to norms higher than his own self-advancement. In later years, Weinfeld was always critical of those "peculiar notions" that "placed personal loyalty above principle and integrity." In particular, his devotion to Herbert Lehman rested on Lehman's "rare courage and impeccable integrity" that always kept him from "swerv[ing] from his plain duty, no matter what the impact upon him personally."[67] Weinfeld's attraction to Woodrow Wilson as a man of principle who dared to fail rather than a man of expediency who failed to dare also cut in favor of his voting against Tammany Hall.

But another interpretation also is possible. Weinfeld was not the only Democrat who voted against the ban on proportional representation; there were five others, including United States Senator Robert F. Wagner, State Conservation Commissioner Lithgow Osborne, and Supreme Court Justice Charles Poletti.[68] It became clear in retrospect that Weinfeld's vote strengthened his ties with these prominent Democratic leaders and others with whom they were closely associated. Perhaps Weinfeld voted as he did, at least in part, to achieve that end. Becoming an ally of these high-ranking Democrats required, in any event, that Weinfeld be perceived as a man of principle, and, even if he was not originally such a man, his self-portrait, combined with Tammany's retribution against him for placing principle above loyalty, made him one.

Thus, shortly after the convention ended, Weinfeld sent Poletti notes congratulating him on his nomination to be lieutenant governor on the Lehman ticket and, later, on his and Lehman's electoral victory. Poletti sent back the following:

I am glad that it was possible for you to help the Governor during the campaign.

This summer I told you that I think one can only get along in public life by adhering with complete honesty and with maximum courage to the principles in which he believes. I have had and hope will continue to have that faith.

Senator Wagner likewise acknowledged a congratulatory note that Weinfeld had sent him and thanked him for help in the campaign.[69]

Thus, as Weinfeld's ties to Tammany loosened, he began to ally himself with a more elevated and more principled crowd. As a result, he and his wife received invitations to attend Governor Lehman's inauguration and the luncheon at the executive mansion thereafter.[70] He also served on a committee with Charles Abrams, former counsel to the City Housing Authority, and Herbert Wechsler, a professor of law at Columbia, to draft a bill that Assemblyman Robert F. Wagner, Jr., the Senator's son, introduced into the state assembly to implement the new constitution's housing article.[71] And, it was not surprising that, after the bill had been enacted, Governor Herbert H. Lehman appointed Weinfeld to the new job created by the law he had helped to draft administering $150 million in state funds to clear slums and build low-rent housing.[72]

As New York's first commissioner of housing, Weinfeld had the highest-paying job in public service that he would ever hold—a salary of twelve thousand dollars per year,[73] plus added perks such as a chauffer-driven state car,[74] at a time when the salary for a federal district judge was only ten thousand dollars annually.[75] He was able to keep the job from July 1939 to the end of December 1942, when a Republican, Thomas E. Dewey, succeeded the Democrat, Charles Poletti, who himself had taken over from Herbert H. Lehman, as governor.[76]

Rarely did Weinfeld have opportunities in the post of commissioner to protect the civil liberties of individuals against government encroachment. There were occasional cases, however, such as one involving the Eisenberger family, and Weinfeld took advantage of them. Management, seeking to evict the Eisenbergers from middle-income public housing, gave three reasons for not renewing their lease: (1) that their two-year-old "twins were holy terrors who destroyed shrubbery, stepped on the lawn, and in wet cement, etc.," (2) that Mr. Eisenberger was "arrogant because he wrote them a letter complaining about their using a certain fertilizer on the lawn outside [the Eisenbergers'] window," and (3) that Mrs. Eisenberger "had sued them for negligence because of an accident [she] had on the stairway." The Eisenbergers claimed that the role of Mr. Eisenberger, a chemistry instructor at City College, in organizing a tenants' union was the real reason for management's hostility.[77]

But, on the whole, Weinfeld's task as housing commissioner was the old-fashioned, progressive one of uplifting the poor. He achieved some successes in that task, but as a result of the outbreak of World War II no low-rent subsidized housing was completed during his term in office.

Construction had begun on the Fort Greene Houses in Brooklyn when the war started, but the site was converted into a defense housing project in view of its proximity to the Brooklyn Navy Yard, and plans to place low-income tenants in the project were postponed for the war's duration. Meanwhile, the start of construction on other projects planned for the city—the Lillian Wald Houses, Bronxville House, and the Amsterdam Houses—and on the Winyah Gardens project in New Rochelle was deferred. Two defense housing projects in Tonawanda and North Tonawanda, which Weinfeld oversaw, were nearly completed when he left office, and other projects were underway in Elmira, Niagara Falls, and Schenectady.[78] On one of his final days in office, Weinfeld signed contracts for postwar construction projects that exhausted the $150 million the legislature had appropriated when he assumed office. In doing so, he noted not only the need "to build additional homes and clear up substandard areas, but also to cushion the impact of post-war readjustment by giving employment to thousands of men on the job and in the building materials industry."[79]

But Weinfeld's work only scratched the surface. When he left office, an estimated three hundred thousand families still lived in what were called "old-law tenements";[80] without counting the units for which he contracted in his final days in office, construction of only 17,142 new residences had been contemplated during his three-and-one-half-year term.[81] Meanwhile, neither Weinfeld nor anyone else of his era had any idea of how the low-income housing projects that were constructed in quantity in the aftermath of the war would develop into dilapidated, crime-infested slums. While the new projects may have been substantially better than the old-law tenements they replaced, they never became the thriving communities that Weinfeld and other public housing advocates anticipated.

Dedication of Fort Greene Housing Project, September 9, 1942. Governor Herbert H. Lehman, Brooklyn Borough President John Cashmore, and Housing Commissioner Edward Weinfeld.

However ambivalent the reality of Weinfeld's accomplishments as housing commissioner may have been, his friends and colleagues did not see it that way. Upon his resignation in December 1942, Governor Poletti called him "a splendid Housing Commissioner," with "vision, resourcefulness and courage," and offered him the "best of luck" in the future. John J. Bennett, Jr., the New York attorney general, wrote that Weinfeld had "done a splendid job for housing in this State," while the chairman of the New York City Housing Authority wrote of Weinfeld's "excellent service" and his contributions "to the advancement of the public housing program." Federal officials agreed. The administrator of the National Housing Agency told Weinfeld that "you and your office [have been] our main reliance in moving forward on the war housing job in New York State," and the agency's regional representative wrote "of the splendid cooperation that you have given me since I started my job six months ago. You have been a rod and staff to me."[82]

Others tried to keep Weinfeld in the housing post. Assemblyman William T. Andrews informed Weinfeld of "efforts [to] induce you to stay." Charles L. Fleece, a vice-president of three projects under Weinfeld's supervision, reported that he had sent a letter "to Governor-elect Dewey, urging that he reappoint you as Commissioner of Housing. . . . You have been likened to the old-fashioned bowler-hatted cop who knows everyone living in the block, but commands and exacts strict discipline, and at the same time understands everyone's problems." Concluding that "we, too, have felt the sting of the stick across the seat of our pants," Fleece ended that "we don't want our cop resigning because of a new chief." The Republican majority leader in the state assembly wrote "to tell you how deeply I regret your departure from the role you have been playing in our state . . . and I only hope that events will be of such a nature that you may again be with us."[83]

Robert R. Hartley, a Presbyterian minister and chairman of the New Rochelle Housing Authority, in what Hartley described as "a Republican community," sent Weinfeld a copy of a letter he had addressed to Governor-elect Dewey, asking him to keep Weinfeld in office:

> The members of our Authority feel that his retention in that office is a "must." . . . In our dealings with Mr. Weinfeld, we have found him to be a wise counsellor and a faithful guide, as well as an interested friend of all those who for years have been struggling to better the housing conditions of the under-privileged in our community. His wise knowledge of housing problems, his genuinely inspired humanitarianism and his unusual abilities qualify him in every way for this important post. We speak from experience and urge you to consider these qualifications before you accept his resignation.
>
> I do not know, and I may be speaking out of turn, but I believe that Mr. Weinfeld might be persuaded to reconsider his resignation if the matter were presented to him by you, and where the poor are concerned, politics should be of secondary consideration.[84]

Dewey, in fact, was prepared to ask Weinfeld to remain on as housing commissioner, but Weinfeld "had no desire or purpose to serve in the Dewey administration."[85] Such service would not have furthered Weinfeld's subsequent career, since it would have resulted in the attenuation of the relationship that had been built during the previous three and a half years and that would be crucial in the future—his relationship with the man who had first appointed him as commissioner, Herbert H. Lehman. Weinfeld was fully aware of the importance of his ties to Lehman. Thus, even before he wrote Governor Poletti officially of his resignation, he informed Lehman of it and expressed his "very grateful appreciation for the opportunity which you gave me" and "the extraordinary cooperation and help which at all times I had from you."[86] Lehman's response was even more telling. "I want you to know," he wrote,

> that I very greatly appreciate your splendid service. It has been a great satisfaction to have had the privilege of working closely with you for the past several years. Your loyalty and encouragement have been a great help to me.[87]

As Lehman added several years later, Weinfeld

> was an unusually efficient and devoted public servant. During the years he was part of my administration, I consulted with him very frequently, not only on matters relating to housing, but on many legal matters as well. I found his judgment and his knowledge of the law excellent.[88]

Thus, on December 31, 1942, Edward Weinfeld left the employ of the state of New York and, until he became a judge, was never again on a government payroll. During the decade of the 1940s, he turned down two opportunities for government service and was unable to obtain the one opportunity that he sought.

Sometime in 1941, while still housing commissioner, he was approached by a committee of political leaders in his district and urged to run for a congressional seat vacated by the sudden death of the incumbent; he rejected the suggestion because he felt "an obligation to finish" his housing work as well as "a deep sense of loyalty to the Governor."[89] Six years later, New York City's mayor, William O'Dwyer, offered to appoint Weinfeld chairman of the City Planning Commission—a post that would not have permitted Weinfeld to maintain any law practice on the side. Because he did not want to close down his practice, he rejected the offer.[90]

The one job Weinfeld wanted turned out to be unavailable, at least on terms he found acceptable. In August 1943, he learned that he had been suggested for an army commission in the Military Government Division of the Provost Marshall General's Office, which would take over "the military government of hostile areas ultimately to be occupied by the American Armed Forces."[91] He eagerly applied for the commission, at the rank of Lieutenant Colonel, and indicated his preference for foreign service. He solicited letters of recommendation, including one from Senator Robert F. Wagner, who called Weinfeld "a man of unusual ability and high character . . . anxious to serve his country."[92] But, in the end, the commission did not materialize because the Secretary of War directed that high-level officer requirements be met by the reassignment of current officers rather than new appointments of civilians.[93]

Thus, Weinfeld reentered and remained in the private practice of law for the decade of the 1940s. But he reentered private practice with new friends, new relationships, and new connections that made his new practice very different from that in which he had been engaged in the early 1930s. He also had a new image: he was no longer the young lawyer striving to move upward through his Tammany connections but a mature former public servant who could be relied on, even at personal cost, to do what was right. We now need to turn to this new image and these new friendships and to probe the transforming impact they had on Weinfeld's professional and personal life.

6

Friendship

Friends were central to the life of Edward Weinfeld—both to his professional life and to his private one. Weinfeld always had time for the men who became his friends, and he enjoyed conversation with them about their lives, their concerns, and the subjects that interested them. He was intensely loyal to his friends, and they reciprocated his loyalty. Even though Weinfeld's many friendships (too many to discuss in this chapter) consumed a good deal of his time, ultimately they helped him to relax. Friends also played key roles in the advancement of his career.

Some of Weinfeld's friendships went back as far as his days in law school and even high school and his early years in practice, but many of the most important ones either grew out of or matured during the course of his public service in Albany, as a member of the 1938 constitutional convention and as New York State housing commissioner. Many of Weinfeld's friends, especially from this later period, were also his patrons: they often worked to advance his career, and in some instances, he worked to advance theirs. And, since Weinfeld outlived nearly all of his friends, he ended up consoling and sometimes caring for their widows and children.

One of his oldest friends was Joseph Eichler, whom he met in 1918 when Joe "was a freshman at the School of Commerce of New York University and . . . [Weinfeld] was at its law school." They soon became fraternity brothers, and, as Weinfeld declared fifty-six years later in his eulogy at Eichler's funeral, "There was then born a friendship that grew in richness through the years and continued undiminished even after he left New York for California. It was sustained and nourished . . . by correspondence which covered so many subjects which reflected his interests."[1]

Eichler was not an intellectual. As he himself said, he was "almost completely free of any intellectual pursuits." His "discussions" with his

California "friends" were "not very profound," and he "read very little"; in his own words, "It usually takes me three days to finish 'Time.'"² But his relationship with Weinfeld was different. According to Weinfeld, Eichler "had an inquiring mind" and "curiosity about men and events." Since Eichler and Weinfeld resided on opposite coasts, they saw each other only rarely and carried on their friendship through "correspondence cover[ing] a wide spectrum that ran the gamut from economic, financial, political, industrial and labor problems, to the ultimate of social reform and social justice."³

Eichler felt comfortable confiding in Weinfeld. He wrote Weinfeld, for example, about his "simple" "philosophy" of "*try[ing] to treat other people decently, especially those who work for me*" and of working "*for the improvement of the lot of the common man.*"⁴ He also sent Weinfeld a copy of his letter resigning from Associated Home Builders of California, a trade organization of which Eichler, as the most prominent building contractor in the San Francisco Bay area, was a leading member; Eichler refused to tolerate the racial discrimination practiced by the association. On other occasions, he wrote about politics. Of course, Weinfeld always sent him a sympathetic and thoughtful response, as, for example, when he congratulated Eichler on his "vigorous and forthright stand" in resigning from Associated Home Builders—a stand that Weinfeld was "sure . . . will have a wholesome effect whether or not the organization accepts your position."⁵

The relationship between these two friends was not, however, solely one of Weinfeld being a sympathetic listener for Eichler. Their relationship was far more reciprocal, with each ministering to the other's needs. For nearly thirty years, Weinfeld, whenever he needed money, turned to Eichler, who advanced loans to cover Weinfeld's requirements. Weinfeld borrowed from Eichler because "as a matter of personal policy . . . [he] preferred not to have . . . [his] personal note with any bank"; as Weinfeld recognized, Eichler also was especially "generous . . . in stating that as far as the principal itself is concerned, I can set the length of time and terms of repayment in any manner I wish."⁶ Weinfeld's first major loan, for the sum of three thousand dollars, appears to have occurred in 1934;⁷ his final loan from Eichler, in the amount of fifteen thousand dollars, took place in 1961.⁸

Another early friendship that had a profound and lasting impact on Weinfeld's life and career was that of Bernard Botein, who was "like a brother" to Weinfeld.⁹ Weinfeld and Botein first met, according to

Botein's son, when they were opposing counsel in a case, and they immediately took a liking to each other.[10] After they had served together in the
Lehman administration, they became especially close. They developed a
tradition, for example, that when either of them began a new job—and
received appropriate stationery—he would send the first letter on the new
stationery to the other.[11] Further evidence of the warm social relationship
between Weinfeld and Botein can be found in the facts that Botein asked
Weinfeld to be godfather for his son Michael[12] and that the Boteins were
social guests at Weinfeld's apartment nearly twice as often as anyone
else.[13]

The professional side of the friendship was even deeper. On one occasion, for example, the Boteins, along with the lieutenant governor and his
wife, spent "a memorable evening" at Weinfeld's apartment, at which
"whispering of Bernie's appointment" as an interim judge took place. A
year later, the Boteins were at the Weinfelds on election night "listening
to the Election Returns" that gave Botein a permanent seat on the Manhattan Supreme Court bench.[14]

Botein repaid Weinfeld in a financial manner on at least two occasions,
when he appointed him as a special master in litigation pending before
the state Supreme Court and Weinfeld earned substantial fees. For example, in *Mahler v. Oishei*, a shareholders' derivative action that was resolved in 1947, Weinfeld received a fee of $32,500[15]—a quite large sum
for that era. Similarly, in *Continental Bank & Trust Co. v. 150 Broadway
Corp.*,[16] Weinfeld acted as a referee in connection with insolvency proceedings involving the 150 Broadway Corp., proceedings that lasted from
March 10, 1945, when Botein first appointed him, until October 27,
1949. Weinfeld received another substantial fee in connection with this
matter.

The professional association between Botein and Weinfeld only deepened when in 1950 Weinfeld finally ascended to the federal bench, and he
and Botein settled into careers as two of the leading judges in New York.
They never became rivals, in part because they strove for judicial excellence and acclaim in different fashions—Botein, as an author of books
and an inventive judicial administrator, and Weinfeld, as an adjudicator
of disputes and teacher and mentor for young lawyers. Thus Weinfeld
and Botein could easily celebrate each other's achievements. Weinfeld, for
example, could offer Botein "special congratulations" on his "Court reform and reorganization efforts" and on a review of one of Botein's
books, an inscribed copy of which Weinfeld had presented to Governor

Edward Weinfeld and Bernard Botein, February 1960.

and Mrs. Lehman, while Botein could express his "great pride" in reading about one of Weinfeld's opinions in *Time* magazine and could urge him to relax and "do the work of only three average judges" rather than four or five.[17]

Bernard Botein, like Joseph Eichler, died many years before Weinfeld did, and Weinfeld offered Botein's family "thoughtfulness, help, and general support" after his death. Mrs. Botein, in particular, thanked Weinfeld for his "strength and guidance and loving concern in our sorrowful time," and then added that "if Bernie could have chosen one person to stand with us, it would have been you."[18] Her affection for the Weinfelds and her need for their support were further demonstrated when, after her husband's death, she moved from her old apartment and into the same apartment building in which Judge and Mrs. Weinfeld resided.[19]

Another of Weinfeld's oldest friends was Louis Lefkowitz, who served as attorney general of New York from 1957 to 1978. Weinfeld and

Lefkowitz first came to know each other when they were district captains—Weinfeld, for the Democrats, and Lefkowitz, for the Republicans—on the Lower East Side.[20] Later, they ran in opposition to each other for a seat in New York's 1938 constitutional convention[21]—a seat that Weinfeld won. They remained friends thereafter, for as long as they both lived.

In 1957, soon after Lefkowitz had assumed the post of attorney general, Weinfeld delivered a speech at a dedication ceremony in Lefkowitz's honor. It is a speech that displays the qualities of generosity and empathy that made Weinfeld so close to the men he befriended.

Though Lefkowitz had been a political opponent, Weinfeld nonetheless spoke of his "personal affection for a dear friend, who by sheer merit, ha[d] achieved high and exalted position." "[P]ersonal affection" is a rare quality for political opponents to display toward each other; even rarer is the compliment Weinfeld paid to Lefkowitz—that he had attained his office through "sheer merit." Weinfeld continued his public display of generosity as he expressed "sentimental pride in what the years have brought" and acknowledged the presence in the audience of Lefkowitz's wife "and all your wonderful family," especially Lefkowitz's mother, who was "still basking in the sunshine reflected by his achievements."[22] Weinfeld simply knew how to make a friend feel wonderful.

He also could express "with nostalgia" what he, Lefkowitz, and his audience shared in common—"our youth, our neighborhood, [and] our community." Weinfeld spoke, in particular, of many childhood experiences that he and Lefkowitz had shared and then of "the political soil" of the Lower East Side, "where votes . . . were grown from the seedings of friendship."[23] By his empathic observations, Weinfeld displayed the bonds that made it possible for him, Lefkowitz, and other men of their generation from the Lower East Side to be such special friends.

With his election to the constitutional convention of 1938, Weinfeld's orbit expanded beyond the upwardly mobile, often immigrant Jewish communities of the Lower East Side, New York University, and the solo-practitioner New York City bar. He took on new friends, mostly in high places. But he lavished on them the same love and care that he had given his old friends, and they helped him professionally just as his old ones had done.

The first of his new friends was Charles Poletti, a justice of the state supreme court and a fellow delegate to the convention. In a letter written shortly after the convention had ended, Weinfeld expressed his gratitude for "the rare privilege of association with" Poletti "at the Constitutional Convention." He then continued,

> I have learned to know you, and of your genuine and sincere interest in progressive and liberal causes. Indeed, the memory of your forceful advocacy of so many forward-looking and progressive measures, shall always remain a treasured memory with me.[24]

Poletti responded in a note written shortly after election day, 1938: "One of the best things of the Constitutional Convention was the opportunity of forming your friendship and during the next four years I want to see a lot of you."[25] During the next four years, and, indeed, for many decades thereafter, Weinfeld and Poletti did see a lot of each other.

Poletti was the one who arranged for that to happen. At the conclusion of the convention, Poletti accepted a place on Governor Herbert Lehman's reelection slate as the Democrats' candidate for lieutenant governor. Several days later, Weinfeld received a telegram inviting him to "attend a luncheon at the Executive Mansions in Albany . . . to discuss certain phases of the campaign";[26] Poletti subsequently indicated how pleased he was "that it was possible for you [Weinfeld] to help the Governor during the campaign,"[27] and there is reason to believe that it was Poletti who made the initial connection between Weinfeld and Governor Lehman—a connection that within a year brought Weinfeld into the Lehman administration and would determine the course of Weinfeld's career.

The connection also led to the most important friendship of Weinfeld's life—with Governor Herbert Lehman and his wife, Edith. Initially, upon his assumption of the office of state housing commissioner in July 1939, Weinfeld's relationship with Lehman was a purely professional one that did not extend beyond housing matters. But as time progressed, Lehman increasingly recognized Weinfeld's talents and added to his responsibilities.

Within less than two years of his assumption of office, Weinfeld was drafting speeches for the governor.[28] Although Weinfeld's earliest draft was written for a public housing ground-breaking ceremony, it extended well beyond housing and into issues of foreign policy. As drafted by Weinfeld and delivered by Lehman, the speech contained the following language:

We are a peace loving people. We have worked and work today only so that all the free peoples of the world may live in peace and security—a peace and security that will insure the continuance and progress of those free institutions, those personal liberties which are the life-blood of our nation and the very being of each of its citizens. There are forces loose in the world which threaten both our peace and our free institutions. Against that threat from abroad we are doing everything needful. We will meet that threat no matter what direction from which it may come.[29]

Another speech a year later likewise addressed issues beyond housing, as it spoke of the need for "the most efficient, the most economical, the fullest possible use of our every resource of man power, of machinery, of plant capacity."[30]

Shortly after he had resigned as governor, Lehman wrote Weinfeld to express appreciation for "your splendid service." Lehman continued, "It has been a great satisfaction to have had the privilege of working closely with you for the past several years. Your loyalty and encouragement have been a great help to me."[31] One of Lehman's staff members added that it had been "fellows like you upon whom I must rely."[32]

Even after he had ceased to be governor, Lehman continued to rely on Weinfeld. When Lehman ran for a seat in the United States Senate in 1946,[33] Weinfeld was again writing speeches for him.[34] In the fall of 1947, Weinfeld wrote another speech for the former governor,[35] and when Lehman decided to run for the Senate seat vacated by Robert F. Wagner in 1949, Weinfeld sent a telegram, signed "Eddie," congratulating him and "add[ing] I am at your full command." Lehman responded that he "look[ed] forward to availing myself of your offer of assistance during the campaign," and, in fact, Weinfeld "play[ed] an active part in the campaign," forwarding the ideas of others,[36] submitting draft speeches, and critiquing the governor's performance at events.[37] Lehman won the 1949 election, and, as we shall see in the next chapter, Lehman reciprocated within a matter of months by recommending that Weinfeld be appointed as a federal district judge.

The friendship between Lehman and Weinfeld involved much more, however, than their mutual advancement of each other's careers. After Weinfeld had ascended to the bench and Lehman had retired from public office, they grew increasingly close to each other. Indeed, the authentic

Herbert H. Lehman, with inscription, "To my friend Eddie Weinfeld—a loyal and efficient public servant—with my best wishes and proud regards." Herbert H. Lehman.

quality of Weinfeld's friendships is perhaps best illustrated by his ties to Lehman after Lehman could no longer advance his career and especially by his ties to Lehman's widow after the governor's death. During the final decades of the Lehmans' lives, Weinfeld's relationship to them was transformed from that of political protégé to surrogate son—a surrogate son who spoke to them daily by telephone.[38]

A handwritten note that Weinfeld sent on the tenth anniversary of his ascension to the bench evidences his changing relationship with the Lehmans. In this note to the governor, Weinfeld attributes his "exciting and enriching" decade on the bench to "your devotion and faith in me," "pray[s] I shall always be worthy of that faith," and ends by toasting "the warmth of your friendship." Less than a year later, Weinfeld sent another handwritten note to Lehman thanking him for his "constant devotion" and expressing how "blessed" he felt "to have such as friend" as the governor.[39]

Several months before Lehman died, he gave Weinfeld a special gift on the occasion of the latter's sixty-second birthday. It was a manuscript document from the 1735 *Zenger* case, but what made the gift particularly special was that Herbert Lehman's brother Irving, then chief judge of the New York Court of Appeals, had given it to Herbert as a gift for his sixtieth birthday. The Zenger document was precisely the sort of family treasure that a father might pass down to a son, and Weinfeld thanked Lehman accordingly, noting that he was "move[d] . . . beyond adequate expression."[40]

Weinfeld continued in his filial role when, several months later, he delivered the eulogy at the governor's funeral. He spoke of the "warmth of the friendship of the Governor and his beloved Edith" as "one of life's richest blessings." He characterized Lehman as "a man of intense family devotion," for whom "'family' meant more than immediate family," even "extend[ing] to friends."[41] When he learned a month later that he had received a bequest from the Lehman estate, Weinfeld wrote a longhand note to Edith Lehman:

> I hardly know what to say or write. You know how much the Governor meant in my life and that I treasure his and your friendship as the richest blessing which ever came to Lillian and me. And now to receive a final generous expression of friendship from him moves me beyond words.
>
> My prayer is that I shall always prove worthy of that friendship and his faith in me.[42]

During the years following the governor's death, Weinfeld remained a dutiful surrogate son to Edith Lehman. He telephoned her every day when they both were in New York City; on Mrs. Lehman's many trips out of town, he corresponded with her frequently. When she requested copies of his correspondence with the governor as evidence of "a friendship which he cherished so deeply," Weinfeld sent all he could find. When Mrs. Lehman needed political advice in connection with a third person's campaign literature containing an old endorsement from Herbert Lehman, Weinfeld provided it instantly.[43] And, when Mrs. Lehman died more than a decade after the governor, she reciprocated with a bequest for Weinfeld in the amount of fifty thousand dollars, which was in addition to the bequest from Herbert Lehman's estate and a one hundred thousand dollar gift that she had given him earlier.[44]

Throughout his life, Weinfeld displayed the same sort of compassion and understanding toward friends that he did toward his immediate family. Indeed, his gracious assistance to friends went back to his youth. One early friend who owed his career to Weinfeld was Henry Waldman, a fellow student and fraternity brother at NYU, who, as we saw, dropped out of law school and only returned because of Weinfeld's encouragement. The Waldman-Weinfeld friendship continued for years, until Waldman's death in 1962, with a series of admiring letters from Waldman to Weinfeld bearing informal salutations such as "dear jurist," "dear judgie," and "dear jedge" and with Weinfeld "kind enough to intervene" with Senator Lehman's staff in an effort to obtain a federal job for Waldman's uncle.[45]

Weinfeld provided similar assistance to many other friends. When Bernard Rothman, the son of Weinfeld's pharmacist for forty years, had his pharmacy license suspended, Weinfeld spoke to him, examined the entire file in the case, and wrote to the State Board of Pharmacy urging his reinstatement, as "the type of pharmacist so sorely needed in many neighborhoods today, with a sincere interest in his patrons and a genuine concern for their wellbeing."[46] He provided help in a family matter to Irving Felt, another close friend, who wrote to thank Weinfeld for "your warm and wise advice to me when I needed the timely, personal help and understanding you provided."[47] Another close friend, Burt Zorn, sought Weinfeld's advice in connection with the decision of his son, Steven Zorn, to seek conscientious objector status during the Vietnam War.[48] A third friend, John Lichtenberg, sought Weinfeld's assistance with the Immigration and Naturalization Service in regularizing his wife's mother's immigrant status in the United States; although the obstacle to her regularization was her brother's affiliation with the Brazilian Communist Party, Weinfeld nonetheless appears to have provided advice and encouragement.[49] For a fourth friend, Pierre Leval, Weinfeld wrote a letter recommending his appointment as a federal district judge.[50]

Weinfeld loved and cared for Burt Zorn, John Lichtenberg, and Pierre Leval, as well as innumerable other protégés, such as his pharmacist's son. Ultimately, however, he was too modest to be comfortable in a role of potentate dispensing wisdom, knowledge, and favors to others and recognizing no one as his peer. He needed and wanted friends who were his equals and from whom he could draw sustenance. For this reason he was drawn into friendships with strong men, like Bernard Botein, who did not need his help, and dominant men, like Herbert Lehman, with whom he could remain in the role of protégé. He formed two such friendships after he had come to the bench—with Learned Hand and with Henry Friendly.

In Weinfeld's own words, his "friendship with Chief Judge Learned Hand . . . began soon after I took office and grew with the years." On one afternoon when he had kept a trial in session one half-hour beyond the time fixed by local court rules, Weinfeld returned to his chambers a few minutes after five o'clock to find an ashen-white and frightened secretary who could scarcely stammer out that shortly before she had been roundly bawled out by the chief judge—didn't Judge Weinfeld know what the prescribed hours for court sessions were?

Hand indicated that he would return as soon as Weinfeld came off the bench, but Weinfeld instead called Hand's chambers and proposed that he come upstairs to visit Hand.

> In about two minutes there was a terrific pounding on the door of my room and in walked the Chief, jabbing a finger at me as he crossed the room and said: "Young man, when I want to pay my respects to a colleague, I call on him. He does not come up to see me." What I thought would be a brief courtesy visit of perhaps a few minutes went on for more than an hour, and the range of subjects was far and wide. . . . A friendship was then born that gave me some of the richest experiences of my life. . . . "There was no stage of acquaintance ripening into friendship; we understood one another and were friends without more ado."[51]

For the next five or six years, Hand and Weinfeld had lunch nearly every Saturday at one of two local cafeterias. Their lunch

> discussions were of a broad spectrum—some on the light side, some on the more serious side, and some gossip of the day. There were times when the chief soared into the highest realms of philosophy, and other times when mundane affairs impelled him to language that would have made the roughest-speaking longshoreman look to his laurels. At some of these sessions he expressed in the colorful language of which he was so capable his disagreement with recent rulings by the Supreme Court and applied pet names he had coined for particular justices.[52]

Learned Hand, with inscription, "To Edward
Weinfeld—Who makes the rest of us feel like
drones." Learned Hand, October 30, 1957.

Similar discussions took place at a number of luncheons in Weinfeld's
chambers, which began when Weinfeld introduced two historic figures
who, although totally unlike each other, were both his friends—Learned
Hand and Herbert Lehman. This unusual threesome (the upstate Republican, the patrician Democrat, and the fellow from the Lower East Side)
hit it off so well together that Weinfeld's secretary reports that raucous
laughter constantly emerged through the closed door of the room in
which they were lunching.[53]

Learned Hand's irreverence undoubtedly contributed to cementing his
friendship with Weinfeld. Weinfeld was a man of always polite and formal bearing. He told one story, for example, of a luncheon he had at a
local Horn and Hardart cafeteria with Learned Hand and John M. Harlan, shortly after the latter had been appointed to the Supreme Court. In

the story, after a young African-American man had become excited at the "great honor" of "meet[ing] the grandson of the man who wrote the dissent in Plessy v. Ferguson," Weinfeld turned to the young man and said, "[Y]ou know that Chief Judge Hand is one of the greatest judges of this country in its entire history."[54] Hand, in contrast, rode roughshod over all such formality, and Weinfeld enjoyed it. For example, when Weinfeld informed Hand that Arthur Schlesinger, Jr., had reported him as criticizing a Supreme Court opinion as "'pettifoggery'" and as stating that "'[t]o trick up a lot of international stuff as though it were law frankly makes me puke, as dear old Holmes used to say,'" Hand responded, "I am amused that my harsh statement should have been quoted. I had forgotten all about the case now, but I have no doubt that what I said represented what I thought at the time."[55] Weinfeld was sufficiently impressed by Hand's response to tape it into his commonplace book—the book to which he looked for guidance as to proper judicial behavior.

But above all, Hand, like Lehman, was a figure to whom Weinfeld looked up. In Weinfeld's condolence note to Hand's widow following his death, Weinfeld remarked on how he had "sat at the feet of a great man" and "for a long time . . . enjoyed the rich pleasure of his company and great intellect." Although Weinfeld never became the son to Learned Hand that he ultimately was to Herbert Lehman, their relationship was a similarly hierarchical one; while there was no doubt "how much B [Learned Hand] thought of" him,[56] Weinfeld was not the heroic figure to Hand that Hand was to Weinfeld.

In contrast, the relationship of Weinfeld to a second great judicial figure with whom he served, Henry J. Friendly, was an equal one. Friendly and Weinfeld recognized each other as great judges. But they never competed with each other, since both knew they differed from one another immensely and that their talents lay along different dimensions.

In one of his earliest letters to Friendly, Weinfeld thanked him for a reprint of an article in the *Yale Law Journal*, which Weinfeld praised for its "scholarly attainment."[57] Subsequently, Weinfeld identified Friendly as one "of this century's 'giants' in American jurisprudence" whose "breadth of . . . erudition ha[d] earned for him a place of preeminence in the history of the American judiciary."[58] On yet another occasion, he "compliment[ed]" Friendly "on the brilliance of your performance" in drafting "a magnum opus in a difficult area of administrative law."[59] In conclusion, Weinfeld saw Friendly "as an outstanding judge and the most remarkable legal mind of his generation."[60]

In contrast, Friendly focused on the "extraordinary human qualities" that made Weinfeld great—his "concept of the high seriousness of the role of a judge," his "peculiar intensity of disinterest," his "fairness," his "courtesy,"[61] and his "thoroughness." These human qualities "radiate[d] through . . . [Weinfeld's] courtroom and produce[d] courtesy and dignity on the part of all."[62] Because it was "such a perfect fit," Friendly applied to Weinfeld words that Learned Hand had once used about Benjamin N. Cardozo:

> "He is wise because his spirit is uncontaminated, because he knows no violence, or hatred, or envy, or jealousy, or ill-will." And it is "this purity that chiefly makes him the judge we so much revere; more than his learning, his acuteness, and his fabulous industry."[63]

According to Weinfeld, he and Friendly became fast friends as soon as the latter came to the bench in 1959. As Weinfeld wrote,

> I regard as one of my life's most meaningful experiences the deep and warm friendship we share. . . . Though we had not met until he came to the Court of Appeals, our first conversation reminded me of Woodrow Wilson's comment on his first meeting with Colonel Edward M. House. When the Colonel observed that soon after their meeting they shared confidences which men usually exchange only after years of friendship, the President-to-be remarked, "My dear friend, we have known one another always." I had the same feeling after meeting Judge Friendly, and our friendship has grown with the years.[64]

Friendly agreed that the Wilson quote "aptly characterize[d] our relationship,"[65] which, on another occasion, Friendly had described as "the warmest of friendships."[66]

Indeed, their friendship was so close that, when the court of appeals reversed in part an opinion Weinfeld had written, Friendly sent the following note: "I am sorry we could not affirm your fine opinion 100 percent—I came the closest that I could." Weinfeld responded, "It was so nice of you to write. . . . As I often told you before, to a soldier in the ranks it is all part of the day's work."[67] The exchange was all part of what Friendly called Weinfeld's "special gift for friendship." He continued,

Once you are within . . . [his] fortunate circle, he identifies with you completely; your joys are his joys, your sorrows his sorrows. If occasion demands, he will give his precious time without stint or limit. It is this quality that established his truly filial relation with Herbert and Edith Lehman. It is this which has made him beloved by so many.[68]

Nothing better illustrates how much Edward Weinfeld treasured friendship than an exchange he had in 1972 with Warren Moscow, with whom he had been closely acquainted since the 1930s. It began with the following 1972 letter from Moscow, written in response to comments Weinfeld had made at a luncheon with Moscow and several others:

The adage that old soldiers never die, but simply fade away, apparently can apply to friendships as well. . . . I presume—for the last time—to speak as bluntly as only an old and good friend may dare, about you at Tuesday's lunch. From its outset you carped and picked much as a nagging shrike would hit at a husband, not for what he was doing at the moment, but for some sin of the past fresh, at least in her mind.

As I sat there among other friends who could not and should not have been involved, the onset was incomprehensible, even irrational. I know of no sins of omission or commission which warranted it, and if my character was so basically sleazy, how did we ever become friends in the first place?

But enough of that. Our friendship was too close too long to end with either a whimper or a snarl. It deserves a decent requiem and I now say in its honor that I shall always cherish its memory.

I neither want nor will welcome a response to this. I prefer to recall the unblemished happy years during which I was the receiver of so many of your kindnesses as well as the occasional times that I was able to reciprocate.[69]

Contrary to Moscow's instructions, Weinfeld did respond both by letter[70] and by telephone. In the phone conversation, Weinfeld strove to convince Moscow that he had been misunderstood and then added, "I have always been proud of my friendships. I pride myself in them—and I hope you will accept my statement. . . . I am sorry. I can't thrust myself upon you; I can't force my friendship on you or anybody else."[71] Nonetheless, he asked

Moscow to "reconsider, and I hope you will."[72] Moscow ultimately did, and he and Weinfeld remained friends.[73]

Friends were just too valuable to lose. It was difficult to find friends who offered "word of deep encouragement" and were "always quick . . . to lend a helping hand," who shared "the good times and the bad," and who did not "run when trouble comes."[74] Weinfeld's life and career were built upon friendships with key men such as Bernard Botein, Joseph Eichler, Belmont Friewald, Henry Friendly, Learned Hand, and, above all, Herbert Lehman. Weinfeld's friendship, in turn, improved the lives of many others.

It is fitting to end this chapter with one last note about a friend of twenty-seven years, Marie Vollrath, who began work with Judge Weinfeld as his secretary in 1960 and remained with him until his death. On the day of a law clerks' dinner celebrating his thirtieth anniversary on the bench, she wrote a note that captures as well as anything why Weinfeld mattered so much to friends:

> I'm sure you know how much I want to be with you tonight; I'm also sure you know why I cannot.[75]
>
> However, I join in spirit with "all your family" on this happy occasion to extend to you our respect, admiration and affection. You are a teacher and an advisor, but most important—a friend. Your "door is always open"—for this, I especially thank you.[76]

7

The Making of a Judge

From his earliest years at the bar, Edward Weinfeld had always wanted to be a judge and had "actively aspire[d] to" a "place . . . on the bench."[1] He worked extremely hard to develop the skills and stature that would merit his appointment. And he did so with great success. By the time he was named to the District Court in 1950, at the age of forty-nine, a widely shared consensus had formed among New York City elites that Weinfeld would bring exceptional talent to the court and would make an outstanding judge. In the words of the *New York Times*, Weinfeld was a "man of warm sympathies, of fairness and high personal integrity," who had "worked tirelessly in innumerable civic causes" and would be "a respected," "able and just United States judge."[2]

Some fifteen years later, after Weinfeld had served on the Southern District, a vacancy occurred on the Second Circuit Court of Appeals, and Weinfeld was mentioned as a candidate to fill the vacancy. Again, the plaudits came. The *Times* called Weinfeld a "truly distinguished . . . jurist" who offered the president "a splendid opportunity to make an outstanding appointment."[3] The *Herald Tribune* declared him "the outstanding jurist sitting in United States District Court" and noted that the American Bar Association "gave him the rare recommendation of 'exceptionally well qualified'" when his name was put forward for elevation to the Second Circuit.[4] And, Charles Wyzanski, a distinguished federal judge in Boston, wrote Weinfeld that "ABOVE ALL you are THE GREATEST LIVING JUDGE IN THE USA—and every qualified observer gives you that rating because of your wisdom, steadiness, learning, tact, and strength."[5] Even a woman whose only connection to him was that she had served "as a juror under your guidance" told Weinfeld how "impressive your courtroom was" and thanked him for his "careful instructions," which enabled her to understand "the import of what I had to do."[6]

Despite this praise, Edward Weinfeld almost failed to obtain a judgeship, and after fifteen outstanding years of service as a trial judge, he was not elevated to the Second Circuit Court of Appeals, when nearly everyone thought he ought to be. The reason is that obtaining a federal judicial appointment is an intensely political process.

Weinfeld's files offer us a very special glimpse into that process. As a young lawyer, Weinfeld had learned shorthand, which he had polished by transcribing speeches of Franklin D. Roosevelt and Winston Churchill during World War II.[7] Using his shorthand, he was able to record many conversations that he had with individuals involved in the judicial appointment process, and he saved typewritten transcriptions of his shorthand notes in his files. Using these transcriptions, this chapter will examine in depth the political processes that denied Weinfeld judicial appointments in the 1940s and later in 1965.

Then, we will turn to the piece of luck that placed Weinfeld on the bench in 1950. Even his good luck had a political component, however, connected to his friendship with Herbert Lehman. In some respects, Weinfeld's successful 1950 appointment was as political as his earlier and later failed appointments were. But, once Weinfeld was on the bench, politics ceased, as he sought wisdom from nonpolitical sources so as to make himself into an outstanding judge.

The Failed Appointments

Edward Weinfeld began to campaign for an appointment to the federal bench in 1946, when the death of a sitting District Court judge had left a vacancy. His greatest strength, which in the short run also constituted a significant weakness, lay in his ties to former governor Herbert H. Lehman. Throughout the four-year campaign it took to elevate Weinfeld to the bench, Lehman was an unfailing supporter. He provided Weinfeld with advice about how to manage his candidacy, contacted people and wrote numerous letters on Weinfeld's behalf, and offered solace at moments when the campaign seemed stalled. As Weinfeld told the governor in January 1947, "of all the friends upon whom I had called he was the only one who I felt had acted sincerely and directly." And when Weinfeld commented that he was "keenly disappointed in some others whose support I expected would be more sincere and more enthusiastic," Lehman reassured him, "out of long experience in political life these things do happen" and told him "not to be so discouraged."[8] A few months later, Lehman also told Weinfeld that he "deeply resented" the failure of others "to go along with his recommendation"; Lehman added that "he resented that and a number of other things but it did not seem to make a damned bit of difference to them." The governor concluded that, as long as a "position was open here, he would not make any other recommendation as he did not want to detract from his support of me. . . . His final words were . . . not to worry—that he would not waiver [*sic*] in the slightest degree no matter who called."[9]

Unfortunately for Weinfeld's ambitions, Lehman was retired from active politics in 1947 and thus was unable to obtain the judgeship Weinfeld so wanted. Indeed, Lehman's backing was probably a liability—as one Bronx Democratic leader commented when informed of Lehman's support for Weinfeld, "What the hell did Lehman ever do for us[?]"[10] The key person whose support Weinfeld needed was Robert F. Wagner, the senior and sole Democratic senator from New York, who by virtue of the practice of senatorial courtesy controlled federal judicial appointments in the state.

Weinfeld had known Wagner at least since 1938, when Weinfeld had been a delegate to the state constitutional convention over which Wagner had presided. He also was close to Wagner's son, Robert F. Wagner, Jr., who would become mayor of New York City several years after Weinfeld had managed his successful campaign in 1949[11] to become Manhattan borough president. The problem, however, was that Weinfeld had little to offer Wagner in return for Wagner's support—support that the senator was not completely free to grant. As the holder of the highest statewide office to which a Democrat had been elected,[12] Wagner had responsibility for maintaining party unity; even more important, his concern for the budding political career of his son prevented him from antagonizing any faction within the party. And, advancing Weinfeld for a judgeship might antagonize others who wanted it.

Working initially through Robert Wagner, Jr., Weinfeld initiated a delicate negotiation with the senator. In a December 1946 meeting with Junior, Weinfeld learned that state and local party leaders and the mayor of New York City were promoting someone else's candidacy; the young Wagner promised to try to arrange a meeting between his father and Weinfeld.[13] Several days later Weinfeld learned from Herbert Lehman that, although the Senator was very fond of me and would very much like to see me get the appointment . . . [,] if others failed to submit my name . . . he was [not] prepared to go to the bat and fight for me. The Governor had the feeling that the Senator did not want to get mixed up in the situation although it would please him very much if the political leaders recommended me and . . . he would be very eager to go along.[14]

On January 3, 1947, Robert Wagner, Jr. confirmed that his father had told Governor Lehman that "he felt I was head and shoulders above most of the other persons, particularly the one who apparently had been designated," but "he was afraid to get into a fight on account of it."[15] Several weeks later, Junior again spoke with Weinfeld about a deal put together by local leaders and reported that a close friend of President Harry Truman had indicated that the president "will not go along" and "talked about their getting together and agreeing upon a high-type man."[16]

Armed with this information, Weinfeld met with Senator Wagner two days later, on February 11, 1947. Weinfeld pushed hard, but delicately, for a commitment of support from the senator, and the senator, with equal delicacy, declined to commit:

EW: The thing here has gotten a bit snarled up.
RFW: I know. . . .
EW: . . . I was hoping you would talk to the President.
RFW: Well—
RFW: When I come back I will talk to you—you and I were at the Convention together and you and I know each other very well and we can discuss our problems.
EW: I would like to tell you my problem—my strong feeling is that with the thing snarled up it would be easier now than before.
EW: If nomination would be made I would have a good chance—it would close the matter—If when you are down there if you get an inspiration, maybe you will call the President.
RFW: That is what I want to talk to you about—I am always very careful—I do not want to make any mistakes.
EW: They won't do anything while you are gone? They need your approval.
RFW: No, they won't do anything—they need my approval.
RFW: I had a tough time at the convention.

EW: I realized it—I think the convention took more out of you than perhaps you realized at the time and I think for personal reasons because there were men there whom you expected to be on your side but who were not.

RFW: Yes. It disappointed me very much.

EW: I think our relationship was a close one because of it [the convention].

Following some conversation about a mutual friend, Wagner announced that his car had arrived, that he must leave, and that "as soon as I get back I will talk to you." Weinfeld then concluded that conversation by saying, "I am depending upon you—I do hope it is going to come through."[17]

The "snarl" continued for several more months. On one occasion in April, Junior reported that his father had asked Irving Ives, the Republican senator from New York, "What about Ed Weinfeld?" and suggested that Weinfeld identify some intermediaries who could speak on his behalf to Ives. When Weinfeld asked whether he could tell one intermediary "that R.F.W. Sr. was for me," Junior responded "that while he is for me, he is not sure that it ought to be known publicly."[18] Weinfeld continued to press. He told Junior that he was "as eager for the job as anything" and that he did "not want to give up on this," since he thought he "fit into the picture in all ways." Junior's only response was, "Dad is dealing with a tough crowd."[19] In the end, the tough crowd prevailed and Weinfeld was not appointed.

The next year, Weinfeld tried again to get himself appointed a federal district judge. On April 8, 1948, he met with Frank Sampson, a local Democratic Party boss, and stated he "would appreciate if you would go along with me." The boss responded,

> I could not promise it because I promised one fellow that I would go along with him. If he does not click there is another fellow that is waiting that I told if number one man does not click he would be considered. I am in a box and do not want to make any further promises.[20]

Again, Senator Wagner did not interfere, the "matter . . . was left to the organization in New York County," and Weinfeld did not receive an appointment to the bench.[21]

Weinfeld's best chance for an appointment came in 1949, when Congress enacted legislation creating four new judgeships in the Southern District of New York. While the bill was pending, Junior reported that he "had a chance to talk with Dad and he said we ought to go all out for Ed again." "'So Dad says he would like to do all he can.'"[22] But, in July 1949, illness forced Robert F. Wagner to retire from the Senate, and Governor Thomas E. Dewey appointed a second Republican, John Foster Dulles, to an interim seat pending the November 1949 election. Without any New York Democrat in the Senate, the four new positions were filled without recourse to the practice of senatorial courtesy, and Weinfeld again did not receive one of them.

As of mid-October 1949, the prospects of Edward Weinfeld ever becoming a judge seemed dim indeed. Despite nearly universal acclaim for his outstanding legal talents, he had failed in two consecutive years to obtain appointment to vacant seats on the district court. Even worse, he had failed in the third year of his efforts to obtain one of four available seats on the court; four other individuals were appointed in preference to him.

To his friends, Weinfeld admitted his "disappointment," while at the same time assuring them that the "good wishes and help of friends ha[d] meant a great deal."[23] But his elder daughter, Ann, then a college freshman, probably expressed his feelings more poignantly than he himself could have in a letter she sent home upon receipt of the news. Ann wrote, in part,

> I tried somewhat unsuccessfully to tell you what your not getting the judgeship first meant to me. It was more than just one of life's expected disappointments. It was a disillusionment. . . . I'm not at the naive idealistic state of thinking that only the most qualified lawyers get to be judges. . . . But I'm still enough of a dreamer to hope that somehow, somewhere, the best, (no matter how they have to get themselves appointed) come out where they should be—and—in the long run the majority of the time that does happen. But—when men like you, Daddy, are completely forgotten about, when just speaking from a judicial point of view you could be more than just another judge, that's when my little dream world begins to shudder. . . .
>
> I write this as a disappointed dreamer, a hopeful citizen and one of your loyal supporters. But most of all I write this as your daughter who

had hoped one of your biggest dreams would be realized. I can't help thinking though that there will be other things and that will in time heal the disppointment of this.[24]

Time would, indeed, cure Weinfeld's disappointment; in fact, the cure would come quite quickly. But before we turn to the appointment he did obtain as a federal judge in the Southern District of New York, we need to examine another position he did not receive—a seat on the United States Court of Appeals for the Second Circuit—a seat for which all recognized that he would have been a uniquely qualified appointee.

The possibility of his elevation occurred in July 1965, when Thurgood Marshall, who only recently had begun service as a judge on the Court of Appeals, resigned from the court to become solicitor general of the United States, a post from which he would be elevated to the Supreme Court in 1967. The name of Edward Weinfeld immediately surfaced as the leading candidate to succeed Marshall on the Circuit Court.

Rumors of an impending vacancy on the Court of Appeals had begun surfacing more than a year earlier, and at that time Edith Lehman, the widow of Herbert, had written a personal note to President Lyndon Johnson in support of Weinfeld's elevation, stating that she did "not want to neglect to do what I am sure Herbert would be doing were he here." On July 21, 1965, Mrs. Lehman wrote a second letter that concluded that "I cannot too strongly recommend Eddie for this advancement" after stating that "no appointment would have given Herbert greater satisfaction than to have seen his friend advanced to the Court of Appeals."[25]

Weinfeld had some powerful people working on his behalf. One of them, Robert F. Kennedy, the newly elected Democratic senator from New York, had put Weinfeld's name forward as his exclusive recommendation.[26] Congressman Emanuel Celler, the chairman of the House Judiciary Committee, agreed with Senator Kennedy that "Weinfeld tower[ed] above all" of "the candidates for the Court of Appeals"—that Weinfeld was "a judge of rare distinction, excellent judicial poise, a man of erudition."[27] Arthur J. Goldberg, the United States ambassador to the United Nations and a former Supreme Court justice, similarly told the president that Weinfeld was "the outstanding District Judge in the country."[28] In fact, before the end of September, the Department of Justice had sent Weinfeld's name to the White House with its recommendation that he be nominated for the vacant seat.[29] Meanwhile, throughout the entire process, Judge Henry J. Friendly worked quietly behind the scenes to obtain the appointment for Weinfeld.[30] Indeed, his commission was on the president's desk waiting to be signed.[31]

But another candidate meanwhile had emerged. Wilfred Feinberg, whose brother, Abe Feinberg, had been a major fundraiser for the Democratic Party since the election of 1948, also sought the vacant judgeship.[32] In early October, Weinfeld learned that Feinberg was a serious candidate, that Senator Kennedy had "talked to the P and pleaded my case, but that he [wasn't] willing to stick his neck out by exercising senatorial veto." Weinfeld also learned that the president had "told him [i.e., Kennedy] that there wasn't any question affecting me personally; that the other fellow had political support which I didn't have."[33] Although Congressman Celler also had favored Weinfeld, he too indicated that he would not oppose the president's nomination of Feinberg.[34] In light of the frailty of Weinfeld's political support and the "tremendous pressure" being "exert[ed]" on Feinberg's behalf,[35] the president appointed Feinberg.

Weinfeld was not especially disappointed by his failure to obtain a seat on the Second Circuit. As soon as he learned of Feinberg's candidacy, he predicted to those around him that Feinberg would get the appointment.[36] Moreover, Weinfeld gained great satisfaction sitting as a District Court judge: as Judge Wyzanski reminded him, "the life of a trial judge" was "rarely deadly," and as a trial judge he served "as a model for the rest of us," whereas on the Court of Appeals he would be "no better than Henry Friendly."[37] Thus, the view that Weinfeld communicated to his friends was that the "incident [was] closed. We must," he wrote, "accept history as it is written, and so far as my personal involvement in the incident is concerned, it is now history."[38] But, as he then added to one close friend,

> my philosophical acceptance of events is not so detached that I can ignore the implications attendant upon the circumstances of the nomination, which have been exposed in the public press and adverted to in a number of editorials. When one contemplates that such factors played any part, let alone the decisive part, in the nomination it is not only saddening and distressing, but demeaning of a great court.[39]

Or, as he wrote in 1978 to another friend who had written him about the 1965 events,

I am sure you must know that I am much happier at the District Court than I would have been at the Court of Appeals—and this is not a case of sour grapes.

I think I told you I reluctantly allowed my name to be considered and the thing moved forward very quickly and was all set until the final event happened.

I have a strong feeling that my contribution here has been a much greater one than it would have been at the higher level. My only feeling is about the method that was used which brought about the result—that is, political power based on financial contributions.[40]

Weinfeld, in short, did not want judicial office to become a matter of political barter and sale. Indeed, anything political produced in him a certain ambivalence. He wondered, for example, whether "the word 'politician' can be applied properly to men who in public office assume the role of statesmen," of whom there were "remarkably few."[41]

It was an ambivalence that he never worked through. On the one hand, he respected the right of the people, by virtue of the votes they cast, to enact their will into law. He began his life in public service as a Tammany worker and, until he ascended the bench, worked in various capacities on a number of political campaigns. He cast the decisive vote of his life, at the 1938 constitutional convention, in favor of proportional representation because, he said, the people of New York City had voted for it. On the other hand, he believed that leaders should always follow their principles. His belief was revealed in his admiration for Woodrow Wilson, who had moved forward with the League of Nations because he thought it right, despite the fact that the public was hesitant. It was revealed more deeply when, in the aftermath of his 1938 vote, he gravitated toward "high-type" men[42] such as Herbert Lehman, who always placed "principle . . . [,] integrity," and "courage" above political expediency.[43]

But, whatever ambivalence Weinfeld may have had about politics in general, he was never ambivalent about the place of money in politics: he thought those who donated money should seek no rewards. Thus, he was comfortable in his belief that, although he was happy remaining on the District Court and Wilfred Feinberg was well qualified to be a circuit judge, Abe Feinberg had obtained the appointment for his brother illegitimately.

Weinfeld never had to resolve his deeper ambivalence about the political process, however, because, in the end, it had brought him what he wanted most—an appointment as a United States district judge. As we shall see when we next turn to the mechanisms of Weinfeld's own appointment, he was chosen only in part for his ability. His mentor and backer, Herbert Lehman, undoubtedly had a well-founded belief in the strength of Weinfeld's qualifications for the bench. But, as we also shall see, Weinfeld's appointment owed a great deal to politics and luck.

The Successful Appointment

The event that precipitated Weinfeld's appointment was the June 29, 1949, retirement from the United States Senate, on account of ill health, of Robert F. Wagner. His retirement required the holding of a special election in November 1949 to fill out the remainder of his term, which ran to January 1, 1951. On the very day Wagner retired, it was clear that Herbert Lehman would be the choice of the Democratic Party to run in the election.[44]

In November, Lehman won a one-year term in the Senate. Since the other New York senator was a Republican, the practice of senatorial courtesy meant that Harry Truman, the Democrat in the White House, would have to obtain Lehman's approval of judicial appointments in New York during that year. In light of Lehman's loyalty and commitment, Weinfeld had his opportunity. But questions remained. Would a vacancy develop on the Southern District bench during the calendar year 1950? If a vacancy developed and political pressure for another candidate emerged, would Lehman be able to resist that pressure?

These questions were quickly answered when, on April 1, 1950, Herbert Lehman sent the following letter on the stationery of the United States Senate:

The President of the United States
The White House
Washington, D.C.

I understand that Judge Simon Rifkind of the Federal District Court of the Southern District of New York, will shortly resign. When and if a vacancy occurs, I strongly endorse Mr. Edward Weinfeld of New York for appointment to this Court.

You may recall that I have recommended Mr. Weinfeld on a

number of previous occasions. I have known Mr. Weinfeld a great
many years. He served as State Commissioner of Housing during
the time I was Governor. He was an unusually efficient and devoted public servant. During the years he was part of my administration, I consulted with him very frequently, not only on matters
relating to housing, but on many legal matters as well. I found his
judgment and his knowledge of the law excellent.

Mr. Weinfeld is an attorney in New York and a member of
the Judiciary Committee of the New York Bar Association. I am
confident that he would receive the endorsement of that and other
bar associations in New York State.

His appointment would be very pleasing to me and I take
pleasure in strongly endorsing his candidacy.[45]

President Truman nominated Edward Weinfeld to be a United States district judge on June 10[46] because, as he wrote in response to a thank-you
letter from Weinfeld, "I am of the opinion that you will make a good
Judge." Truman then added, "I think Judge appointments are the most
important appointments I make and I am very careful about the people I
do appoint."[47] The Senate confirmed the nomination on August 1, and
Weinfeld was sworn in and took his seat on August 14.[48]

The Creation of a Judicial Persona

When most people obtain an office or a job, it never occurs to them that
they should study in a systematic fashion how others in the past have performed that and similar jobs, as a means of preparing themselves to perform well. Even if it did occur to them, they would conclude that they
lack the time. However, as we have seen, Edward Weinfeld always believed in exhaustive preparation as the key to success, and he always
made time to prepare properly.

Upon his appointment to the district court in 1950, Weinfeld acquired
a green, leather-bound book that he made into something similar to the
commonplace books of earlier lawyers and judges.[49] In the book, he
placed excerpts, which he usually copied in his own hand, from materials
he had read about the qualities of good judges. As much as anything, the
entries reveal his qualities as a judge—qualities to which the entries gave
form and shape. Weinfeld's first entries appear to have been made in the

THE WHITE HOUSE
WASHINGTON

July 14, 1950

Dear Judge:

I appreciate very much your letter of the eleventh.
I am of the opinion that you will make a good Judge
and that is why I appointed you.   I think Judge appointments are the most important appointments
I make and I am very careful about the people I do
appoint.

Sincerely yours,

Harry Truman

Honorable Edward Weinfeld
39 Broadway
New York 6, New York

Letter from President Harry Truman to Edward Weinfeld, July 14, 1950.

Following the induction ceremony. From *left to right*, Fern Weinfeld, Judge
John C. Knox, Judge Weinfeld, Lillian Weinfeld, and Ann Weinfeld.

summer of 1950; his final entry was made in the autumn of 1986, thirty-six years later and only one year before his final illness forced him off the bench. Throughout the thirty-six years, Weinfeld was always preparing—and, always learning.

It is not surprising that Weinfeld began with Moses and the Old Testament, which has a good deal to say about judging. Although not an observant Jew, Weinfeld had celebrated his bar mitzvah,[50] had performed religious ceremonies after his parents' deaths,[51] and, at least in his later years, read a passage from the Bible every morning.[52] He was without doubt aware of the wisdom about judging contained in the Great Book.

The new judge's first entry was chapter 1, verses 16 and 17 of the Book of Deuteronomy, where Moses explained the law to the leaders he had appointed for Israel:

And I charged your Judges at that time, saying: "Hear the causes between your brethren and judge righteously between a man and his brother, and the stranger that is with him. Ye shall not respect persons in judgment; ye shall hear the small and the great alike; ye shall not be afraid of any man; for the judgment is God's; and the cause that is too hard for you ye shall bring unto me, and I will hear it."

Weinfeld's second entry was from Leviticus, chapter 19, verse 15: "Ye shall do no unrighteousness in judgment; thou shall not respect the person of the poor, nor honour the person of the mighty; but in righteousness shalt thou judge thy neighbor." His final biblical entry, from Deuteronomy, chapter 16, verses 18 and 19, read,

Judges and officers shall thou make thee in all thy gates, which the Lord thy God giveth thee throughout thy tribes; and they shall judge the people with just judgment. Thou shalt not wrest judgment; thou shalt not respect persons, neither take a gift: for a gift doth blind the eyes of the wise, and pervert the words of the righteous.

These biblical quotations reflect the core of Edward Weinfeld's values during his thirty-seven years on the bench. Of course, Weinfeld never took a gift, "for a gift doth blind the eye of the wise, and pervert the words of the righteous." Moreover, Weinfeld's transcendent concern was to give "just judgment," which he always strove to find by searching for factual truth and unquestioned law. He never based his treatment of a case on the identity of the litigants before him; he heard "the small and the great" alike and treated "strangers" just as he did American citizens and residents of the City of New York. He knew, as he quoted from Piero Calamandrei's *Eulogy of Judges,*[53] that a

> good judge takes equal pains with every case no matter how humble; he knows that important cases and unimportant cases do not exist, for injustice is not one of those poisons which, though harmful when taken in large doses, yet when taken in small doses may produce a salutary effect.[54]

Weinfeld also found parallel values to which he adhered in the writings of earlier American jurists. For instance, he recorded and absorbed the insight of Chief Justice John Marshall that the judge "should be rendered perfectly and completely independent, with nothing to control him but God and his conscience." Weinfeld agreed with Marshall "that the greatest scourge an angry Heaven ever inflicted upon an ungrateful and sinning people was an ignorant, a corrupt, or a dependent judiciary."[55] Similarly, he agreed with Chief Justice Charles Evans Hughes that judges should "work in an objective spirit"[56] and "that the dignity, esteem and indeed the aloofness, which attach to them . . . , should be jealously safeguarded."[57] Finally, he agreed with Professor Philip Kurland that a judge "must purge his mind and will of those personal presuppositions and prejudices which almost inevitably invade all human judgments; he must approach his problems with as little preconception of what should be the outcome as it is given to men to have." In short, the "prime condition" of being a good judge was a "capacity for detachment."[58]

A notably heroic figure for the newly appointed Judge Edward Weinfeld was Justice Oliver Wendell Holmes. Weinfeld's notes on Holmes report that, although Holmes "would disclaim being religious," nonetheless, "in the unyielding fidelity to truth, to right conduct, to the tolerant treatment of his fellow men, he [was] essentially religous."[59] In later years, Weinfeld agreed with an author who wrote about two of his colleagues, Judge Learned Hand and Judge Augustus N. Hand, that "the greatest of judges are those" who inspire in their "brethren on the bench, at the bar, and among the public . . . the conviction that the decision of every question, the weighing of every argument, the resolution of every discretionary issue, will be made selflessly, fearlessly, [and] wisely," with a "disciplined mind, disinterested conscience, and that elevated common sense which we call wisdom."[60] Weinfeld agreed with Cardozo that a "Judge, even when he is free, is still not wholly free. He is not to innovate at pleasure" or "to yield to spasmodic sentiment, to vague and unregulated benevolence. He is to exercise his discretion informed by tradition, methodized by analogy, and subordinated to 'primordial necessity of order in social life.'"[61]

In addition to recording the often-repeated sentiment that judges must "be absolutely honest, [and] absolutely courageous," Weinfeld also took note of the notion that good judges were "blessed by God with an understanding heart."[62] This view was elaborated in a long quotation from the work of Piero Calamandrei, who wrote,

> It has been said that too much intelligence is harmful to a Judge, but I do not subscribe to this. I do say, however, that the best judge is one in whom a ready humanity prevails over a cautious intellectualism. A sense of justice, the innate quality bearing no relation to acquired legal techniques, which enables the judge after hearing the facts to feel which party is right, is as necessary to him as the good ear of the musician; for if this quality is wanting, no degree of intellectual pre-eminence will afford adequate compensation.[63]

Arthur T. Vanderbilt, the chief justice of New Jersey and dean of Weinfeld's alma mater, New York University School of Law, agreed that

> [w]e need judges learned in the law, not merely the law in the books but, something far more difficult to acquire, the law as applied in action in the courtroom; judges deeply versed in the mysteries of human nature and adept in the discovery of the truth in the discordant testimony of fallible human beings; . . . judges, above all, fired with consuming zeal to mete out justice according to law to every man, woman and child that may come before them and to preserve individual freedom against an aggression of government; judges with humility born of wisdom, patient and untiring in the search for truth.[64]

A trial judge, in particular, "should be a man of even temper and one who can be trusted to display courtesy to the litigants and bar; in short, . . . he should be a gentleman. . . . Another quality devoutly to be wished for is the ability to keep reasonably silent while trying a case."[65]

One final quality came to Weinfeld's attention as he tried to identify what he could do to be a good judge. Here he quoted Newton D. Baker, an advisor to his preeminent hero, President Woodrow Wilson. Baker asked,

> Who is fit to be a judge? A man of learning who spends tirelessly the weary hours after midnight acquainting himself with the great body of traditions and the learning of the law.
>
> A man who bears himself in his community with his friends but without familiars; almost lonely, devoting himself exclusively to the most exacting mistress that man ever had, the law as a profession in its highest reaches.[66]

Edward Weinfeld, as we shall see, was obsessed with the idea that a good judge was a hard-working judge. He bought totally into a statement of Felix Frankfurter that

> [w]ithout adequate study there cannot be adequate reflection; without adequate reflection there cannot be adequate discussion; without adequate discussion there cannot be the searching and fruitful interchange of informed minds which is indispensable to wise decision and which alone can produce compelling opinions.[67]

He thought it imperative during the course of deliberation on a case, as he indicated by quoting Benjamin Franklin, to remain open to the possibility, upon "better information or fuller consideration," of "chang[ing] my opinion even on important subjects, which I once thought right, but found to be otherwise."[68] As with Charles Evans Hughes, "[t]he qualities that he sought to infuse into his opinions were accuracy, clarity, conciseness and power. These were the four corners of good judicial craftsmanship." Like Hughes, Weinfeld never thought it "the function of the Judge to write literature." The ultimate "test" of a good opinion was "whether it made the Court's judgment unmistakably plain."[69]

Above all, Weinfeld ascended the bench with a postulate that he should engage in intense, painstaking revision of everything he wrote. No idea appeared as fequently in his judicial commonplace book as this axiom. Thus, he agreed with Edward H. Warren that one should "[g]o over drafts as they come back from the typist and rub and rub and rub again until you have massaged away every muddy word and every waste word. . . . Read much, discuss much, ponder most, write a little."[70] He believed that "[l]egal writing" should be "precision writing," which could "be accomplished without resort to legalese and euphemistic language."[71] But to achieve clarity and precision, it was necessary to revise. In one of his final entries in his book—copied from a 1986 article in the *ABA Journal*, Weinfeld maintained that, when examining a draft, it was necessary to

> [f]irst, eliminate. Examine each word sitting there on your page and ask, "What do you do for me?" If the answer is that it merely loiters, doing nothing, make the superfluous word get up and move along. Let lazy language take its ease elsewhere, but never in your writing.
>
> Second, boil down. A briefer version is always better than a longer. Remember, verbosity endangers. Language is as precious as any coinage and as easily debased. The spendthrift of words risks a fate even worse than that awaiting the spendthrift of money. All the latter need fear is an empty pocket; the former hazards an empty head. . . . Clear ideas make clear writing. Think about your meaning before trying to express it.[72]

Such advice, of course, was not new; William Cullen Bryant had given it in the nineteenth century, and Weinfeld had duly recorded it, as follows:

> Never use a long word when a short one will do. Call a spade a spade, not a well known oblong instrument of manual industry.
>
> Let a home be a home, not a residence; a place a place, not a locality. Where a short word will do, you lose by using a long one. . . . Write much as you would speak; speak as you think. . . . After you have written an article, take your pen and strike one half the words, and you will be surprised to see how much stronger it is.[73]

The judge whom Edward Weinfeld probably held in the greatest esteem—and who, incidentally, was in many ways the mentor of Weinfeld's opinion-writing style—was Justice Louis D. Brandeis. As Felix Frankfurter wrote about Brandeis,

> Even after the long incubating process of maturing an opinion—the wide range of investigation, the toilsome study within it, the slow, care-

ful writing of findings and conclusions—it was routine for him to revise his draft opinion again and again, often more than a dozen times.[74]

It was "no secret" that Brandeis's "opinions went through dozens, even scores, of painstaking revisions. If they have a quality about them that is monumental and massive, it is only because they were granite-hewn and sculptured with infinite care."[75] Weinfeld similarly took note of the opinions of Justice Hugo Black, who, he noted, "worked his opinions through draft after draft [not] to make them more elaborate but simpler; an opinion was likely to peak for complexity at the second draft and to be smoothed out and simplified by attention to every single word in the drafts that followed."[76]

There was, of course, much overlap between the characteristics that Weinfeld possessed before he came to the bench—his work ethic, his writing ability, his facility in synthesizing facts, his strategic sense, his compassion and dedication to helping others, his avoidance of conflict, and his adherence to principle—and the qualities of good judging that he recorded in his book. The first two qualities were captured everywhere in the book, as was the importance of neutrality and adherence to principle. Piero Calamerdrei focused on the importance of facts and adherence to principle, while Chief Justice Hughes's emphasis on the importance of judicial dignity and aloofness, and Arthur T. Vanderbilt's advice about being courteous, reflected good counsel about how to avoid conflict. The one quality of Weinfeld that was not picked up by his quotes in the commonplace book was his strategic sense.

Thus, becoming a judge in many respects simply reaffirmed characteristics that Weinfeld already possessed. But, in other respects, the judge-making process made him a changed man. He had always worked hard, but as a judge he worked even harder, always "prefer[ring] to do the 'leg-work'" himself.[77] More importantly, there was a change in his personal qualities. The youthful student and attorney who had been an active member of a fraternity, who had climbed in the cellar window of a house on which he had just completed a closing, and who had struggled to make financial ends meet to support his young family was transformed into a figure on the bench of nearly biblical proportions—a figure with unusual compassion and empathy for but nonetheless profound distance from the other people in his courtroom. Above all, his ascension to the bench stripped Weinfeld of all further ambition—a man who always had found

132 | The Making of a Judge

it necessary to strive to advance his career now became satisfied with the job he held and tried only to do it well.

Becoming a judge—something for which Weinfeld had been "consciously and subconsciously . . . training . . . all . . . [his] life"—produced "a complete blending of . . . [him] and . . . [his] life." He "experienc[ed] that mystic sense of rightness we encounter now & then in life. As when you visit a spot you feel you've known all your life; or meet a person with whom you immediately establish a rapport."[78] Ascension to the bench made Weinfeld a different person.

While Weinfeld's transformation may have been more pronounced than the transformation of many others who have assumed judicial robes, it was not unique. His transformation is significant not because it was atypical but because it was characteristic of the experience that so many others have undergone in becoming federal judges. The one big difference between Weinfeld and most others is that Weinfeld left an unusually complete record—of the political ambitions with which a person seeking to be a judge must be consumed, of the political hurdles that such a person must vault to be appointed, and of the post-appointment seepage of ideas that transforms a politically successful person into a figure unique in American if not world government—a hard-working, disinterested, reflective, compassionate, yet righteous Article III judge.

8

The Patriarch
Edward Weinfeld's Judicial Style

The green, leather-bound volume into which Weinfeld placed
his excerpts about the qualities of good judges was not a trivial diversion.
The entries in the book resurfaced constantly as he performed his job; ultimately they created the core of Weinfeld's judicial persona. It is that persona which this chapter seeks to begin to comprehend.

First, we must strive to recapture the image of Judge Weinfeld seated
in his courtroom conducting a judicial proceeding. "On the bench, he was
single-minded and even austere. Especially in his later years, his high
cheekbones, piercing eyes, and bushy eyebrows gave him the appearance
of a biblical patriarch." There was "an extraordinary dignity in the trials
over which Judge Weinfeld preside[d]"—a "dignity . . . palpably present
in the jury box, on the witness stand, at the Judge's bench" that could be
"sensed by all the participants." "[W]hen you appeared before Judge
Weinfeld, you knew you were before the majesty of the law."[1]

Even jurors who served in Weinfeld's court were impressed by his dignity in dealing with them. For example, there was a special speech he
crafted for jurors as he discharged them following a verdict—a variant of
which is still in use on the Southern District. In this speech, Weinfeld observed that he

> adhered to a fixed policy of not thanking jurors for their services. . . .
> You took a solemn oath to render justice. . . . I happen to believe that
> one who faithfully and conscientiously discharges his duty neither is
> entitled to, nor must he or she expect, thanks. You did what you
> were required to do as you understood your duty. Your reward must
> come from the knowledge that you responded to the call of duty as a

citizen and were privileged to play an important part in the administration of justice.[2]

Jurors were euphoric when they left Weinfeld's courtroom. One commented that the judge "was the living example of my idea of a true American," while another told Weinfeld how "serving as a juror in your court
. . . helped restore my confidence in our judicial system."[3] A third juror
wrote that Weinfeld

> would have been tremendously pleased at the extremely high opinion
> the jurors held of your ability, impartiality and method of handling the
> case. There was so much comment about this that I felt you ought to
> know you had earned an outstanding amount of respect from this group
> that had an opportunity to watch your work.[4]

Above all, however, Weinfeld's "courtroom was a place of justice."
Even the "litigants . . . emerge[d] with the belief that the trial ha[d] been
a classically just adjudication." They

> realize[d] that their arguments ha[d] been thoughtfully considered and
> that the decisions reached were good faith attempts to provide them
> with everything to which they were entitled. Indeed, opposing advocates
> describing Judge Weinfeld's conduct of a trial [would] often raise a hand
> and draw an imaginary line through the air as they [said], "Right down
> the middle." . . . Nor [was] respect for Judge Weinfeld's impartiality lim-
> ited to attorneys; it [was] not . . . uncommon for the Judge to receive un-
> solicited statements from convicted defendants that they had received a
> fair trial before him.[5]

However "impossible" it might be "to capture the reality of the dignity
and fairness that [were] hallmarks of a Weinfeld trial," it nonetheless is
clear that concepts of dignity and fairness manifested themselves to those
present "as a tangible thing in the courtroom."[6]

Examples are legion. One illustration of the dignity of Weinfeld's
courtroom occurred during a criminal prosecution of defendants who
"claimed they were political revolutionaries who did not recognize the le-
gitimacy of the government." Yet "every time the Judge walked into the
courtroom, they stood up in respect."[7]

Weinfeld had to work hard to orchestrate this dignity. According to one clerk,

> After a conviction in a criminal case, the Marshal called and asked me to come to his office. The Marshal said that the convicted defendant was an unusually strong and violent man and requested permission to keep the defendant in handcuffs during sentencing. I told the judge, and as might be expected, his response was, ". . . you know my rule." When I told this to the Marshal, he asked to see the judge. Again, as might be expected, the judge said to the Marshal, "No, and I have every confidence that you will maintain order and decorum in the courtroom." On sentencing day, in addition to ten deputy marshals, there were six or seven city detectives, each about six feet four and 250 pounds. There was no incident.[8]

By acting consistently with an entry in his commonplace book, which mandated "that the dignity, esteem and indeed the aloofness, which attach to" judges "be jealously safeguarded,"[9] Weinfeld, who fully understood the importance of maintaining appearances, thus managed to preserve the image of the courtroom as a place of justice rather than raw coercive power.

A key ingredient of justice—fairness—was another hallmark that Edward Weinfeld worked hard to maintain in his courtroom. He "had a passion for fairness." Paraphrasing an entry in his commonplace book that a "good judge takes equal pains with every case no matter how humble" and "knows that important cases and unimportant cases do not exist," the judge "was fond of saying that each case was important, no matter how small the amount at issue."[10] He also insisted that the people who appeared before him, whether famous or ordinary, receive equal treatment. Thus, when the famous appeared in his court—Richard Burton and Elizabeth Taylor,[11] Mickey Mantle,[12] the New York Football Giants, Inc.,[13] State Supreme Court Justice James Vincent Keogh,[14] and U.S. Attorney Elliott Kahaner[15]—Weinfeld treated them exactly as he did every other litigant or witness.

Similarly, when the well-known band leader, Skitch Henderson, after conviction for income tax evasion, urged that his sentence be reduced because the adverse publicity he had received was punishment in itself, Weinfeld responded, quoting the first entry in his green commonplace book,

It is true that the activities of those who enjoy public status are the subject of extensive publicity; publicity is generated in proportion to one's public standing—the greater one's public status, the greater the publicity. However, a plea that the extensive publicity which follows upon exposure of a public figure's shortcomings is a sufficient punishment and adequate to vindicate the public interest is utterly without substance. Any such concept would set a double standard in dealing with those who violate the law. Evenhanded justice requires that in imposing a sentence upon a conviction of a crime a single standard be applied to public figures as well as to the unpublicized citizen. They stand as equals at the bar of justice. The biblical injunction applies: "Ye Shall Not Respect Persons in Judgment." Deuteronomy 1:17[16]

Weinfeld likewise strove to maintain an even balance between rich and poor litigants in civil cases. Thus, when a wealthy corporation sought to impose large litigation costs on an individual litigant, Weinfeld responded,

> Undoubtedly, parties to a litigation may fashion it according to their purse and indulge themselves and their attorneys, but they may not foist their extravagances upon their unsuccessful adversaries. To sanction such a policy may result not only in harassing a litigant, but may even deprive him of his day in court, particularly where, as in the instant case, there is great disparity in the financial resources of the parties. Fear of imposition of astronomical costs should not be a deterrent against the assertion of legitimate disputes.[17]

Weinfeld was deeply committed to the proposition that "the requirement of an independent fact-finder, capable of evaluating all the evidence, and only the evidence, in coming to a determination is a fundamental element of our concept of fairness."[18] Accordingly, "he disciplined himself to be impartial." His vision of how "to be fair [also] had . . . to do with listening attentively, correcting for his own views and feelings, [and] taking the necessary time . . . to decide." He "spent enormous time on each case" and "heard oral argument on all motions." In the interest of fairness, "he would not discuss settlement with the parties" because he "did not want to be seen as bringing about a settlement when a jury might reach a different conclusion." Similarly, his practice was not to read a law "clerk's bench memo on a motion until he had read the briefs and formed a tentative judgment," because, as he explained, it "would be unfair . . . for the side that his clerk favored to have two advocates."[19]

His fairness and impartiality were well known. In one case, for example, in which a Wall Street investment banking firm was suing a multinational oil company and both sides were represented by leading members of the New York bar, the parties waived the right to trial by jury and "agreed that the outcome be left to Judge Weinfeld," upon whom they could rely to be fairer and more impartial than a jury. Even a criminal defendant, who had been convicted and sentenced to prison by Weinfeld, was willing to take his chances again when, after serving his prison term, he was indicted on a new charge. Although the judge offered to recuse himself, the accused declined his offer, only to be convicted and again sentenced to prison.[20]

Nearly as important to Weinfeld as the reality of fairness was the appearance thereof—a subject on which he wrote in *United States v. Ferguson*.[21] The *Ferguson* case involved a series of suppression motions, all turning on whether an informant for the government named Brown had given evidence implicating the defendants voluntarily or had testified under threats and coercion by the government. In an in camera submission, the government had included affidavits from FBI agents and prosecutors; in addition, it submitted a transcript of a statement before the grand jury by one Mark Pomerantz, an assistant United States attorney who had served as law clerk to Judge Weinfeld several years earlier. When Weinfeld, in preparing for a hearing on the defense motions, came across the Pomerantz transcript, he suggested that the government disclose it to defense counsel who, upon disclosure, moved that the judge recuse himself from the case.

Weinfeld had consistently refused in the past to recuse himself from cases in which a former law clerk was counsel.[22] He knew he had the ability to reject his clerks' legal arguments.[23] But could he find that a former clerk was not telling the truth? Counsel for the defendants argued that resolution of the issue of the voluntariness of Brown's statements depended, in part, on the credibility of the government's witnesses, including Pomerantz, and that Weinfeld could not render an impartial judgment on the credibility of a former clerk. The government responded by agreeing not to call Pomerantz as a witness at any hearing the court might direct and urging that his grand jury statement not be considered on the suppression motion.

Weinfeld observed that there was "sufficient matter before the Court . . . , exclusive of Pomerantz's grand jury testimony, to resolve the disputed issues" and that he could "bring to bear a disciplined mind" so that the voluntariness of Brown's statements could be determined "solely upon the evidence exclusive of Pomerantz's testimony." Then Weinfeld continued,

> But is that the answer? More is required. The defendants express great concern of a spillover effect of Pomerantz's testimony. . . . The defendants contend that despite the Court's announced exclusion of Pomerantz's testimony, it will have a subtle if not subliminal influence.[24]

Although Weinfeld did not doubt his ability to maintain a balance between prosecution and defense and decide the defense motions solely on the law and the facts in evidence before him, he also knew that the issue was

> not whether the Court can be impartial in fact; there are other matters to be considered.
>
> Despite the Court's subjective view that all matters can be resolved impartially, a judge has an independent duty to disqualify himself "in any proceeding in which his impartiality might reasonably be questioned." The issue then is not the Court's own introspective capacity to sit in fair and honest judgment with respect to the controverted issues, but whether a reasonable member of the public at large, aware of all the facts, might question the Court's impartiality. . . . My relationship to Pomerantz is so intimate and my esteem for him so high, as it is for all my many clerks through the years, that the "average person on the street" might reasonably conclude that no matter how strongly the Court states that Pomerantz's testimony will not enter into its judgment, nonetheless, in some imperceptible manner his testimony will intrude itself.[25]

Accordingly, Weinfeld granted the motion for disqualification.

As the *Ferguson* case demonstrated, being fair and maintaining the appearance of fairness required hard work. A judge who did not prepare carefully for hearings on motions might never have learned in timely fashion that a former law clerk had given grand jury testimony; as a result, he might have found it difficult to withdraw from the case without embarrassment to himself or added inconvenience to the parties. Weinfeld, in contrast, understood that "the most underrated component of justice is the hard work of getting to it"—that the essential rudiment "of the human desire for justice" is "the modest dignity of self-sacrificing work" and "the endless willingness to take pains to get it right."[26] He regularly put into operation the advice in his commonplace book that only "a man . . . who spends tirelessly the weary hours after midnight . . . devoting himself exclusively to the most exacting mistress that man ever had, the law as a profession in its highest reaches," was "fit to be a judge."[27]

But work alone—even the "work in an objective spirit"[28] commanded by Weinfeld's green, leather-bound book—could not by itself produce just results. Weinfeld also developed a style of opinion writing in which he strove to avoid intruding his personal policy predilections into his decisions. It was a style that aimed to decide cases on the basis of fundamental legal principles—but always in the context of the specific facts of the cases before him. We must now turn to an in-depth examination of Weinfeld's style as well as to a number of his opinions that illustrate it.

Foremost in Weinfeld's approach was a belief, reflected in the entries of his judicial commonplace book and grounded in his years of experience as a litigator, that a good "judge after hearing the facts" will instinctively "feel which party is right."[29] Thus, he called himself a "fact judge."[30] To the casual reader, any single Weinfeld opinion often seems merely to decide disputed issues of fact and to apply the law as discovered by following professional norms of research and analysis. The reader of his opinions will almost never find the judge engaged in the self-conscious making of new law. On the contrary, he exhibited a strong faith that existing law would suffice to decide every case coming before him—a belief that, if he only used his energy and intelligence, he would be able to find that law, and that failure to find it would reflect on his capacity as a judge, not on the majesty of the law.

The essence of Weinfeld's opinion-writing style was to avoid deciding unresolved questions of law or questions of social policy. When parties to a case posed such a question, he attempted either to resolve the case on its facts or to probe the law more deeply, searching for a bedrock legal principle that would make decision of the more specific, unresolved issue superfluous. If he had to decide unresolved issues of law, he strove to address them in alternative holdings. Only as a last resort would he rest a judgment on the resolution of a single, novel point of law, and then only after thorough and painstaking research.

Weinfeld's approach to writing opinions manifested itself in one of the earliest cases to come before him, *Austrian v. Williams*. The case arose when trustees in bankruptcy brought suit on behalf of a corporation against several defendants, including a principal shareholder, Harrison Williams, whom the trustees accused of controlling the corporation and using his power of control to loot its assets. Weinfeld tried the case without a jury from October 3 to November 30 of his first year on the bench and ultimately disposed of it a year later in a fifty-five-page opinion.[31]

The opinion turned first to the trustees' claim that Williams controlled the corporation. It concluded that he did. Weinfeld found that every officer of the corporation was "Williams' personal designee," who "looked to . . . him, as 'the real guide.'" He received daily reports on corporate affairs, even while abroad, and he often carried out negotiations for the corporation, after which "the board members invariably gave their pro forma approval." "Every important action affecting" the corporation "was initiated by Williams or by directors or officers under his immediate supervision and instruction," who merely "carried out the administrative details which implemented the plan or program" adopted by Williams. Even when he directed that all corporate records pertaining to him be destroyed, his order was obeyed. In sum, Williams's "wish was a command, faithfully executed by officers and directors alike."[32]

Next, Weinfeld turned at length to the trustees' claim that Williams and others in thirteen separate transactions had wrongfully misappropriated corporate funds. After analyzing every one of the transactions minutely, he found that Williams had breached his fiduciary duty in regard to four of them. He dismissed the claims against Williams in connection with the other nine transactions and against his codefendants in connection with all thirteen.

Williams argued, however, that he was not liable even in connection with the four claims that remained because suit had not been filed in a timely fashion under the applicable statute of limitations. Unlike the earlier claims, this argument raised a pure issue of law—an issue of what statute of limitations applied to the suit. If New York's statute of limitations applied, the suit was time-barred. On the other hand, if the traditional federal equitable doctrine of laches applied, suit was not barred. Weinfeld could not avoid the issue by finding facts.

It was undisputed that the trustees had brought suit under federal bankruptcy law to recover for breaches of fiduciary duty grounded in state common law. The basic issue, as delineated by the judge, was whether *Erie R.R. v. Tompkins*[33] required the district court to apply federal or state law "in an equity suit involving state created rights where federal jurisdiction [was] based, not on diversity of citizenship but upon a statute enacted by Congress under its constitutional power."[34]

"It should be stressed" that resolution of this issue, in any direction, had to "break . . . new ground—that nothing in the exposition of the Erie doctrine" prior to the time of Weinfeld's decision "compel[led]" any particular result.[35] Accordingly, Weinfeld felt comfortable in ruling that the "uniform and efficient enforcement of rights of debtor-estates and creditors [was] a matter of important federal public policy"; that federal law therefore trumped his "mechanically [applying] the New York statute of limitations";[36] and that, under federal law, Williams, though none of the other defendants, was liable on four of the plaintiffs' specifications. But his comfort was misplaced as the Court of Appeals, over a dissent by Judge Charles Clark, reversed and held New York's limitation law binding.[37]

The reversal in *Austrian v. Williams* only confirmed Weinfeld's instinct that he should avoid, whenever possible, the determination of unresolved issues of law. Indeed, in later years, he nearly always succeeded in circumventing them. *United States v. Toney*,[38] decided during his last several years on the bench, will illustrate.

The *Toney* case arose out of the practice of the then United States attorney, Rudolph Giuliani, of delaying the arraignment of individuals arrested for crime in order to give government agents time to question them and extract evidence from them. Weinfeld himself abhorred the practice,[39] but he also understood that some "Judges of the Court of Appeals ha[d] expressed contrary views" about its legality, and he was not prepared to declare the judgment of those panels incorrect. Thus, he decided to dispose of the case on limited factual grounds, in a way that made it "unnecessary to consider the general attack leveled on the practice."[40]

The judge concentrated on the motion of Luis Perez to suppress a statement made without counsel during a twenty-three-hour period of incarceration following his arrest. The key fact for Weinfeld was that Perez was processed—i.e., fingerprinted, strip-searched, photographed, and checked for prior record—within two and a half hours of his arrest, and that at the conclusion of his processing he was not taken before a magistrate, even though one was then available. Indeed, he did not see a magistrate for another twenty hours. Weinfeld examined seriatim all the reasons the government advanced for this delay, found that there was "no adequate explanation for the delay,"[41] held that it was unreasonable, and hence ruled that the statements made by Perez were inadmissable. On the facts found by Weinfeld, the Court of Appeals affirmed.[42]

Another case that illustrated Weinfeld's preference for finding facts rather than deciding issues of law was *United States v. Bethlehem Steel Corp.*[43] The government had brought suit under section 7 of the Clayton Act[44] to enjoin the merger of Bethlehem Steel and Youngstown Sheet and Tube Company, which were the nation's second- and sixth-largest steel companies, respectively. The defendant companies argued that they should be permitted to merge in order to enhance their ability to compete effectively with United States Steel, the largest company and acknowledged trend setter in industry pricing policies. Moreover, Bethlehem and Youngstown maintained that a merger would permit them to increase their production capacity in the general vicinity of Chicago in response to a long-felt shortage of certain steel products in that area—an expansion neither company desired to undertake individually.

Weinfeld did not immediately turn to the resolution of the important and, at that time, unresolved legal issue of whether necessity to compete could justify an otherwise impermissible merger.[45] Instead, he began by explaining the central goal of section 7 of the Clayton Act as it had been amended in 1950—the prevention of any significant reduction of competition in any market in which two merging companies were competing. He then resolved two factual issues. The first was whether any markets existed in which the merging companies were competing; the second was whether a merger would substantially lessen competition in any of those markets.

Resolution of these highly complex issues raised subsidiary issues that could have been treated as questions of law, but Weinfeld did not treat them that way. For example, the government contended that each of the defendants' product lines that had peculiar physical characteristics and uses constituted a separate market, while the defendants claimed that markets had to be determined with reference to the ability of steel producers to shift from product to product. The judge did not consider the defendants' claim, because it had no factual basis. He pointed out that the evidence had established that "the defendants' production flexibility or mill product line theory [was] indeed pure theory. In practice, steel producers ha[d] not been quick to shift from product to product in response to demand." He also remarked that "continuing relationships between buyers and sellers in the steel industry ma[d]e such shifts unlikely."[46] Noting in addition the inconsistency with which the defendants advocated their position, Weinfeld adopted the government's approach toward delineation of product markets. Of course, in favoring the government's market theory, Weinfeld implicitly accepted its legal sufficiency, but he never actually ruled that the defendants' position was legally insufficient. By finding a lack of factual support for the argument rather than ruling that the theory was bad law, the judge completely undercut the defendants' argument and precluded them from advancing it on appeal.

Another issue that the judge resolved on factual rather than legal grounds was whether the defendants' or the government's theory of the relevant markets should govern. The government contended that the nation as a whole or, alternatively, certain sections of the country into which both Bethlehem and Youngstown shipped steel and steel products, should be denominated the relevant market for the steel industry and for the component lines of commerce. Defendants asserted that it would be more appropriate to view the nation as divided into three sections or markets—east, west, and midcontinent. They argued that Bethlehem was an effective competitor only in the two coastal sections, while Youngstown was effective only in the midcontinent area. Weinfeld declined to decide whether such a division of the country was appropriate as a matter of law. He turned instead to a review of industry practice and statistics.

The judge found that Bethlehem's shipments of over two million tons of finished steel products into the midcontinent area represented almost 5 percent of total shipments in the area and exceeded the capacity of several major local producers. The volume of Bethlehem's sales indicated that it was without question nearly as effective in the midcontinent area as was Youngstown, which accounted for 7 percent of that area's total shipments. Naturally, the factual determination that Bethlehem was a competitor to reckon with in the midcontinent region also involved a legal assumption that a supplier of nearly 5 percent of the total goods in any given market was a substantial competitor—but few would disagree with such an assumption. Nevertheless, Weinfeld was not content to rest his decision solely on his findings about the midcontinent region. His alternative basis for finding that Bethlehem and Youngstown competed in the same markets derived from a concession by the defendants' witnesses that Michigan, the largest steel-consuming state in the nation, was sufficiently important to be considered a separate market and that Bethlehem, which supplied almost 12 percent of Michigan's total steel needs, was an effective competitor in that state.

To summarize the judge's reasoning up to this point: first, he made findings of fact about the product and geographical markets in which the parties competed. Then, he reached a legal conclusion that followed almost inevitably from the facts: because there was substantial competition between Bethlehem and Youngstown, their merger would substantially decrease competition in the steel industry. Since section 7 specifically prohibits mergers that would "substantially . . . lessen competition," the merger between the two companies was prohibited by that statute.

Once he had reached these conclusions, the judge tackled the defendants' principal claim that the merger should be permitted because it was necessary to enable Bethlehem and Youngstown to compete with U.S. Steel. He did not initially rule on that claim as a matter of law; instead, he examined the practical likelihood that only the merger could achieve the defendants' aims and that the need for additional capacity in the Chicago area could not be met without the merger. He found that Bethlehem had successfully met past challenges and was well equipped to "keep pace with the demands of our national economy." Only after arriving at that conclusion of fact, which implied that Bethlehem could compete effectively even if it did not merge with Youngstown, did Weinfeld reject the defendants' claim as a matter of law, holding that "[i]f the merger offends the statute in any relevant market then good motives and even demonstrable benefits are irrelevant and afford no defense."[47]

The judge thus wove a complex tapestry of law and fact in the *Bethlehem Steel* case. The main threads, on which his decision rested, were factual, deeply grounded in the record of the case, and hence largely immune from appellate review. Indeed, the defendants in the case did not bother to appeal from his judgment. Weinfeld thereby achieved his task of resolving the dispute between the parties justly and definitively, although the new law made by his opinion was not nearly as authoritative as it might have been if the Court of Appeals and Supreme Court had affirmed it.

United States ex rel. Elksnis v. Gilligan[48] was a similarly masterful tapestry. Almars Elksnis, a Latvian immigrant, had been convicted on his own guilty plea in state court of killing his common-law wife. Ten years later he brought a habeas corpus action in federal court on the ground that his plea before the state court judge had been taken in violation of the Constitution and was therefore void. Weinfeld set aside Elksnis's conviction, upholding his claim on three alternative grounds.

One ground was that any plea offered in return for a promise by the judge as to the maximum penalty he would impose was not a voluntary plea and hence was unconstitutional. Essentially this holding was one of law, yet it was closely intertwined with the facts. Weinfeld observed that before Elksnis met with the judge to discuss his sentence, he had resolutely refused to plead guilty and thereby waive trial. From this fact Weinfeld inferred that the judge's statement must have had compelling force, explaining that, in light of the petitioner's obvious determination to plead not guilty, there was every reason to believe that the interview with the judge did in fact unduly influence his plea. As Weinfeld then added,

> When a judge becomes a participant in plea bargaining he brings to bear the full force and majesty of his office. His awesome power to impose a substantially longer or even maximum sentence in excess of that proposed is present whether referred to or not. . . . [N]o matter how well motivated the judge may be, the accused is subjected to a subtle but powerful influence. A guilty plea predicated upon a judge's promise of a definite sentence by its very nature does not qualify as a free and voluntary act. The plea is so interlaced with the promise that the one cannot be separated from the other; remove the promise and the basis for the plea falls.[49]

Weinfeld was not, however, content to base his decision on this argument alone, particularly in view of its apparent novelty and its seeming inconsistency with a contemporary decision of the court of appeals.[50] Consequently, he put forward two other grounds for invalidating the plea.

The first was the state trial judge's failure to abide by his promise when he imposed a longer maximum sentence than the one he had agreed would be imposed. The state agreed that under normal circumstances a sentence inconsistent with a promise upon which a plea had been based would be void. It argued, however, that in this case the judge was released from his promise because it had been based upon a misunderstanding about Elksnis's prior record that had been induced by his attorney and because Elksnis had acquiesced in its withdrawal.

Weinfeld answered the state's initial argument by showing that it was factually incorrect. A careful and thorough review of the record—in particular, of the testimony of the state trial judge who had made the promise—established that the state judge must have known of Elksnis's prior record at the time the guilty plea was entered. Concerning the claim of acquiescence, Weinfeld observed that acquiescence meant a waiver of a constitutional right and thus had to be measured against the controlling standard of "intentional relinquishment."[51] A review of the circumstances surrounding the plea showed that Elksnis never had explicitly acquiesced in the sentence that had been imposed, nor had he relinquished his right to reinstate a plea of not guilty. Indeed, at the first opportunity he had attacked his sentence on the ground that the judge had broken his promise. Thus, both because Elksnis had never actually waived his right to reinstate his plea of not guilty and because the guilty plea had been induced by the judge's promise, Weinfeld found that Elksnis's plea could not be viewed as voluntary. Since the accepted constitutional standard unambiguously required that a guilty plea be voluntary,[52] Elksnis's plea had to be set aside.

Weinfeld's final alternative ground for finding that the plea was invalid was that it was not knowledgeable. The record showed that when asked by the state trial judge about the crime with which he had been charged—the fatal stabbing of his wife—Elksnis had claimed that he had acted in self-defense or in a fit of temporary insanity. Since Elksnis had never deliberately chosen to abandon these defenses, Weinfeld found that the plea was "not understandingly and knowingly made."[53] On this ground, too, unambiguous constitutional law required that the guilty plea be set aside.[54]

To appreciate fully the craftsmanship of *Elksnis* and the law that it made, we must review the state of the law at the time the opinion was announced. Only three years earlier, in *United States ex rel. McGrath v. LaVallee*,[55] the Second Circuit had held that a plea was not invalid simply because it was induced by a judicial suggestion of leniency. *Elksnis* appeared to take issue with that holding.[56] Although Weinfeld could have readily distinguished *Elksnis* from *McGrath*—in the former case the promise of a ten-year maximum sentence was explicit, whereas in the latter the judge had merely advised that a more lenient sentence might follow from a guilty plea to a lesser offense—he did not take that approach. Instead, he left language in the *Elksnis* opinion that suggests that any judicial discussion of sentencing, whether or not it results in an explicit promise by the judge, invalidates a guilty plea that is a product of the discussion.

Despite this broad language, it should be noted that after the state attorney general's office had studied Weinfeld's *Elksnis* decision, the opinion was found to be so persuasive that the office withdrew its notice of appeal to the Second Circuit.[57] The chief difficulty the opinion must have presented for the state was that the only actual point of law Weinfeld relied on was the proposition that a guilty plea must be voluntarily and knowingly made to be constitutionally valid. That legal conclusion had been affirmed many times by the Supreme Court.[58] Every subsidiary issue that Weinfeld decided resulted from the measurement of the facts against this controlling standard. It would have been impossible, for example, for the Court of Appeals to have reversed the alternative legal holding that a plea made with a reservation of defenses is constitutionally invalid, without at the same time reversing Weinfeld's finding of fact that at the time Elksnis reserved his defenses he did not understand what he was doing. Because that finding had unquestioned support in the record, the Second Circuit would have had no power to reverse it. Thus, *United States ex rel. Elksnis v. Gilligan* is a typical Weinfeld opinion in that, rather than making new law, it seems merely to resolve questions of fact that guide decision of the ultimate legal issues, as to which the recognized controlling standard is not in doubt.

Perhaps the most factually dense case of Weinfeld's career was the Penn Central merger case, on which Weinfeld sat from 1966 to 1969 on a three-judge district court with his colleague and close friend, Henry J. Friendly. The case produced two lengthy opinions by the three-judge court, from both of which Weinfeld dissented.

The issue in the first[59] was whether the merger of the New York Central and Pennsylvania Railroads should go forward while the Interstate Commerce Commission (ICC) determined the conditions that were needed to protect smaller railroads in the Northeast from the destructive competition that the newly merged Penn Central would create. The ICC voted to let the merger proceed, and Judge Friendly, with Judge Richard H. Levet concurring, was ready to defer out of recognition that "administrative agencies are not held to a standard of perfection that would render them unique among organs of government." In Friendly's view, the court was "not truly empowered to engage in this case in the same kind of weighing and balancing and then making our own decision as . . . we would be if we were reviewing the action of a lower court."[60]

Weinfeld, in contrast, could not tolerate the serious errors he found in the ICC proceedings. He was not prepared to defer on the basis of "the Commission's devotion to duty, its expertise, its knowledgeability and its broad administrative powers as against the Court's limited powers of judicial review." Always a stickler for finding facts accurately and precisely, Weinfeld declared that the uncertainties in the ICC findings, which he examined in detail, undermined "the foundation for its ultimate finding . . . that the proposed merger will be consistent with the public interest, and hence the validity of the Commission's order authorizing the merger [was] cast in grave doubt."[61] Accordingly, he was prepared to enjoin the merger. When the case was appealed to the Supreme Court, it agreed with him by a five-four vote.[62]

Within a year of the Supreme Court's decision, the case was back before the three-judge court, this time on the issue of the dollar amount that the Penn Central would be required to pay for the assets of the bankrupt New York, New Haven, and Hartford Railroad, which had been included by the ICC in the newly merged rail system as one of the conditions deemed necessary to preserve competition.[63] After a remand to the commission, the case came back up to the court.[64] Writing again for himself and Judge Levet, Judge Friendly began "by reiterating the severe limitations on the scope of our review"[65] and then proceeded to uphold the ICC's decision.

Weinfeld had a different view of the court's function in reviewing the Commission—"'to guard against the possibility of gross error or unfairness.'" Because he found on a detailed and carefully crafted evaluation of the evidence that the commission's findings not only "contain[ed] more than a 'possibility' of, but . . . [were] pockmarked with, gross error and unfairness,"[66] he again dissented. He simply could not defer in the face of severe factual error. Again, the Supreme Court agreed with Weinfeld's dissent and reversed Judge Friendly's ruling.[67]

Yet another Weinfeld opinion in the same mold of careful, detailed evaluation of the facts is *Vulcan Society v. Civil Service Commission.*[68] *Vulcan* was a class action brought by black and Hispanic individuals to challenge the constitutionality of the examination administered to applicants for the position of New York City firefighter. The judge found that the plaintiffs had made out a prima facie statistical showing that the test discriminated against blacks and Hispanics. The principal remaining issue was whether the test was sufficiently job related—whether the skills it examined were needed to perform the job of firefighter. Judge Weinfeld noted that there were three professionally accepted techniques for establishing job-relatedness and thus the validity of examination—predictive validation, concurrent validation, and content validation. The defendant conceded that it had used neither of the first two methods, but had relied solely upon content validation, which consists of nothing more than a check whether "the content of the examination matches the content of the job."[69] The major legal issue in the case was whether content validation alone was a sufficient indicator of job-relatedness; in its leading case on the subject, the Second Circuit had left the issue open,[70] and other circuits were divided.[71] Weinfeld, however, found it unnecessary to resolve this knotty question of law. Instead, after a careful examination of the facts, he concluded that the content validation in which defendant had engaged was inadequate.

The main theme here, as elsewhere in this chapter, is meticulous examination of the facts; it was a practice in which Weinfeld engaged again and again.[72] Thus, in a prosecution occurring in his first decade on the bench, against a former congressman named Vincent Quinn, who was accused of accepting money to influence the outcome of a matter pending before the Internal Revenue Service, Weinfeld combed the trial record for evidence that Quinn had known that his law partner was representing a client before the IRS and that money paid for that representation had been deposited to general partnership funds, a portion of which was later paid to Quinn. When he found no evidence of actual knowledge, he entered a judgment of acquittal at the close of the government's case.[73]

Some two decades later, Weinfeld similarly combed a trial record in connection with a contempt charge against an attorney, Stanley Cohen, who had represented a defendant accused and ultimately convicted of smuggling weapons on behalf of the Jewish Defense League. In a twenty-three-page opinion summarizing the two-thousand-page trial record, Weinfeld found that the acts and conduct committed by Cohen constituted misbehavior in the presence of the trial judge, that the misbehavior interfered with the progress of the trial, and that Cohen had engaged in it deliberately and with intent to obstruct the administration of justice. Thus, Weinfeld held Cohen in contempt.[74]

Of course, Weinfeld could not always write opinions resolving cases on the facts. At times, he had to decide unresolved issues of law,[75] as in *Austrian v. Williams*,[76] discussed above. This was especially true in cases involving construction of ambiguous legislation. The judge decided a number of such cases,[77] but two will suffice to set out his approach, which was to engage in what can be seen in a sense as a sort of factual inquiry— a meticulous, detailed examination of legislative text and history.

United States ex rel. Casanova v. Fitzpatrick[78] was a habeas corpus proceeding commenced by an attaché of the Cuban mission to the United

Nations who had been arrested on a charge of conspiracy to commit sabotage and to violate the Foreign Agents Registration Act. Casanova claimed he was entitled to diplomatic immunity either under article 105 of the UN Charter or, alternatively, under the headquarters agreement locating the United Nations in New York. After examining the language and history of both the charter and the agreement, testimony before congressional committees, and House and Senate committee reports, Weinfeld rejected the claim. His examination of the headquarters agreement is particularly illustrative: it granted immunity in section 15(1) to specified high-ranking diplomats, of whom Casanova was not one, and in section 15(2) to "such resident members of their staffs as may be agreed upon between the Secretary-General, the Government of the United States and the Government of the Member concerned."[79] Weinfeld observed that section 15(2) had been accepted by the UN under pressure from the United States in place of a draft provision that would have given all staff members immunity and thus could not be interpreted, as advocated by Casanova, to give immunity to the entire diplomatic staff.

Another statutory interpretation case decided at almost the same time as *Casanova* was *Wagio Kong Tjauw Wong v. Esperdy*.[80] The issue was whether Wong, who sought admission to the United States as a permanent resident, should be placed in the Asia-Pacific triangle quota, in which event he would be admitted, or in the quota for Chinese persons, in which event the quota already was exhausted and he would not be admitted. Wong, who had been born in Surinam,[81] a Dutch colony in South America, had a full-blooded Chinese father and a full-blooded Indonesian mother. Under old legislation, an individual of at least one-half Chinese ancestry was considered a Chinese person, but that legislation had been repealed in 1952, and thereafter statutory law contained no definition of a Chinese person. But the 1952 immigration act did contain a provision that a person such as Wong, at least one-half of whose ancestors were indigenous to the Asia-Pacific triangle (which included Indonesia) but who was born outside the triangle, fit under the triangle's quota. Weinfeld held that the specific statutory provision of the 1952 act governed and hence admitted Wong to permanent residence.

On rare occasions, careful, detailed examination of legislative text and history did not help Weinfeld give meaning to incomplete or ambiguous statutes. But, even then, he tried to resort to principled adjudication. For example, in *Stonehill Communications, Inc. v. Martuge*,[82] the issue was whether a book describing nude beaches violated the manufacturing clause of the Copyright Act—a clause that prohibited the importation into the United States of works "consist[ing] preponderantly of nondram[a]tic literary material . . . in the English language"[83] unless they had been manufactured in Canada or the United States. Nowhere did the statute define the word "preponderantly," and the Customs Service, which sought to bar importation of the book, accordingly urged that it possessed discretion to determine whether the literary material in the book, which in this instance occupied far less space than the book's many photographs of nude beaches, was "preponderant," based on its judgment of whether the literary material was "important."[84]

Weinfeld, hesitant, as always, about yielding broad discretion to administrators, rejected any such standardless determination. As he wrote,

> This case is a prime example of the problems of allowing an administrative agency to exercise uncontrolled discretion in determining what is important in a book. . . . There are obviously any number of interpretations one could make about what is "important" in a book. Such a vague standard leaves authors and publishers without any guide while not providing any significant advantage to printers, the intended beneficiaries of the clause.

Carefully examining the context of the legislation, the judge noted that the "purpose" of the manufacturing clause was "purely economic in support of the American printing industry" and that this purpose could best be advanced, "[i]n the absence of congressional or duly authorized guidelines," by "an objective test—in this instance, a 'mechanical' one." "In the absence of any other standards," Weinfeld supplied his own—that a book would be defined as consisting preponderantly of literary material in the English language when that material occupied more than half the surface area of the book, exclusive of margins.[85]

As Weinfeld understood it, the exercise of unbridled discretion was simply inconsistent with the doing of justice. Justice required that individuals be aware of and have the opportunity to conform their behavior to government's requirements; vesting officials with discretion meant that individuals would not know how to behave or how to plan their affairs. Discretion made Weinfeld uncomfortable, not only because its holder might abuse it, but more importantly because no one could predict how it would be used or discern whether it had been abused.

Discomfort with the exercise of discretion was connected, in turn, to one of Weinfeld's most deeply held values—his abhorrence of conflict. He understood that when a rule of law is uncertain, those governed by it, citizens and officials alike, will have incentives to conform their behavior to their own self-interest and to stretch the rule to cover their behavior. Eventually, those who have divergent interests will find themselves in conflict as they stretch rules in opposite directions. Worst of all, there will be no obvious resolution to the conflict. In contrast, when rules of law are clear, they will create a matrix in which everyone except those willing to break the law will obey it and conflict will be minimized.

Because Weinfeld was concerned more with legal uncertainty and conflict than with bureaucrats abusing their discretion, he was as uncomfortable with his own exercise of discretion as he was reviewing its exercise by someone else. Nonetheless, there were occasions when the law required him to exercise it. On those occasions, though, he strove to make his exercise of discretion as similar as possible to his performance of any other judicial function by carefully compiling the facts and thereby elaborating the context of the case and only then specifying the precepts on which his exercise of discretion was based. He strove, that is, to bring the rule of law even to the exercise of discretion.

United States v. Greater Blouse, Skirt & Neckwear Contractors Ass'n[86] offers an example. The opinion in the case decided a motion by the government to file a nolle prosequi to an indictment against multiple defendants charging antitrust violations in the production of women's blouses. Pursuant to Rule 48(a) of the Federal Rules of Criminal Procedure, the judge before whom the motion was made was required to exercise discretion in deciding whether or not to grant the motion. But the rule set forth no criteria to guide the court, nor did it indicate the purpose to be served by requiring judicial approval of a nolle prosequi.

One defendant opposed the government's motion. It argued that, during the five years in which the indictment had been pending, the alleged antitrust violations had ceased and, as a result, its business had improved. It expressed concern that the violations would begin again once the indictment was dismissed. Weinfeld concluded, however, that the purpose of the criminal justice system was "not to aid the private interests of a party engaged in controversy with others, although, to be sure, at times an indictment, prosecution and conviction [might] achieve that incidental result." After doing his homework, he expressed the view that Rule 48(a) required judicial approval of a nolle so there would be "public exposure of the reasons for abandonment of an indictment . . . to prevent abuse of the uncontrolled power of dismissal previously enjoyed by prosecutors."[87] Once he was satisfied that the reasons given by the government for dropping its prosecution were authentic, he exercised his discretion favorably and granted the motion to dismiss.[88]

The law also required Weinfeld to exercise discretion in *United States v. DeParias*,[89] where he had sentenced a woman alien who had pleaded guilty to a conspiracy to kidnap to a prison term of forty years, to run concurrently with a forty-year term she was already serving for extortion. Since DeParias had committed two felonies, she would be automatically deported, unless Weinfeld exercised discretion conferred on him by statute and filed a recommendation against deportation.

Weinfeld engaged and wrote about his engagement in the "painstaking consideration" of all the circumstances, including the heinous nature of DeParias's crimes and the hope that "her imprisonment [would] result in rehabilitative benefits." But, above all, he focused on the fact that DeParias was the mother of two young children, who were American citizens, were being raised by their grandmother, and would be in their late teens at the earliest time their mother could be released from prison. If DeParias were deported at that time, her

> children will then be faced with a grisly choice. If they decide to live with their mother, they must forego the benefits and advantages of our society and leave our shores. If they opt to remain here and stay with the grandmother who has raised them, they will be burdened by the harrowing thought that they have abandoned their mother to a land and life of exile.

In light of the competing concerns, Weinfeld concluded that "our society can afford the risk of allowing her to remain in this country to share her life with her children" and exercised his discretion in favor of issuing a recommendation not to deport.[90]

United States v. Kaplan[91] presented a somewhat different twist. Nathan Kaplan, who had been convicted and served time for a crime to which another man subsequently had pleaded guilty and also served a prison sentence, moved under section 2255 to vacate his conviction. "Upon the evidence," Weinfeld thought it appropriate to "set aside the conviction since, as the United States District Attorney now acknowledges, the facts now known nullify the theory upon which the defendant was convicted and render that conviction erroneous and unjust." But section 2255 gave him no jurisdiction, since it allowed a court to set aside a conviction only for constitutional defects, and Kaplan had proved no such defects in his conviction. Essentially, Kaplan was moving for relief on the basis of newly discovered evidence, but his motion was untimely under the applicable rule, Rule 33 of the Rules of Criminal Procedure. Accordingly, Weinfeld was "forced to the conclusion that . . . [he was] without power to grant the application."[92]

Of course, he could "not exceed the limits of authority," but he also "would be shirking . . . [his] responsibility if the denial of the motion were made without further comment." He observed that in "those exceptional cases where the rules of law of broad application work an injustice in an individual case, our institutions provide redress through the pardoning power," and he accordingly "expresse[d] the hope that prompt consideration will be given to the pending application" by Kaplan for a pardon, "so that the interests of justice may be served."[93] With that expression of hope, Weinfeld was thereby able to fight for justice while still adhering rigidly to fixed bounds of the law.

These rare cases in which he was required to think about exercising discretion illustrate as well as anything Edward Weinfeld's conception of judicial duty. For Weinfeld, judging was not about the exercise of power for political ends, but about the rule of law—about the "judge's prime responsibility to maintain the integrity of the judicial system; to see that the due process of law, equal protection of the laws and the basic safeguards of a fair trial [were] upheld."[94] According to Weinfeld, the community had

> a right to expect that those it trusted with high public office will scrupulously and religiously live up to their oath of office. Indeed, those so honored should by exemplary conduct set the standards for others to follow. . . . A civilized society is strong only as long as its laws are administered honestly, fairly and impartially by those who are sworn to do so, and none [is] under a more positive duty of scrupulous allegiance to law and order than the judge.[95]

Whether in his green, leather-bound commonplace book, in his published opinions, or in the intimacy of his chambers and courtroom, Weinfeld always worked tirelessly both to further the rule of law and to mete out evenhanded justice.

In so striving for law and justice, Weinfeld simply blended the characteristics he had long possessed as a person and lawyer with the aspirations recorded in his commonplace book. Several elements were obvious, as already noted, in everything he did: his hard work, clear writing, emphasis on facts, and sound strategic judgment. But his judicial work also reflected something more; somehow, Weinfeld fused adherence to principle, sensitivity to factual context, and compassion for others into doing justice. His unfailing courtesy and dignity and his undeviating efforts to base his decisions on meticulous fact finding and bedrock legal principles typically led to the resolution of conflict rather than its exacerbation. After Weinfeld had spoken, litigants recognized that usually there was nothing more to be said. They knew they had received justice under law.

9

The Liberal
Edward Weinfeld's Judicial Values

In analyzing Edward Weinfeld's judicial style in the preceding chapter, we focused on how he decided cases, whenever possible, by applying a fixed body of existing legal principles in the context of facts found in a careful, painstaking manner. At the core of his vision was the impartial judge who insured that due process of law, equal treatment of litigants, and the basic safeguards of a fair trial were upheld. As we saw particularly in his cases involving statutory construction and the exercise of discretion, Weinfeld sought to avoid making policy choices; he always tried as a judge to be the instrument of policies dictated by other institutions, never of his own.

Weinfeld, however, was not naive. He sat on the bench in the aftermath of the legal realist critique. He was aware of the realist argument that the sources of law typically reflect conflicting social policies and that, in elaborating legal doctrine, judges often choose policies consistent with some set of social values. As he wrote on the front flyleaf of a book he had read, "Judges do bring to their work certain moral values and views of social policy."[1]

How did Weinfeld reconcile his consistent refusal, on the one hand, to incorporate his own policy preferences into his decisions with his awareness, on the other, that policy was an inevitable ingredient of law? Several factors explain his method of reconciliation.

First, Weinfeld never resolved a pending case by facilely identifying a policy in which he believed—for example, the policy of not allowing judges to participate in plea bargaining—and then announcing that he was deciding the case to advance that policy. Instead, as we saw in *United States ex rel. Elksnis v. Gilligan*,[2] he unearthed established legal principles and then painstakingly analyzed the record in the proceedings before him to elucidate why judicial participation in the case had violated those principles. He also took the time to develop alternative reasons in support of the result he had reached.

Second, Weinfeld developed a conception of his role that diverted his attention from policy issues. The judge did not see himself as a social engineer whose task was to resolve conflicts among competing social classes or interest groups. Nor did he understand himself as a managerial judge whose role was to supervise structural reform litigation or to efficiently administer a docket within a judicial bureaucracy. Instead, he viewed his responsibility as the resolution of disputes between litigants in discrete cases. Generally, he avoided thinking about the impact his decisions would have on groups or individuals other than the immediate litigants. As a result, as the last chapter's analysis of the *Bethlehem Steel* case[3] showed, he did not write opinions in order to maximize the societal impact of his views or consciously to foster social change. On the contrary, he wrote for the purpose of justifying his decisions to the litigants before him, and he focused on what had most meaning to them—the facts through which they had lived and the application of preexisting law, under which they had planned their affairs, to those facts.

Of course, Weinfeld's practice of handling cases as disputes between particular litigants rather than as clashes of interest between larger social groups was facilitated by his sitting as a trial rather than an appellate judge. It enabled him to speak of cases in terms of their importance to the parties, and indeed, it is true that much litigation in the district court does consist of matters having little immediate significance to anyone other than the parties. Weinfeld's status as a trial judge also bred caution. He often worried that as a single federal district judge he lacked the breadth of information and experience or the moral authority to change social and political practices and policies instituted by elected public officials. The judge knew that he could master the facts and find established law. That was the realm of a trial judge: he was comfortable within it and knew that trouble awaited him if he strayed outside it.

Still, there remained a third, and far more important, reason why Edward Weinfeld felt no conflict between his duty of fidelity to law and the advancement of sound social policy. This reason lay in the nature of the societal policy that he believed he had authority to enforce—the maintenance of due process of law and equal protection of the laws and the holding of those entrusted with high public office to their oaths of office. "A civilized society," as he saw it, "is strong only as long as its laws are administered honestly, fairly and impartially,"[4] and he always insisted that judges and other public officials so administer law. He envisioned no conflict between this policy and the law—he understood the policy already to be incorporated into the law.

Weinfeld expressed himself with clarity in *United States ex rel. Lee Till Seem v. Shaughnessy*,[5] in which the Immigration and Naturalization Service (INS) sought to prohibit a woman from China who claimed she was married to an American citizen of Chinese ancestry from entering the United States. The INS was holding the woman at Ellis Island on "strong suspicion concerning . . . [her] fraudulent claim" for entry, but "[n]ot a single fact buttresse[d] the charge," and, over a period of four months during which it kept Lee Till Seem in detention, the government had done nothing to obtain evidence. "The substance of the affidavit" in opposition to her writ of habeas corpus was "an apologia to justify failure of the immigration authorities to move expeditiously in the conduct of investigations" due to "shortage of administrative and investigative personnel and the alleged inexperience of inspectors at the New York Port of Entry."[6] Weinfeld responded,

> The Immigration Service is entitled to every reasonable opportunity to follow through on leads which it believes will be productive of results, but this may not be used as an excuse to detain one an unreasonable length of time on a mere allegation of suspicion, unsupported by evidential facts. Volume of work, personnel shortages and other related administrative problems may present an administrator with understandable difficulties; *they do not, however, relieve him of his paramount duty to comply with and enforce the law. . . . To permit her continued detention under the present circumstances and without a hearing comes close to those concepts of State power which are abhorrent to our way of life.* "[7]

Weinfeld expressed himself in a similar, albeit less strong, fashion in *United States ex rel. Kusman v. District Director of Immigration and Naturalization at Port of New York*.[8] Kusman had been imprisoned for five months at Ellis Island under a final order of deportation, the validity of which was unquestioned, when Weinfeld granted his writ of habeas corpus. Kusman's argument was that his detention was for the sole purpose of effecting deportation, that it had become evident that he could not be deported since no country would accept him, and hence that his continued detention, in effect, "constituted imprisonment in contravention of the Fifth Amendment." Weinfeld agreed. He concluded that "the immigration authorities ha[d] failed to move with reasonable dispatch," and, when he learned that, while the writ was pending, they had ceased in their efforts to locate a country to which to send Kusman, he complained that an "appeal to the Courts to inquire into the cause of detention should not serve as an excuse to delay action required under the express terms of the statute."[9]

Weinfeld again chastised the Immigration and Naturalization Service for opposing the naturalization of Paul Gourary because he had sought and obtained a deferment from military service. Gourary, who had migrated to the United States from Austria in 1939, registered for the American military draft in 1941 and ultimately was classified I-A, available for induction. He thereupon appeared before his local draft board and requested a temporary deferment due to his father's serious illness. He was handed form 301 by a clerk and told to file it for a deferment. Upon its filing, he received the deferment. However, form 301 plainly indicated that any alien who completed and filed the form would thereafter be ineligible for citizenship.

The problem was that Gourary should not have been given form 301, which was available only to neutral aliens seeking to avoid the World War II draft. Gourary came from a country that had been annexed to Germany in 1938 and thus was an enemy alien. Unlike neutral aliens, enemy aliens had no right to avoid American military service, although as a practical matter the military did not induct them if they did not wish to serve and so indicated by completing form 304. Filing form 304, unlike filing form 301, did not bar an individual from applying subsequently for citizenship.

The government conceded that if the clerk had given Gourary the correct form, he would have been eligible for citizenship. But it argued that, since he obtained a draft deferment in return for his agreement not to apply for citizenship, he should be barred. Weinfeld was not impressed:

> I think it quite irrelevant that the petitioner was relieved of military duty. . . . Whatever one's personal views may be of his avoidance of service, such rights as the law accords him may not be denied simply because his conduct would readily be condemned by the many. Any diminution of his rights solely because his conduct did not find popular favor is a diminution of the integrity and the majesty of the law. Only in the exact and equal administration of the law can justice be done and public confidence in its administration maintained.[10]

The INS was not alone in receiving Weinfeld's knocks;[11] as the *Gourary* case suggests, the Selective Service System was another federal agency into whose proceedings Weinfeld was prepared to inquire. For example, in *United States v. Burlich*,[12] Weinfeld acquitted a defendant charged with failure to report for induction into military service because his local draft board had failed to follow proper procedures in classifying him I-A, even though it was conceded that a sufficient basis in fact existed to sustain the I-A classification. And, in *United States v. Clare*,[13] Weinfeld granted a motion for a judgment of acquittal on a similar charge when the government refused at trial to submit an FBI report on which a Selective Service hearing examiner had relied in denying Clare's request to be classified either as a minister of religion or as a conscientious objector.[14]

Indeed, no institution of government was immune from Weinfeld's gaze; he was prepared to criticize any individual or entity that failed to abide by proper legal standards. One of his classic critiques arose out of a proceeding to expunge from the records of the court a "presentment" issued by a grand jury.[15]

The grand jury had been investigating possible violations of conspiracy and perjury laws with reference to affidavits of union leaders, required under the Taft-Hartley Act, affirming that they were not Communists. It returned no indictments, but nonetheless filed a report declaring that union officials had invoked their privilege against self-incrimination and that the Taft-Hartley affidavits of those officials were not "worth the paper they [were] written on." The grand jury recommended that the National Labor Relations Board (NLRB) revoke the certification of the unions whose leaders had invoked the Fifth Amendment, and the NLRB began proceedings to do so. Some of the union leaders also were questioned about religious matters, such as their "belief in the Supreme Being, baptism, their particular religious faith, the length of adherence to it, atheism and agnosticism."[16]

Weinfeld granted the motion to expunge the grand jury's presentment or report from the records of the court. "A fundamental purpose of the Founding Fathers," he wrote, "was to confine the courts to the performance of their judicial duties"—"the decision of issues between litigants"—and thereby "to secure the fair and impartial administration of the laws." A grand jury, which was merely "an appendage of the court," possessed a "jurisdiction . . . coextensive with the court's and [could] not exceed it." But this grand jury had exceeded its jurisdiction. Its presentment had given political advice to the NLRB and in the process had shed

the "'principal attributes'" of a "'judicial document'—'the right to answer and to appeal'" and to "'know . . . upon what evidence the findings
are based.'" The "Court's processes," in Weinfeld's view, could not be so
"used to defeat that fundamental fairness which must mark all judicial
proceedings"—in this case, the rule "that a man should not be subject to
a quasi-official accusation of misconduct which he cannot answer in an
authoritative forum."[17]

When he addressed the remaining issue in the case concerning the
grand jurors' inquiries into religious beliefs of witnesses, Weinfeld became almost livid. "Questions as to religion," he wrote,

> may have a place in closed societies with official requirements as to reli-
> gious belief, where conformity is the rule of life—such societies, in a
> word, as our forefathers fled from; but in a free society such as ours,
> where a man's faith is his own affair, the questions asked were highly im-
> proper.[18]

Weinfeld was equally disturbed when Congress, or more particularly
the Senate's Subcommittee on Investigations chaired by Joseph Mc-
Carthy, acted outside the law. The judge heard two cases arising out of
the activities of the Wisconsin senator.

One was *United States v. Lamont,*[19] involving an indictment against
Corliss Lamont and others for refusing to answer questions asked by the
senate subcommittee. The defendants moved to dismiss the indictment on
various constitutional grounds (the Fifth Amendment privilege against
self-incrimination not being among them), but Weinfeld never reached
the constitutional issues. Instead, he turned to a proposition central to his
jurisprudence and conceded by all—that the power of every American institution, even Congress, was bound by law. He declared,

> While the Congress is possessed of broad powers to conduct investiga-
> tions necessary for the performance of its constitutional functions . . . [,]
> the congressional power to investigate is not boundless. . . . "It cannot
> be used to inquire into private affairs unrelated to a valid legislative pur-
> pose."[20]

Thus, "not every willful refusal to answer," but only a "contumacious
refusal . . . to answer a question pertinent to an inquiry before a law-
fully constituted committee, acting within the scope of its authority,"

constituted an offense for which an indictment would lie. When Weinfeld searched through congressional materials, he failed "to find any reference to the Permanent Subcommittee, let along any delegation of power to it"; as a result, he ended up taking note of the "obscurity of the committee's origin" and observing that "[i]t may well be that some resolution or authorization exists but thus far it has not been revealed." In light of the lack of evidence that the McCarthy committee had any authority whatever to ask any questions, Weinfeld dismissed the indictment against Lamont and others for failing to answer them.[21]

The second case in which Weinfeld challenged the McCarthy committee was *United States ex rel. Belfrage v. Shaughnessy*.[22] Belfrage was being detained on Ellis Island without bail, pending deportation on charges of being affiliated with the Communist Party. For many years, the government had investigated Belfrage on similar charges but had failed to uncover evidence sufficient to justify proceedings against him. Then, early in 1953, Belfrage was called to testify before the McCarthy committee, where he refused on Fifth Amendment grounds to answer questions. The day after his refusal, the government arrested him and began deportation proceedings, claiming in essence that an alien's refusal to answer questions about alleged Communist affiliations was a sufficient ground for deportation.

It would have been tempting for most district judges to do what the Court of Appeals did when it affirmed Weinfeld's issuance of a writ of habeas corpus: to hold as a matter of law that an alien's taking the Fifth Amendment before a congressional committee was not a sufficient ground for deportation. Weinfeld, however, took a different approach: he examined the facts to determine whether Belfrage was an active participant in the Communist movement. He found that the government had long advanced general allegations that Belfrage was an active member of the Communist Party and the world Communist movement, that he had associated with principal party leaders, and that he had traveled to the Soviet Union and engaged in espionage activities. But over a period of seven years, the government had never availed itself of an opportunity to supplement its allegations with evidentiary fact, nor had it made any effort to take Belfrage into custody. The only new fact occurring in 1953 was Belfrage's refusal to testify, and Weinfeld did not understand how "his assertion of a constitutional privilege" made him "such a menace to the nation's safety that it [was] now necessary to jail him without bail."[23]

Prosecutors and police constituted two other groups of public officials whose frequent misconduct proved troubling to Weinfeld. For example, in *United States v. Wilson*,[24] he expressed his qualms about the U.S. attorney's practice of levying multiple charges against a defendant who had committed a single act that happened to violate several statutes. Such "fragmentation of charges," in his opinion, "serve[d] to extend a trial, . . . distract[ed] the jury from basic central issues in the case by dispersion of factual aspects, . . . and place[d] an unduly heavy burden upon the jury to concentrate on the proliferated issues."[25]

Weinfeld expressed his views about police misconduct most explicitly in *Handschu v. Special Services Division*,[26] in which he declined to dismiss a complaint alleging unlawful activities by undercover members of the New York City Police Department. Weinfeld wrote,

> The use of secret informers or undercover agents is a legitimate and proper practice of law enforcement. . . . The use of informers and infiltrators by itself does not give rise to any claim of violation of constitutional rights.[27] However, those so engaged may not overstep constitutional bounds; the Bill of Rights protects individuals against excesses and abuses in such activities. . . . [T]he initiation and inducement of criminal activity by government agents is proscribed. . . . [T]he complaint alleges that the informers and infiltrators provoked, solicited and induced members of lawful political and social groups to engage in unlawful activities[,] including a scheme "to plan the bombing of a government facility."

Indeed, the complaint alleged that infiltrators urged members of lawful organizations to participate in unlawful conduct at demonstrations as part of a plan fostered by the police department's Security and Investigation Section (SIS) to create an atmosphere among its members of mistrust, suspicion and hostility so as to prevent their free and lawful association with one another and to chill their interest in the exercise of their right of free expression and association. Weinfeld continued,

> The complaint further charges that the agents, in their reports to SIS, which in some instances are daily, include information concerning persons, places and activities entirely unrelated to legitimate law enforcement purposes, such as lists of those attending meetings of lawful organizations. . . . The essence of the claim is that SIS systematically engages

in these excesses and abusive tactics with the purpose and effect of sow-ing distrust and suspicion among plaintiffs and other[s] who espouse un-orthodox or dissenting political and social views, thereby discouraging them from associating for that purpose.[28]

Not surprisingly, Weinfeld condemned such police activity. He likewise condemned coercive or fraudulent police practices that induced confes-sions;[29] as he wrote in one case involving police interrogation of a defen-dant after counsel had requested that no questioning occur in his absence,

I see little point in well-intentioned utterances denouncing in-custody in-terrogation of an accused person known to be represented by counsel without affording counsel an opportunity to be present, or in condemn-ing prosecuting attorneys who take part in such interrogation in viola-tion of professional ethics and then allowing the government to become the beneficiary of the condemned conduct. The only effective way to ter-minate this unfair and at times unethical practice is to prohibit the gov-ernment from using its illicit fruits.[30]

He also denounced violations of constitutional rights by the government in other contexts.[31] As he said in one case involving an unauthorized wiretap,

The majesty of the law demands that constitutional guarantees and statutory rights be fully enforced even though at times it may result in one charged with crime escaping just conviction. The history of freedom has been the history of respect for and enforcement of due process of law. Our judgments must not be warped by the fact that the defendant is charged with an offense which involves a sordid and shabby business. It is well to recall that "the safeguards of liberty have frequently been forged in controversies involving not very nice people."[32]

Weinfeld adhered to this view not only in cases involving wiretapping but also in a line of cases arising out of an apparent policy on the part of New York City of closing down bookstores selling pornographic material by seizing both illicit and licit material.[33]

In short, Edward Weinfeld regarded the protection of constitutional rights as part of the essence of his judicial duty. As his pornography cases show, he was a strong proponent of First Amendment rights. This was true even in other contexts. Thus, in *Boe v. Collelo*,[34] he granted an injunction on behalf of distributors and readers of *The Call*, a "revolutionary newspaper,"[35] against municipal enforcement of an ordinance requiring a license to sell anything within the town,[36] and in *Fortune Society v. McGinnis*,[37] he upheld the right of inmates in state prisons to receive *Fortune News*. In *Adey v. United Action for Animals, Inc.*,[38] he ruled that the plaintiff, a public official, had failed in his libel action to offer sufficient proof of malice to overcome the defendants' First Amendment right to publish their statement about him.

Weiss v. Willow Tree Civic Ass'n[39] presented First Amendment claims in a more complex procedural context. Plaintiffs, a group of Hasidic Jews seeking to construct residential housing in the town of Ramapo, New York, for themselves and their fellow Hasidim, brought a civil rights action against the Willow Tree Association, an organization of private individuals that sought to persuade town authorities to deny the necessary permits for the project. The complaint alleged that the defendant and its members were acting on the basis of ethnic and religious prejudice against the Hasidim. Weinfeld nonetheless granted the defendant's motion to dismiss the complaint. He held that the plaintiffs' claims all were grounded in the Fourteenth Amendment, and thus required a showing of state action to succeed, and that plaintiffs had not pleaded that governmental agencies were in any way involved in the Willow Tree Association's activities. But then the judge added that "other considerations of more compelling force" also required dismissal of the complaint—namely, that the activities of the Willow Tree Association were "inextricably bound up with the defendants' exercise of First Amendment rights of assembly, petition, and association." Finally he held that the civil rights laws

> do not afford a remedy for injuries that may be sustained as an incident
> to private individuals' exercise of their fundamental rights to assemble,
> petition and associate for the purpose of influencing—openly and without force—officials of state and local governments.[40]

Again, First Amendment rights had trumped.

Weinfeld also showed regard for constitutional rights of a more novel sort. Sitting in *Hall v. Lefkowitz*,[41] brought as the first case to test the constitutionality of state legislation outlawing abortion and also one of the first cases in which women staged a courtroom demonstration,[42]

Weinfeld, only months after Earl Warren had retired as chief justice, quoted a circuit court opinion as follows:

> In this day and time of dynamic expansion of constitutional principles and their application to new and sometimes unheard of situations it takes judicial prescience of a Delphic order to say with certainty that the attack [on a state statute] is insubstantial. It is the better course . . . to forego the doubts, constitute a 3-Judge Court, and allow that court to determine initially [a statute's constitutionality].[43]

With these words, Weinfeld granted a motion to convene a three-judge court to examine the constitutionality of New York's anti-abortion legislation, to which the New York legislature responded by repealing the laws in question.[44]

There were many other cases in which Weinfeld protected constitutional rights that often were of a novel variety. Thus, he upheld complaints alleging the unconstitutionality of New York's eleven-month residency requirement for voters in primary elections,[45] of New York's Mental Hygiene Law, which permitted emergency confinement of twenty-one days in a mental hospital without judicial review of persons alleged to be mentally incompetent,[46] and of the New York State Education Law, which required physicians to be citizens of the United States or to become citizens within ten years of licensure.[47] He upheld a complaint by a Spanish-speaking worker who claimed that New York discriminated against him when he applied for unemployment benefits because its forms were all printed only in English.[48] He also upheld a complaint by a woman alleging that she had been denied First and Fourteenth Amendment rights when the Police Department refused to appoint her as a police officer because the father of her child had a criminal record.[49] And he was extremely critical of state and city officials in a case involving the termination of services to nursing home patients without a hearing.[50] The case that provoked his criticism, he wrote,

> does not belong in this court. It involves three governmental agencies—federal, state and city—and centers about regulations so drawn that they have created a Serbonian bog from which the agencies seemingly are unable to extricate themselves. An attorney representing one agency describes the situation as in "a confusing state of flux," a gross understatement. It is a mess. . . . It borders on the absurd that federal, state and

local officials charged with the administration of the Social Security Act cannot reach an accommodation as to the meaning of the regulations which they drafted themselves but instead force a court action for their interpretation.[51]

Weinfeld thereupon examined the federal regulations with his usual care and thoroughness and concluded that they would be violated by transferring patients to facilities providing a lower level of care without first providing notice and an opportunity for a hearing.

Even when he declined to rule on the merits in favor of individuals claiming violations of their constitutional rights,[52] the judge insisted that they receive a hearing on their claims. A classic case was *Ledesma-Valdes v. Sava*,[53] where several aliens seeking to enter the United States at New York brought a writ of habeas corpus and then were immediately transferred by INS officials to El Paso, Texas, before their case could be heard. Although he refused to direct the return of the aliens to New York, Weinfeld held that, since the district director of INS in New York had control over the aliens when they filed their writ, the Southern District of New York retained jurisdiction of the case. He thereby made it clear that he would hear the merits of the case when the time came to hear the merits and thus that the INS could not avoid adhering to the law.

Weinfeld reached an analogous result in *Chenkin v. Bellevue Hospital Center, New York City Health & Hospitals Corp.* [54] Plaintiff, Paul Chenkin, brought an action for a judgment declaring unconstitutional the defendant's policy of randomly searching employees' possessions when they left the hospital. The judge held that the plaintiff had an expectation of privacy in connection with his possessions and hence that he was potentially protected by the Fourth Amendment. He then held, however, that the hospital's search policy was not unconstitutional, since the hospital had a compelling interest in preventing employee pilferage and since employees had an option of checking possessions before entering and thereby avoiding any search.

He did the same in *Sellman v. Baruch College of the City University of New York*,[55] where the plaintiff sought a judgment that a provision of the Baruch College student government constitution, requiring students for elective positions to be registered on a full-time basis and to maintain a minimum grade-point average, was void. Weinfeld first declared that, since Baruch College was a public institution, its student government was subject to federal constitutional constraints. But he then held that the full-time and grade-point-average requirements were reasonable and hence constitutional ones.

Then there was *In re Ullman*,[56] an application by the United States attorney for an order directing William Ludwig Ullman to answer possibly incriminating questions in return for receiving a statutory grant of immunity from prosecution. Ullman refused to answer on the ground of the statute's unconstitutionality, but Weinfeld, ruling against him on every one of his constitutional claims, directed him to answer. Nonetheless, Weinfeld made a significant concession to Ullman. One issue in the case was whether Congress was constitutionally required, in return for compelling a person to give testimony to federal authorities, to grant immunity from future state as well as federal prosecutions. Weinfeld declined to find such a constitutional requirement. Nonetheless, he did hold that Congress had constitutional power to immunize federal witnesses from state prosecution, and he construed the statute in question as granting Ullman such immunity.

Weinfeld's amenability to giving serious consideration to claims of individual rights, whatever his ultimate conclusion on the merits, emerged most clearly, perhaps, in *United States v. States Marine Lines*.[57] The case was a criminal prosecution under a recently enacted statute for the protection of animal rights—a statute making it a crime to ship animals by sea in an unsafe fashion. The government offered little evidence to counter testimony on behalf of the defendants that the animals in question had been shipped from East Africa to New York in a customary fashion; instead, it relied mainly on a statutory presumption that the presence in a vessel of a "substantial ratio" of dead, diseased, or starving animals was prima facie evidence of a violation. The judge, however, was not impressed with the political correctness of the statute: he understood that human defendants would suffer criminal conviction and punishment if he found the defendants guilty. He therefore turned to his traditional liberal values and insisted on evidence before he was willing to find guilt. Accordingly, he concluded,

> Upon the whole record, in view of the adequate crates, the adequate food, [and] the adequate care afforded the animals . . . , the government has failed to prove beyond a reasonable doubt that the defendants knowingly caused or permitted any wild animals to be transported to the United States under inhumane or unhealthful conditions.[58]

Although it was neither more nor less important to him than any other case he had ever heard, *United States v. States Marine Lines* is especially important to us, as interpreters of Edward Weinfeld's life and career, because it forces us to confront the nature of his liberalism. It shows that Weinfeld was not a liberal of a Great Society or postmodern sort; issues such as animal rights had no particular traction for him. Weinfeld's jurisprudence reflected a more traditional liberalism in which he adhered to legal principle and avoided deciding cases by recourse to contested policy preferences.

As the cases discussed in this chapter show, Weinfeld never had any doubt that judges should adapt the law to the progressive directions in which society was moving. But the judge never considered himself free to lead society in whatever direction he believed best. Weinfeld did not pursue a liberal judicial agenda because his own moral values or views of social policy dictated it; he pursued his agenda because he understood he was living in a "'time of dynamic expansion of constitutional principles.'"[59] He distinguished, that is, between his own and society's beliefs.

Weinfeld regarded judges who pursued their own personal beliefs as less authoritative than those who ascertained the values of society. He hesitated, for example, to rely on cases from the District of Columbia Circuit Court of Appeals because the high rate of division and dissent in that circuit, in his view, undermined its authority: it demonstrated that the circuit's judges were pursuing personal jurisprudential agendas rather than working together to identify society's collective agenda.[60]

Of course, Weinfeld's distinction between his own and society's beliefs was a slender one: people tend to assume that others agree with their deepest values. Nonetheless, in the context of the mid–twentieth century, the distinction made sense for Weinfeld,[61] who was living at a time when constitutional rights were being broadly extended to members of society who had not previously enjoyed them. As late as the 1970s, when it was deciding cases such as *Roe v. Wade*[62] and *University of California Regents v. Bakke*,[63] the Burger Court could be perceived as expanding the domain of rights, albeit more slowly than the Warren Court had. Until the decade of the Reagan presidency, Weinfeld never needed to rely on his own personal beliefs as a basis for law because the culture in which he lived had adopted beliefs similar to his and was putting them into practice.

Ronald Reagan did pose a problem for Edward Weinfeld, as is illustrated by an incident during one of Weinfeld's hospital stays several years before his death. Weinfeld and a former law clerk who was visiting him were watching the evening news together, when the president appeared on the television screen. Weinfeld's response was immediate and peremptory: "'Please turn the television off,'" he said. "'As a judge, I have an obligation to respect the president, and I can't do it if I watch him.'"[64] The problem was that the Reagan presidency undermined Weinfeld's assumptions about America's direction; Weinfeld, who by the time of Reagan was old and firmly set in his ways, dealt with the problem simply by tuning it out. What we cannot know is how Weinfeld would have responded to a presidency like Reagan's if it had occurred two decades earlier.

Weinfeld's particular conception of progress was also important in another way. Weinfeld understood that his heroes—Louis Brandeis, Herbert Lehman, and Woodrow Wilson—had striven to advance the cause of all humanity, not the causes of specific groups such as African Americans, women, or immigrants. Of course, he recognized that specific underclasses might benefit from a progressive effort to improve the lot of all humanity and hence that, in the world beyond the law, there was little difference between viewing progress as a moral imperative to make humanity as a whole better off and seeing it as a practical imperative for advancing the interests of particular groups. Nevertheless, there is a vital jurisprudential distinction between the two approaches. A liberal judge who understands her task as working to uplift particular groups might find the interests of those groups coming into conflict, and at that point her jurisprudence might fail to identify which group she should prefer. Weinfeld, in contrast, never faced this problem. He viewed progress as a unitary good, and, as long as the law was pointing toward a better world, he saw no need to ask specifically whether it was advancing the interests of any one group more than the interests of others.

Weinfeld could maintain his unitary vision of progress because of his conception of equality—the good toward which American law and society were, in his view, progressing. Unlike many legal thinkers today, Weinfeld did not pursue a vision of equality that divides society into classes and interest groups at war with each other. Thus, he never had to focus on the perverse question whether a judgment in a case would give a particular group or class more or less than its fair share of the societal pie. This question is perverse because it creates a sharp dichotomy in the thinking of a judge between fidelity to law and considerations of social policy. Judges who focus on the question can never decide any issue of law without favoring some social groups or interests over others: once a judge, that is, identifies a particular societal distribution as just, she will necessarily test proffered legal doctrine by the standard of how well it achieves that distribution. She will follow existing doctrine when it is consistent with her vision of justice and reject it when seriously inconsistent. But her vision of justice will always be controlling—it will prescribe how much of a role preexisting legal doctrine will play in the determination of cases.

Weinfeld, who had a different view of equality and justice, never thought in such a fashion. He saw only individuals, not groups and classes, in the litigants who came to his court. For him, equal justice was not about the distribution of wealth and power, but about the behavior of government towards citizens. Due process of law, equal protection of the laws, and the honest, fair, and impartial administration of law all required the same behavior on the part of judges and officials—that they "not respect persons in judgment" but "hear the small and the great alike," and neither "respect the person of the poor, nor honour the person of the mighty; but in righteousness" render judgment. Weinfeld had faith that the principles instinct in law would provide all Americans with the substance of liberty and justice as long as judges and officials applied law equally.

Thus, Weinfeld's vision of justice and equality, like the visions of other judges, controlled the way he approached legal doctrine. But, since his vision was different—it required only that he adhere consistently to the rule of law—it never created a conflict with the imperative of fidelity to law that a judge with a vision of equality as distributional justice would face. Instead, it directed fidelity to law.

Weinfeld's vision of justice was a product more of his life experience than of sophisticated analysis. Although Weinfeld undoubtedly was stung by ethnic and religious discrimination in his youth, he never saw himself as a victimized Jew. Perhaps discrimination made it more difficult for youths like himself to rise out of Lower East Side obscurity, but, if so, Weinfeld adapted to the difficulty by working harder and recalibrating his goals. His was an individual, not a class struggle for equality, in which he strove to improve his own life by taking advantage of what America had to offer, not by asking for fundamental transformations of society that would make it easier for him to achieve his objectives.

Of course, Weinfeld understood that America contained classes and interest groups; in his youth, he could not ignore the fact that America consisted of two societies: the one composed chiefly of male, white, Protestant, middle-class descendants of northwest Europeans, and the other composed of women, blacks, immigrants from southern and eastern Europe and their children, and left-wing political dissidents. Although wealth was more common in the first society and poverty in the second, the key distinction between the two, as Weinfeld saw it, was not economic; there were many poor people in the first and some wealthy ones in the second. In the mind of Edward Weinfeld, the principal difference between the two societies was that members of the second did not receive the same protection from the law as did members of the first. Indeed, citizens of the second society tended to live without law and sometimes amid violence: their lives were ordered through extralegal, often religious norms,[65] and they were frequently harassed by the authorities, notably the Immigration and Naturalization Service and local police forces.[66]

Weinfeld's legal and judicial career can best be understood as a continuing effort on his part to extend the equal protection of the law to members of this second society—to individuals who in his youth had not enjoyed it. From the divorcées whom he had represented as a young attorney, through the victims of the McCarthy inquisition, to the draft resisters of the Vietnam era, Weinfeld brought the protection of the law to those who had been forced to function outside it until their arrival at his office or courtroom.

Thus, for Weinfeld, there was no inconsistency between adherence to fixed, unchanging legal principles and the better attainment of justice. Eliminating injustice did not require change in the law; it demanded only that existing law be extended to people who had not previously been its beneficiaries. As a judge, he did not need to change law but only to apply it equally to all cases, no matter how humble.

The judge's jurisprudential position was a tenable one. Although it surely is possible to view the divisions in American society as conflicts between classes and interest groups that can be rectified only by fundamental legal and social redistribution made on the basis of contested policy judgments, Weinfeld's own rise from obscurity to professional success and honor suggests that, at least for some, there is an alternative route to equality. That route is to demand the protection of existing law and to take advantage of the benefits it offers, as Weinfeld did first for himself and his clients and then for the litigants who appeared before him. In this deep sense, Edward Weinfeld's jurisprudence grew out of his life experience.

His jurisprudence also grew out of his life experience in another sense. As we saw when we examined Weinfeld's relationship to his wife and family, compassion and avoidance of conflict were values about which Weinfeld cared deeply. Weinfeld's jurisprudence likewise displayed compassion and evaded conflict. Those who entered his courtroom had to focus their attention not on the values and policies that divided them, but on proving detailed facts through the careful pursuit of established procedures. No one could disagree with Weinfeld's axiom that all parties in his courtroom were entitled to equal protection of the laws, nor could anyone doubt that life would be more just if government officials accorded to everyone the equal protection they deserved. Of course, few officials were prepared to make the necessary efforts to insure equal protection for all, but Weinfeld never demanded that they make them. His only requirement was that officials not deny individuals their rights, and an official usually could meet that requirement by releasing from custody or otherwise proceeding compassionately against the individual who had sought Weinfeld's help. Officials thus had little reason to pursue conflict with Weinfeld rather than effectuate his judgments.

By focusing on individual litigants and on the relationship of government to individuals, Weinfeld was able to avoid thinking about conflict among diverse social groups. By averting his attention from conflict, he was able, in turn, to avoid deciding contested issues of law. That left him free to resolve cases under widely accepted, preexisting, though compassionate, legal norms.

In the end, Weinfeld's approach reflected a late-eighteenth-century rather than a late-twentieth-century vision of judging. He was, in the words of James Madison, a "man . . . connected with the constitutional rights of the place" or office that he occupied.[67] His core judicial virtues mirrored the constitutive values of Article III, which directs judges to decide only specific cases and controversies by recourse to impartial norms reflecting the best values of society as a whole. In his fierce devotion to the job of judging and his deep immersion in it, Weinfeld became the institution of judge itself, as distinguished from someone standing outside the institution who used it to manage society or control social policy. He used it only to do equal justice under law.

10

Teacher and Mentor

As the last two chapters have shown, Edward Weinfeld formulated a distinctive jurisprudence of potential importance to scholars
and judges of today. But his judicial career is also important for a second
reason—for the role he played in teaching and mentoring young attorneys, who during his years on the bench transformed the New York bar
and ultimately became its leaders. This chapter will examine the relationship between Weinfeld and the law clerks whom he trained and men-
tored. In particular, it will examine the backgrounds of the clerks, the
processes by which they were appointed, and their impact on the legal
profession subsequent to their tenure with the judge. The chapter will
then examine what the judge taught his clerks while they were with him
in chambers.

Very good students, mainly from the New York metropolitan region
and often of ethnic, usually Jewish, background applied to clerk for
Judge Weinfeld. Rarely did students with a white, Anglo-Saxon, Protestant history who had been raised outside New York and performed at the
very top of their class in the nation's leading law schools apply to clerk
for the judge, especially during the first half of his tenure on the bench.
Thus, particularly during the 1950s and 1960s, Weinfeld did not have
law clerks who, it would have been predicted, were most likely to attain
the highest levels of success at the New York bar. Nonetheless, Weinfeld's
teaching and counseling transformed these clerks into extraordinary
young lawyers and inspired them, once they had left his chambers, to go
forth and create or conquer what are now the elite law firms of New
York City.

Of course, a few years passed before the patterns by which good law
students came to clerk in Judge Weinfeld's chambers became established
and much longer before the judge's enormous impact on his clerks be-

came visible to the outside world. Indeed, the judge's first law clerk, Joseph Tekulsky, came to the judge in a manner in which no other clerk ever would.

Tekulsky, who was practicing law with a small New York City firm when he applied to the judge, had a sound educational background: he had attended a suburban New York high school, Harvard College, and Columbia Law School. The resumé he submitted with his application revealed that he was on the dean's list at Harvard, but it offered no evidence that his record in law school had been distinguished. He was not on the *Columbia Law Review*.[1] Tekulsky's file does not contain letters of recommendation from any professors at Columbia; letters came only from Ben Hartstein, for whom Weinfeld had worked while in law school and against whom Tekulsky's firm had litigated a case,[2] and from Tekulsky's father, Sol Tekulsky, who was an attorney[3] and one of Weinfeld's old friends.[4]

Judge Weinfeld's second law clerk, Frederick B. Boyden, began to establish what would become the mold out of which future Weinfeld clerks would emerge, even though he was not a native New Yorker. After attending Harvard and Columbia for his undergraduate work, Boyden went to Columbia Law School, where he ranked ninth in his class at the end of his second year and was an editor of the *Columbia Law Review*.[5] The judge hired him on the recommendations of Assistant Dean James P. Gifford and Professor Herbert Wechsler,[6] who had come to know Weinfeld when they had served together as advisors to a legislative committee that had drafted the New York legislation under which Weinfeld became housing commissioner.[7]

Maurice Nessen, the judge's third law clerk, anchored the pattern more firmly. Although a native of Brookline, Massachusetts, rather than New York,[8] Nessen was dating and would soon marry a woman from New York, the daughter of a judge of the New York Court of Appeals with whom Weinfeld was, of course, acquainted. Nessen wanted to clerk for a judge based in New York City.[9] Initially, Yale Law School, at which he was managing editor of the *Yale Law Journal*,[10] had recommended him to Jerome Frank, a distinguished member of the Second Circuit Court of Appeals, but Frank selected someone else.[11] Nessen then went to speak with Professor Boris Bittker, whose seminar he had taken. Bittker had known Weinfeld since the 1940s through Bittker's father-in-law, Carl Stern, and Carl Stern's brother-in-law, Louis Weiss, both of whom were friends of Weinfeld. Bittker remembers praising Weinfeld to Nessen.[12] Yale then recommended Nessen to Weinfeld, who interviewed him several times and finally offered him the position.[13]

Upon the termination of his clerkship with the judge, Nessen established a pattern followed almost precisely by his three immediate successors. First, he maintained the closest of personal ties to the judge, who "sponsored his admission to the bar," "followed his career with fatherly interest," and became "godfather of his oldest child."[14] Second, he spent several years after his clerkship working as an assistant United States attorney[15]—an office in which a person can hone litigation skills. Third, he formed a partnership with a close friend from law school who also had worked with him in the U.S. attorney's office, Arthur Kramer,[16] and established a small firm that by the end of the 1990s had grown into the twenty-eighth largest firm in New York,[17] a firm—Kramer, Levin, Naftalis, Nessen, Kamin, and Frankel[18]—in which for many years he was a name partner. Few attorneys in the city have enjoyed comparable success over the last four decades.

Nessen's successor was Stephen Wise Tulin, who clerked in 1954–1955. Tulin, who ranked fourth in his class at Yale Law School at the end of two years and had been elected comment editor of the *Yale Law Journal*, was a friend of Nessen who, it appears, had urged him to apply for the Weinfeld clerkship.[19] Like Nessen, Tulin came with a recommendation from Professor Bittker, who described him as "one of our top men" and "a most pleasant companion as well."[20] He was also the grandson of Rabbi Stephen S. Wise, whom Weinfeld admired as "the greatest orator of my time,"[21] the son of Judge Justine Wise Polier of the Domestic Relations Court, and the adopted son of attorney Shad Polier; Weinfeld had known the Polier family, which he described as "a family the members of which have long been devoted to the public welfare and interest," for many years before coming to the bench.[22]

Tulin followed in Nessen's footsteps not only into the clerkship but also thereafter. Like Nessen, Tulin had the closest of personal relations with the judge; when Tulin's adoptive father died, Weinfeld came to the Polier home and helped "get my mother over the very rough moments at the house before we went to the cemetery." As Tulin added, Weinfeld was "the only one for whom I feel rather much the way I felt about Shad."[23] Like Nessen, Tulin had a distinguished legal career—in his case, as the partner of his father, Shad Polier, an eminent civil rights lawyer active in the affairs of the American Jewish Congress and of the NAACP Legal and Educational Defense Fund.[24] Tulin surely did not accumulate as much wealth as Nessen, but he continued his family's distinguished tradition of "devot[ion] to the public welfare and interest."[25]

A third man from Yale, Barry Garfinkel, succeeded Tulin as Weinfeld's law clerk. Like Tulin and the judge's first clerk, Joseph Tekulsky, Garfinkel had a relative—in this instance, a cousin—who was an attorney and a friend of Weinfeld and who wrote a letter of recommendation on his behalf.[26] Garfinkel also received recommendations from Yale professors Myres S. McDougal[27] and Fowler V. Harper, who observed that Garfinkel had been "elected Managing Editor of the Yale Law Journal" and was "in the top quarter of his class."[28] With his typical attention to detail, Weinfeld followed up Harper's letter with a phone call, in which Harper, according to Weinfeld's notes, declared Garfinkel to be "very capable but would not put him in the very top group. Personal relations would be excellent."[29] Weinfeld also telephoned Bittker, who "considere[d]" Garfinkel "a pretty good man," although not as able as another Yale applicant that year and no better than a third.[30]

Like Nessen and Tulin, Garfinkel remained close to the judge after his clerkship. That closeness was evidenced, for example, by an invitation to the "Judge & Lillian" (i.e., Mrs. Weinfeld) from "Gloria" (i.e., Mrs. Garfinkel) to attend "a surprise party for Barry's 50th Birthday"[31] and by a party for the Weinfeld family and close friends that Garfinkel cohosted on the occasion of Weinfeld's eightieth birthday.[32] A note from Weinfeld to Garfinkel thanking that him "for arranging that 'the family' [i.e., the attending law clerks] were seated at one table at the wind-up dinner of the [Second Circuit Judicial] Conference" further evidences their relationship. As Weinfeld added, "you know what joy it gave Lillian and me that all of us were to-gether."[33]

Unlike Nessen and Tulin, Garfinkel did not want to become an assistant United States attorney following his clerkship. Nor did he go out and found his own firm. Like Tulin, Garfinkel, following advice of Judge Weinfeld at the conclusion of his clerkship,[34] joined a small firm, now Skadden, Arps, Slate, Meagher & Flom, which had been founded in 1948.[35] When Garfinkel joined the firm, he became its ninth lawyer.[36] Today, Skadden, Arps has grown to become the largest law office in New York, with 1,602 attorneys[37] and with double the total revenues of its nearest rival.[38] During its growth, Garfinkel served for many years as managing partner of its litigation department. For a man whose father died at the age of nine, who worked his way through college and law school "as a waiter at various restaurants in New York City" and "during summers . . . at mountain resorts,"[39] and who was "not in the very top group" at Yale Law School,[40] the clerkship with Judge Weinfeld marked the beginning of a remarkable professional career.

All of Judge Weinfeld's first five law clerks were graduates of two of the top law schools of their era—Columbia and Yale. The sixth law clerk was not. Instead, he was a graduate of New York University School of Law (Weinfeld's alma mater), which in the mid-1950s would not have ranked in the top ten nationally. Nonetheless, his clerkship with the judge would mark the start of the most remarkable professional career that any of the clerks would enjoy.

Martin Lipton had made an outstanding record for himself at NYU, where he ranked second in the class and served as editor-in-chief of the *Law Review*.[41] One of his NYU professors, Charles Seligson, wrote that in seventeen years of teaching he had "come across very few students who are his equal" and "only one other student who might perhaps be regarded as having a keener legal mind."[42] Nonetheless, at the conclusion of his NYU education, Lipton had moved uptown to Columbia Law School, to begin study for a J.S.D.,[43] to work as a legal writing instructor in connection with Columbia's first-year Legal Method course, and thereby to obtain the certification of a leading school. His supervisor at Columbia, Professor Harry W. Jones, thought well of Lipton but did not identify him as one of the very top recent graduates in the nation. All Jones wrote was that Lipton had "led his class at NYU Law School last year, and I am sure that he would have done quite well at any law school."[44]

During the three decades after leaving Weinfeld's chambers, Lipton probably maintained the closest relationship with the judge of any of the clerks. Lipton was part of a very small group present at Weinfeld's apartment the day before he died, when the American Law Institute presented the judge with the Henry Friendly Medal.[45] Earlier, when New York University School of Law had honored Lipton with its Vanderbilt Associates Medal, the school's highest award to an alumnus, it was Weinfeld who made the presentation, during which he took note of Lipton's "great capacity for friendship and a strong sense of loyalty to those with whom he worked."[46] Lipton, in response, wrote the judge that the presentation was "the most moving thing I have ever heard about me and the firm. It actually brought tears to my eyes."[47] Weinfeld and Lipton would serve together for many years after the presentation both on the NYU Law School's Law Center Foundation and on the university's board of trustees, and Lipton, along with Barry Garfinkel, would host the judge's eightieth birthday celebration.

When Lipton finished his clerkship with the judge, he, like Garfinkel, joined a small firm,[48] where he remained for several years. Then, in the mid-1960s, Lipton joined with three of his fellow members of the *New York University Law Review*—Herbert Wachtell, Leonard Rosen, and George Katz, who, according to legend, felt "'excluded' from the large New York firms at the time because they were Jewish"[49]—to found Wachtell, Lipton, Rosen & Katz, which has become the fifty-third largest firm in New York[50] and the most profitable of all, measured in terms either of revenue per lawyer or of profits per partner, which average well over one million dollars annually. As one legal consultant has observed, Wachtell, Lipton "has simply become . . . 'the best at whatever they've tried.'"[51] Lipton himself has been described as "'the most prominent corporate lawyer in the country.'"[52]

This sequence of four law clerks—Maurice Nessen, Stephen Tulin, Barry Garfinkel, and Martin Lipton—would never be duplicated, in Weinfeld's chambers or probably in any other judge's chambers in America. None of the four had been graduated with the highest grades in his class, and only one had been editor-in-chief of his law review—and that law review was not a top-ranking one. Perhaps, when they arrived in Judge Weinfeld's chambers, they already possessed unrevealed talents that would make one of them into an eminent civil rights attorney and the other three into transforming instruments of New York legal practice. An alternative hypothesis is that Weinfeld's clerks absorbed invaluable skills during their year of training at his hands. Before examining this alternative, however, we first must survey the backgrounds and careers of the other men and women who clerked for Judge Weinfeld between 1958, the year Lipton left, and 1988, the year the judge died.

Within the next group of clerks were three individuals—Judith T. Younger, a graduate of New York University School of Law; William B. Pennell, a graduate of the University of Pennsylvania Law School; and Daniel P. Levitt, a graduate of Harvard Law School—whose backgrounds bore much similarity to those of the judge's first six clerks: none of the three stood first in his or her class, and all three held officers' positions other than editor-in-chief on their respective law reviews. All three, however, would pursue different career paths during their postclerkship years from those followed by Weinfeld's earlier clerks and would thereby break ground that many of the subsequent clerks would similarly tread.

Reunion of Judge Weinfeld's Law Clerks, 1969. *Front row seated at far left:* Daniel P. Levitt. *Second row seated at far left:* Steven Wise Tulin; *third from left:* Marie Vollrath (Judge Weinfeld's secretary); *fourth from left:* Judge Weinfeld; *fifth from left,* Lillian Weinfeld; *at far right,* William B. Pennell. *First row standing:* first woman from left, Judith T. Younger. *Rear row standing: at far right,* William E. Nelson (author); *second from right,* Martin Lipton; third from right, Maurice Nessen; sixth from right, Barry Garfinkel.

Younger would be the first Weinfeld clerk to become a law professor and subsequently a law school dean;[53] Pennell, the first to become a partner in an established New York law firm; and Levitt, the first to clerk for a justice of the Supreme Court of the United States.

Beginning with Judith T. Younger, a total of forty-nine men and women[54] served as Judge Weinfeld's law clerks. Of the forty-nine, eleven clerked subsequently with eight different justices of the Supreme Court of the United States.[55] Eleven became law professors, holding tenured or tenure-track appointments at Buffalo, Columbia, Cornell, Georgetown, Hofstra, Michigan, Minnesota, New York University, Pennsylvania, Rutgers, Southern California, Syracuse, Virginia, Wisconsin, and Yale.[56]

Three of the eleven have taken leave from their academic careers to hold public office: Frank M. Tuerkheimer, who served as United States attorney for the Western District of Wisconsin during the Carter administration;[57] T. Alexander Aleinikoff, who served as general counsel of the Immigration and Naturalization Service in the Clinton administration;[58] and Mark F. Pomerantz, who left the Columbia Law School faculty to found a small criminal defense firm, Fischetti, Feigus & Pomerantz,[59] then moved to Rogers & Wells, next became chief of the Criminal Division of the U.S. attorney's office for the Southern District of New York, and now is a partner at Paul, Weiss, Rifkind, Wharton & Garrison.[60] A twelfth clerk, John H. F. Shattuck, was a vice-president of Harvard, after serving as director of the Washington office of the American Civil Liberties Union and before becoming assistant secretary of state for human rights in the Clinton administration and later United States ambassador to the Czech Republic.[61] And, a thirteenth clerk, Stephen J. Suffern, after working as a public-interest lawyer for groups such as Legal Aid and the New York Law Commune, left the United States in 1974 and eventually moved to Paris, where he has been teaching American law and politics to French undergraduates since 1984 and has recently begun practicing immigration and human rights law on behalf of refugees.[62]

Four of Weinfeld's younger clerks have spent all or most of their careers to date in the practice of public interest law without ever turning to academia. The most senior of them, Irving Berger, who clerked in 1971–1972, has spent much of his career as an attorney for municipal governments in Cleveland, Ohio, and Orange County, California.[63] Kenneth T. Roth, who worked for the judge in 1980–1981, has become executive director of Human Rights Watch.[64] Steven Michaels, from the 1984–1985 term, moved to Hawaii following his clerkship, where he spent eleven years in the state attorney general's office and rose to the position of first deputy attorney general and solicitor general; in 1996, he moved back to New York for personal reasons and joined the firm of Debevoise, Plimpton, Lyons & Gates.[65] After clerking for Judge Weinfeld in 1986–1987 and Justices Lewis F. Powell and Anthony M. Kennedy in 1987–1988, Robert W. Werner became an assistant United States attorney in Connecticut, special counsel for Connecticut governor Lowell Weicker, associate attorney general of Connecticut, and, after a brief stint in private practice, moved to Washington, D.C., where he joined the Office of Legal Counsel in the Department of Justice.[66]

Four of the judge's post-1960 law clerks followed the pattern of clerks from the 1950–1960 decade and either founded their own firm or joined existing small firms. Christopher Norall, from the 1970–1971 term, founded the firm of Forrester & Norall in Brussels, Belgium, to specialize in European Community law.[67] William P. Casella, from 1973–1974, opened his own solo practice in the tiny upstate hamlet of Narrowsburg, New York.[68] Jerry S. Chasen, from 1977–1978, founded his own firm in Miami, Florida,[69] and Robert L. Plotz, from 1980–1981, after working for five years in the U.S. attorney's office for the southern district, joined the small New York City litigation firm of Orans, Elsen & Lupert.[70]

Two other clerks from the 1980s, Nina Gillman and Philomena A. Burke, work in the office of general counsel of major corporations—Colgate Palmolive and Mobil Oil, respectively.[71] Janet Hurley, who under the name of Janet Taber was clerking for the judge at the time of his death, first went to the law firm of Hughes, Hubbard and then to the legal department of Morgan Stanley. From there, she was recruited into the business side of Lehman Brothers and then Goldman, Sachs, where she structures equity derivatives contracts.[72]

Judge Weinfeld's remaining twenty-five clerks have become partners in major New York City or national law firms, including Arnold & Porter; Covington & Burling; Cravath, Swaine & Moore; Davis, Polk & Wardwell; Shearman & Sterling; Sullivan & Cromwell; Wilkie Farr & Gallagher; Williams & Connolly; and Wilmer, Cutler & Pickering, as well as firms mentioned above.[73] One of the twenty-five, John G. Koeltl, who clerked for Weinfeld in 1971–1972 and then for Supreme Court Justice Potter Stewart, was elevated to the bench of the United States District Court for the Southern District of New York in 1994.[74]

One might expect to find a comparable record of extraordinary success among former clerks of Supreme Court justices and former clerks of a few especially distinguished circuit judges, such as Judge Henry J. Friendly. But no other district judge and few circuit judges have produced an equally notable body of alumni. The extraordinary success of the former Weinfeld clerks is especially striking given that, with occasional exceptions, the very top law school graduates in America choose to clerk directly with Supreme Court justices or with distinguished circuit judges rather than on the district court level. Weinfeld, after as well as before 1959, usually obtained very good but not the absolutely best law school graduates to serve as his law clerks. Of his total of fifty-five clerks, only three, all from NYU, graduated first in their law school class,[75] and only four served as editors-in-chief of their law review, three of them from NYU[76] and one from Michigan.[77] Weinfeld rarely had what Henry Friendly, for one, routinely had—the very best students from Harvard, Yale, Stanford, Chicago, or Columbia applying to be his law clerk.

How, then, can we account for the fact that the very good group of young men and woman who entered Judge Weinfeld's chambers emerged one or occasionally two years later as a group that no other collection of former clerks has surpassed and few have equaled—a group that would join and, on occasion, even found leading law firms or pursue distinguished academic and public-interest legal[78] careers? The obvious answer is that Edward Weinfeld was an astounding teacher, who impressed himself on the students who held office as his clerks. Weinfeld's clerks became, in significant ways, young Edward Weinfelds.

The judge, as Alfred D. Youngwood has written, "expected a great deal of his clerks, and he gave even more in return as a teacher and mentor."[79] Earlier Youngwood had told Weinfeld how he had "always considered my year with you to have played a very special and important part in my development as a lawyer, and the work habits and insights that you instilled into me have played significant roles in my practice over the years."[80] Barry Garfinkel agreed that "the work habits and ethos of . . . [his] professional life were formulated during my one year with the judge."[81] Similarly Charles Mulaney wrote how he had "been spoiled by a year of learning from you,"[82] and Bruce Yannett thanked the judge "for making this past year more rewarding, both intellectually and personally, than I ever imagined a single year could be."[83] In the words of Vicki Been, "You taught me an enormous amount during the year, both professionally and personally,"[84] while, according to Bob Warner, the judge "taught me an approach . . . that I know I could never have gotten from any other person."[85] Writing six months after his clerkship about a murder case to which he had been assigned *pro bono* to assist another lawyer, Thomas F. Connell wrote, "I have been told that at trial I will be given a major responsibility for preparing witnesses, eliciting testimony, and conducting cross-examination. Naturally, I am petrified, although I am sure I would be much more so had I not spent so fruitful a year under your tutelage."[86]

Perhaps the collective feeling of Judge Weinfeld's law clerks was best summed up by Eben Moglen and John Shattuck in the 1980s. Shattuck told the judge how every clerk would agree that "he had learned more during the year with you than at any other time in his life."[87] And, in a note to the judge when he ended his clerkship in June 1986, Moglen wrote,

> Entering these Chambers for the first time as your clerk is a momentous feeling, but it is nothing compared to the sense of imminent departure, and the accompanying knowledge that nothing will ever be quite the same again. . . . [I]n a year lived with you, . . . one cannot help but change, and change profoundly. I came to these Chambers, I think, "well-schooled"; I leave here truly educated in priceless ways.[88]

A decade later, John G. Koeltl, the only clerk who has followed Weinfeld to the bench, wrote, "The Judge's presence is real for me every day in my life as a judge. I think about how the Judge has helped to shape my life and how I try to emulate him."[89]

"Weinfeld's strongest lessons," according to his 1970–1971 clerk, Christopher Norall, were twofold—"how to solve problems and how to be fair."[90] The remainder of this chapter focuses on these two teachings— first, what the judge taught his clerks about practicing law and solving legal problems, and second, what he taught them about integrity and justice.

Weinfeld's approach to solving legal problems, wrote Chris Norall, was to

> just lay out all relevant elements carefully, and most of the time the solution followed naturally, without much need for elaborate or dazzling mental acrobatics. This was not an easy lesson for a proud young man just graduated with a good law degree, as I frequently noticed when I tried to pass the message on to others. It was one of the most useful pieces of professional and, indeed, personal equipment I ever acquired.

Other clerks have commented on how the judge "taught us to be rigorously careful in assuring that we got our facts right"—about "the need to pay attention to all details, the importance of always being careful, that the facts of a case, not just the law, were crucially important." "Hyperbole and rhetoric informed little, sloppiness not at all. . . . The facts of the case were crucial, because the Judge knew that if he started from solid understanding of facts, the law would lead to a just result."[91]

He followed that approach, as always, in *United States v. Toney*,[92] the case in which the government, following a practice instituted by then

United States Attorney Rudolph Giuliani, had held a defendant for nearly twenty-four hours before presenting him to a magistrate, who then appointed counsel to represent him. During the interval, as discussed earlier, an assistant United States attorney had interviewed the defendant and obtained a confession. Believing that Giuliani's "practice was an unprincipled and strategic end run around the defendant's right to counsel,"[93] Weinfeld directed his then clerk, Vicki Been, to draft an opinion suppressing the confession. "I poured my soul into a full attack on the constitutionality of the practice," Been writes, but the judge "took one look at the draft, patiently explained that he was a district judge, not the Supreme Court of the United States, and sent me back with instructions to write about the facts of the delay and leave the law and the appropriateness of the practice itself for 'higher authorities.'"[94] As the opinion took final shape, the judge permitted Been to include only one footnote on what she viewed as the "complicated and controversial" issue "whether a court could suppress a confession solely because of unreasonable delay in presenting the defendant to the magistrate."[95] Weinfeld added another footnote explicitly declining to express an "opinion about the Southern District United States Attorney's practice," which, according to the judge, "involve[d] a policy decision as to judicial supervision of the administration of criminal practice in the Federal Courts" that "should be left for determination by higher authority."[96]

When the government sought the opinion of higher authority by filing a mandamus action against the judge, Been became "very nervous about the opinion" and "lost a great deal of sleep over the following weeks, worrying that I would be the infamous clerk who had worked on the first Weinfeld opinion to be reversed in no telling how many decades."[97] When the Second Circuit decided the case, it handed down an affirmance, on the ground that it had "no firm conviction that any of his [Weinfeld's] findings of fact were erroneous."[98] But the Court of Appeals "stopped short" of finding Giuliani's "practice inherently unconstitutional."[99]

Weinfeld's emphasis on facts remained in the forefront of his law clerks' minds long after they had left his chambers. Nearly a decade after completing his clerkship, Frank Tuerkheimer sent Weinfeld a brief on which he was working; in a detailed response, the judge queried, "Are you satisfied that the factual portrayal is objective? . . . Of course, if the facts are correct, it follows that . . . [the] conclusion is correct—but are the facts conceded?"[100] Tuerkheimer's successor, Dan Levitt, likewise reported to the judge how, as a law clerk to Justice Fortas in one case, he made a Weinfeldian study of the trial record and produced a memo—circulated to the Court—which turned the tide. Then we circulated a draft opinion (mostly mine), complete with record references, which built up such an overwhelming factual basis . . . that it converted three votes to nine. Almost none of the crucial facts were to be found in the Government's brief; indeed, I think they were deliberately omitted in an effort to force the Court to decide the broader question. But they were there in the record—where I was taught last year to find them.[101]

Ken Roth, a clerk from 1980–1981 who since has become executive director of Human Rights Watch, initially found it difficult to accept Weinfeld's teaching that "it was enough simply to state the facts and explain the obvious judgment they demanded." Arriving "from a Yale Law School education, steeped in theoretical analysis, policy debates and the skepticism of a confirmed legal realist," Roth found the notion that "the facts of a case spoke to a Natural Law—an inherent moral order" and that there "was no need for the kind of theoretical analysis that made judicial opinions candidates for law school texts" a "quaint anachronism." He thought that "only a man born of a simpler world, . . . before the moral ambiguity of the twentieth century had fully unfolded, could maintain such an unwavering ethical perspective." But two decades later, as a human rights advocate, Roth "appreciate[s] the sustaining value of the Weinfeld moral vision." Human Rights Watch, he notes, operates in "situations where, for all practical purposes, there is no law because the judiciary lacks the will, independence or power to restrain governmental encroachments on basic rights." Nonetheless,

> by investigating, documenting and exposing human rights abuses, we establish the facts of the case and expose them to public scrutiny. These facts have power—sufficient to restrain many a tyrant—not because of statute books, legal precedents or academic theories, but because they speak to a deeper and widely shared moral judgment. One does not need a refined legal education to know that murder, torture, censorship or discrimination are wrong. Most people worldwide share these basic moral judgments.

Thus, "exposure" of human rights violations has "work[ed] even in distant corners of the globe" to restrain tyrannical governments.[102]

Roth's observation requires that we pause, however, to examine what "the Weinfeld method"[103] can and cannot accomplish and how its capacities relate to the career paths in which his former clerks have succeeded. The judge's method of finding the facts and the comparable postmodern method of constructing narratives[104] constitute powerful means by which those who possess coherent ideologies can impose them on those who lack the ability, incentives, or resources to formulate alternatives. Recourse to facts and stories can smooth out the rough edges of a social order and keep it functioning in elegant fashion. But finding facts and constructing narratives cannot alone produce fundamental legal or social change.

Thus, Judge Weinfeld's recitation of the facts of the arraignment delay in *United States v. Toney*[105] left the Court of Appeals, which itself was without jurisdiction or incentive to reexamine the facts, without any "firm conviction that any of his findings of fact were erroneous."[106] But Weinfeld's opinion did not change the law or put a stop to Giuliani's "unprincipled and strategic"[107] practice. Likewise, Human Rights Watch has achieved invaluable success in restraining the behavior of petty tyrants who depend on Western support and cannot risk exposure in Western media. The People's Republic of China, on the other hand, feels free to ignore Human Rights Watch and the West. With its different "social system, ideology, historical tradition and cultural background," China pursues "different means and ways in realizing human rights and fundamental freedoms," with "top priority . . . be[ing] given to [the] right to subsistence and the right to development."[108] Thus, it continues, among other things, to persecute members of the Falun Gong sect for practicing their religious beliefs.[109]

Weinfeld's clerks, as we have seen above, have succeeded as law professors and public-interest lawyers. But their success, measured either in terms of the number of clerks entering teaching or public-interest practice or in terms of the prestige of the positions they hold in either field, is not extraordinary in comparison with the success that former clerks of many other judges have enjoyed. What is remarkable is that twenty-eight out of the thirty-five former Weinfeld clerks who have spent all or most of their careers in private practice either founded or became partners in major New York City or national law firms.

This 80 percent rate of successful big-firm practice may be unusual, but it is not fortuitous. By training his clerks to patiently and painstakingly construct facts into coherent narratives, Judge Weinfeld taught them a skill that the well-heeled clients of big firms need and for which they are able to pay. A lawyer who possesses the time, ability, and resources to structure facts at the outset of litigation or of the planning of a transaction typically will serve his or her client well; the combination of the skill imparted by Weinfeld to his clerks with the time available in big firms and the resources provided by their clients is a prescription for success.

Weinfeld also trained his clerks for success in private practice, and indeed, in all legal endeavors, by his "exacting standards and his extraordinary devotion to work"—by his "day-in and day-out dedication to the highest legal standard. . . . The Judge," according to Mark F. Pomerantz, "never took shortcuts. He read all the briefs. He read all the significant precedents. He gave every matter his utmost attention. And his personal professional standard was perfection." John G. Koeltl relates how, after Weinfeld had revised a draft opinion that Koeltl had turned in even though it still had problems, Koeltl tried to congratulate the judge by saying, "'I did what I could, but it was not quite right. You've solved these problems.' In my brashness, I beamed at the judge. The Judge responded, in one of the few cold comments I can recall in the course of the clerkship: 'Don't ever, ever let me do something that's not quite right.'"[110]

"The quest for perfection, day in and day out," was, according to Robert L. Plotz, "exhausting" and, "at least initially, intimidating." But, as a result, Plotz "learned not only the importance of thorough fact-finding but that there were no shortcuts in the process."[111] When Bob Litt left Weinfeld's chambers to clerk for Justice Stewart, he wrote the judge about how he "realize[d] the virtues of the training you put us through," because "unlike some of the others here I am painfully aware of the incompleteness of the memos I am doing. I keep expecting to have you buzz me and chide me for not being thorough enough."[112] After Steven Reisberg had left chambers to join a big firm, he likewise wrote the judge how he was "trying to represent our clients as best I can, and following your advice, that means 'doing my homework.'"[113]

Lessons about practicing law and solving legal problems, however, were only a part of Weinfeld's legacy to his law clerks. Of equal or greater importance is what he taught them about integrity and justice.

"Our first lesson" in justice, according to Kevin T. Baine, "was one of scrupulous fairness." Other clerks agreed. John Koeltl, for one, has taken note of Weinfeld's "joy in doing what was right and just and fair . . . in the context of what the law provided," while Chris Norall has written that "his lessons on how to go about trying to be fair had something to do with listening attentively, correcting for his own views and feelings, taking the necessary time (neither more nor less) to decide. The Judge was freer than most men of vanity, and he disciplined himself to be impartial."[114]

But more than merely fairness was involved. For Bruce Yannett, "the values you attempted to instill throughout the year . . . [were] honesty, fairness, patience, diligence, attention to detail, enthusiasm for the law, and compassion for those around you."[115] Robert W. Werner likewise came away from his year "with a sense of the integrity, honesty, and dedication that is so essential to a system of justice,"[116] while Eben Moglen "came fully to appreciate the role played by qualities of character in the doing of justice: patience, modesty, and capacity for making hard decisions without haste and without vacillation."[117] According to Frank M. Tuerkheimer, "there was nothing imperious about the judge," while Leonard Becker added that "far from treating lawyers with contempt or disrespect, Judge Weinfeld engaged them with a stern courtesy, tempered only by his intolerance for lack of preparation [and] his almost physical revulsion at sleazy or slippery litigators." "All who came before him," added Steven H. Reisberg, "were not simply equal, but each had an equal demand to be treated fairly, with dignity and respect, and have their case adjudicated with the same degree of care and concern."[118]

Alfred D. Youngwood similarly recognized Weinfeld's "care, his compassion, his love of the law and his understanding of the impact it had on society—individual by individual. The Judge, with all of his authority and all of his stature, treated everybody who appeared before him with respect and dignity."[119] He "never forg[o]t that we are ultimately dealing with people, not numbers or goods,"[120] and he "taught, by example, the rare qualities of graciousness, caring, humility, and generosity."[121] Weinfeld's "qualities of mind and heart," said another clerk, were "transmitted to your clerks day by day and hour by hour, as examples for a lifetime."[122]

At the end of her clerkship, Victoria Nourse left the judge an especially eloquent note about what she had learned. "Someone once said that it is only unreasonable men who become famous. Well, judge, you are famous, and you are unreasonable, unreasonable in the best of senses, in demanding of yourself what most of us are not willing to give."[123] After quoting a dissenting opinion of Jerome Frank to the effect that "all our complicated judicial apparatus yields but a human judgment,"[124] Nourse concluded, "I would trust a single 'human judgment' of yours, Judge, over a stack of Supreme Court cases and the opinion of a handful of law professors—and that is said by a born 'conceptualizer.'"[125]

Again, there is a need to pause. Judge Weinfeld surely possessed integrity and exhibited a powerful vision of justice, but it was a vision with which not everyone would agree. Stephen Suffern, who worked for Weinfeld in 1969–1970 and had a more "tense relationship with the Judge" than any other clerk, found Weinfeld's vision of justice "representative of the best in classical New Deal liberalism." He found the judge "tremendously tolerant and open minded" and a paragon of "equanimity in face of the chaos" spawned by black and anti–Vietnam War activism. Suffern recalls one incident where the judge declined to revoke the passport of an activist who had been charged with crime, even though he recognized that the activist might jump bail and flee the country. He also notes that Weinfeld did not object to "my continuing my anti-war activities" even while clerking.[126]

But Suffern is critical of Weinfeld for "not being open to new intellectual trends." "I tried," Suffern reports, "to push him toward new ideas, anti-war stuff, but he just wouldn't budge. I confronted him on his sentencing—that he let white collar people get away easier than poor people—and he refused to listen."[127] No doubt, Suffern is right about Weinfeld's rigidity. In a splendid memoir, the judge's daughter Fern, who, as we have seen, holds a Ph.D., teaches, and is a practicing psychologist, agrees that her father was "closed to change in general" and comments on his "reluctance to cross the boundaries of his known world" and his "inflexibility once he had internalized a belief." She adds that he "was so grounded in his beliefs about how a person should behave and conduct himself" that he could not "imagine alternative ways." In particular, as discussed earlier, Fern notes that her father never had read Freud and never had internalized any contemporary psychological values;[128] on the contrary, he commented to one correspondent on what he "regard[ed] as the errant [*sic*] nonsense of Freud."[129]

An example is provided by *United States v. Ferguson*,[130] the case analyzed above that entailed a motion by the defense that Weinfeld disqualify himself because a former law clerk, Mark F. Pomerantz, had given testimony in the government's favor. Because the judge's "relationship to Pomerantz" was "intimate" and his "esteem for him . . . high," the defense was concerned, even though Weinfeld had announced that Pomerantz's testimony would be excluded from the record, that it could "have a . . . subliminal influence." As we have seen, Weinfeld, with his negativity toward Freud, would have none of this argument. "The Court," he wrote, "does not doubt that it can bring to bear a disciplined mind" nor "that in fact it can hold the 'balance nice, clear and true.'"[131]

In the end, Weinfeld's "capacity for making hard decisions without haste and without vacillation"[132] was not unrelated to his "inflexibility" and "reluctance to cross the boundaries of his known world."[133] The very New Deal tolerance for disagreement that made it possible for Weinfeld to allow Steve Suffern to continue his antiwar activities precluded his accepting Suffern's ideology. The judge's patience, humility, generosity, and compassion made his "human judgment" more trustworthy than the judgments of most "conceptualizer[s],"[134] but his judgment nonetheless remained human, imperfect, and tied to a fixed and finite world view. Above all, as Steve Suffern has suggested, Weinfeld's jurisprudential view left little room for fundamental legal or social change—which made it a view that future partners in major law firms could comfortably absorb.

Whatever its shortcomings, Edward Weinfeld's vision of justice possessed a "magnetic pull, the power to entice others to dedicate themselves, most especially the clerks who were willing and able to throw themselves into and under his spell."[135] How can this magnetic pull be explained? The answer, it is submitted, is that Weinfeld not only preached his vision but lived it nobly as well. He was constant, as Victoria Nourse put it, "in demanding of [himself] what most . . . are not willing to give."[136] More than anything, the generosity he exhibited to his law clerks—sometimes bordering on impropriety—put them forever under his spell.

Weinfeld wrote countless letters of recommendation on behalf of clerks and former clerks who wanted to serve at the Supreme Court,[137] become law professors,[138] judges,[139] or other public officials,[140] or obtain some sort of public recognition.[141] He followed their careers with gratification[142] and was always available to discuss career issues and offer advice when asked.[143] The judge also used his old connections in the world of public housing to try to obtain an apartment in New York City housing for the grandmother of one former clerk,[144] and wrote Henry N. Ess, a partner in Sullivan and Cromwell, in order to provide the Cromwell Foundation with information it might find helpful in deciding whether to subsidize publication of a book by another former clerk.[145] He agreed to telephone Martin Lipton on behalf of a third former clerk, who was considering whether to leave academia and enter private practice.[146]

Weinfeld also provided personal financial assistance that helped one law clerk move to Washington to begin his Supreme Court clerkship.[147]

Most significant of all was the way Weinfeld treated the law clerks during their day-to-day labors in chambers. Before he would turn his own attention to a pending matter, his practice was to ask one of the clerks to write a memo or a draft opinion on the case. Once the memo or draft was completed, Weinfeld would write his own tentative disposition, without, however, reading what the clerk had done. Only after he had put his own thoughts into writing would he examine what the clerk had written. If they agreed on the essentials, they would then work together to combine and polish their two drafts.

Two clerks report a remarkably similar story, which undoubtedly reflects the experience of many others: "Only once," writes Mitchell A. Lowenthal, "do I recall a disagreement that was not promptly resolved. Each of us continued to draft divergent opinions. Ultimately, I persuaded him to change his view slightly, but even then he completely rewrote my draft, strengthening the arguments before he was done."[148] The present author had a similar experience with Weinfeld in connection with *United States ex rel. Elksnis v. Gilligan*,[149] where the judge initially hesitated to grant habeas corpus on Elksnis's behalf. Ultimately, he was persuaded, but once he was, he completely ignored the clerk's memos and drafted his brilliant opinion entirely by himself.[150]

Enormous ego gratification undoubtedly resulted for the young men and women like Mitchell Lowenthal who persuaded the legendary figure for whom they were working to change his view of a pending matter. But, along with the ego gratification, there came a powerful lesson—namely, that the judge could be persuaded to change his mind not by policy debate but only by hard work and an appeal to reasoned factual and doctrinal analysis. Subsumed within this lesson were Weinfeld's own deep-seated assumptions about law and justice—assumptions accepted by all the law clerks, except perhaps Stephen Suffern, largely without great thought.

This is not to say that Judge Weinfeld consciously toyed with the minds of his law clerks; as we have seen, he never thought about life in such a psychological fashion. He simply understood, as he wrote when he recommended Maurice Nessen for a judicial appointment, that "a top flight lawyer" was a person whose "preparation is thorough, [and] his analysis penetrating," with "the capacity to listen and to bring to bear an informed judgment on difficult matters."[151] The judge merely followed his own beliefs religiously and by doing so spread them to his clerks.

Weinfeld's vision of justice and generosity proved additionally compelling to his clerks because he never compromised it. The judge, as they all knew him, "never took shortcuts."[152] His refusal to compromise standards remained true even during the final months of his life, when he was suffering from terminal cancer. Less than two months before he collapsed while leaving the courthouse and was hospitalized, for instance, he received a lengthy letter from the prior year's clerk, who had only recently moved on to Justice Powell's chambers, in which the clerk described various happenings at the Supreme Court. As always, Weinfeld answered the letter in detail, without giving any indication of his declining state of health, even in the midst of a two-month trial of "about the most difficult criminal case I have ever tried."[153] "The Judge," as Philomena Burke, his last clerk has written, "was magnificent until the end, penning his last opinion a week before his passing."[154]

Burke's immediate predecessor, Dori Hanswirth, has written about Weinfeld's funeral, which occurred some two weeks before her wedding. "I felt," she writes,

> like I had lost a member of my own family. . . . His funeral was a very emotional event. By the end of the funeral day, I was physically and emotionally drained. When I arrived home that evening, in the mail was a wedding card and gift from the judge. The Judge had written a long and beautiful note about the meaning of marriage and all of the good wishes he had for us. He wrote the letter the day before he died. That a man in so much pain, so close to death could write such a life-affirming message showed me a level of human spirit and kindness that I did not think existed.[155]

No wonder that Edward Weinfeld possessed a "magnetic pull" over his law clerks, that he was able "to entice" them "to throw themselves into and under his spell,"[156] and that they thereby became remarkably successful lawyers in his image.

11

The Judge as Societal Advisor

This chapter examines the quasi-judicial and extrajudicial jobs of Edward Weinfeld following his appointment to the bench. These jobs ranged from the essentially judicial one of serving for a decade on the Multidistrict Litigation Panel to counseling friends with legal or legal-personal difficulties. The chapter begins with consideration of Weinfeld's work on the Multidistrict Panel. Next, it surveys his role as an advisor to his alma mater, New York University, through service on its board of trustees and as president of its Law Center Foundation. Then, it turns to his work as a member of both a judicial committee and a national commission deliberating reform of the nation's bankruptcy laws. Finally, it probes the various ways he assisted personal friends with problems.

Except for service as a member of the Bankruptcy Committee of the Judicial Conference and some instances of giving personal advice to friends, Weinfeld did not begin serving in his various advisory capacities until the late 1960s, when he had been on the bench for nearly two decades and was almost seventy years old. By that time, his ways as a judge had been firmly set. Indeed, by the late 1960s Weinfeld could not conceive of himself as anything but a judge.

As a result, Weinfeld brought to his quasi- and extrajudicial roles the mindset of a judge. He addressed the issues that came before him by reference to fixed standards and traditional ways of solving problems. Creativity and extended vision were not his strengths. Arguably, the best way to think about Weinfeld's various advisory roles is to understand that he brought to them the tunnel vision of a trial judge rather than the broad, inventive genius of a dynamic and enterprising political or corporate leader. His was a valuable, but therefore limited contribution.

His work on the Multidistrict Litigation Panel, which had been created by 1968 legislation giving it jurisdiction to consolidate before a single judge in a single district for pretrial purposes multiple actions containing common questions of fact,[1] was essentially judicial in nature. The panel consisted of seven circuit and district judges appointed by Chief Justice Earl Warren in May 1968 to serve for staggered one-, two-, or three-year terms. Weinfeld, who was one of the initial seven judges appointed to the panel, was to serve for a term of three years.[2]

Weinfeld, in fact, remained on the panel for more than ten years. During that time, he was "a tower of strength"[3] for the multidistrict body and participated actively in its deliberations.[4] Weinfeld's greatest contribution to the work of the panel arose out of his insistence that it function and be regarded as a court rather than a committee of the Judicial Conference. This insistence reflected both his greatest strength and simultaneously his greatest weakness: by the end of the 1960s, Weinfeld could address issues only in a judicial framework and had lost, if he had ever possessed, the capacity to think outside the judicial box. Serving in this judicial mode, Weinfeld undoubtedly played a leading part as the panel "built up a large body of law and worked out appropriate standards for the consolidation or coordination of cases having common issues of fact."[5] The panel thereby gained stature and the kind of broad acceptability that courts possess as a result of the legal community's faith that, through law, courts will do justice. But, at the same time, the multidistrict body must have lost some of the flexibility and opportunity to impose creative solutions that it might have possessed if it had functioned less judicially and more as an informal committee.

The decision, made by Weinfeld and the other judges who served initially on the Multidistrict Litigation Panel, to launch the body in a judicial direction was not without controversy. It was connected, in turn, to another controversial issue—the length of its judges' tenure. Section 1407 of the Judicial Code, which was the legislation creating the panel, did not specify the tenure of the judges; it provided only that they would be appointed by the chief justice and that no two members of the body could be from the same judicial circuit. When Earl Warren appointed Weinfeld and the other initial judges on the panel, he clearly contemplated that no one would serve for more than three years.[6] However, when Warren Berger replaced Earl Warren as chief justice in 1969, he appeared to change the policy when he refused to accept resignations from panel members, telling them "that the Panel was doing a good job and to hang on."[7]

Chief Justice Burger later claimed he was unaware of the three-year limitation that Chief Justice Warren had placed on panel membership, and accordingly he decided in 1976 to rotate existing members off and to appoint new ones. Indeed, he confessed that he "could be fairly accused of 'gross negligence' for my lack of attention to the subject" and for his failure to "to acquaint myself with the history of the Panel."[8] Weinfeld did not dispute this confession, but he did disagree with the chief justice's view that the sitting judges on the Multidistrict Litigation Panel should be replaced.

Along with John Minor Wisdom, the presiding judge of the Multidistrict Litigation Panel, Weinfeld met personally with Chief Justice Berger and "expressed the unanimous view of the Panel that it was a court and would function more effectively if rotation came about by attrition rather than by treating the Panel as a committee with a membership subject to frequent change." Weinfeld and Wisdom "felt pretty good when" they left their "meeting with the Chief Justice" and believed that the "problem is primarily one of communication."[9] In the end, however, Weinfeld and Wisdom, on the one hand, and Berger, on the other, disagreed about the tenure of judges on the Multidistrict Panel and perhaps about the panel's nature itself, and Berger determined that Weinfeld and his colleagues should be rotated off and replaced with new blood.

Weinfeld, however, resisted and refused to grant the chief justice either an easy or a gracious resignation. Instead, he forced the chief to proceed slowly and by indirection. Over the course of a year, Berger placed pressure on Judge Wisdom to resign and, upon receiving his resignation in October 1978,[10] wrote back, with great solicitude: "I am glad to see that you have decided to relinquish the chairmanship of the Judicial Panel on Multidistrict Litigation since, as I expressed to you a year ago, I have felt that you were carrying too heavy a burden."[11] Berger next appointed Judge Murray Gurfein of the Second Circuit Court of Appeals as the new presiding judge of the Multidistrict Panel, following which he wrote Weinfeld:

As you may know, Judge Wisdom has asked to be relieved of his duties as Chairman of the Judicial Panel on Multidistrict Litigation. I have asked Judge Murray Gurfein of the Court of Appeals for the Second Circuit to take over the duties of chairman. Since the statute precludes more than one member of the panel from the same circuit this will, unfortunately, require the termination of your services as a member of the panel. In view of your long service as a member I assume that you will in a sense be relieved to be able to step down. I do want you to know, however, of my sincere appreciation for your dedicated efforts to the work of the Judicial Panel on Multidistrict Litigation.

Weinfeld, of course, had no choice but to yield to the chief justice's power, but he could let Berger and others know his true feelings. In an utterly frigid, albeit proper, letter, he informed the chief, "I think you made an excellent choice in the appointment of Judge Murray Gurfein to serve as Chairman of the Judicial Panel on Multidistrict Litigation. He is a worthy successor to a worthy predecessor."[12] Weinfeld said nothing else; in particular, he offered no acknowledgment of his resignation. The only other thing he did was to enclose the Chief Justice's correspondence with judges Gurfein, Wisdom, and himself, with the following cover memorandum to his colleagues on the Multidistrict Panel: "I enclose correspondence which is self explanatory. I think all of you know how much I enjoyed our relationship and working with you."[13] With that, Weinfeld's decade of extra service on the multidistrict court was sadly over.

In that decade of service, as I have already suggested, Weinfeld displayed many of his defining personal and professional characteristics. The most important was his unremitting socialization as a judge: he could conceive of the assignment of the Multidistrict Litigation Panel and of his own role on the panel only in judicial terms. This meant finding the facts and applying the law to the facts as his conscience commanded; it included the filing of dissents[14] and other separate opinions[15]—at times, even lone dissents[16]—rather than striving for a consensus aimed at maintaining easy working relations among panel members and at solving and avoiding problems. Weinfeld never compromised or "placed personal loyalty above principle and integrity."[17] He also manifested a sort of obduracy when he refused to yield graciously to the chief justice's desire that he resign. Finally, he demonstrated his lawyerly skills in his dispute with Berger, when he mailed correspondence to fellow judges revealing how the chief justice had pressured members of the multidistrict body into resigning contrary to their own better judgment.

Weinfeld behaved similarly when he served on the board of trustees of New York University and as president of its Law Center Foundation. He was first elected to the Law Center Foundation in 1967 and was chosen as president in 1973; he joined the university's board of trustees in 1975.[18] As a member of the university's two boards, Weinfeld always prepared thoroughly and meticulously and exercised careful judgment on the matters brought to his attention, even at the level of correcting errors in minutes of meetings.[19] During his time as president of the Law Center Foundation, "[n]o major decision was made without his careful study, advice and approval."[20]

Nevertheless, the minutes of board meetings show that Weinfeld was not an initiator; he waited for the president of the university or the dean of the law school to seek his views, whereupon he gave them. In this respect, he acted in a familiar judicial mode of letting others formulate issues and then responding to them.

He never proposed or otherwise initiated creative new policies, and only once did he support such a policy—when a former law clerk proposed that the law school use some of the money from the Mueller sale, discussed below, to found a research center modeled after the old Johns Hopkins Institute of the 1930s.[21] But Weinfeld was never a "passive"[22] board member. He had no difficulty disagreeing with administration proposals and presenting his own divergent views when he thought them right. On one occasion, for instance, his opposition to the law school's purchase of land for construction of a new dormitory almost halted the project. Weinfeld thought the price for the land was too high and that the law school could not afford to pay it. He relented only when the president of the university promised that, if the price could not be lowered, the university would pay the difference between the price to which Weinfeld was willing to agree and the price that had to be paid.[23]

By far, Weinfeld's most important task as a university trustee and as president of the law school's board arose out of the sale of the C. F. Mueller Company for over $100 million and the division of the proceeds of the sale between the law school and the university. Weinfeld's role in these complex transactions, again, was not that of an initiator. But he was kept fully informed of ongoing negotiations, and no decisions were made or actions taken without his approval.[24] Throughout the negotiations, he "was always a loyal and forceful representative of the law school community, but he insisted that the Law School's position be fair and fully cognizant of its role in the larger community." He set "an example of how to fulfill fiduciary responsibilities to the Law School and to the University without sacrificing the interests of either."[25]

There was still more of the same from Weinfeld in his years on the Bankruptcy Administration Committee of the Federal Judicial Conference and on a statutorily created national commission to revise the bankruptcy laws. He began his service on the Bankruptcy Committee in 1956 and became its chairman in 1967. Then, in 1971, he was appointed a member of the Commission on the Bankruptcy Laws of the United States, which had been created by act of Congress in order to study and propose revisions to the bankruptcy laws. On that commission, he served with members of Congress, judges, and prominent bankruptcy lawyers. Finally, in 1977, he was asked to serve as a member of the Judicial Conference's Ad Hoc Committee on Bankruptcy Legislation.[26] Thus, by the time Congress enacted a new bankruptcy statute in 1977, Weinfeld had about as much expertise in bankruptcy law as a federal judge could possibly have.

From the moment he first began publicly to address bankruptcy issues, he did so from the perspective of a judge and in the interests of his fellow judges. In July 1968, only eight months after he had become chairman of the Judicial Conference's Bankruptcy Committee, Weinfeld testified before Congress about a proposal to establish a commission to recommend changes in bankruptcy law. After testifying in favor of giving the commission a broad rather than a narrow mandate to study possible changes in bankruptcy, Weinfeld addressed the issue of the makeup of the commission. One proposal was that the commission consist of two Senators, two members of the House of Representatives, three referees in bankruptcy, and three businesspeople. Weinfeld, on behalf of the Judicial Conference, instead urged that the commission contain three members appointed by the president, two appointed by the chief justice of the United States, and two each from the Senate and the House.[27]

In recommending the different makeup, Weinfeld was striving to place Article III judges rather than businesspeople and bankruptcy referees on the commission. He gave two reasons for his proposal. One was that "men who have so-called expertise judgment" should be called as witnesses by the commission rather than being given decision-making power. He continued,

> You must bear in mind that the experts have points of view reflecting at times their separate interest—I don't mean this special interest in any invidious sense—but men sometimes become wedded to their particular ideas. It would seem to me that . . . in the determination of . . . broadgaged [*sic*] policies, the Commission would necessarily call in men of varying points of view from the bar, from the credit associations, and call upon referees to give their points of view.

At the opposite extreme, Weinfeld opposed "the inclusion of men who were beyond the immediate day-by-day activity" and thus "might have [only] theoretical concepts" to offer during the deliberations of the commission. The right people for the commission, according to Weinfeld, were "judges[,] [who] were far more experienced, understanding the problems" that occurred in bankruptcy, since they regularly reviewed the decisions of referees, while at the same time they were not tied to the narrow perspectives that referees typically held.[28]

It is important to appreciate how Weinfeld's testimony to Congress reflected his view of judging. The most important quality of a judge, according to Weinfeld, was disinterestedness; because judges of general jurisdiction dealt with myriad problems, they did not have preconceived views that would get in the way of dispassionate analysis. The second essential quality of a judge was rootedness; judicial analysis was grounded in the specific facts and specific circumstances of specific problems and did not evaporate into the ether of theoretical speculation. In arguing for the presence of judges on a commission to study reform of the bankruptcy laws, Weinfeld was making a claim about the importance of disinterested, rooted analysis in the law-making process and about the unique capacity of judges to engage in such analysis.

Congress accepted Weinfeld's argument and structured the membership of the bankruptcy commission as he proposed. The chief justice thereupon appointed Weinfeld to the commission.

As a member of the commission, Weinfeld saw no reason to stop thinking like a judge; indeed, he had argued that people like him should serve on the commission so that it would have the benefit of judicial thinking. Thinking like a judge, however, profoundly limited the contribution Weinfeld could make. First, it meant that he could not bring to analysis of bankruptcy code reform the creative, theoretical insights of the academics, practicing attorneys, and even congresspeople with whom he worked. Second, his judicial perspective blinded him to the fact that judges are not always dispassionate arbiters; even they can "become wedded to their particular ideas"[29] when their interests are sufficiently threatened. Thus, on one issue Weinfeld would end up standing, initially alone, representing what appeared to be essentially the partisan interests of federal district judges.

The issue involved the office of bankruptcy referee. Under the Bankruptcy Act of 1898, the first federal bankruptcy law to become permanent, jurisdiction of bankruptcy cases lay in the district court. As the number of bankruptcy filings increased during the first two-thirds of the twentieth century, district judges were authorized to appoint referees in bankruptcy, who served for a term of years and were assigned the task of assisting the judges in the administration of bankruptcy cases.[30] By the late 1960s, however, concerns were growing about the efficacy of this system. Some urged that the office of bankruptcy referee was "a step child . . . without prestige and ordinarily [did] not attract highly qualified attorneys to accept appointment to the bench," since the "best lawyers [did] not want to be assistants to district judges." Attorneys who practiced before the referees complained that, since "the appointing judge" in many districts was "also the judge who review[ed] the referee's orders and judgments," it was sometimes the case "that the relationship between the judge and referee compromise[d] the possibility of obtaining an independent review of the referee's rulings." In sum, many reformers felt a "pressing" need "for an independent, prestigious bankruptcy court with broad jurisdiction and powers."[31]

Accordingly, proposals were advanced to transform bankruptcy referees into bankruptcy judges, appointed by the president and confirmed by the Senate. Some proposed that the new judges be given Article III status, with life tenure, although others proposed the bankruptcy courts should be legislative or Article I courts, with judicial tenure for a term of years. Under both schemes, however, appeal would lie directly to the circuit courts of appeal rather than to the district courts.

Weinfeld disagreed. Thus, when he read one memo arguing that able attorneys did not seek appointment to the office of bankruptcy referee because the office lacked prestige, he wrote in the margin, "Not so." Similarly, during discussions in the Bankruptcy Commission on whether to create a new Article I or Article III bankruptcy court, Weinfeld was explicit. He

> felt that there was no need to restructure the court. He did not agree with the reasons being advanced to support the change, and accordingly he would abide by his earlier decision that the referees should remain as part of the United States district courts.[32]

And, when the Bankruptcy Commission recommended that Congress create new bankruptcy courts independent of the district courts, Weinfeld took the very unusual step of publishing a separate statement dissenting from the commission's recommendation.

Weinfeld's dissent was a factually grounded, tightly reasoned document. In it, he wrote,

> A principal reason advanced for establishing an independent court structure is that it will correct alleged deficiencies in the present system. Generally, the majority accepts the view that attorneys who specialize in bankruptcy law and appear regularly before referees, as well as trustees who receive their appointments from referees, refrain from filing petitions for review from referees' orders because of fear of reprisal by referees. This assumption is without factual support. The majority also accepts the view that the relationship between the referee and a reviewing district court judge tends to undermine the integrity of the judicial process; that a district court judge is unlikely to reverse an appointee and so reviews or appeals are discouraged. This premise, based upon "impression or belief," [footnote omitted] again is groundless and improperly gives credibility to an argument that a United States District Judge will render decisions on review based on his relationship to the referee whose decision is under review rather than on the merits of the issues before him. The assumption has as little force to it as would a claim that the court of appeals would hesitate to reverse a district court judge because he was known to the members of the panel. . . .
>
> I do not believe, based on my experience in my own busy metropolitan district, which has seven full-time referees, that attorneys are supine or that any reputable attorney would forebear to file what he considered a meritorious review of a referee's order for fear of incurring a referee's displeasure. Equally groundless are the assumptions which attribute to referees and judges lack of impartiality based on the present method of appointment.

Weinfeld then went on to correct "[a] basic erroneous assumption . . . that the referee is appointed by the judge." He explained that "[u]nder section 34 of the Bankruptcy Act appointments of referees are made by concurrence of a majority of the judges of the court," not by the individual judge who would hear a particular appeal. Accordingly, Weinfeld concluded that the "referee system has worked well and efficiently through the years and I find no justifiable reason for a change which would add another tier of judges to the federal judicial system."[33]

Even though Weinfeld clearly was a "distinguished" and arguably "the most knowledgeable member" of the Bankruptcy Commission, his dissent did not carry the day. In part, that was because Weinfeld's dissent read like "a judicial opinion sustaining [his] position" rather than "a clear statement capable of being understood by a Congressman or a Senator" who "probably shudder[ed] at the thought of getting mixed up in bankruptcy laws" and thus was eager to defer to a "'good old boy' congressional scenario" that would treat the commission as having "made a detailed study of the solution; it's noncontroversial, so we'll go along with it."[34]

Like most Weinfeld opinions, his dissent began with a broadly shared major premise—that absent good cause the law should not be altered. He next turned, as he invariably did, to the facts in order to rebut claims that the bankruptcy system required alteration because it was operating unfairly or inefficiently. But here Weinfeld faced a problem—namely, that the facts were in dispute and that he did not have the jurisdiction that he typically possessed as a trial judge to adjudicate the dispute.

Moreover, Weinfeld never made a clear statement addressing the real issue in the controversy over the proper status for bankruptcy judges. Perhaps he never perceived the issue clearly, although he must have felt it instinctively. The issue, as his friend James L. Oakes, a judge on the Second Circuit Court of Appeals, expressed it, was that appointment of bankruptcy judges by the president "serve[d] to denigrate the authority of United States District Judges."[35] The policy issue, which congresspeople and senators clearly could have comprehended, was whether to enhance the position of bankruptcy judges at the expense of lowering the status of district judges. Weinfeld, however, never identified this issue, and, of course, he offered no arguments in support of preserving the status of his court. His decades of experience on the trial bench had not prepared him to take such an approach.

Thus, we can understand that Weinfeld failed in his efforts to persuade Congress not to undermine the status of district judges because, in arguing his case, he could not escape the mentality of a district judge. Indeed, he did not even try to escape that mentality. There remains a question, though, of whether he should have tried. Perhaps, Weinfeld understood that he had been invited, as a member of the Bankruptcy Commission, to draft new bankruptcy legislation because Congress wanted a judicial perspective on the commission and thus that his duty, as a commission member, was to act judicially. In this view, it was more important to play his role judiciously than to take every available step to win. Put differently, Weinfeld may have thought, however wrongly, that the best way to persuade Congress to protect the district court bench was by demonstrating how outstanding district judges behave and by hoping that Congress could appreciate the value of encouraging such behavior.

In addition to serving on the Multidistrict Panel, acting as a fiduciary for NYU, and participating in the redrafting of the bankruptcy laws, Edward Weinfeld performed numerous advisory and service functions for fellow judges, former clients, family members, and friends.

On some occasions, he acted in a quasi-official capacity, as when Chief Judge Lloyd MacMahon of the Southern District asked for his views on Chief Justice Warren Berger's proposal "that cases of exceptional length and difficulty [be] assigned to an effective judge." Responding in a fashion typically protective of the judiciary and of the judicial function as he had long understood it, Weinfeld wrote,

> I am of the view that the proposal . . . has the potential of further erosion of the independence of the judiciary and contains within it the seeds of dissension among judges who serve within a particular district. . . . Each judge of this court . . . has a certificate signed by the President of the United States which states he was nominated by the President and, with the advice and consent of the Senate, appointed because of his or her wisdom, uprightness and learning.
>
> Each judge must be deemed competent to handle any case and effectively, whatever its nature or ramification. . . . The fact that some judges may be more efficient than others does not mean that they decide cases with greater judicial acumen than their peers.[36]

Weinfeld also performed other sorts of quasi-official duties. For example, he spoke at a luncheon to lawyers on the staff of the United States attorney, who "were particularly delighted to have a chance to see the human side of a member of the bench they have admired from afar." And, he allowed his name to be used as a reference by candidates for the district court bench, such as Pierre Leval, who thanked Weinfeld and acknowledged "that your good opinion will carry great weight."[37]

Weinfeld routinely served as an advisor for his fellow judges. They were constantly seeking his advice about the substance of the law; in particular, they regularly borrowed his old jury charges and adapted them to their own cases.[38] They also turned to Weinfeld with their ethical dilemmas. For example, Judge Irving Ben Cooper sought Weinfeld's advice in connection with publication of an article that declared, "Law clerks, lawyers, even other judges roll their eyes when the subject of Judge Cooper's 'judicial temperament' comes up."[39] Another judge, Samuel M. Rosenstein, who had taken senior status but wanted to continue sitting in districts that needed help, sought Weinfeld's intervention upon learning that Chief Justice Berger was blocking his assignment to those districts; Weinfeld responded that he "hope[d]" Rosenstein would "understand" that "there are considerations which preclude my taking any action."[40] Henry Friendly put the matter most succinctly, in print, when he declared, "When I have occasionally been confronted with a problem on which I felt the need for objective advice, Judge Weinfeld was usually the first to whom I turned; after he had spoken, there was generally no need to consult anyone else."[41]

Then, there was advice and assistance to former clients and friends. A note from Irving Felt, for instance, thanked Weinfeld for his "warm and wise advice to me when I needed the timely, personal help and understanding you provided."[42] He discussed with his friend Burt Zorn, apparently at some length, the application of Zorn's son to avoid military service in Vietnam on grounds of being a conscientious objector.[43] And, there was the request from a former secretary for help in finding a lawyer who could draft her will.[44]

Weinfeld was especially solicitous of young people entering the legal profession. At the request of an old friend,[45] Weinfeld met with the friend's son to discuss the son's plans to attend law school and to introduce him to a former law clerk then on the Yale Law School faculty.[46] For many years, Weinfeld met in his chambers with a group of NYU law students during the week of their orientation.[47] And, he wrote countless letters of recommendation on behalf of children of family and friends seeking admission to law school.[48]

Throughout all these activities, Weinfeld adhered to a fine line and abided by the proprieties demanded of a judge. In writing a letter of recommendation urging the admission of a relative's son to NYU Law School, he made it clear that he had not "had an intimate acquaintanceship with him" and could not comment on his academic record; he attested only that his father's "prideful references to his son indicate that he is a serious and dedicated student," that "his intellectual curiosity is broad-gauged," and that his "family life has been exemplary."[49] Similarly, when a former client called Weinfeld's attention to the difficulty that one of his relatives was having obtaining an immigrant visa to the United States, apparently because her brother had been a member of the

Communist Party of Brazil, Weinfeld spoke with family members and obtained additional information from them.[50] When the visa finally was issued, he wrote a note stating, "I was delighted to hear the news" and "hope you are all relaxed."[51] But there is no evidence that he ever intervened with the Immigration and Naturalization Service. And, when a distant relative asked him to intervene on his behalf in a civil service matter connected with his post office employment, Weinfeld wrote back that the relative should "appreciate that I am in no position to take any action relative to your request."[52]

Thus, Edward Weinfeld's quasi-judicial and extrajudicial activities were of a piece with his work as a judge and his career as a lawyer before he became a judge. He worked especially hard and paid close attention to facts. He used language carefully, effectively, and, when he wanted, eloquently. He avoided creative artistry and cautiously trod well-worn paths. He always paid attention to ethical proprieties and the demands of etiquette, although he never hesitated to speak out and express his own viewpoint, however unpopular it might be. And, he was loyal to the institutions and individuals he was helping, even to the extent, perhaps, of permitting his loyalties to get the better of his disinterestedness, as in the instance of his work at the Bankruptcy Commission on behalf of district judges. But Weinfeld never let his loyalties, or anything else for that matter, trump principle or "'let [him] do something that [was] not . . . right.'"

12

The Blessings and
Tribulations of Age

Approximately every decade, profound changes had occurred in Edward Weinfeld's life. In his early teens, he had left the confines of home and the Lower East Side and entered the mainstream of Manhattan life at DeWitt Clinton High School. In his early twenties, he had begun the practice of law, and a decade later, just a few months shy of his thirtieth birthday, he had married and begun a family. Several years thereafter, in his late thirties, he had assumed public office, and the decade after that, at the age of forty-nine, he had ascended the federal bench. Thereafter, Weinfeld remained a United States district judge and he and his family prospered. Nonetheless, change continued.

The next stage in Weinfeld's life began some two months after his sixtieth birthday, with the loss of a dear friend, and then a month later, with his first serious illness. I shall address the illness first.

Weinfeld was attending the Second Circuit Judicial Conference when he became ill and had to be taken back to New York City for emergency surgery.[1] Until that time, Weinfeld had enjoyed extraordinarily good health. Unlike many men of his time, he watched his caloric intake and exercised religiously through walking, swimming, and tennis. But like many other successful professionals, he also abused his body—he worked too hard, failed to get sufficient sleep, and, arguably, imbibed more cups of coffee and double martinis than doctors recommend. For the first sixty years of his life, he nonetheless continued to live as he had throughout his youth, with no untoward consequences. Time inevitably takes its toll, however, and as he passed through the decade of his sixties, Edward Weinfeld lost his youth. Age brought health problems—for him and for Lillian Weinfeld—but, remarkably, he fought them and overcame

208 | *The Blessings and Tribulations of Age*

them. Weinfeld accepted his declining health, made the necessary personal adjustments, and went on with his life and career. Above all, he never let health problems diminish his concern for others or his faith that he could make their lives better.

Another aspect of growing older did, however, depress him. Beginning with the deaths of Learned Hand and Herbert Lehman in the early 1960s and ending with the suicide of Henry Friendly shortly before he himself died, Weinfeld lost nearly all his lifetime friends. These losses caused him grief, although at first he was able to contain it. But ultimately, like nothing else in his life, the loss of nearly all his friends left him depressed.

At the same time, though, age had its rewards, chiefly in the form of honors and recognition. During his thirty-seven years on the federal bench, Weinfeld received virtually every honor available to a judge, and by the end of his career, he had attained a unique level of respect and recognition. He clearly appreciated the honors he received and the fame that came with them. By the time he died, he was able to know something of which few mortals can be certain—that he had performed his life's work successfully and that everyone who had been watching knew of his success.

His first three awards came from his alma mater, New York University, in the form of a Presidential Citation in 1965, an Alumni Meritorious Service Award in 1966, and an honorary Doctor of Laws in 1970. NYU also would honor him in later years by publishing a special issue of the *Law Review* in his twenty-fifth year on the bench, by dedicating an issue of the *Annual Survey of American Law* to him, by constructing a seminar room in his memory, and lastly by creating a chaired professorship in his name.[2]

Other honors began in 1973, when he received the Learned Hand Medal. Then, in 1977 he was given the Herbert Lincoln Harley Award of the American Judicature Society "for providing throughout his career on the bench an impeccable model of judicial conduct, temperament and decisiveness." In 1981 he received the Samuel E. Gates Award of the American College of Trial Lawyers for his "contribution to the improvement of the litigation process" and in 1984, the Fordham-Stein Award for his "professional integrity and leadership." Among the honors in the last three years of his life were a Medal for Outstanding Service to Law from the Riot Relief Fund, an honorary membership in the Association of the Bar of the City of New York, the Gold Medal Award from the New York State Bar Association, and the LaGuardia Medal from the City of New York.[3]

But the greatest tribute to Weinfeld was an article about him in the *New York Times* in recognition of his thirty-fifth anniversary on the bench. The article noted that Weinfeld was "routinely showered with . . . praise" and "likened to New York's other noted 20th-century jurists, Benjamin Cardozo and Learned Hand." The article added that "[f]ellow jurists regularly seek his counsel," that "appellate courts rarely reverse him," and that the "United States Supreme Court often mentions Judge Weinfeld by name, a rare tribute for a trial judge." It also quoted Justice William J. Brennan, who called Weinfeld "'a day-by-day living example of what we want our judges to be.'" What had especially distinguished Weinfeld's career, according to Brennan, was "'the purity of its devotion and its quiet dedication to the business of judging.'"4

Before this stream of awards began, however, other signs of the aging process had materialized. First came the death in August 1961 of a friend and colleague of a decade, Learned Hand. Hand, of course, was something of a father figure to Weinfeld; he was Weinfeld's elder by some twenty-nine years. Hand was also eighty-nine years old when he died. Hence Weinfeld did not react to his death as he might have reacted to the death of one of his own contemporaries closer to him in age. Nonetheless, Hand's death deprived Weinfeld of a close friend. As Weinfeld wrote to Frances Hand, "a friendship was born" on the very first occasion when he met Learned Hand, and thereafter they regularly had lunch together every Saturday. Weinfeld concluded that on those occasions he had "enjoyed the rich pleasure of his [Hand's] company and great intellect" and that "[t]he warmth of his friendship shall always remain a treasured memory." Mrs. Hand responded, "I know how much B [Learned Hand] thought of you."5

Within weeks of Judge Hand's death, Weinfeld underwent his first surgery. It was only the beginning of his health difficulties that fall. As he wrote to a friend some six weeks later in mid-October, it was only a week since he had "returned home after that long and unanticipated, protracted siege at the hospital." He had "hardly expected (and neither did the doctors) when I entered [the hospital] that I would have to undergo a second major operation." Although that was now "all behind" him, he still had "a long way to go before I reach normalcy" and was "anemic and run-down." Eight days later Weinfeld was still complaining to the same friend that he was "still at home; progress has been somewhat slow and I am trying very hard to be patient" and "hop[ing] I will be permitted to go to chambers for several hours a day." Two weeks later, Weinfeld reported that his "rate of progress" still "was quite slow," but he had accepted the fact that he would not be permitted to return to the courthouse for another month.[6]

Ultimately Weinfeld did make continued progress and recover fully, but untoward events continued to strike. Two years later, on December 5, 1963, the most important friendship of Weinfeld's life ended with the death of Herbert H. Lehman, the former governor and senator who had appointed Weinfeld to statewide office and later procured his appointment to the federal bench. Lehman, like Hand, was older than Weinfeld—in this instance, some twenty-three years older—and by the time of Lehman's death at the age of eighty-five his relationship to Weinfeld had become very much one of a surrogate father. Lehman's death, like Hand's, was thus in the nature of life, and Weinfeld accepted it as such. Nonetheless, Weinfeld was "saddened . . . very much" since Lehman "was a truly wonderful man" with whom Weinfeld had developed a very close relationship—they "talked . . . at least two or three times a week." Indeed, Weinfeld had telephoned Lehman merely "a half hour before he passed away," and "[t]he startling suddenness of his passing made the news the more shocking." At the same time, he "was deeply touched that Mrs. Lehman asked me to deliver the eulogy, but greatly concerned whether I would measure up and say in a simple way what we all felt about this warm and gentle friend of impeccable integrity."[7]

In the eulogy, delivered before an assemblage including President Lyndon Johnson and Chief Justice Earl Warren,[8] Weinfeld's first goal was to do justice to the reputation of his late friend, and he accordingly focused his remarks mainly on Lehman's public career. But he also made his tribute "personal" by hinting at what Lehman had meant to him. Thus, Weinfeld began the eulogy by referring to the "need within ourselves to commune with all the people he loved and who loved him—and to share our sense of loss which is so great," and he continued by pointing to the "warmth of the friendship of the Governor," who always found time to "share the joy or, if the occasion required, to express the sorrow and sympathy of a friend." And, he ended with an eloquent testament of how Lehman's lifetime of accomplishment enabled him to accept his death: "Because of him and his achievements, the world is a better place in which to live. This shall be a comfort to his family and friends. Herbert Lehman is forever enshrined in our hearts."[9]

With his own first serious illness and the deaths of his two close, elderly friends, Weinfeld had begun learning how to face the the limitations of life and the inevitability of death. Although Weinfeld would never let illness or other weakness interfere with the duty he owed others to perform his judicial tasks at his best, resignation and acceptance of whatever fate had in store had begun to replace ambition and efforts to control the course of events. Of course, acceptance had been made somewhat easier by the benignity of fate: Weinfeld had enjoyed excellent health for sixty years, his first illness was neither life-threatening nor permanently debilitating, and his two friends had lived long and full lives that they had used to create magnificent functional and aesthetic legacies.

The next untoward event, however, seemed somewhat less fair. Less than a year after Herbert Lehman's death, Sol Sklar, a long-time friend of Weinfeld who was one year younger, died of cancer. At his funeral, Weinfeld spoke on behalf "of Sol's lifetime friends—those who knew him in the days of his youth, at college, at law school, in professional life and communal affairs." He praised Sklar as someone who "was able to bring all the warmth, color, understanding and compassion of the family lawyer into his relationship with his business clients." But above all, Weinfeld, talking "as an intimate friend" of Sklar who could "presume to speak his thoughts," emphasized the need, even when death seemed premature and unfair, to "accept final judgment with understanding."[10]

Only a year passed before trouble struck even closer to home. After a difficult autumn of 1965, in which Weinfeld had been seeking but failed to receive an appointment to the Second Circuit Court of Appeals, Mrs. Weinfeld became ill over the winter of 1965–1966 with a mysterious lung ailment. Fearing cancer, her doctors ordered her hospitalized for tests that for some time proved inconclusive. Finally, after performing exploratory surgery, the doctors concluded that she did not have cancer, but she still had to recover from the surgery before being permitted to return home. In all, she underwent several weeks of hospitalization, which produced a major scare in the Weinfeld family, even though in the end all was well.[11]

Annual troubles continued. On February 1, 1967, exactly a year after Mrs. Weinfeld's hospitalization, Weinfeld delivered a eulogy for Hilda Altschul Master, the sister of Edith Lehman. Hilda Master was not a public figure, and thus Weinfeld's eulogy had to focus on her private virtues. Naturally, he reported on his own values as much as Hilda's in observing that, although "[s]ome say the world is a kind of jungle," Hilda "made it a place of peace" and "protected those she loved from the harsh realities of life." "She believed that Happiness is the only good; Reason the only torch; Justice the only worship; Humanity the only religion."[12]

The next February was more difficult, when a close friend of nearly half a century, Burt Zorn, died of cancer at the age of sixty-three. "[H]is passing," as Weinfeld wrote to another friend, was "a crushing blow—somehow it has hit me more than the passing of other close friends."[13] Although it was "hard" for Weinfeld "to stand before his poor, stilled body—before all who loved him—had worked or played with him—and try to speak calmly about him," he agreed to give Zorn's eulogy. Publicly, Weinfeld emphasized that Zorn had "had a full life; had a wonderful family and shared great friendships"; and "even had fun in the midst of a busy life." "[W]hat more," Weinfeld added, "can one ask?" For, as Weinfeld responded, "The measure of a man's life is not his calendar years, but the life he lived and shared with others, and the contribution he made to his time."[14]

But bleaker ideas had crossed Weinfeld's mind. In a draft of the eulogy, after giving expression to the ideas just quoted that remained in the public version, Weinfeld added, "And yet as we understand that, we still cannot accept his passing without that sense of loss." Moreover, in speaking of Zorn's friends, Weinfeld's rough draft observed that "each was the fuller for having known him; each is the lesser for his passing."[15] We can never know why Weinfeld omitted these bleaker thoughts from his public statement. Perhaps, the aim of his omission was to make the funeral service easier for Zorn's family and even himself to bear.

Death kept coming, and when, on December 17, 1969, Weinfeld spoke at the memorial service at the federal courthouse for his late colleague William B. Herlands, the bleakness that had remained secreted in the rough draft of the Zorn eulogy emerged. On this occasion, Weinfeld took note of "the decree of fate [that had] cut short his [Herlands's] stay with us." Of course, Weinfeld then ended on a more upbeat note, taking stock of all that Herlands had accomplished as a judge and asking, "What more can one who labored in the judicial vineyard ask at the end of his life's journey?"[16]

Fifteen months later, another friend, James Felt, who was two years younger than Weinfeld, died, and Weinfeld found himself delivering yet another eulogy for one of his peers. Of course, the eulogy for Felt contained the usual catalogue of his accomplishments, followed by the question, "What more can one ask?" After the obvious answer that nothing more could be asked, Weinfeld continued, "Nonetheless, we are here to pay our respects to our dear friend," and he continued with the observation that, when a friend "passes on, . . . our lives are diminished—that each, perhaps in a different way, suffers a personal loss."[17]

In short, as his friends kept dying around him, Weinfeld's perspective on death slowly began to change. He became more ready to express his feelings of loss, even as he continued simultaneously to accept the inevitability of human mortality. As Weinfeld outlived his contemporaries, his circle of friends narrowed and life grew increasingly sad.

If Herbert Lehman had been Weinfeld's most important friend, Bernard Botein was his "closest friend,"[18] and that closeness made his death in 1974 particularly sad. Botein and Weinfeld were the same age. They had first met as young lawyers, had served together in the Lehman administration, and had both achieved fame as judges. As one mutual friend wrote to Weinfeld, he "always thought of" Botein "in connection with you, and of both of you, together, as two of the finest members of the legal profession; dedicated men of outstanding ability, with the highest integrity, and expressing the best ideals of legal and public life." Others also recognized the closeness of the Weinfeld-Botein friendship. A former law clerk wrote Weinfeld a sympathy note that observed, "I know how close you were, and how much his passing must mean to you"; another friend remarked, "I know how close you were," while a colleague on the federal bench observed, "No one can ever fill the loss you suffer by his passing."[19]

Weinfeld responded to Botein's death as he previously had to so many others. In an oration at a memorial service at the Association of the Bar of the City of New York, Weinfeld observed that Botein had "live[d] a full life of service to his time and community," "had led as worthwhile and fulfilling a life as was within his power," and thus "was prepared for the final judgment." At the same time, Weinfeld did not deny that Botein was a special, "loyal and concerned friend"; "[f]riends' problems became his problems; their joys were his joys; their sorrows were his sorrows." "Those of us who shared his friendship," he added, "were indeed blessed."[20]

As Weinfeld also acknowledged privately, he had "indeed lost a dear friend whom I shall miss very much." To another, Weinfeld wrote that "I have indeed lost a very dear friend and I do miss him very much. It all came on suddenly and the last few days were difficult."[21] At the first meeting of NYU's Law Center Foundation following Botein's death, Weinfeld gave "a most moving testimonial about his long friendship with Bernie and the serious loss to all of us and to the cause of justice." Finally, Weinfeld spent considerable time with Botein's family during his brief illness and after his death, prompting his son to note that he was "like a brother to Father" and to thank him for his "thoughtfulness, help, and general support," his "words [that] were a source of wisdom to all of us, and . . . calm conduct [that] was a wonderful example."[22]

After the 1974 death of Bernard Botein, life, as Weinfeld well understood, still went on. So too did death, as Weinfeld's friends continued to die and he continued delivering their eulogies. But at least in some of the eulogies, the old ritualistic acceptance of death's inevitability was missing. Increasingly, Weinfeld spoke chiefly of the loss that death brings. For example, at the 1976 funeral service of Edith Lehman, Weinfeld began by noting that Mrs. Lehman's mourners were "assembled to commune with one another and to give public expression to our shared regard for one who enriched the lives of all who knew her." Then, after observing that "we have reached the last page of the final chapter of a book that encompassed two lives"—that of Governor Lehman as well as Edith Lehman—Weinfeld concluded, "Now both have passed from the scene. And we are at the moment of parting and we say farewell to our beloved—a truly noble lady."[23]

Among other friends who died were Richard Korn, about whom Weinfeld remarked that "the final parting from those we love is never easy," and Norman Simon, one of Weinfeld's doctors who, he said, "had a rare capacity for deep and warm friendship, and through that gift of friendship . . . gave each of us a part of himself" that would "remain a treasured memory." When Weinfeld eulogized Justine Wise Polier, the daughter of Rabbi Steven Wise, the mother of one of Weinfeld's law clerks, and later a state court judge who became one of Weinfeld's friends, he focused on "the privilege of her personal friendship" and the "memories of her talents, her idealism, [and her] tenacity of purpose." In the instance of a close friend, Myron Greene, Weinfeld focused on his "loyalty" and on how "[t]he lives of all who knew him had been diminished by his passing." Even at the 1986 memorial service of his ninety-six-year-old colleague, Judge Edward Dimock—one of the few people Weinfeld eulogized in the 1980s who was older than he was—he no longer told his listeners that they should rejoice in the distinguished career of the deceased; instead, he urged that "[w]e all treasure his memory."[24]

Thus, as more of Weinfeld's friends died, his perspective on death continued to change. He placed less emphasis on the need to prepare for the final judgment by leading as worthwhile and fulfilling a life as possible; his attention moved to the deprivation that death wrought and on the need to cherish the memories of those who had passed on. As he wrote to the wife of a former colleague, "While we know that a time of parting must come from those with whom we have shared life's journey—when it does come, it is never easy."[25] Although Weinfeld had not fully abandoned his recognition of the inevitability of death, he appears to have become somewhat less accepting.

Indeed, death became something to fight, and it is remarkable how well Weinfeld fought it. During the final decade of his life, his body was racked with cancer, but he refused to succumb. During the course of the late 1970s and early 1980s, Weinfeld had surgery for skin cancer, stomach cancer, and breast cancer. He also had phlebitis, gout, a bout of Legionnaires' disease, and then in 1984 had to be flown by helicopter from Montauk, Long Island to Mount Sinai Hospital in Manhattan for an emergency removal of his gall bladder.[26] He accepted the treatments his doctors prescribed for these diseases; Weinfeld was an obedient patient who always was totally respectful toward doctors and never questioned them. At the same time, he refused to let illness interfere with his life or his work. He never used the word "cancer" in referring to his ailments, and, in essence, dealt with the disease by denying that he had it. He was impatient with people who complained about aches and pains and had no time for that nonsense himself or for the nonsense of being sick with cancer.[27]

But Weinfeld's fight could not be won and his health continued to decline. By the mid-1980s, he knew his cancer was incurable. He learned that he had a tumor in a liver duct that could not be surgically removed; surgeons could at best remove the part of the tumor that was causing an obstruction and hope that it would grow back slowly. He underwent surgery to alleviate the obstruction, but refused either radiation or chemotherapy treatments. In his view, "There was no point. The most it would do is prolong my life a little longer, and I don't think it's living life to move from the chair to the bed."[28] Weinfeld simply went back to work. Still, his level of well-being sank. His doctors ordered him to forego his evening martinis, which he did, but stopping the martinis deprived him of the evening relaxation that had enabled him to go to bed and sleep for at least a few hours a night.[29] The lack of sleep, in turn, along with the slow progress of his cancer, left Weinfeld frail and exhausted virtually every day during the final years of his life.

Meanwhile, old friends and contemporaries continued to die. With one of them, Weinfeld had kept in touch since he had first met the friend when he was a senior in high school.[30] Another old friend was Abe Wolf, who in neat handwriting in May 1986 informed Weinfeld that his wife had just died "after ailing quite a while with a heart condition."[31] Eight months later, Abe himself was failing badly, as he wrote Weinfeld the following in a weak hand:

> As time hangs heavily on my lonely life I think of you and Lillian often. I also think of the many times your warm comfortable words helped me through trying moments. I am so very grateful to you for all this. I keep your news article before me—it is outstanding! I would give anything to be close to you. [Wolf lived in Lenox, Massachusetts.][32]

Four months later, Abe Wolf died.[33]

Death was visibly approaching, and Weinfeld needed to make arrangements to face it—always and for anyone, a difficult matter. The difficulty was compounded for Weinfeld, however, by two out-of-the-ordinary deaths of friends. These two deaths forced him to think hard as he worked his way toward his own final place of rest.

Weinfeld found it easier to cope with what most readers would find the more traumatic of the two deaths—that of Stephen Botein, the son of Weinfeld's late friend, Bernard Botein, who had been felled by a sudden, fatal heart attack at the age of forty-four. Because Stephen Botein was so young, Weinfeld could not treat his death merely as the conclusion of a long and successful life. Botein's death was simply tragic, in that he left two young daughters and a great deal of unfinished work behind. And the conclusion of Weinfeld's talk at Botein's memorial service reflected that tragedy:

> Words and public tributes can never diminish the loss of one who has lived with us, nurtured us, played with us and shared in our joys and sorrows.
>
> Yet, one may draw solace that each of us did share life's experiences with Steve and that he was a part of, continued, and passed along a tradition of learning, intellect, integrity, affection and warmth to those he loved.
>
> Each of us was enriched by that experience.

And, as Weinfeld added in a private letter to Stephen Botein's young wife, "you should each cherish his memory."[34]

With the death of the young Stephen Botein, Weinfeld's views reached their ultimate fruition. Twenty-five years earlier, when old men such as Learned Hand and Herbert Lehman had died, death had provided Weinfeld with a reason for celebrating life. In his early eulogies, Weinfeld had talked of the accomplishments of the deceased, had emphasized how the deceased were undoubtedly satisfied with those accomplishments, and had urged the living likewise to be satisfied and to permit the deceased to pass on. Death, like hard work leading to accomplishment, was merely an inevitable part of life, in which the living should jubilantly acquiesce.

When Weinfeld became old and the young began dying around him, he did not entirely abandon his early views. He still gave praise to those who had nurtured, played with, and shared in the joys and sorrows of family and friends and who had performed their part in passing along a tradition of learning, intellect, integrity, affection, and warmth. But the praise was no longer jubilant; it no longer sufficed to make death acceptable. In Weinfeld's later eulogies, death had become sad—death had become something to be mourned. Weinfeld's later eulogies emphasized the difficulty of parting, the feeling of loss, and the finality that death brings. The only thing that could survive death was memory, and thus he urged the living to remember.

It was these views that Edward Weinfeld brought to a death that pained him more than any other—the death of his fellow jurist Henry Friendly. Shortly after Friendly's death, Weinfeld wrote that "[a] noble man has left our midst and left a deep void."[35] And, some two weeks later, he made a statement unlike any other he had ever made about someone's death. It was a simple, direct statement—namely, "I have not yet been reconciled to his departure."[36]

One reason Friendly's death was so difficult for Weinfeld was that it took his last true peer. As an earlier chapter showed, many of Weinfeld's friends were his protégés and dependents. They came to him needing help and advice that he always graciously—indeed, lovingly—provided, as one provides help for children, even adult children. But Weinfeld needed more from friends. He needed friends like Learned Hand and Herbert Lehman, for whom he could serve as a son, and Bernard Botein and Henry Friendly, to whom he could relate as an equal brother. Indeed, as we saw earlier, many of Weinfeld's friends going back as far as college were surrogate brothers of a sort. With Friendly's death, his last brother was gone. As he remarked to one former clerk, he now had no one left except his family and "the boys" (i.e., the law clerks).[37]

The death was made even more difficult because Friendly had committed suicide. Friendly possessed a "temperament . . . deeply melancholic" and an "outlook on the world deeply pessimistic to the point of despair." The death of his wife, Sophie, who had been "his rock and staff" for fifty-five years and without whom "he was bitterly lonely," in conjunction with a corneal ulcer that temporarily exacerbated "longstanding visual difficulties," undermined the "grit and will power" that had "maintained" his life "against serious obstacles" in the past. "Although suicide—eventual suicide—[had been] no stranger to his thoughts even in healthier, less unhappy days," he began contemplating it "with ever greater seriousness in his final months"[38] and discussing it with his friends, including Weinfeld. Those friends, especially Weinfeld, tried to dissuade him. But, as another friend observed after Friendly had completed his plan, "he never wanted to be talked out of his decision, but rather to be sure that I understood the motives behind that decision."[39]

Weinfeld could not understand, however, because understanding would have undercut the very basis on which Weinfeld himself was barely managing to survive. Obstacles similar to those that drove Friendly to suicide were also impacting Weinfeld. Weinfeld's marriage, like Friendly's, was coming apart as Lillian Weinfeld's loss of self-discipline with respect to alcohol was driving a wedge between her and her husband. And, Weinfeld had even worse health problems: he knew he had an incurable disease that sooner or later would prevent him from continuing his life's work. But Weinfeld would not let these obstacles stop him: he understood the difficulty of parting and the feeling of loss that his death would bring to others, as well as the capacity to help and serve others that still remained within him. Suicide, for Weinfeld, was an unacceptable act of selfishness deserving of no respect. At the very core of his being, Weinfeld rejected Friendly's solution and went on, however difficult it became, keeping death at bay for as long as possible.

But death could only be postponed, not beaten back. Near the end of a six-week criminal trial—the sort of judicial proceeding that saps a trial judge's energy more than any other—Weinfeld collapsed, fell down the front steps of the courthouse, and was taken to the hospital. Informing him that they could do nothing to restore his energy or improve his un-

Henry J. Friendly, with inscription, "To Ed
Weinfeld, embodiment of all that is best in a
judge, who had made these years, through his
friendship, a well of satisfaction and delight."
Henry J. Friendly, February 28, 1980.

derlying medical condition, the doctors made it clear that the end was
near. He would never return to his beloved chambers.

Weinfeld, who at the time was eighty-six years old, initially felt cheated
by the impending presence of death because, as he told visitors, he had
planned to serve as an active judge until the age of ninety and then to take
senior status.[40] But his self-pity soon departed, and his old will to nurture
and serve others returned. His first step was to will his way out of the
hospital. Initially, his doctor was not willing to discharge him because, the
doctor said, he was not eating enough. In an act of will, Weinfeld ate
enough so that the doctor would let him out.

Once he was home, he returned to nurturing others. He knew he would die soon, and he wanted family and friends to be comfortable about his passing. Thus, to every one who visited him in his final weeks, he repeated, with appropriate variations, a theme first expressed in his eulogy of Herbert Lehman a quarter-century earlier: "Dear family and friends, do not trouble yourselves. I had a full and rewarding life. I saw the fulfillment of many of the ideals and principles that I believed in and fought for. And when my time came, it came"[41] in the presence of loved ones. Weinfeld wanted no one to be saddened by his forthcoming death, since he had done all the things he had wanted and had had a wonderful life.

A few more extraordinary acts of will were still required. One was the signing of his last opinion only a week before he died.[42] A second occurred when Weinfeld learned that he would be the first recipient of the Henry J. Friendly Medal by the American Law Institute. In a bizarre twist of fate, Friendly, by dying before Weinfeld, had performed an unselfish service to his friend, and Weinfeld wanted to reciprocate by receiving the medal, in person, while he was still alive. Accordingly, he arranged to have the award ceremony in his home.

He prepared for the ceremony as he always had. He spent several days formulating his acceptance speech with the aid of a former law clerk who for twenty years had helped him draft speeches.[43] He spent the evening before the ceremony going over his acceptance, to insure that he would be comfortable and familiar with it. The next day he got up from his bed, dressed himself in a suit, received the Friendly Award, and delivered, standing, his ten-minute acceptance speech in his living room before a group containing family, American Law Institute officials, a colleague on the bench, former law clerks, and other friends.[44] He then returned to bed and to his nurturing tasks, as he wrote by hand "a long and beautiful note about the meaning of marriage" and sent it to a former law clerk whose marriage was scheduled for the following week.[45]

The next day, in a final act of will, he summoned his wife, his two daughters, and his grandchildren to his bedside. He told them how much he loved them. And, then, he stopped breathing.

13

And the Just Shall
Bring Forth Wisdom

Two days after Edward Weinfeld died, eighteen hundred mourners attended his funeral at Temple Emanu-El.[1] The funeral service truly captured Edward Weinfeld, the judge and the man. Morris Lasker, who was Weinfeld's colleague on the district court bench, spoke of his commitment

> always to do right without being presumptuous; to serve the public with all your strength, without craving power; to use the law as an instrument for justice, without sacrificing stability. And your uniqueness (for you were unique) consisted in fulfilling that commitment day after day, year after year, without pretentiousness. . . . Your creed was to do justly and to walk in the path of your God.

Quoting the words that Learned Hand had written of Cardozo, Lasker concluded that Weinfeld was "wise because his spirit [was] uncontaminated; because he [knew] no violence, or hatred or envy, or jealousy or ill-will."[2]

Martin Lipton, a former law clerk, likewise spoke of Weinfeld's

> dedication to mastering the facts of each case so that he could apply the law in the way that was right and fair to the parties. . . . However careful and thorough we thought we were, the Judge was more careful and thorough. Good was never good enough. Great was not great enough. Perfect was the goal. No one was more realistic about the impossibility of perfection, but no one worked harder to achieve it.[3]

Alvin H. Schulman, his son-in-law, spoke of Edward Weinfeld as a friend. Schulman related how

> if you wanted to talk with him about a personal or private affair, he brought to the conversation a rare intelligence and depth of experience. His suggestions—and he gave them only if asked—were at the same time informed with an uncompromising moral sense and a sense of the practical possibilities. And you could tell him anything. He disproved the cynical adage that a secret is a fact known only to one person. In the "bosom of the family" or in the "privacy of this room," to use the phrases Eddie used, he might unburden himself of a private opinion; but he never sought the cheap attention that comes from betraying a confidence. . . . He made us better than we were. When we were with him, the force of his personality required of us purposes of dignity. When we were with him, he required of us a clarity of thought and precision of language that, with luck, would last until we were with him again.[4]

And, Amy Weinfeld Schulman, the judge's granddaughter, summed it all up, as she tried to convey what made the love of the man she called "Grandpar" special. As she explained,

> just as his devotion to public service and prowess on the bench did not lie in the big case or in intricate abstractions, so too intimacy with Grandpar was not contained in self-conscious gestures or sudden revelations. The symmetry between the two is not accidental, for above all his devotion to public service was personal—it *was* Edward Weinfeld the man. And intimacy with him was to share his commitment to fair play, his eye for detail and his sense of loyalty. . . .
>
> I once asked Grandpar, in an attempt to find the man behind the man: Don't you ever get lonely being the repository of so many other people's confidences and struggles? I asked him whom he turned to. He looked at me, somewhat perplexed. And then I realized that his capacity to give and to listen, to be there for others, was the source of his strength and how he felt at home in the world.[5]

There was more of the same three months later at a memorial service at the United States Court House. Wilfred Feinberg, the chief judge of the

Second Circuit Court of Appeals, spoke of Weinfeld's "dedication, his fairness, his common sense, his compassion, his thoroughness, . . . his courage" and "[h]is continued enthusiasm about the law." "He operated," in the words of an old friend, Warren Moscow, "without fanfare, with keen intelligence and judgment, diligently, with a commitment to doing what was right. He sought no personal publicity." Manhattan District Attorney Robert Morgenthau, another old friend, said,

> His oath of office was the biblical injunction: "Ye shall not respect persons in judgment; ye shall hear the small and the great alike." Edward Weinfeld followed that oath perhaps better than any man or woman who has ever been appointed to any bench. Never did he use his public office to promote his name, his views, or his personality. He used it to do justice. . . . "It is his purity of spirit that makes him the judge we so much revere, even more than his learning, his acuteness, and his fabulous industry. [according to Henry Friendly]"

And, John Koeltl, a former law clerk and now himself a United States district judge, wrote how Weinfeld taught his clerks "thoroughness and care, attention to detail, scrupulous adherence to the facts, integrity, and an unerring sense of justice."[6]

It was a remarkable set of tributes that were accorded to Edward Weinfeld on his death. They show that the boy born in obscurity on the Lower East Side had led "a great life and . . . had accomplished his life's work." Indeed, it "was a magnificent life and will continue to live in the memories of his family and his friends."[7]

But, will Edward Weinfeld leave a timeless legacy? Will anyone remember his deeds after those who knew him personally are gone? Will Weinfeld's distinctive style of judging be important in the future? Can we, as the Bible suggests, gain wisdom by studying how Weinfeld achieved justice for those who came before him?

At the outset, it must be noted that Weinfeld's style is out of favor with many current thinkers. When Richard Nixon campaigned for the presidency in 1968 by attacking the Warren Court, he began a process of politicizing the judicial function.[8] Since that time, the classical distinction between law and politics has come under increasing attack, and judges have been seen as inevitably preferring some groups in society over others on the basis of essentially political, substantive values external to established legal doctrine. Current thinkers disagree not about the policy-making role judges should assume, but about the substantive values judges should choose in performing that role.

Weinfeld never had a theory of what substantive justice was or of how it could be fully attained. But he had faith that substantive justice existed and manifested itself through law. He also had faith that others shared his faith. Both faiths were deeply rooted in traditional religious and cultural values.

The most ancient source of the judge's faiths was, as we have seen, biblical: Weinfeld consciously tried to model his judicial behavior on that of Old Testament judges. That does not mean that Weinfeld saw himself as applying the law of the Mosaic God in his decision making; he knew that, as a United States district judge, his sources of law must be American common law and legislation. It was the attitude—especially the *gravitas* and impartiality—of Old Testament judges, not the substance of their decisions, that Weinfeld wished to emulate.

This Old Testament attitude precluded Weinfeld from seeing himself as a judicial lawmaker who made hard choices among competing substantive, political values. He understood that a truly impartial judge could not have an instrumental agenda for the transformation of society: impartiality demands the absence of the very sort of policy preconceptions that a judge adhering to an instrumental agenda inevitably will hold. Weinfeld also understood that mortal judges who take seriously a concept of higher law cannot themselves make law; only God can give the law. Judges in an Old Testament mode can only find facts that call the relevant precepts of transcendent law into play and interpret those precepts when they are vague or otherwise imprecisely applicable. Even these interpretations, however, do not themselves make law, again, because only God can make law.

The Old Testament was not the only backward-looking source of Judge Weinfeld's jurisprudence. His judicial approach also was consistent with that of one of his heroes, Louis D. Brandeis. Weinfeld, as we saw, found Brandeis's Supreme Court opinions "painstaking" and "monumental";[9] he also must have been aware of the justice's reputation as the twentieth-century incarnation of the Old Testament Isaiah.[10]

Brandeis was even more important to Weinfeld for his work as a lawyer—as the creator of the Brandeis brief. The first such brief, it will be recalled, was filed in the case of *Muller v. Oregon*,[11] where Brandeis advised that emphasis be placed, not on urging the Court to change the law, but on showing how the facts of the case dictated a result in his client's favor within the bounds of then-existing law. The Brandeis brief, in effect, became a tool for progressive lawyers to achieve societal reform when legal doctrine and judicial institutions supported maintenance of the status quo.

As we saw when we examined Weinfeld's early career in private practice, Weinfeld took Brandeis's method to heart. He often represented underdogs who had to circumvent hostile legal doctrines in order to win their cases; in representing them, Weinfeld developed a habit not of making creative and imaginative legal arguments but instead of developing factual bases that led to victory under the law as it then existed. His approach as a young lawyer, like the approach of Brandeis, was to achieve just results—in this instance, results favorable to his clients—by searching for and establishing facts that he could fit within preexisting rules of law or bedrock legal principles.

From roots in the Old Testament, his own experience as a young litigator, and his admiration for Louis D. Brandeis, Edward Weinfeld developed the distinctive judicial style that reflected the values of independent, individualized judgment implicit in Article III of the Constitution. The Old Testament taught him that an impartial judge striving for justice between litigants ought not have an instrumental law-making agenda designed to promote social change. His experience as a litigator further informed him that, even if he had wanted to make law, he typically would lack effective power to do so. Above all, Weinfeld learned from Brandeis that he could almost always achieve the result he found appropriate in a case—that is, he could do right and justice—by focusing on facts and showing, on the facts, how the case fit within existing law as understood in the context of ongoing societal progress.

Thus, study of Weinfeld's life and juridical method can offer useful insight for judges in the coming twenty-first century. However, there are two difficulties with Weinfeld's approach that those who are attracted to it must address.

The first, as already suggested, is that Weinfeld's juridical method can only produce justice in individual cases; it cannot produce transformative social change. Even if everyone who comes to court receives justice from judges like Weinfeld, the world at large will still remain unjust. The poor will still be with us, and powerful individuals will still advance their well-being by taking advantage of the weak. Judges who want to help the poor and the weak as classes, rather than only the few poor and weak individuals who happen to appear before them, need a jurisprudence other than Weinfeld's.

This first difficulty, however, provides no reason to undervalue what Weinfeld has to offer. The judge never presumed that his jurisprudence would, in fact, make everyone equal. It never occurred to him that it was within the power of the judiciary to change society comprehensively rather than merely apply legal principles justly and equally in the specific factual contexts of the cases before him. And Weinfeld ultimately may be right: judges may, indeed, have little power to engineer social change.[12]

The limits of the judicial power are especially apparent in Third World and former Communist nations, where preexisting judiciaries were sometimes so corrupt or politically manipulated that the task now at hand is to establish faith in the judiciary's integrity. Where people are accustomed to judicial impartiality, they can look beyond it and ask their judges to further social progress or to achieve social justice. But where, as in newly emerging democracies, legal transparency, predictability, and impartiality have never existed, the judiciary must expend all its energies to secure them before pursuing any broader governmental role.

Moreover, even in America, judges are not omnipotent. They do not always possess sufficient power to push legal doctrine into greater conformity with their views of social policy and, even if they have power, the political and social costs of exerting it may be too high. Perhaps judges who face limits on their power should continue striving to promote the legal and social changes in which they believe, even though they know they will fail to attain them. On the other hand, they could decide to accept only half a loaf, to follow the approach of Brandeis the lawyer and Weinfeld the judge, and to engage in factual analysis that will persuade their colleagues to join them in reaching just results in pending cases even while leaving legal doctrine as a whole, from their point of view, imperfect.

Thus, the incapacity of Weinfeld's juridical method to bring about transformative social change should not prevent judges from using it for more limited ends. A second difficulty with the approach, however, is more troublesome.

Edward Weinfeld always acted as if law existed transcendentally, so that, once the facts of a case were determined, the outcome became obvious. In Weinfeld's drill, "the facts of a case spoke to a Natural Law—an inherent moral order" reflective of human progress.[13] Most scholars today doubt, however, whether any inherent moral order exists. They are inclined to reject the proposition that some master culture, from which a judge can derive standards for adjudicating cases, sets norms for all. These jaded scholars see Weinfeld's jurisprudence as quaint and out of vogue and can only laugh at a man who strove to become a good judge by purchasing a leather-bound book and inscribing therein all the maxims he could find about judging.

In order to find Weinfeld's juridical method useful, readers must conclude that they do not yet reside in such a rigidly multicultural world, in which adjudication in accordance with norms that transcend any one culture has become impossible. They need to have faith that there remains "a deep . . . and widely shared moral judgment . . . that murder, torture, censorship or discrimination [among other things] are wrong." Some, perhaps, can have such faith. For those who do, there is a place, as one former law clerk has suggested, for an old-fashioned judge "born," as Weinfeld was, "of a simpler world, . . . before the moral ambiguity of the twentieth century had fully unfolded, . . . [to] maintain such an unwavering ethical perspective."[14]

Thus, the juridical method of Edward Weinfeld can provide some twenty-first-century judges with a jurisprudence for deciding individual cases justly under legal rules that reflect whatever progress society, viewed as a coherent whole, is making. As the preeminent trial judge in twentieth-century America, Weinfeld surely can serve as a model of excellence for the thousands of trial judges who are striving today to do their jobs well. Likewise, judges in emerging democracies that have never enjoyed the rule of law need to emulate his *gravitas*, impartiality, and faith that the legal norms of society as a whole can resolve conflict. Finally, Weinfeld's jurisprudence offers specific content and illustration for sophisticated judges and scholars who want to make American appellate judging less political and more concerned, in the tried and tested words of Lon Fuller, with the forms and limits of adjudication.[15] While Weinfeld's jurisprudence offers no model for the creation of utopia, it constitutes an exemplary paradigm for fidelity to law, right, and justice.

Notes

NOTES TO THE INTRODUCTION

1. *Washington Post*, January 19, 1988, B6; *Los Angeles Times*, January 19, 1988, 20; *San Francisco Chronicle*, January 19, 1988, Box 36, Scrapbook 3, Weinfeld Papers.

2. "Judge Edward Weinfeld, 86, Dies: On U.S. Bench Nearly 4 Decades," *New York Times*, January 18, 1988, A16.

3. "The Devotion of Judge Weinfeld," *New York Times*, January 19, 1988, A26.

4. *See Edward Weinfeld: A Judicious Life* (New York: Federal Bar Foundation, 1998), 106.

5. 244 Fed. 535 (S.D.N.Y.), *rev'd*, 246 F.2d 24 (2d Cir. 1917).

6. 159 F.2d 169 (2d Cir. 1947).

7. *See* Gerald Gunther, *Learned Hand: The Man and the Judge* (New York: Knopf, 1994), x.

8. Robert Litt to William E. Nelson, June 4, 2001 (e-mail on file with author).

9. *See* Laura Kalman, *The Strange Career of Legal Liberalism* (New Haven, Conn.: Yale University Press, 1996), 42.

10. *See* Morton J. Horwitz, *The Warren Court and the Pursuit of Justice* (New York: Hill and Wang, 1998), xii; Kalman, *Legal Liberalism*, 2–5, 42–51, 230–39.

11. *See* Gunther, *Learned Hand*, 257, 270, 278.

12. The easiest way to begin addressing the vast literature on legal process theory is to consult William N. Eskridge, Jr., and Philip P. Frickey, "An Historical and Critical Introduction to *The Legal Process*," in Henry M. Hart, Jr., and Albert M. Sacks eds., *The Legal Process: Basic Problems in the Making and Application of Law* (Westbury, N.Y.: Foundation Press, 1994), li, xcvii–cxxxiv. The most important early argument in favor of judicial deference to the political branches was Alexander M. Bickel, *The Least Dangerous Branch: The Supreme Court at the Bar of Politics* (New York: Bobbs-Merrill, 1962), 111–98.

NOTES TO CHAPTER I

1. Joshua B. Freeman, *Working-Class New York: Life and Labor since World War II* (New York: New Press, 2000), 292.

2. *Id.*, xv.

3. *Id.*, xv.

4. Available sources do not agree on the precise year in which either Weinfeld's father or mother was born. As to his father, see passport application of Edward Weinfeld, cc. 1977, Box 3, Weinfeld Papers (dating father's birth as 1861); *In the Matter of Abraham Weinfeld on his Naturalization*, Jan. 12, 1894 (microfilm in Federal Records Center, New York, N.Y.) (dating father's birth as 1863); Census of 1900, vol. 144, E.D. 383, sheet 8, line 58 (microfilm in Federal Records Center, New York, N.Y.) (dating father's birth as 1864). As to his mother, see passport application of Edward Weinfeld, cc. 1977, Box 3, Weinfeld Papers (dating mother's birth as 1874); Census of 1900, vol. 144, E.D. 383, sheet 8, line 58 (microfilm in Federal Records Center, New York, N.Y.) (dating mother's birth as 1875).

5. On Gorlice and Lelesz, *see* Gary Mokotoff and Sallyann Amdur Sack, *Where Once We Walked: A Guide to the Jewish Communities Destroyed in the Holocaust* (Teaneck, N.J.: Avotaynu, 1991), xvi, 103, 183. On DeWitt Clinton High School, *see* Stephan F. Brumberg, *Going to America, Going to School: The Jewish Immigrant Public School Encounter in Turn-of-the-Century New York City* (New York: Praeger, 1986), 182–83. In 1929, the school moved to Mosholu Parkway and 205th Street in the Bronx, and in 1983, it became coeducational. *See* Kenneth T. Jackson, ed., *The Encyclopedia of New York City* (New Haven, Conn.: Yale University Press, 1995), 332.

6. *Edward Weinfeld: A Judicious Life* (New York: Federal Bar Foundation, 1998), 1.

7. *See In the Matter of Abraham Weinfeld on his Naturalization*, Jan. 12, 1894 (microfilm in Federal Records Center, New York, N.Y.) (stating that Abraham first came to New York in 1879). The census of 1910 and his son's recollection are that he arrived permanently in 1888. *See* Census of 1910, Roll 1101, pt. 2, 85A (microfilm in Federal Records Center, New York, N.Y.); *A Judicious Life*, 1.

8. Author's telephone interview on May 6, 2003 with Rabbi David Posner of Temple Emanu-El, New York, N.Y., a descendant of one of those children.

9. *See A Judicious Life*, 1; Census of 1910, Roll 1011, pt. 2, 85A (microfilm in Federal Records Center, New York, N.Y.); Posthumous Transcription of Tape-Recorded In-Person Conversation between the Honorable Edward Weinfeld, United States District Court, Southern District of New York, and Amy Schulman (His Granddaughter), September 3, 1988, Tape 4, 14–16 (transcript on file with the author).

10. *See* Thomas Kessner, *The Golden Door: Italian and Jewish Immigrant Mobility in New York City, 1880–1915* (New York: Oxford University Press, 1977), 26–32, which indicates that this pattern was less true, however, for Jews than for Italians.

11. *See* Norma Basch, *Framing American Divorce: From the Revolutionary Generation to the Victorians* (Berkeley: University of California Press, 1999), 107, 114; Hendrik Hartog, *Man and Wife in America: A History* (Cambridge, Mass.: Harvard University Press, 2000), 282.

12. Fern W. Cohen, *Included Out (Excluded In) . . . Mostly about My Father, Tennis, Me, and Freud . . .* (ms. dated March 4, 2000 in possession of the author), 139.

13. *See* Arch C. Gerlach, ed., *The National Atlas of the United States of America* (Washington, D.C.: United States Department of the Interior Geological Survey, 1970), 241; Allon Schoener, ed., *Portal to America: The Lower East Side, 1870–1925* (New York: Holt, Rinehart, 1967), 210–11. *See generally* David C. Hammack, *Power and Society: Greater New York at the Turn of the Century* (New York: Columbia University Press, 1987), 60–65.

14. Jacob A. Riis, *How the Other Half Lives: Studies among the Tenements of New York* (New York: Dover Publications, 1971), 27, 131, 145. This 1971 edition was an unabridged republication of the text of the 1901 edition of the work originally published by Charles Scribner's Sons, New York, in 1890.

15. Riis, *The Other Half*, 229; Stephen Fox, *The Mirror Makers: A History of American Advertising and Its Creators* (New York: William Morrow, 1984), 100; *Town of Manlius v. Town of Pompey*, 250 N.Y.S. 690, 692 (Sup. Ct. 1930).

16. Charles N. Fay, *Business in Politics: Suggestions for Leaders in American Business* (Cambridge, Mass.: Riverside Press, 1926), 103, 164; Elbert Hubbard, *A Message to Garcia and Thirteen Other Things* (East Aurora, N.Y.: Roycrofters, 1901), *quoted in* Peter Baida, *Poor Richard's Legacy: American Business Values from Benjamin Franklin to Donald Trump* (New York: William Morrow, 1990), 241; James W. Prothro, *The Dollar Decade: Business Ideas in the 1920s* (Baton Rouge: Louisiana State University Press, 1954), 210.

17. Fox, *Mirror Makers*, 101; Howard M. Sachar, *The Course of Modern Jewish History* (Cleveland: World Publishing, 1958), 339, 341; Baida, *Poor Richard's Legacy*, 205; *see generally id.*, 203–6; Brumberg, *Going to America*, 4–7. On the late-nineteenth-century origins of prejudice against Jewish immigrants, *see* Edwin G. Burrows and Mike Wallace, *Gotham: A History of New York City to 1898* (New York: Oxford University Press, 1999), 1087–88, 1114–26.

18. Oscar Handlin, "Race and Nationality in American Life," *quoted in* Melvin Steinfeld, ed., *Cracks in the Melting Pot: Racism and Discrimination in American History*, 2d ed. (New York: Glencoe Press, 1973), 186. On the connection of Jews to socialist movements, *see also* Nathan Glazer and Daniel

Patrick Moynihan, *Beyond the Melting Pot: The Negroes, Puerto Ricans, Jews, Italians, and Irish of New York* (Cambridge, Mass.: MIT Press, 1963), 169.

19. Quoted in Ronald Takaki, *A Different Mirror: A History of Multicultural America* (Boston: Little, Brown, 1993), 283.

20. *Id.*, 283–85.

21. *See A Judicious Life*, 1, 17; Census of 1910, Roll 1011, pt. 2, 85A (microfilm in Federal Records Center, New York, N.Y.).

22. *A Judicious Life*, 1, 17.

23. *Included Out*, 61.

24. *A Judicious Life*, 97.

25. *Id.*, 97–98.

26. Personal experience of the author with Weinfeld following a New York University School of Law graduation ceremony. I accompanied Weinfeld on the subway and subsequent walk to chambers, after which I was exhausted and soaked with perspiration. He, of course, was fresh and ready for work upon his arrival in chambers.

27. Conversation between Edward Weinfeld and Amy Schulman, Tape 5, 7.

28. One of the author's duties as law clerk was to stop by the cafeteria on my way in to work and pick up a muffin for the judge; he arrived in chambers too early, before the muffins had been baked.

29. *See* Conversation between Edward Weinfeld and Amy Schulman, Tape 5, 5.

30. Author's interview with Ann Schulman, May 27, 2003.

31. Conversation between Edward Weinfeld and Amy Schulman, Tape 5, 7.

32. *See* Edward Weinfeld to Sobel Affiliates, August 17, 1967, and attached claim form, Box 3, folder—Insurance, Weinfeld Papers; Edward Weinfeld to New York City Transit Authority, May 15, 1975, Box 3, folder—Insurance, Weinfeld Papers.

33. *See* Freeman, *Working-Class New York*, 169–76.

NOTES TO CHAPTER 2

1. Posthumous Transcription of Tape-Recorded In-Person Conversation between the Honorable Edward Weinfeld, United States District Court, Southern District of New York, and Amy Schulman (His Granddaughter), September 3, 1988, Tape 4, 19 (transcript on file with the author).

2. *Id.*, 4–5.

3. *See Edward Weinfeld: A Judicious Life* (New York: Federal Bar Foundation, 1998), 17; Fern W. Cohen, *Included Out (Excluded In) . . . Mostly about My Father, Tennis, Me, and Freud . . .* (ms. dated March 4, 2000 in possession of the author), 57, 87.

4. *A Judicious Life*, 17.

5. *Included Out,* 57–58.

6. *A Judicious Life,* 17.

7. *Id.,* 17–18.

8. *Id.,* 18.

9. *Id.,* 12–13; Interviews with Abraham Lass, *quoted in* Stephan F. Brumberg, *Going to America, Going to School: The Jewish Immigrant Public School Encounter in Turn-of-the-Century New York City* (New York: Praeger, 1986), 133.

10. *Quoted in* Brumberg, *Going to America,* 7.

11. Brumberg, *Going to America,* 6.

12. *See* Ronald Takaki, *A Different Mirror: A History of Multicultural America* (Boston: Little, Brown, 1993), 298–303; Brumberg, *Going to America,* 115–37, 143, 146–47.

13. Norman Podhoretz, *Making It* (New York: Random House, 1967), 4.

14. William H. Maxwell, "The Development of Elementary Schools in the State of New York," *quoted in* Brumberg, *Going to America,* 12–13.

15. "Course of Study in Geography with a Syllabus" (New York: Board of Education, rev. ed., 1907), 52.

16. *A Judicious Life,* 18, 96.

17. *Id.,* 17–19.

18. Conversation between Edward Weinfeld and Amy Schulman, Tape 4, 5.

19. *See* Jon M. Kingsdale, "The 'Poor Man's Club': Social Functions of the Urban Working-Class Saloon," *American Quarterly* 25(4) (October 1973): 472, 482–83.

20. *See* Arthur S. Link, *Woodrow Wilson and the Progressive Era, 1910–1917* (New York: Harper, 1954), 10–11.

21. *See* Philippa Strum, *Louis D. Brandeis: Justice for the People* (Cambridge, Mass.: Harvard University Press, 1984), 291–99.

22. Conversation between Edward Weinfeld and Amy Schulman, Tape 4, 8–9.

23. *Included Out,* 27, 44, 59, 65–66, 69.

24. *See* Link, *Woodrow Wilson and the Progressive Era,* 10.

25. *See* Arthur S. Link, *Woodrow Wilson: A Brief Biography* (Cleveland: World Publishing, 1963), 163–78.

26. Conversation between Edward Weinfeld and Amy Schulman, recalling Wise's eulogy following Wilson's death, Tape 4, 11.

27. *Included Out,* 58.

28. Author's conversation with Edward Weinfeld in 1966.

29. *See* Mac Appleton to Edward Weinfeld, December 29, 1925, Box 36, folder 5, Ideal Scrapbook, Weinfeld Papers.

30. *A Judicious Life,* 24.

31. Speech at Dedication of Community Synagogue to Louis Lefkowitz, April 28, 1957, Box 23, folder 1, Weinfeld Papers.

32. See Kenneth T. Jackson, ed., *The Encyclopedia of New York City* (New Haven, Conn.: Yale University Press, 1995), 332.

33. Edward Weinfeld to William J. Kridel, January 26, 1976, Box 40, folder 10, Weinfeld Papers.

34. Conversation between Edward Weinfeld and Amy Schulman, Tape 4, 21.

35. *A Judicious Life*, 18.

36. See Jackson, *Encyclopedia*, 332; Arthur Markewich to Edward Weinfeld, January 30, 1976, Box 40, folder 14, Weinfeld Papers.

37. *Included Out*, 43.

38. Student Record for Edward Weinfeld, Transcript and Certification Department, New York University, New York, N.Y.

39. *A Judicious Life*, 7, 20–21.

40. *Included Out*, 59.

41. *A Judicious Life*, 19, 21.

42. New York University School of Law has undergone surprisingly little change in the first-year curriculum during the past eight decades.

43. List of Award Recipients, New York University School of Law, Program for Commencement Exercises, May 15, 2003.

44. Student Record for Edward Weinfeld, Transcript and Certification Department, New York University, New York, N.Y.

45. *A Judicious Life*, 21.

46. Student Record for Edward Weinfeld, Transcript and Certification Department, New York University, New York, N.Y.

47. *A Judicious Life*, 21.

48. Conversation between Edward Weinfeld and Amy Schulman, Tape 4, 24.

49. *Id.*

50. Joe Eichler to Edward Weinfeld, October 27, 1936, 4, Box 3, folder— Joseph L. Eichler, Weinfeld Papers.

51. Conversation between Edward Weinfeld and Amy Schulman, Tape 4, 24.

52. *Phi Sigma Deltan*, vol. 3, no. 6 (June 1924), 4, Box 33, Weinfeld Papers; *Phi Sigma Deltan*, vol. 3, no. 12 (Convention Issue, December 1924), 12, Box 33, Weinfeld Papers. See also Dinner-Dance Program for Ruby Anniversary Convention, 1909–1949, December 28, 1949, Box 33, Weinfeld Papers.

53. Conversation between Edward Weinfeld and Amy Schulman, Tape 4, 24–25. In the transcription of the conversation, the word "frater" was erroneously transcribed as "fodder."

54. *Phi Sigma Deltan*, vol. 3, no. 12 (Convention Number, December 1924), 4, Box 33, Weinfeld Papers.

55. *The Central Councillor*, vol. 3, no. 5 (1924), 7, Box 33, Weinfeld Papers.

56. *Phi Sigma Deltan*, vol. 3, no. 12 (Convention Number, December 1924),

4, Box 33, Weinfeld Papers; *Phi Sigma Deltan* (Convention Number, December 1925), 4–7, Box 33, Weinfeld Papers; *Phi Sigma Deltan* (February 1926), 3, Box 33, Weinfeld Papers.

57. *Phi Sigma Deltan* (Convention Number, December 1925), 5, Box 33, Weinfeld Papers.

58. Ben Nurick to Edward Weinfeld, January 13, 1926, Box 36, folder 5—Ideal Scrapbook, Weinfeld Papers.

59. *Phi Sigma Deltan*, vol. 3, no. 12 (Convention Issue, December 1924), 12, Box 33, Weinfeld Papers; *Phi Sigma Deltan* (Convention Number, December 1926), 5, Box 33, Weinfeld Papers; *Phi Sigma Delta* (Convention Number, December 1925), 5–6, Box 33, Weinfeld Papers.

60. *Phi Sigma Deltan* (Convention Number, December 1925), 5, Box 33, Weinfeld Papers.

61. Henry S. Waldman to Edward Weinfeld, April 29, 1924, Box 38, folder 13, Weinfeld Papers.

62. *Included Out*, 35, 59–61.

63. *Id.*, 24, 37.

64. Author's telephone interview with Michael Botein, August 5, 2000.

65. Guest Book—Lillian Weinfeld, May 13, 1951, Box 6, Weinfeld Papers.

66. *Included Out*, 59.

NOTES TO CHAPTER 3

1. "Winners Announced in Tests for Bar," *New York Times*, August 20, 1922, 16. Only 285 out of the 751 who had taken the bar exam passed.

2. *Edward Weinfeld: A Judicious Life* (New York: Federal Bar Foundation, 1998), 7, 21–22.

3. Fern W. Cohen, *Included Out (Excluded In) . . . Mostly about My Father, Tennis, Me, and Freud . . .* (ms. dated March 4, 2000 in possession of the author), 47; *A Judicious Life*, 22.

4. Announcement of Opening of Practice, January 1923, Box 36, folder 5, Ideal Scrapbook, Weinfeld Papers.

5. 123 Misc. 519, 205 N.Y.S. 401 (App. Term 1st Dept. 1924).

6. 123 Misc. at 521, 205 N.Y.S. at 403, *quoting Heaphy v. Eidlitz*, 197 A.D. 431, 432–33 (1st Dept. 1921).

7. 123 Misc. at 520, 205 N.Y.S. at 402.

8. *A Judicious Life*, 22.

9. *See* Order, *Gellert v. Gellert*, File No. 4986, Supreme Court, Kings County, March 12, 1926 (name of Morris Weinfeld on stationery crossed out and name of Edward Weinfeld typed above); Affidavits in Opposition to Resettlement of Order, *id.*, April 3, 1926 (name of Morris Weinfeld on stationery); Order and Notice of Entry, *id.*, September 28, 1926 (name of Edward Weinfeld

on stationery). On all three documents, the given address was 217 Broadway, New York, N.Y.

10. File No. 4986, Supreme Court, Kings County, 1925–1926. A reported opinion resolving one issue in the case appears at *Gellert v. Gellert*, 128 Misc. 146, 218 N.Y.S. 555 (Sup. Ct. Kings Co. 1926).

11. "Plaintiff Uses Lipstick, But Does Not Consider It a Cosmetic," Newspaper Article dated December 1925, Box 36, folder 5, Ideal Scrapbook, Weinfeld Papers; "Forced to Remove Lipstick, Woman Wins Separation," newspaper article dated December 1925, Box 36, folder 5, Ideal Scrapbook, Weinfeld Papers.

12. Resettled Order, *Gellert v. Gellert*, File No. 4986, Supreme Court, Kings County, April 2, 1926.

13. Memorandum of Law on Behalf of Plaintiff, *Gellert v. Gellert*, File No. 4986, Supreme Court, Kings County, undated. In a later matter in which Weinfeld represented a husband, the wife received a weekly payment of thirty dollars per week for herself and her three children, which was to be reduced to twenty-one dollars per week in the event that the husband's gross income fell below thirty-five hundred dollars per year. *See* Agreement between Tillie Fassler and Saul Fassler, 4–6, vol. 10, Box 31, Weinfeld Papers.

14. *See* Memorandum of Law on Behalf of Plaintiff, *Gellert v. Gellert*, File No. 4986, Supreme Court, Kings County, undated.

15. *Gellert v. Gellert*, 128 Misc. 146, 218 N.Y.S. 555 (Sup. Ct. Kings Co. 1926).

16. *See* "Plaintiff Uses Lipstick"; "Forced to Remove Lipstick."

17. *Gellert v. Gellert*, August 20, 1934, *Cases and Points*, vol. 9, Box 31, Weinfeld Papers.

18. *See* Resettled Order, *Gellert v. Gellert*, File No. 4986, Supreme Court, Kings County, April 2, 1926; Order, *Gellert v. Gellert*, File No. 4986, Supreme Court, Kings County, December 9, 1926; *Gellert v. Gellert*, August 20, 1934, *Cases and Points*, vol. 9, Box 31, Weinfeld Papers.

19. *See* Agreement between Tillie Fassler and Saul Fassler, *Cases and Points*, vol. 10, Box 31, Weinfeld Papers.

20. In connection with the Agreement between Tillie Fassler and Saul Fassler, *Cases and Points*, vol. 10, Box 31, Weinfeld Papers, where the wife's attorney is mentioned on page 10 of the agreement, it appears that Weinfeld represented the husband. In *Glover v. Glover*, *Cases and Points*, vol. 10, Box 31, Weinfeld Papers, where a wife sought a separation on the ground that her husband, in private, had accused her falsely of infidelity, Weinfeld definitely represented the husband. In every other matrimonial matter for which the author has been able to obtain evidence of Weinfeld's involvement, he represented the wife.

21. "Sued Dentist, a 'Free Love' Disciple," *New York Journal*, March 1930, Box 36, Scrapbook 1, Weinfeld Papers.

22. *Franklin v. Franklin, Cases and Points,* vol. 10, Box 31, Weinfeld Papers.

23. *Weinstein v. Weinstein, Cases and Points,* vol. 10, Box 31, Weinfeld Papers.

24. Memorandum in Opposition to Motion, 32, *Udko v. Udko, Cases and Points,* vol. 10, Box 31, Weinfeld Papers.

25. *Id.*

26. *Id.,* 30.

27. *Id.,* 31.

28. *See* Appellant's Brief, *Udko v. Udko,* 1–2, *Cases and Points,* vol. 14, Box 31, Weinfeld Papers. The brief herein cited was written subsequent to the parties' divorce, on a successful appeal from a denial of a motion by Mrs. Udko for reimbursement for expenses incurred during a medical emergency suffered by her child.

29. 232 A.D. 569, 251 N.Y.S. 111 (1st Dept. 1931).

30. Appellant's Brief, 2, *Lowenstein v. Lowenstein,* 232 A.D. 569, 251 N.Y.S. 111 (1st Dept. 1931).

31. *Id.,* 2–3, 39.

32. *Id.,* 40.

33. *Id.,* 5–6.

34. *Id.,* 8–11.

35. *Id.,* 14–20.

36. *Id.,* 20–22.

37. *Id.,* 10.

38. Appellant's Reply Brief, 39, *Lowenstein v. Lowenstein,* 232 A.D. 569, 251 N.Y.S. 111 (1st Dept. 1931).

39. *Id.,* 10–11 (quoting opinion of trial court).

40. *Id.,* 12–13; Appellant's Brief, 16–17, 31.

41. Appellant's Reply Brief, 12–13.

42. Appellant's Brief, 14.

43. *Id.,* 3, 5.

44. *Lowenstein v. Lowenstein,* 232 A.D. 569, 251 N.Y.S. 111 (1st Dept. 1931).

45. Edward Weinfeld to Joseph L. Eichler, December 25, 1935, Box 3, Weinfeld Papers.

46. *See* Commencement Speech at Vermont Law School, May 23, 1981, Box 22, Weinfeld Papers.

47. Advice to Lawyers, Box 35, Green Leather Bound Scrapbook, Weinfeld Papers.

48. Rose Sperber to Edward Weinfeld, August 26, 1950, Box 16, folder 3, Weinfeld Papers.

49. Author's telephone interview with Ann Schulman, July 15, 2000; author's conversation with Fern Cohen, May 7, 2003.

50. "Deathbed Statement Void: Murder Suspect Freed," *New York Herald Tribune*, April 4, 1928, 2.

51. *See People v. Corey*, 157 N.Y. 332, 347–49, 51 N.E. 1024, 1028–29 (1898).

52. *See* "Dying Man's Belief He Would Recover Clears a Suspect," *New York Evening World*, April 3, 1928, Box 36, Scrapbook 1, Weinfeld Papers; "Freed as Murder Suspect, Though Named by Dying Man, *New York Times*, April 4, 1928, 31.

53. Weinfeld would have been surprised unless he himself had bribed Nammack or at least knew that he had been bribed. Everything known about Weinfeld compels the rejection of this possibility.

54. *See* "Judge Denounces Jury," *New York Evening Telegram*, April 20, 1928, Box 36, Scrapbook 1, Weinfeld Papers; "Judge Denounces Auto Death Jury," *New York Evening Post*, April 20, 1928, 3; "Judge Rebukes Jurors Who Free Motorist of Charge His Car Killed Boy in Speeding," *New York Times*, April 21, 1928, 1.

55. *Filangeri v. State, Cases and Points*, vol. 10, Box 31, Weinfeld Papers.

56. *People v. Lutterman and Kutner, Cases and Points*, vol. 10, Box 31, Weinfeld Papers.

57. *United States v. Weinberger, Cases and Points*, vol. 10, Box 31, Weinfeld Papers.

58. *People v. Kestenbaum, Cases and Points*, vol. 10, Box 31, Weinfeld Papers.

59. *People v. Leik*, 265 N.Y. 580, 193 N.E. 329 (1934) (per curiam).

60. Brief for Appellant, *People v. Leik, Cases and Points*, vol. 9, Box 31, Weinfeld Papers.

61. *Id.*, 13–14.

62. Brief in Support of the Application Made by the Petitioners Herein, *People v. Goodman, Cases and Points*, vol. 10, Box 31, Weinfeld Papers.

63. Author's conversation with Edward Weinfeld, sometime in the spring of 1966.

64. Author's telephone interview with Ann Schulman, July 15, 2000.

65. Edward Weinfeld to Joseph L. Eichler, December 25, 1935, Box 3, Weinfeld Papers.

66. Memorandum in Support of Motion to Vacate, etc., *Artloom Corp. v. Robbins Bros., Inc.*, 5–6, *Cases and Points*, vol. 10, Box 31, Weinfeld Papers.

67. *Id.*, 7–8.

68. Memorandum in Opposition to Motion to Vacate Notice of Examination, *Bernstein v. Fan & Bill's, Inc.*, 1–2, *Cases and Points*, vol. 10, Box 31, Weinfeld Papers.

69. *Bernstein v. Fan & Bill's, Inc., New York Law Journal*, June 19, 1934, *Cases and Points*, vol. 10, Box 31, Weinfeld Papers.

70. Memorandum in Support of Motion to Vacate Notice of Examination before Trial, *Mosberg v. Trattner*, 11–12, *Cases and Points*, vol. 10, Box 31, Weinfeld Papers.

71. *Id.*, 30.

72. Memorandum in Opposition to Defendants' Motion to Vacate the Notice for the Examination of the Defendants before Trial, *Avgerinos v. Worthland Realty Corp.*, and Memorandum in Support of Application for an Order Directing the Defendants to Submit to an Examination before Trial, *Dubin v. Maron*, *Cases and Points*, vol. 9, Box 31, Weinfeld Papers. For other essentially procedural motions in which Weinfeld was involved, *see* Memorandum in Support of Motion to Consolidate, *Lovett v. Schwabach*, and Defendant's Supplemental Memorandum of Law, *Maltbie v. Kookogey* (on issue of timeliness of motion), *Cases and Points*, vol. 10, Box 31, Weinfeld Papers.

73. Memorandum in Opposition to Defendant's Motion, *Rosenthal v. Simon Ackerman Clothes, Inc.*, 1, 5, *Cases and Points*, vol. 9, Box 31, Weinfeld Papers.

74. *Rosenthal v. Simon Ackerman Clothes, New York Law Journal*, undated, *Cases and Points*, vol. 9, Box 31, Weinfeld Papers.

75. Memorandum in Opposition to Defendants' Motions to Dismiss the Complaint, *Gebert v. Fairchild*, 2–3, *Cases and Points*, vol. 9, Box 31, Weinfeld Papers.

76. *Raives v. United States*, 39 F.2d 142, 144–45 (E.D.N.Y. 1930).

77. Appellant's Points in Reply, *Raives v. Raives*, 2–3, Files of United States Court of Appeals for the Second Circuit, Case No. 11437, Federal Records Center, New York, N.Y. *See also* Appellant's Points, *Raives v. Raives*, 2–3, Files of United States Court of Appeals for the Second Circuit, Case No. 11437, Federal Records Center, New York, N.Y.

78. *Raives v. Raives*, 54 F.2d 267, 269 (2d Cir. 1931).

79. Respondent's Brief, *Smith v. Fischer*, *Cases and Points*, vol. 10, Box 31, Weinfeld Papers.

80. *Id.*, 4–5.

81. Memorandum, *Grossinger v. Mittman*, *Cases and Points*, vol. 10, Box 31, Weinfeld Papers.

82. Memorandum on Behalf of the Defendant, Morris Sadof, *Rosenstein v. Sadof*, *Cases and Points*, vol. 10, Box 31, Weinfeld Papers.

83. Respondent's Brief, *Dubin v. Shander*, 9–10, *Cases and Points*, vol. 11, Box 31, Weinfeld Papers.

84. *Dubin v. Shander*, 248 A.D. 897, 291 N.Y.S. 407 (App. Div. 1936).

85. *See* Memorandum in Opposition to Motion, *Dubin v. Shander*, *Cases and Points*, vol. 11, Box 31, Weinfeld Papers.

86. Memorandum in Support of Motion by Plaintiff for a Bill of Particulars, and in Opposition to the Cross-Motion by the Defendant, *Dubin v. Shander*, *Cases and Points*, vol. 11, Box 31, Weinfeld Papers.

87. *Dubin v. Shander, New York Law Journal*, July 21, 1936, *Cases and Points*, vol. 11, Box 31, Weinfeld Papers.

88. Memorandum in Support of Motion, *Irving Trust Co. v. White Star Coal Co., Inc., Cases and Points*, vol. 10, Box 31, Weinfeld Papers.

89. *Feist v. Druckerman*, 70 F.2d 333 (2d Cir. 1934).

90. *People ex rel. Ryan v. Graves, New York Law Journal*, October 19, 1935, *Cases and Points*, vol. 10, Box 31, Weinfeld Papers. For Weinfeld's involvement in the case, *see* Memorandum in Support of Motion, *People ex rel. Ryan v. Graves, Cases and Points*, vol. 10, Box 31, Weinfeld Papers.

91. *Horvath v. Brettschneider*, 131 Misc. 618, 227 N.Y.S. 109 (City Ct. of N.Y. 1928).

92. *See* Plaintiff's Memorandum, *Buvel v. Naman, Cases and Points*, vol. 10, Box 31, Weinfeld Papers; Defendant's Memorandum, *Buvel v. Naman, Cases and Points*, vol. 10, Box 31, Weinfeld Papers.

93. *Buvel v. Naman, New York Law Journal*, February 1, 1936, *Cases and Points*, vol. 10, Box 31, Weinfeld Papers.

94. Memorandum in Support of Defendant's Motion to Dismiss Complaint, *Loder v. Alexander Hamilton Institute*, 3–4, 6–12, *Cases and Points*, vol. 10, Box 31, Weinfeld Papers.

95. *Id.*, 12–17, *quoting Grant v. New York Herald Co.*, 138 A.D. 727, 123 N.Y.S. 449 (1st Dept. 1910) (emphasis added by Weinfeld).

96. Memorandum on Behalf of Plaintiffs in Opposition to Defendant's Motion, *Loder v. Alexander Hamilton Institute*, 8, *Cases and Points*, vol. 10, Box 31, Weinfeld Papers.

97. *Loder v. Alexander Hamilton Institute, New York Law Journal*, March 21, 1935, *Cases and Points*, vol. 10, Box 31, Weinfeld Papers.

98. Harry Field to Edward Weinfeld, September 29, 1936, Box 3, folder— Joseph L. Eichler, Weinfeld Papers. For the papers that Weinfeld filed on the plumbers' behalf, *see* Order to Show Cause, Affidavits, Summons and Complaint and Exhibits, *Field v. Rice, Cases and Points*, vol. 11, Box 31, Weinfeld Papers.

99. Memorandum in Opposition to Plaintiff's Motion for Injunctive Relief, *Mosberg v. Trattner, Cases and Points*, vol. 10, Box 31, Weinfeld Papers.

100. Memorandum of Law, In the Matter of the Butterick Company, 1, 17, *Cases and Points*, vol. 10, Box 31, Weinfeld Papers. For a second brief in the same case, *see* Memorandum in Opposition to Motion to Vacate Service of Subpoena and Complaint, *Cases and Points*, vol. 10, Box 31, Weinfeld Papers.

101. *In re Meyerberg*, 249 A.D. 149, 291 N.Y.S. 519 (1st Dept. 1936).

102. Memorandum in Opposition to Motion to Dismiss Complaint, *Lautman v. American Woolen Co.*; Reply Memorandum of Plaintiff in Opposition to Motion to Dismiss Complaint, *Lautman v. American Woolen Co.*; Memorandum in Support of Motion to Remand, *Lautman v. American Woolen Co.*; Reply Memorandum in Support of the Motion to Remand, *Lautman v. American*

Woolen Co.; Memorandum in Opposition to Petition Filed by American Woolen Company for Removal, *Lautman v. American Woolen Co.*, all in *Cases and Points*, vol. 10, Box 31, Weinfeld Papers.

103. Edward Weinfeld to John C. Knox, October 4, 1935, *Cases and Points*, vol. 10, Box 31, Weinfeld Papers.

104. Edward Weinfeld to Joseph L. Eichler, December 25, 1935, Box 3, folder—Joseph L. Eichler, Weinfeld Papers.

105. Appellant's Points, *Shapiro v. Gough, Cases and Points*, vol. 10, Box 31, Weinfeld Papers.

106. In a letter that Weinfeld sent to Joseph L. Eichler on June 12, 1940, Box 3, folder—Joseph L. Eichler, Weinfeld Papers, about a year after he had assumed the office of housing commissioner, which paid a salary of twelve thousand dollars per year, Weinfeld wrote that "public service has involved some financial sacrifice," especially since "my office is almost at a complete standstill with expenses continuing, and no new business coming in, and my office is operating at a loss." In addition to his practice income, we know that Weinfeld earned some money from his work as counsel to a state legislative committee and as a delegate to the 1938 state constitutional convention.

107. Edward Weinfeld to Joseph L. Eichler, August 18, 1937; Joe Eichler to Ed Weinfeld, October 2, 1935; Eddie to Joseph Eichler, October 2, 1935; Edward Weinfeld to Joseph L. Eichler, December 25, 1935; Edward Weinfeld to Joseph L. Eichler, June 12, 1940, all in Box 3, folder—Joseph L. Eichler, Weinfeld Papers.

108. Edward Weinfeld to Pelham St. George Bissell, September 4, 1935; Edward Weinfeld to Pelham St. George Bissell, October 23, 1935; Pelham St. George Bissell to Edward Weinfeld, October 24, 1935; Pelham St. George Bissell to Edward Weinfeld, April 24, 1936, all in *Cases and Points*, vol. 10, Box 31, Weinfeld Papers.

109. Memorandum on Behalf of Plaintiff, *Wolfsont v. Bennett, Cases and Points*, vol. 10, Box 31, Weinfeld Papers.

110. "Meet the Delegates," *Knickerbocker News*, July 7, 1938, Box 36, Scrapbook 1, Weinfeld Papers.

NOTES TO CHAPTER 4

1. Joshua B. Freeman, *Working-Class New York: Life and Labor since World War II* (New York: New Press, 2000).

2. *Edward Weinfeld: A Judicious Life* (New York: Federal Bar Foundation, 1998), 9.

3. Fern W. Cohen, *Included Out (Excluded In) . . . Mostly about My Father, Tennis, Me, and Freud . . .* (ms. dated March 4, 2000 in possession of the author), 64.

4. *A Judicious Life*, 20.

5. Author's conversation with Ann Schulman, January 27, 2001.

6. *Included Out*, 64.

7. *A Judicious Life*, 20.

8. *Id.*, 20.

9. *Phi Sigma Deltan* (Convention Number, December, 1925), 5, Box 33, Weinfeld Papers.

10. *A Judicious Life*, 20.

11. The leading history of twentieth-century dating patterns in America, *see* Beth Bailey, *From Front Porch to Back Seat: Courtship in Twentieth-Century America* (Baltimore: Johns Hopkins University Press, 1988), suggests that the familiar pattern of a single man taking a single woman on a date had emerged in middle-class America by the 1920s. *Id.*, p. 13. Weinfeld's dating of Lillian Stoll simply did not conform to this pattern.

12. *Included Out*, 133.

13. Author's telephone conversation with Ann Schulman, January 27, 2001.

14. *See* wedding invitation, in *A Judicious Life*, 9.

15. *A Judicious Life*, 9.

16. *Included Out*, 63, 138.

17. *A Judicious Life*, 36

18. Author's telephone conversation with Ann Schulman, January 27, 2001.

19. *A Judicious Life*, 36

20. *Included Out*, 138.

21. Author's telephone conversation with Ann Schulman, January 27, 2001.

22. *A Judicious Life*, 9.

23. *Included Out*, 261.

24. Guest Book—Lillian Weinfeld, February 14, 1950, Box 6, Weinfeld Papers.

25. *Included Out*, 261.

26. *Id.*, 109, 138; author's conversation with Fern Cohen, May 7, 2003.

27. *See* Guest Book—Lillian Weinfeld, November 19, 1942, November 20, 1942, April 21, 1951, Box 6, Weinfeld Papers.

28. *A Judicious Life*, 10.

29. *See* Guest Book—Lillian Weinfeld, January 21, 1941 to December 31, 1941, Box 6, Weinfeld Papers.

30. *Id.*, November 14, 1941; December 19, 1941; January 25, 1942; May 6, 1945; December 12, 1947; February 22, 1948; February 11, 1949; February 2, 1951; February 9, 1951; December 12, 1952.

31. *Included Out*, 135, 185.

32. Edward Weinfeld to Joseph Eichler, November 23, 1942, Box 3, folder— Joseph L. Eichler, Weinfeld Papers.

33. Guest Book—Lillian Weinfeld, Intermission, Summer 1942, Box 6, Weinfeld Papers.

34. *Included Out*, 52.

35. Edward Weinfeld to Joseph Eichler, November 23, 1942, Box 3, folder—Joseph L. Eichler, Weinfeld Papers.

36. Author's conversation with Ann Schulman, June 6, 2001.

37. "Theatre Party at 'No Strings' Will Benefit LENA March 30," *New York Times*, March 10, 1962, 10.

38. Lillian Weinfeld, handwritten speech, undated, Box 44, folder 22, Weinfeld Papers.

39. Single handwritten page of notes for a speech, undated, Box 44, folder 22, Weinfeld Papers.

40. Ann received a bachelor's degree from Vassar, and Fern from Radcliffe.

41. *Included Out*, 178–80; author's conversation with Fern Cohen, June 7, 2003.

42. *Id.*, 125.

43. *Id.*, 178.

44. *Id.*, 226; author's conversation with Fern Cohen, June 7, 2003.

45. *Included Out*, 227.

46. Author's conversation with Ann Schulman, May 27, 2003 (concerning, in particular, the husband of Weinfeld's client, Ralphina Lowenstein).

47. Author's conversation with Ann Schulman, June 6, 2001.

48. Author's conversation with Ann Schulman, June 6, 2001.

49. *See* Remarks of Alvin H. Schulman, Judge Edward Weinfeld, 1901–1988, Service at Temple Emanu-El, New York, N.Y., January 19, 1988, Box 25, Weinfeld Papers.

50. Author's conversation with Ann Schulman, May 27, 2003.

51. *Included Out*, 31.

52. *Id.*, 34.

53. *Id.*, 35.

54. *Id.*, 33.

55. Author's conversation with Edward Weinfeld, sometime in 1965–1966.

56. *Included Out*, 32.

57. Posthumous Transcription of Tape-Recorded In-Person Conversation between the Honorable Edward Weinfeld, United States District Court, Southern District of New York, and Amy Schulman (His Granddaughter), September 4, 1988, Tape 5, 10 (transcript in possession of the author).

58. *Id.*, 11.

59. Edward Weinfeld to Philip Baum, Associate Executive Director, American Jewish Congress, July 18, 1977, Box 43, folder 19B, Weinfeld Papers.

60. Conversation of Edward Weinfeld with Amy Schulman, Tape 5, 11–12.

61. *Id.*, 7.

62. For information on Weinfeld's Long Island and Carribean vacations, *see* Box 43, folders 8, 9, 10, and 16, Weinfeld Papers.

63. Conversation of Edward Weinfeld with Amy Schulman, Tape 5, 11.

64. *See* invitation from Samuel L. Lewis, American Ambassador to Israel, Box 43, folder 19B, Weinfeld Papers.

65. *A Judicious Life,* 9.

66. *Included Out,* 124, 126.

67. *A Judicious Life,* 10.

68. Inscription from Eddie to Bubs on reprint of New York University Law Review Symposium in Honor of Judge Edward Weinfeld, Box 37, Weinfeld Papers.

69. Bubs to My Darling, October 27, 1981, Box 44, folder 18, Weinfeld Papers.

70. From Bubs to My Darling, December 22, 1959, in Box 44, folder 18, Weinfeld Papers.

71. *See* Amy Schulman to Grandma & Grandpa, June 8, 1977; Amy to Grandmar & Grandpar, undated; Elizabeth to Grandma & Grandpa, undated, all in Box 44, folder 18, Weinfeld Papers; *A Judicious Life,* 11.

72. Wedding speech for Amy Schulman and David Nachman, undated, Box 44, folder 23, Weinfeld Papers.

73. Nina Schulman to Edward Weinfeld, December 15, 1982, Box 44, folder 23, Weinfeld Papers.

74. *A Judicious Life,* 20.

75. Author's conversation with Ann Schulman, May 27, 2003.

76. *Included Out,* 21, 178–80.

77. *Id.,* 31, 126.

78. *Id.,* 59.

79. Edward Weinfeld to Mrs. Harold Faber, February 10, 1971, Box 39, folder 12, Weinfeld Papers.

80. Author's conversation with Ann Schulman, June 6, 2001.

NOTES TO CHAPTER 5

1. *See* "Democrats Hold 62 Assembly Seats," *New York Times,* November 7, 1928, 6.

2. *Application of Dolen,* 225 A.D. 78, 79, 231 N.Y.S. 617, 618 (1st Dept. 1928).

3. Appellant's Brief, *People v. Leik,* 4, 17, 60, *Cases and Points,* vol. 9, Box 31, Weinfeld Papers.

4. *Id.,* 60, quoting remarks of trial judge.

5. *Id.,* 5–6, 14–16.

6. "Liberal Party Granted Appeal in Strong Case," *New York Telegram,* October 25, 1934, 18.

7. *Id.*

8. *Peel v. Cohen,* 242 A.D. 264, 275 N.Y.S. 91 (2d Dept. 1934).

9. *Peel v. Cohen,* 265 N.Y. 312, 192 N.E. 785 (1934).

10. *See* Respondents' Memorandum in Appellate Division; Respondents' Brief and Record on Appeal in Court of Appeals, both in *Cases and Points,* vol. 9, Box 31, Weinfeld Papers.

11. "Democrats Win State Assembly," *New York Times,* November 7, 1934, 1, 7.

12. "Liberal Party Granted Appeal in Strong Case," 18.

13. "State to Broaden Mortgage Inquiry," *New York Times,* September 5, 1935, 38.

14. "Bond Committee Probe Launched," *New York Post,* September 30, 1935, Box 36, Scrapbook One, Weinfeld Papers.

15. Edward Weinfeld to Joseph L. Eichler, December 25, 1935, Box 3, folder—Joseph L. Eichler, Weinfeld Papers.

16. Private Hearings of Committee, vol. 4, 1568–70, Box 28, Weinfeld Papers.

17. *Id.,* vol. 5, 1745–82, Box 28, Weinfeld Papers.

18. "Pounds Forgets $45,000 Fee Details at Quiz," *New York Herald Tribune,* November 10, 1935, Box 36, Scrapbook 1, Weinfeld Papers.

19. "L. H. Pounds Scored on Straus Bonds," *New York Times,* November 2, 1935, 23.

20. "Inquiry Shows Inflated Price for Hotel Rent," *New York World Telegram,* November 19, 1935, Box 36, Scrapbook 1, Weinfeld Papers.

21. "'Finance Doctor' Sold Bond List," unidentifiable newspaper, November 20, 1935, Box 36, Scrapbook 1, Weinfeld Papers.

22. "Saul S. Streit Is Dead at 86; Ex-Judge and Assemblyman," *New York Times,* September 5, 1983, 30.

23. "Protective Groups Urged to Reform," *New York Times,* December 12, 1935, 39.

24. "Straus Bond Group Backs Supervision," *New York Times,* December 18, 1935, 39; "Pounds in Agreement with Streit Group," *New York Times,* January 4, 1936, 23.

25. "Bill Up to End 'Shocking' Evil in Mortgages," *New York Post,* January 10, 1936, Box 36, Scrapbook 1, Weinfeld Papers; "Mortgage Law to End Abuses Is Introduced," *New York Sun,* February 10, 1936, Box 36, Scrapbook 1, Weinfeld Papers.

26. "5 State Laws Enacted to Aid Bondholders," *New York Herald Tribune,* June 15, 1936, 23.

27. "Saul S. Streit Is Dead," 30.

28. "Legislative Board Weighs Need for Securities Agency in State," *New York Herald Tribune,* February 19, 1937, 31.

29. Edward Weinfeld to Joseph L. Eichler, December 25, 1935, Box 3, folder—Joseph L. Eichler, Weinfeld Papers.

30. "Streit Report," *New York World Telegram*, February 11, 1936, Box 31, Scrapbook 1, Weinfeld Papers.

31. "How the Suckers Were Milked Twice," *New York Post*, February 20, 1936, Box 36, Scrapbook 1, Weinfeld Papers.

32. "Legislators Want Model State 'SEC,'" *New York Times*, March 21, 1937, sec. 3, 6.

33. "Weinfeld Urges Additional Laws for Securities," *New York Herald Tribune*, March 22, 1937, Box 36, Scrapbook 1, Weinfeld Papers.

34. "Legislators Weigh Plan for State SEC," *New York Times*, February 19, 1937, 27.

35. "Weinfeld Urges Additional Laws for Securities," *New York Herald Tribune*, March 22, 1937, Box 36, Scrapbook 1, Weinfeld Papers.

36. "Tiger Opens Fight in City on New Deal," *New York Mirror*, August 4, 1937, 2.

37. *See* "Primary Thursday to Draw a Big Vote," *New York Times*, Sept. 12, 1937, 2; "Civic Union Backs 59 for Convention," *New York Times*, October 25, 1937, 3.

38. *See* Application for Commission in the Military Government Division of the Provost Marshall General's Office, November 20, 1943, Box 44, folder 10, Weinfeld Papers.

39. *Record of the Constitutional Convention of the State of New York, 1938* (Albany: J. B. Lyon Co., 1938), 878.

40. *Id.*, 2734–35.

41. *People v. Fisher*, 14 Wendell 9, 28 Am. Dec. 501 (N.Y. 1835).

42. The case cited by Weinfeld was *People v. Amana*, 203 A.D. 548, 196 N.Y.S. 606 (1st Dept. 1922). The convention reporter apparently misheard Weinfeld.

43. *Record*, 2736.

44. *Id.*, 1763.

45. 281 U.S. 439 (1930).

46. "Meet the Delegates: Edward Weinfeld, New York Lawyer, Keen Student of Convention Problems," *Knickerbocker News*, July 7, 1938, Box 36, Scrapbook 1, Weinfeld Papers.

47. "A Good Appointment," *Watertown Daily Times*, July 14, 1939, Box 36, Scrapbook 1, Weinfeld Papers.

48. "In Politics," *Knickerbocker News*, July 27, 1938, Box 36, Scrapbook 1, Weinfeld Papers.

49. "A Good Appointment."

50. *Record*, 1864, 2725.

51. *See id.*, 72, 108–9, 271, 434–35, 1336, 1726, 1754, 1814, 1997, 2044–45, 2207, 2650, 3055.

52. *Id.*, 1629.

53. *Id.*, 1629, 1632.

54. *Id.*, 3069–70.

55. *Id.*, 3071, 3088.

56. *Id.*, 733–35, 2265.

57. *Id.*, 1331–34, 1339, 1341, 2265.

58. *Id.*, 1857–59, 1863.

59. *Id.*, 456, 462–463.

60. *Id.*, 462–463, 2265.

61. *See* William E. Nelson, *The Legalist Reformation: Law, Politics, and Ideology in New York, 1920–1980* (Chapel Hill: University of North Carolina Press, 2001), 119–29.

62. *Record*, 3422–23.

63. Ira S. Robbins to Edward Weinfeld, August 31, 1938, Box 36, folder 1, Scrapbook 1926–1941, Weinfeld Papers.

64. Seymour Ellenbogen to Edward Weinfeld, September 15, 1938, August 31, 1938, Box 36, folder 1, Scrapbook 1926–1941, Weinfeld Papers.

65. "The Back Room," *New York Post*, May 13, 1939, Box 36, Scrapbook 1, Weinfeld Papers.

66. Seymour Ellenbogen to Edward Weinfeld, September 15, 1938, Box 36, folder 1, Scrapbook 1926–1941, Weinfeld Papers.

67. Edward Weinfeld to Edith Lehman, February 2, 1968, Box 27, folder 1, Weinfeld Papers.

68. "After the Public Took a Hand," *New York World Telegram*, August 27, 1938, Box 36, Scrapbook 1, Weinfeld Papers.

69. Edward Weinfeld to Charles Poletti, October 3, 1938; Edward Weinfeld to Charles Poletti, November 9, 1938; Charles Poletti to Edward Weinfeld, November 10, 1938; Robert F. Wagner to Edward Weinfeld, November 17, 1938; Robert F. Wagner to Edward Weinfeld, November 22, 1938, all in Box 36, folder 1, Scrapbook 1926–1941, Weinfeld Papers.

70. Invitations, Box 36, folder 1, Scrapbook 1926–1941, Weinfeld Papers.

71. "New Housing Bill Limits State Fund," *New York Times*, January 28, 1939, 3.

72. "New Housing Head to Begin His Task," *New York Times*, July 15, 1939, 2.

73. "Lehman Names Housing Head," *New York Post*, July 14, 1939, Box 36, Scrapbook 1, Weinfeld Papers.

74. Author's conversation with Ann Schulman, July 5, 2000.

75. *See* An Act to Fix the Salaries of Certain Judges of the United States, 44 Stat. 919 (1936).

76. Poletti, who had been elected lieutenant governor on a ticket led by Herbert H. Lehman, succeeded Lehman when Lehman resigned to become the State Department's director of foreign relief and rehabilitation operations.

77. "Twins, 2, Star in Housing Row Put Up to State," *New York Post*, September 27, 1939, Box 36, Scrapbook 1, Weinfeld Papers.

78. "Post-War Housing Advanced in State," *New York Times*, December 14, 1942, 25.

79. "City Building Fund Needs More Money," *New York Times*, December 29, 1942, 36.

80. *Id.*

81. "Weinfeld Resigns State Housing Job," *New York Times*, December 21, 1942, 17.

82. Charles Poletti to Edward Weinfeld, December 19, 1942; John J. Bennett, Jr., to Edward Weinfeld, December 21, 1942; Edmond B. Butler to Edward Weinfeld, December 24, 1942; John B. Blandford, Jr., to Edward Weinfeld, December 21, 1942; Charles S. Ascher to Edward Weinfeld, December 21, 1942, all in Box 18, Weinfeld Papers.

83. William T. Andrews to Edward Weinfeld, December 22, 1942; Charles L. Fleece to Edward Weinfeld, December 21, 1942; Irving M. Ives to Edward Weinfeld, January 2, 1943, all in Box 18, Weinfeld Papers.

84. Robert R. Hartley to Thomas E. Dewey, December 23, 1942, Box 18, Weinfeld Papers.

85. Edward Weinfeld to William J. Lamont, June 3, 1987, Box 40, folder 11, Weinfeld Papers.

86. Edward Weinfeld to Herbert H. Lehman, December 18, 1942, Box 18, Weinfeld Papers.

87. Herbert H. Lehman to Edward Weinfeld, December 23, 1942, Box 18, Weinfeld Papers.

88. Herbert H. Lehman to Harry S. Truman, April 1, 1950, Box 16, folder 1, Weinfeld Papers.

89. Edward Weinfeld to William J. Lamont, June 3, 1987, Box 40, folder 1, Weinfeld Papers.

90. Edward Weinfeld to Joseph L. Eichler, August 11, 1947, in Box 3, folder—Joseph L. Eichler, Weinfeld Papers.

91. F. M. Bishop to Edward Weinfeld, August 4, 1943, Box 44, folder 10, Weinfeld Papers.

92. Robert F. Wagner to Colonel Norman Lovett, October 11, 1943, Box 44, folder 10, Weinfeld Papers.

93. F. M. Bishop to Edward Weinfeld, August 4, 1943; Robert F. Wagner to

Colonel Norman Lovett, October 11, 1943; Norman F. Lovett to Edward Weinfeld, November 20, 1943, all in Box 44, folder 10, Weinfeld Papers.

NOTES TO CHAPTER 6

1. Edward Weinfeld, "Eulogy for Joseph L. Eichler, July 28, 1974," Box 3, folder—Eichler eulogy, Weinfeld Papers.

2. Joseph Eichler to Edward Weinfeld, October 27, 1936, Box 3, folder—Joseph L. Eichler, Weinfeld Papers.

3. Edward Weinfeld, "Eulogy for Joseph L. Eichler, July 28, 1974," Box 3, folder—Eichler eulogy, Weinfeld Papers.

4. *Id.* (emphasis in original).

5. Joseph L. Eichler to Richard K. Doyle, June 25, 1958; Edward Weinfeld to Joseph L. Eichler, November 6, 1955; Edward Weinfeld to Joseph L. Eichler, July 2, 1955, all in Box 3, folder—Joseph L. Eichler, Weinfeld Papers.

6. Edward Weinfeld to Joseph Eichler, October 16, 1961, Box 3, folder—Loan Data—1961, Weinfeld Papers.

7. Telegraphic Remission from Joseph L. Eichler to Edward Weinfeld, December 8, 1934, Box 3, folder—Joseph L. Eichler, Weinfeld Papers.

8. Promissory Note to Joseph L. Eichler, October 1, 1961, Box 3, folder—Loan Data—1961, Weinfeld Papers.

9. Michael Botein to Uncle Eddy, February 27, 1974, Box 38, folder 1, Weinfeld Papers.

10. Author's telephone interview with Michael Botein, August 5, 2000.

11. *See* Bernard Botein to Edward Weinfeld, January 7, 1969, Box 38, folder 1, Weinfeld Papers; Edward Weinfeld to Bernard Botein, January 3, 1957, Box 38, folder 1, Weinfeld Papers.

12. Michael Botein to Edward Weinfeld, December 31, 1971, Box 38, folder 1, Weinfeld Papers.

13. *See* Guest Book—Lillian Weinfeld, Box 6, Weinfeld Papers.

14. *Id.*, November 14, 1941, November 3, 1942.

15. Judgment, *Mahler v. Oishei*, Index No. 28485/1947, Supreme Court, New York County, *Report and Record*, 10, Box 29, Weinfeld Papers.

16. Weinfeld's copy of the proceedings in this case fills Box 30, Weinfeld Papers.

17. Edward Weinfeld to Bernard Botein, June 10, 1962; Edward Weinfeld to Bernard Botein, September 21, 1956; Bernard Botein to Edward Weinfeld and Lillian Weinfeld, June 30, 1966; Bernard Botein to Edward Weinfeld, August 4, 1958, all in Box 38, folder 1, Weinfeld Papers.

18. Michael Botein to Uncle Eddy, February 27, 1974; Marian Botein to Edward Weinfeld, undated, both in Box 38, folder 1, Weinfeld Papers.

19. Interview with Ann Schulman, May 21, 2003.

20. Speech by Edward Weinfeld at Community Synagogue's Dedication to Louis Lefkowitz, April 28, 1957, Box 23, folder 1, Weinfeld Papers.

21. *See* "Primary Thursday to Draw a Big Vote," *New York Times*, September 12, 1937, 2.

22. Speech by Edward Weinfeld at Community Synagogue's Dedication to Louis Lefkowitz, April 28, 1957, Box 23, folder 1, Weinfeld Papers.

23. *Id.*

24. Edward Weinfeld to Charles Poletti, October 3, 1938, Box 36, folder 1, Scrapbook 1926–1941, Weinfeld Papers.

25. Charles Poletti to Edward Weinfeld, November 10, 1938, Box 36, folder 1, Scrapbook 1926–1941, Weinfeld Papers.

26. Telegram from Walter T. Brown to Edward Weinfeld, October 6, 1938, Box 36, Scrapbook 1, Weinfeld Papers.

27. Telegram from Walter T. Brown to Edward Weinfeld, October 6, 1938; Charles Poletti to Edward Weinfeld, November 10, 1938, both in Box 36, folder 1, Scrapbook 1926–1941, Weinfeld Papers.

28. *See* Edward Weinfeld to Walter Brown, Secretary to the Governor, April 28, 1941, and attached speech draft, Box 27, folder 2, Weinfeld Papers.

29. Address of Governor Lehman at Ground Breaking Ceremony for Fort Greene Houses, Brooklyn, New York, May 6th, 1941, 4 P.M., Box 27, folder 2, Weinfeld Papers.

30. Suggested Notes for Governor Lehman's Address at the Mayor's Conference, Syracuse, June 10th [1942], Box 27, folder 2, Weinfeld Papers.

31. Herbert H. Lehman to Edward Weinfeld, December 23, 1942, Box 27, folder 2, Weinfeld Papers.

32. James J. Mahoney to Edward Weinfeld, August 27, 1942, Box 27, folder 2, Weinfeld Papers.

33. *See* "Lehman for United States Senator," Box 27, folder 2, Weinfeld Papers.

34. *See* Edward Weinfeld to Herbert H. Lehman, October 21, 1946, Box 27, folder 2, Weinfeld Papers; Edward Weinfeld to Herbert H. Lehman, October 26, 1946, Box 27, folder 4, Weinfeld Papers.

35. *See* Edward Weinfeld to Herbert H. Lehman, November 12, 1947, Box 27, folder 3, Weinfeld Papers.

36. Eddie Weinfeld to Herbert H. Lehman, August 31, 1949; Herbert H. Lehman to Edward Weinfeld, September 10, 1949; Edward Weinfeld to Alexander Mintz, October 22, 1949, all in Box 27, folder 3, Weinfeld Papers.

37. *See* Edward Weinfeld to Herbert H. Lehman, October 24, 1949, Box 27, folder 3, Weinfeld Papers.

38. Author's conversation with Ann Schulman, June 6, 2001.

39. Edward Weinfeld to Herbert H. Lehman, August 14, 1960; Edward

Weinfeld to Herbert H. Lehman, April 26, 1961, both in Box 27, folder 5, Weinfeld Papers.

40. Edward Weinfeld to Herbert H. Lehman, May 14, 1963, Box 27, folder 5, Weinfeld Papers.

41. Funeral Service for Hon. Herbert H. Lehman, December 8, 1963, 5, 7, in Box 27, folder 5, Weinfeld Papers.

42. Edward Weinfeld to Edith Lehman, January 11, 1964, in Box 27, folder 5, Weinfeld Papers.

43. *See* Edith Lehman to Edward Weinfeld, October 31, 1966; Edward Weinfeld to Edith Lehman, October 26, 1966; Edith Lehman to Edward Weinfeld, June 19, 1967; Edward Weinfeld to Edith Lehman, June 20, 1967, all in Box 27, folder 5, Weinfeld Papers.

44. Lawrence B. Rodman to Edward Weinfeld, April 13, 1976, Box 3, folder—EAL Bequest, Weinfeld Papers; Edith A. Lehman to Edward Weinfeld, June 27, 1966, Box 3, folder—Edith A. Lehman Gift, Weinfeld Papers.

45. Henry S. Waldman to Edward Weinfeld, Friday morning [ca. August 1950]; Henry S. Waldman to Edward Weinfeld, January 22, 1951; Henry S. Waldman to Edward Weinfeld, Monday [ca. April 1952]; Henry S. Waldman to Edward Weinfeld, February 28, 1951, all in Box 38, folder 13, Weinfeld Papers.

46. Edward Weinfeld to State Board of Pharmacy, October 24, 1966, Box 41, folder 6, Weinfeld Papers.

47. Irving Mitchell Felt to Edward Weinfeld, May 22, [no year], Box 39, Weinfeld Papers.

48. *See* Burton A. Zorn to Edward Weinfeld, May 4, 1966, Box 41, Weinfeld Papers; Burton A. and Fay S. Zorn to Stephen A. Zorn, May 2, 1966, Box 41, Weinfeld Papers; Burton A. and Fay S. Zorn to Whom It May Concern, May 2, 1966, Box 41, Weinfeld Papers.

49. *See* John Lichtenberg to Edward Weinfeld, January 29, 1960, Box 40, folder 11, Weinfeld Papers; Min Lichtenberg to Edward Weinfeld, March 21, 1960, Box 40, folder 11, Weinfeld Papers; John Lichtenberg to Edward Weinfeld, March 25, 1960, Box 40, folder 11, Weinfeld Papers.

50. Pierre Leval to Edward Weinfeld, May 10, 1977, Box 40, folder 11, Weinfeld Papers.

51. Edward Weinfeld to J. Edward Lumbard, June 25, 1985, Box 40, folder 2, Weinfeld Papers.

52. *Id.*

53. Author's conversation with Marie Vollrath, unknown date.

54. Edward Weinfeld to J. Edward Lumbard, June 25, 1985, Box 40, folder 2, Weinfeld Papers.

55. Edward Weinfeld to Learned Hand, November 11, 1960; Learned Hand to Edward Weinfeld, November 14, 1960, both in Box 47, Green Commonplace Book, Weinfeld Papers.

56. Edward Weinfeld to Frances Hand, August 21, 1961; Francis Hand to Edward Weinfeld, undated, both in Box 40, folder 2, Weinfeld Papers.

57. Edward Weinfeld to Henry J. Friendly, December 7, 1961, Box 10, Friendly-Weinfeld Letters, Weinfeld Papers.

58. Edward Weinfeld, "A Tribute to Henry J. Friendly," *Annual Survey of American Law*, vol. 1978, xx.

59. Edward Weinfeld to Henry J. Friendly, October 13, 1967, Box 10, Friendly-Weinfeld Letters, Weinfeld Papers.

60. Weinfeld, "A Tribute to Henry J. Friendly," xx, xxiv.

61. Henry J. Friendly, Speech at Dedication of Seminar Room in New York University School of Law, November 16, 1977, Box 10, Friendly-Weinfeld Letters, Weinfeld Papers.

62. Henry J. Friendly, "Edward Weinfeld," *New York University Law Review* 50 (1975): 977, 978.

63. Henry J. Friendly, Speech at Dedication of Seminar Room in New York University School of Law, November 16, 1977, Box 10, Friendly-Weinfeld Letters, Weinfeld Papers.

64. Weinfeld, "A Tribute to Henry J. Friendly," xx, xxiii.

65. Henry J. Friendly to Edward Weinfeld, April 20, 1979, Box 10, Friendly-Weinfeld Letters, Weinfeld Papers.

66. Friendly, "Edward Weinfeld," 977.

67. Henry J. Friendly to Edward Weinfeld, February 2, 1968; Edward Weinfeld to Henry J. Friendly, February 6, 1968, both in Box 10, Friendly-Weinfeld Letters, Weinfeld Papers.

68. Friendly, "Edward Weinfeld," 977, 979.

69. Warren Moscow to Edward Weinfeld, December 6, 1972, Box 40, folder 14, Weinfeld Papers.

70. *See* Edward Weinfeld to Warren Moscow, December 10, 1972, Box 40, folder 14, Weinfeld Papers.

71. Notes of Phone Conversation between Edward Weinfeld and Warren Moscow, undated, Box 40, folder 14, Weinfeld Papers.

72. Edward Weinfeld to Warren Moscow, December 10, 1972, Box 40, folder 14, Weinfeld Papers.

73. Author's conversation with Ann Schulman, June 6, 2001.

74. Anonymous, "I Have a Friend," undated, Box 41, Weinfeld Papers.

75. Ms. Vollrath was caring for her ill mother.

76. Marie Vollrath to Edward Weinfeld, June 6, 1980, Box 47, Green Commonplace Book, Weinfeld Papers.

NOTES TO CHAPTER 7

1. "Politics," *New York Evening Journal*, January 9, 1933, 8.

2. "An Excellent Appointment," *New York Times*, July 11, 1950, 30.

3. "The Feinberg Appointment," *New York Times*, October 13, 1965, 46.

4. "Appeals Court Choice—Judicial Dismay," *New York Herald Tribune*, October 13, 1965, 29.

5. Charles Wyzanski, Jr., to Edward Weinfeld, October 12, 1965, Box 45, folder 3, Weinfeld Papers (emphasis in original).

6. Vanessa Jalet to Edward Weinfeld, March 28, 1979, Box 40, folder 5, Weinfeld Papers.

7. *See* "Judge Weinfeld at 79," *New York Law Journal*, May 14, 1980, 1. During a trial, he would take shorthand notes that would be picked up on a regular basis and taken upstairs to his secretary, who transcribed them. *Id.*

8. Memo of Substance of Talk with Herbert H. Lehman, January 20, 1947, Box 16, folder 1, Weinfeld Papers.

9. Memorandum of Talk with Herbert H. Lehman, April 12, 1947, Box 16, folder 1, Weinfeld Papers.

10. Memorandum of Conversation with Robert F. Wagner, Jr., April 9, 1947, Box 16, folder 1, Weinfeld Papers.

11. Weinfeld agreed to manage Robert Jr.'s campaign in August of 1949, shortly after Robert Sr. had retired from the Senate because of poor health. Edward Weinfeld to Herbert H. Lehman, August 15, 1949, Box 16, folder 1, Weinfeld Papers.

12. By the late 1940s, the governor, the lieutenant governor, and the other senator from New York were all Republicans.

13. Memo of Conversation with Robert F. Wagner, Jr., December 12, 1946, Box 16, folder 1, Weinfeld Papers.

14. Memo, Sunday Evening, December 22, 1946, Box 16, folder 1, Weinfeld Papers.

15. Conversation with Robert F. Wagner, Jr., January 3, 1947, Box 16, folder 1, Weinfeld Papers.

16. Memo, Sunday, February 9, 1947, Box 16, folder 1, Weinfeld Papers.

17. Talk with Senator Robert F. Wagner, February 11, 1947, Box 16, folder 1, Weinfeld Papers.

18. Talk with Robert F. Wagner, Jr., April 7, 1947, Box 16, folder 1, Weinfeld Papers.

19. Talk with Robert F. Wagner, Jr., April 9, 1947, Box 16, folder 1, Weinfeld Papers.

20. Memo of Conversation with Frank Sampson, April 8, 1948, Box 16, folder 1, Weinfeld Papers.

21. Ed Flynn to Herbert H. Lehman, April 20, 1948, Box 16, folder 1, Weinfeld Papers.

22. Memo of Conversation with Commissioner Robert F. Wagner, Jr., March 11, 1949, Box 16, folder 1, Weinfeld Papers.

23. Edward Weinfeld to Coleman Woodbury, November 14, 1949; Edward Weinfeld to Maxwell H. Tretter, October 7, 1949, both in Box 16, folder 1, Weinfeld Papers.

24. Ann Weinfeld to Edward Weinfeld, October 16, 1949, Box 16, folder 1, Weinfeld Papers.

25. Edith A. Lehman to the President of the United States, February 6, 1964; Edith A. Lehman to the President, July 21, 1965, both in Box 45, folder 3, Weinfeld Papers.

26. *See* Memo of Conversation with Joe Dolan, September 13, 1965, 10:15 A.M., Box 45, folder 3, Weinfeld Papers. *See also* Memo of Henry J. Friendly Conversation with Edward Weinfeld, September 14, 1965, 10 P.M., Box 45, folder 3, Weinfeld Papers.

27. Emanuel Celler to the President, September 28, 1965, Box 45, folder 3, Weinfeld Papers.

28. Memo of Burton A. Zorn Conversation with Arthur J. Goldberg, September 14, 1965, 3:35 P.M., Box 45, folder 3, Weinfeld Papers.

29. Memorandum, September 29, 1965, Box 45, folder 3, Weinfeld Papers.

30. Box 45, folder 3, Weinfeld Papers contains Weinfeld's notes of conversations he had with various people who provided him with information about events leading up to the president's decision and who helped him strategize about how to respond to those events; the majority of Weinfeld's conversations were with Judge Friendly.

31. Statement of Daniel P. Levitt at Symposium on the Life of Edward Weinfeld, New York University School of Law, June 2, 2001.

32. "Appeals Court Choice—Judicial Dismay," *New York Herald Tribune*, October 13, 1965, 29.

33. Memo, Thursday, October 7, 1965, 11:42 A.M., Box 45, folder 3, Weinfeld Papers.

34. "U.S. Court Choice Surprises Some," *New York Times*, Tuesday, October 12, 1965, 27.

35. Memo, Sunday Evening, September 26, 1965, Box 45, folder 3, Weinfeld Papers.

36. Author's conversation with Edward Weinfeld, October 1965.

37. Charles E. Wyzanski, Jr., to Edward Weinfeld, October 12, 1965, Box 45, folder 3, Weinfeld Papers.

38. Edward Weinfeld to David L. Krooth, November 18, 1965, Box 45, folder 3, Weinfeld Papers.

39. Edward Weinfeld to Paul M. Herzog, October 21, 1965, Box 45, folder 3, Weinfeld Papers.

40. Edward Weinfeld to William C. Leff, March 10, 1978, Box 45, folder 3, Weinfeld Papers.

41. Edward Weinfeld to Joseph Eichler, April 16, 1968, Box 3, folder—Joseph L. Eichler, Weinfeld Papers.

42. Memo, Sunday, February 9, 1947, Box 16, folder 1, Weinfeld Papers.

43. Edward Weinfeld to Edith Lehman, February 2, 1968, Box 27, folder 1, Weinfeld Papers.

44. "Senator Wagner Resigns: Fall Election Is Necessary," *New York Times*, June 29, 1949, 1.

45. Herbert H. Lehman to Harry S. Truman, April 1, 1950, Box 16, folder 1, Weinfeld Papers (emphasis added).

46. "Weinfeld Named to Federal Bench Here; Bar, Party Leaders Hail Truman's Choice," *New York Times*, June 11, 1950, 21.

47. Harry Truman to Edward Weinfeld, July 14, 1950, Box 16, folder 1, Weinfeld Papers.

48. *See* "Weinfeld Confirmed," *New York Times*, August 2, 1950, 27; "A New Member of the Federal Bench," *New York Times*, August 15, 1950, 22.

49. The materials quoted below are in the form in which Weinfeld copied them into his Green Commonplace Book, Box 47, Weinfeld Papers, not in the form in which they appeared in the original text.

50. Author's conversation with Ann Schulman, May 21, 2003.

51. *See Edward Weinfeld: A Judicious Life* (New York: Federal Bar Foundation, 1997), 35–36.

52. *See* Edward Weinfeld to Ann Rosman, March 27, 1987, Box 41, Weinfeld Papers; Edward Weinfeld to Mr. and Mrs. James Felt, February 16, 1971, Box 39, folder 12, Weinfeld Papers.

53. Piero Calamandrei, *Eulogy of Judges: Written by a Lawyer* (Princeton, N.J.: Princeton University Press, 1946).

54. *Id.*, 67.

55. Address by John Marshall before Virginia State Convention, 1829–1830, *quoted in O'Donoghue v. United States*, 289 U.S. 516, 532 (1933).

56. Chief Justice Hughes, Response to an Inquiry, *quoted in* 338 U.S. xvii–xviii (1948).

57. *Quoted in* Merlo Jo Pusey, *Charles Evans Hughes*, vol. 1 (New York: Columbia University Press, 1963), 296–97.

58. Philip B. Kurland, "The Appointment and Disappointment of Supreme Court Justices," *Arizona State University Law Journal* 5 (1972): 190.

59. Alpheus Thomas Mason, *Harlan Fiske Stone, Pillar of the Law* (New York: Viking Press, 1956), 326–27.

60. Charles A. Horsky's definition of judicial greatness in "Augustus Noble Hand," 1119, *quoted in* Marvin Schick, *Learned Hand's Court* (Baltimore: Johns Hopkins University Press, 1970), 352 n.13.

61. Benjamin N. Cardozo, *The Nature of the Judicial Process* (New Haven, Conn.: Yale University Press, 1921), 141.

62. Levi S. Udall, "The Essential Characteristics of a Judge," *Journal of the American Judicature Society* 41 (October 1957): 69.

63. Calamandrei, *Eulogy of Judges*, 62.

64. Arthur T. Vanderbilt, *The Challenge of Law Reform* (Princeton, N.J.: Princeton University Press, 1955), 11.

65. Remarks of Chief Justice G. Joseph Tauro of Supreme Judicial Court of Massachusetts to newly appointed judges, *The Judges' Journal* 13(4) (October 1974): 87.

66. Weinfeld did not identify the source of the Baker quotation.

67. *Rosenberg v. United States*, 346 U.S. 273, 309 (1953) (Frankfurter, J., dissenting).

68. Benjamin Franklin, "Final Address at the Constitutional Convention, September 17, 1787," in Max Farrand ed., *The Records of the Federal Convention of 1787*, vol. 2 (New Haven, Conn.: Yale University Press, 1911), 642.

69. Pusey, *Charles Evans Hughes*, vol. 2, 679.

70. Edward H. Warren, *The Rights of Margin Customers against Wrongdoing Stockbrokers and Some Other Problems in the Modern Law of Pledge* (Norwood, Mass.: Plimpton Press, 1941), 30.

71. Elliott L. Biskind, "Write It Right," *New York Law Journal*, October 2, 1979, 2.

72. Irving Younger, "Persuasive Writing," *American Bar Association Journal* 72 (March 1, 1986): 92.

73. *Quoted in* Arthur S. Link, ed., *The Papers of Woodrow Wilson*, vol. 1 (Princeton, N.J.: Princeton University Press, 1966), 118–19.

74. Felix Frankfurter, ed., *Mr. Justice Brandeis and the Constitution* (New Haven, Conn.: Yale University Press, 1932). Weinfeld's Green Commonplace Book fails to indicate the article in this collection from which he extracted the quotation.

75. Paul Freund, "Proceedings in Memory of Mr. Justice Brandeis," 317 U.S. xx (1942).

76. John P. Frank, "Hugo Black: He Has Joined the Giants," *American Bar Association Journal* 58 (1972): 25.

77. Edward Weinfeld to Bernard Botein, August 30, 1950, Box 52, folder 22, Weinfeld Papers.

78. Bernard Botein to Edward Weinfeld, August 18, 1950, Box 38, folder 1, Weinfeld Papers.

NOTES TO CHAPTER 8

1. *Edward Weinfeld: A Judicious Life* (New York: Federal Bar Foundation, 1998), 63, 95; John G. Koeltl and Frank M. Tuerkheimer, "Judge Weinfeld and

the Criminal Law: The *Keogh-Kahaner* Trial—A Case Study in Criminal Justice," *New York University Law Review* 50 (1975): 1008–9.

2. *Quoted in* Koeltl and Tuerkheimer, "Judge Weinfeld and the Criminal Law," 1044.

3. William Rayner Davis to the Editor, *New York Herald Tribune*, April 27, 1951, Box 35, Scrapbook 1950–1957, Weinfeld Papers; Norman J. Rubin to Edward Weinfeld, August 27, 1970, Box 41, Weinfeld Papers.

4. Harvey Picker to Edward Weinfeld, March 2, 1954, Box 35, Scrapbook 1950–1957, Weinfeld Papers.

5. *A Judicious Life*, 64; Koeltl and Tuerkheimer, "Judge Weinfeld and the Criminal Law," 1008–9.

6. *Id.*, 1050.

7. *A Judicious Life*, 115.

8. *Id.*, 91.

9. Merlo Jo Pusey, *Charles Evans Hughes* (New York: Columbia University Press, 1963), *quoted in* Box 47, Green Commonplace Book, Weinfeld Papers.

10. *A Judicious Life*, 103; Piero Calamandrei, *Eulogy of Judges: Written by a Lawyer* (Princeton, N.J.: Princeton University Press, 1946), *quoted in* Box 47, Green Commonplace Book, Weinfeld Papers.

11. *See Twentieth Century-Fox Film Corp. v. Taylor*, 239 F. Supp. 913 (S.D.N.Y. 1965).

12. *See* Fern W. Cohen, *Included Out (Excluded In) . . . Mostly about My Father, Tennis, Me, and Freud . . .* (ms. dated March 4, 2000 in possession of the author), 33, 64.

13. *See Blaich v. National Football League*, 212 F. Supp. 319 (S.D.N.Y. 1962).

14. *See United States v. Keogh*, 271 F. Supp. 1002 (S.D.N.Y. 1967), *modified*, 391 F.2d 138 (2d Cir. 1968), and 289 F. Supp. 265 (S.D.N.Y. 1968), *aff'd*, 417 F.2d 885 (2d Cir. 1969).

15. *See United States v. Kahaner*, 203 F. Supp. 78 (S.D.N.Y. 1962), and 204 F. Supp. 921 (S.D.N.Y. 1962).

16. *United States v. Henderson*, 399 F. Supp. 508, 510 (S.D.N.Y. 1975).

17. *Farmer v. Arabian American Oil Co.*, 31 F.R.D. 191, 193 (S.D.N.Y. 1962), *rev'd*, 324 F.2d 359 (2d Cir. 1963), *rev'd*, 379 U.S. 227 (1964); *Accord, Brager & Co. v. Leumi Securities Corp.*, 530 F. Supp. 1361, 1363 (S.D.N.Y.), *aff'd*, 697 F.2d 288 (2d Cir. 1982); *Cf. Colucci v. The New York Times Co.*, 533 F. Supp. 1011, 1013 (S.D.N.Y. 1982) (attorney fees).

18. *Rastelli v. Warden, Metropolitan Correctional Center*, 622 F. Supp. 1387, 1396 (S.D.N.Y. 1985).

19. *A Judicious Life*, 100, 103, 106. *See also id.*, 116, for a similar description of the judge's procedures a decade later.

20. *A Judicious Life*, 61, 105.

21. 550 F. Supp. 1256 (S.D.N.Y. 1982).

22. *See Hunt v. Mobil Oil Corp.*, 557 F. Supp. 368, 376–77 (S.D.N.Y.), *aff'd*, 742 F.2d 1438 (2d Cir. 1983); *United States v. Ferguson*, 548 F. Supp. 1390, 1391 (S.D.N.Y. 1982). For another case in which the judge refused to recuse himself, *see Markus v. United States*, 545 F. Supp. 998 (S.D.N.Y.), *aff'd*, 742 F.2d 1444 (2d Cir. 1982).

23. Indeed, he had decided *Hunt v. Mobil Oil Corp.*, 465 F. Supp. 195 (S.D.N.Y. 1978), *aff'd*, 610 F.2d 806 (2d Cir. 1979), a suit involving hundreds of millions of dollars in which a former law clerk, Daniel P. Levitt, had served as lead counsel for the Hunts, against Hunt. For earlier opinions on pretrial motions, see *Hunt v. Mobil Oil Corp.*, 444 F. Supp. 68 (S.D.N.Y. 1977); *Hunt v. Mobil Oil Corp.*, 410 F. Supp. 10 (S.D.N.Y. 1975); *Hunt v. Mobil Oil Corp.*, 410 F. Supp. 4 (S.D.N.Y. 1975).

24. 550 F. Supp. at 1259.

25. *Id.*, 1260.

26. *A Judicious Life*, 125–26.

27. Newton D. Baker, quoted in Box 47, Green Commonplace Book, Weinfeld Papers.

28. Chief Justice Hughes, Response to an Inquiry, *quoted in* 338 U.S. xvii–xviii (1948), Box 47, Green Commonplace Book, Weinfeld Papers.

29. Piero Calamandrei, *Eulogy of Judges, quoted in* Box 47, Green Commonplace Book, Weinfeld Papers.

30. William E. Nelson, "Judge Weinfeld and the Adjudicatory Process: A Law Finder in an Age of Judicial Lawmakers," *New York University Law Review* 50 (1975): 980, 982. After reading this article, Weinfeld told the author that the article correctly captured the essentials of his decision-making process.

31. *Austrian v. Williams*, 103 F. Supp. 64 (S.D.N.Y.), *rev'd*, 198 F.2d 697 (2d Cir.), *cert. denied*, 344 U.S. 909 (1952).

32. *Id.*, 74–75.

33. 304 U.S. 64 (1938).

34. *Austrian v. Williams*, 103 F. Supp. 64, 111 (S.D.N.Y. 1952).

35. *Austrian v. Williams*, 198 F.2d 697, 703 (2d Cir. 1952) (Clark, J., dissenting).

36. *Austrian v. Williams*, 103 F. Supp. 64, 112–13 (S.D.N.Y. 1952).

37. *Austrian v. Williams*, 198 F.2d 697 (2d Cir.), *cert. denied*, 344 U.S. 909 (1952).

38. 579 F. Supp. 652 (S.D.N.Y.), *aff'd sub. nom. United States v. Perez*, 733 F.2d 1026 (2d Cir. 1984).

39. See chapter 5 above at note 58.

40. *United States v. Toney*, 579 F. Supp. 652, 654 (S.D.N.Y. 1984).

41. *Id.*, 655.

42. *United States v. Perez*, 733 F.2d 1026 (2d Cir. 1984).

43. 168 F. Supp. 576 (S.D.N.Y. 1958).

44. 15 U.S.C. § 18.

45. This issue was later settled in *United States v. Philadelphia Nat'l Bank*, 374 U.S. 321 (1963) (asserted need to compete with the largest bank in its city and with New York banks would not justify the merger of Philadelphia's second- and third-largest banks). *See also Missouri Portland Cement Co. v. Cargill, Inc.*, 498 F.2d 851 (2d Cir.), *cert. denied*, 419 U.S. 883 (1974) (absent horizontal or vertical effects, merger acquisition that will stimulate competition in an oligopolistic industry does not violate section 7 of the Clayton Act).

46. 168 F. Supp. at 592.

47. *Id.*, 616–17.

48. 256 F. Supp. 244 (S.D.N.Y. 1966).

49. *Id.*, 254.

50. *See United States ex rel. McGrath v. LaVallee*, 319 F.2d 308, 313–14 (2d Cir. 1963) and 348 F.2d 373 (2d Cir. 1965), *cert. denied*, 384 U.S. 923 (1966).

51. 256 F. Supp. at 251.

52. *See Henry v. Mississippi*, 379 U.S. 443, 451 (1965); *Fay v. Noia*, 372 U.S. 391, 439 (1963).

53. 256 F. Supp. at 257.

54. *See Machibroda v. United States*, 368 U.S. 487, 493 (1962); *Kercheval v. United States*, 274 U.S. 220, 223 (1927). Weinfeld had reached a like conclusion in an analogous case involving a defendant convicted in a federal court on a federal charge. *See United States v. Colson*, 230 F. Supp. 953 (S.D.N.Y. 1964). He had also reached that conclusion in two factually analogous cases involving a different issue, deprivation of the right to counsel, when he held that counsel was constitutionally mandated in a case where a defendant had potentially complex defenses to a criminal charge of rape. *See United States ex rel. Brown v. Fay*, 242 F. Supp. 273 (S.D.N.Y. 1965); *United States ex rel. Bowers v. Fay*, 171 F. Supp. 558 (S.D.N.Y. 1958), *aff'd*, 266 F.2d 824 (1959).

55. 319 F.2d 308 (2d Cir. 1963).

56. Weinfeld's only overt expression of lack of sympathy with *McGrath* was his citation from the dissent in that case to support his point that there is a significant difference between a defendant's bargaining with a prosecutor and a defendant's bargaining with a judge, "'who [is] ultimately to determine the length of sentence to be imposed.'" 256 F. Supp. at 255, *quoting* 319 F.2d at 319 (Marshall, J., dissenting). Weinfeld himself had only recently held that federal judges could not participate in plea bargaining in federal prosecutions, *see United States v. Tateo*, 214 F. Supp. 560 (S.D.N.Y. 1963), but he did not cite the *Tateo* case in the *Elksnis* opinion since *Tateo* had not rested on constitutional grounds.

57. *See* Stipulation Withdrawing Appeal, July 28, 1966, *United States ex rel.*

Elksnis v. Gilligan, 65 Civ. 2478, United States District Court, Southern District of New York, Federal Records Center, New York, N.Y.

58. See *Machibroda v. United States*, 368 U.S. 487, 493 (1962); *Kercheval v. United States*, 274 U.S. 220, 223 (1927).

59. *Erie-Lakawana R.R. v. United States*, 259 F. Supp. 964 (S.D.N.Y. 1966), *rev'd sub nom. Baltimore & Ohio R.R. v. United States*, 386 U.S. 372 (1967).

60. 259 F. Supp. at 980–81.

61. *Id.*, 981, 982.

62. *Baltimore & Ohio R.R. v. United States*, 386 U.S. 372 (1967).

63. *New York, New Haven & Hartford R.R. v. United States*, 289 F. Supp. 418 (S.D.N.Y. 1968).

64. *New York, New Haven & Hartford R.R. v. United States*, 305 F. Supp. 1049 (S.D.N.Y. 1968), *vacated in part sub. nom. New Haven Inclusion Cases*, 399 U.S. 392 (1970).

65. *Id.*, 1053.

66. *Id.*, 1065, 1066.

67. *New Haven Inclusion Cases*, 399 U.S. 392 (1970).

68. 360 F. Supp. 1265 (S.D.N.Y.), *remanded in part*, 490 F.2d 387 (2d Cir. 1973). For an earlier opinion in the same case, *see Vulcan Society v. Civil Service Commission*, 353 F. Supp. 1092 (S.D.N.Y. 1973) (denying preliminary injunction).

69. 360 F. Supp. at 1274.

70. *Chance v. Board of Examiners*, 458 F.2d 1167, 1177 n.16 (2d Cir. 1972).

71. *Compare Pennsylvania v. O'Neill*, 348 F. Supp. 1084, 1090–91 (E.D. Pa. 1972), *aff'd in relevant part by an equally divided court*, 473 F.2d 1029, 1030 (3d Cir. 1973) (en banc) (city must attempt to devise a test predictive of on-the-job performance), *with Castro v. Beecher*, 459 F.2d 725, 729 n.3, 737–38 (1st Cir. 1972), *aff'g in relevant part* 334 F. Supp. 930, 942, 945 (D. Mass. 1971) (city must create test valid under either content or "empirical" validation criteria), *and Carter v. Gallagher*, 452 F.2d 315, 320, 326 (8th Cir. 1971), *adopted in relevant part*, 452 F.2d 327, 331 (8th Cir.) (en banc), *cert. denied*, 406 U.S. 950 (1972) (specific adherence prescribed to guidelines of 29 C.F.R. § 1607 (1975)). The EEOC guidelines in question favored "criterion-related" (predictive or concurrent) validation but allowed content relation "where criterion-related validity [was] not feasible."

72. Indeed, Weinfeld was never ideologically driven in cases alleging racial or other forms of discrimination but always let his judgments rest on careful examination of the facts, *see Beverley v. Douglas*, 591 F. Supp. 1321 (S.D.N.Y. 1984); *Zervigon v. Piedmont Aviation, Inc.*, 558 F. Supp. 1305 (S.D.N.Y.), *aff'd*, 742 F.2d 1433 (2d Cir. 1983); *Colucci v. The New York Times Co.*, 533 F. Supp. 1005 (S.D.N.Y. 1982); *St. Lawrence v. Scully*, 523 F. Supp. 1290 (S.D.N.Y. 1981), *aff'd*, 697 F.2d 296 (2d Cir. 1982); *Dopico v. Goldschmidt*, 518 F. Supp.

1161 (S.D.N.Y. 1981), *aff'd*, 687 F.2d 644 (2d Cir. 1982); *King v. Bailar*, 444 F. Supp. 1093 (S.D.N.Y. 1978); *Morpurgo v. United States*, 437 F. Supp. 1135 (S.D.N.Y. 1977), *aff'd sub nom. Morpurgo v. Professional Staff Congress*, 580 F.2d 1045 (2d Cir.), *cert. denied*, 439 U.S. 1000 (1978); *Child v. Beame*, 425 F. Supp. 194 (S.D.N.Y. 1977); *Equal Employment Opportunity Comm'n v. Kallir, Philips, Ross, Inc.*, 420 F. Supp. 919 (S.D.N.Y. 1976), *aff'd*, 559 F.2d 1203 (2d Cir. 1977); *Child v. Beame*, 412 F. Supp. 593 (S.D.N.Y. 1976); *Labat v. Board of Higher Education of the City of New York*, 401 F. Supp. 753 (S.D.N.Y. 1975); or the law. See *Law v. Cullen*, 613 F. Supp. 259 (S.D.N.Y. 1985); *Beverley v. Douglas*, 591 F. Supp. 1321 (S.D.N.Y. 1984); *Obradovich v. Federal Reserve Bank of New York*, 569 F. Supp. 785 (S.D.N.Y. 1983); *Dopico v. Goldschmidt*, 518 F. Supp. 1161 (S.D.N.Y. 1981), *aff'd*, 687 F.2d 644 (2d Cir. 1982); *Sogluizzo v. Local 817, International Brotherhood of Teamsters*, 514 F. Supp. 277 (S.D.N.Y. 1981); *DeFigueiredo v. Trans World Airlines*, 322 F. Supp. 1384 (S.D.N.Y. 1971).

73. *United States v. Quinn*, 141 F. Supp. 622 (S.D.N.Y. 1956).

74. *In the Matter of Cohen*, 370 F. Supp. 1166 (S.D.N.Y. 1973).

75. See, e.g., *United States ex rel. D'Antonio v. Follette*, No. 66 Civ. 51 (S.D.N.Y. Sept. 22, 1966), *rev'd*, 394 F.2d 402 (2d Cir. 1969); *Terry v. Denno*, 254 F. Supp. 909 (S.D.N.Y. 1966).

76. 103 F. Supp. 64, 110–17 (S.D.N.Y.), *rev'd*, 198 F.2d 697 (2d Cir.), *cert. denied*, 344 U.S. 909 (1952).

77. *See, e.g., Self-Powered Lighting, Ltd. v. United States*, 492 F. Supp. 1267 (S.D.N.Y. 1980) (construing Buy America Act to contain an exemption for specified defense products purchased from British contractors); *In re Ullman*, 128 F. Supp. 617 (S.D.N.Y.), *aff'd*, 221 F.2d 760 (2d Cir. 1955), *aff'd*, 350 U.S. 422 (1956) (extending scope of witness-immunity statute in subversion and treason cases to state as well as federal courts); *In re Oddo*, 117 F. Supp. 323 (S.D.N.Y. 1953), *rev'd sub nom. Application of Barnes*, 219 F.2d 137 (2d Cir. 1955), *rev'd sub nom. United States v. Minker*, 350 U.S. 179 (1956) (limiting power to INS to summarily subpoena naturalized citizens for the purpose of revocation of citizenship); *United States v. International Longshoremen's Ass'n*, 116 F. Supp. 262 (S.D.N.Y. 1953) (construing Taft-Hartley Act to authorize joinder of new union in jurisdictional dispute with old union that led old union to call strike); *De La Rama S.S. Co. v. United States*, 98 F. Supp. 514 (S.D.N.Y. 1951), *rev'd*, 198 F.2d 182 (2d Cir. 1952), *rev'd*, 344 U.S. 386 (1953) (finding district court jurisdiction under a wartime ship-insurance statute repealed during the pendency of the action, even though the repealer contained no savings clause).

78. 214 F. Supp. 425 (S.D.N.Y. 1963). Weinfeld also authored another opinion in the *Casanova* case, *United States v. Casanova*, 213 F. Supp. 654 (S.D.N.Y. 1963), which denied a motion to suppress evidence obtained through wiretapping.

79. *Quoted at* 214 F. Supp. at 432.

80. 214 F. Supp. 264 (S.D.N.Y. 1963).

81. Located on the northern coast of South America.

82. 512 F. Supp. 349 (S.D.N.Y. 1981).

83. *Quoted in* 512 F. Supp. at 350.

84. *Id.,* 352.

85. *Id.*

86. 228 F. Supp. 483 (S.D.N.Y. 1964).

87. 228 F. Supp. at 486, 490.

88. *See also United States v. Beckom,* 324 F. Supp. 253, 254 (S.D.N.Y. 1971), where Weinfeld dismissed a criminal prosecution twelve years after the alleged offense had occurred and five years after the government had returned an indictment, with the observation that it was "a case of unwarranted delay to the prejudice of the defendant," and *United States v. Dillon,* 183 F. Supp. 541 (S.D.N.Y. 1960), where he dismissed a prosecution that had been pending for eight years with the observation, "I do not conceive it to be the duty of a defendant to press that he be prosecuted upon an indictment under penalty of waiving his right to a speedy trial if he fails to do so. It is the duty of the public prosecutor . . . to observe the constitutional mandate guaranteeing a speedy trial." *Id.,* 543.

89. 631 F. Supp. 1530 (S.D.N.Y. 1986), *aff'd,* 930 F.2d 908 (2d Cir. 1991).

90. *Id.,* 1532. *But cf. Application of Amoury,* 307 F. Supp. 213, 217 (S.D.N.Y. 1969), where Weinfeld refused to grant an application by a minor child, who, fortuitously, happened to be born while his parents were visiting the United States. The judge noted, "The humanitarian appeal in the instant case is far less compelling than that posed in other cases. . . . [T]he situation which now exists was created by the aliens who, from the time of their admission here, embarked on a program to gain preferential status not accorded them by law."

91. 101 F. Supp. 7 (S.D.N.Y. 1951).

92. *Id.,* 14.

93. *Id.*

94. *United States ex rel. Elksnis v. Gilligan,* 256 F. Supp. 244, 254 (S.D.N.Y. 1966).

95. Stenographer's Minutes of Sentencing Proceedings, *United States v. Kahaner,* 61 Cr. 113, August 2, 1962, 3843–44, Box 15, Weinfeld Papers. For an analysis of Weinfeld's work in the *Kahaner* and *Keogh* cases, which sees his jurisprudence in the same fashion as does the present chapter, *see* John G. Koeltl and Frank M. Tuerkheimer, "Judge Weinfeld and the Criminal Law: The *Keogh-Kahaner* Trial—A Case Study in Criminal Justice, *New York University Law Review* 50 (1975): 1008.

NOTES TO CHAPTER 9

1. Handwritten note by Edward Weinfeld on front flyleaf of Frank M. Coffin, *The Ways of a Judge: Reflections from the Appellate Bench* (Boston: Houghton Mifflin, 1980).

2. 256 F. Supp. 244 (S.D.N.Y. 1966).

3. 168 F. Supp. 576 (S.D.N.Y. 1958).

4. Stenographer's Minutes of Sentencing Proceedings, *United States v. Kahaner*, 61 Cr. 113, August 2, 1962, 3843–44, Box 15, Weinfeld Papers.

5. 104 F. Supp. 819 (S.D.N.Y. 1952).

6. *Id.*, 820.

7. *Id.*, 820–21 (emphasis added).

8. 117 F. Supp. 541 (S.D.N.Y. 1953).

9. *Id.*, 544, 547.

10. Petition of Gourary, 148 F. Supp. 140, 144 (S.D.N.Y. 1957).

11. For other cases in which Weinfeld ruled against INS in either immigration or naturalization matters, *see Petition of Kwong Hai Chew*, 278 F. Supp. 44 (S.D.N.Y. 1967); *Petition of Rosenbaum*, 171 F. Supp. 141 (S.D.N.Y. 1959); *Eelhart v. Dulles*, 135 F. Supp. 12 (S.D.N.Y. 1955); *In re Oddo*, 117 F. Supp. 323 (S.D.N.Y. 1953), *rev'd sub nom. Shaughnessy v. Oddo*, 219 F.2d 137 (2d Cir. 1955); *United States ex rel. Daniman v. Esperdy*, 113 F. Supp. 283 (S.D.N.Y. 1953), *appeal dism. sub nom. United States ex rel. Daniman v. Shaughnessy*, 210 F.2d 564 (2d Cir. 1954); *United States ex rel. Kwong Hai Chew v. Shaughnessy*, 113 F. Supp. 49 (S.D.N.Y. 1953); *United States ex rel. Bittelman v. District Director of Immigration & Naturalization at Port of New York*, 99 F. Supp. 306 (S.D.N.Y. 1951). Of course, INS won some of its cases before Weinfeld. *See Application of Amoury*, 307 F. Supp. 213 (S.D.N.Y. 1969); *Sovich v. Esperdy*, 206 F. Supp. 558 (S.D.N.Y. 1962), *rev'd*, 319 F.2d 21 (2d Cir. 1963); *United States ex rel. Tom We Shung v. Murff*, 176 F. Supp. 253 (S.D.N.Y. 1959), *aff'd sub nom. United States ex rel. Tom We Shung v. Esperdy*, 274 F.2d 667 (2d Cir. 1960); *Petition of Suey Chin*, 173 F. Supp. 510 (S.D.N.Y. 1959); *United States ex rel. Blankenstein v. Shaughnessy*, 112 F. Supp. 607 (S.D.N.Y. 1953).

12. 257 F. Supp. 906 (S.D.N.Y. 1966).

13. 108 F. Supp. 307 (S.D.N.Y. 1952).

14. Of course, there were many draft evasion cases in which Weinfeld convicted defendants. *See United States v. Dolinger*, 384 F. Supp. 682 (S.D.N.Y. 1974); *United States v. Aull*, 341 F. Supp. 389 (S.D.N.Y.), *aff'd*, 469 F.2d 151 (2d Cir. 1972); *United States v. Mangone*, 333 F. Supp. 932 (S.D.N.Y. 1971), *aff'd*, 456 F.2d 1336 (2d Cir. 1972); *United States v. Branigan*, 299 F. Supp. 225 (S.D.N.Y. 1969); *United States v. Planas*, 226 F. Supp. 803 (S.D.N.Y. 1964). *Cf. United States v. Holohan*, 390 F. Supp. 310 (S.D.N.Y. 1975) (motion to dismiss indictment denied).

15. *Application of United Electrical, Radio & Machine Workers of America,* 111 F. Supp. 858, 859 (S.D.N.Y. 1953).

16. *Id.,* 860–61, 869.

17. *Id.,* 864, 867–69.

18. *Id.,* 870.

19. 18 F.R.D. 27 (S.D.N.Y. 1955), *aff'd,* 236 F.2d 312 (2d Cir. 1956).

20. *Id.,* 32–33.

21. *Id.,* 32, 34–35. Lamont was less successful when he came before Weinfeld a quarter-century later in a suit under the Freedom of Information Act seeking disclosure of all FBI records containing information related to him. *See Lamont v. Department of Justice,* 475 F. Supp. 761 (S.D.N.Y. 1979) (granting some, but not all, of the government's requests to withhold material). For another FOIA case in which Weinfeld upheld all the government's requests for nondisclosure, *see Holy Spirit Ass'n for the Unification of World Christianity, Inc. v. United States Department of State,* 526 F. Supp. 1022 (S.D.N.Y. 1981).

22. 113 F. Supp. 56 (S.D.N.Y. 1953), *aff'd,* 212 F.2d 128 (2d Cir. 1954).

23. *Id.,* 60.

24. 565 F. Supp. 1416 (S.D.N.Y. 1983).

25. *Id.,* 1440.

26. 349 F. Supp. 766 (S.D.N.Y. 1972).

27. Indeed, in *Brown v. Matias,* 102 F.R.D. 580 (S.D.N.Y. 1984), Weinfeld acknowledged the importance of nonofficer witnesses to police activity and of maintaining the confidentiality of the information they provided.

28. 349 F. Supp. at 769–70.

29. *See United States ex rel. Caserino v. Denno,* 259 F. Supp. 784 (S.D.N.Y. 1966).

30. *United States v. Wedra,* 343 F. Supp. 1183, 1188–89 (S.D.N.Y. 1972).

31. *See* Leonard H. Becker, "Judge Weinfeld and Constitutional Law," *New York University Law Review* 50 (1975): 1051, 1059–68. *Cf. United States v. One 1974 Cadillac Eldorado Sedan,* 407 F. Supp. 1115 (S.D.N.Y. 1975), *rev'd,* 548 F.2d 421 (2d Cir. 1977) (the use of a vehicle to reach a crime scene does not make the vehicle an instrumentality of crime and hence subject to seizure). Of course, Weinfeld upheld much prosecutorial activity as lawful. *See, e.g., United States v. Ianniello,* 621 F. Supp. 1455 (S.D.N.Y. 1985), *aff'd,* 808 F.2d 184 (2d Cir. 1986).

32. *United States v. Hill,* 149 F. Supp. 83, 86 (S.D.N.Y. 1957).

33. *See G.I. Distributors, Inc. v. Murphy,* 336 F. Supp. 1036 (S.D.N.Y.), *rev'd,* 469 F.2d 752 (2d Cir. 1972). *Accord, Star Distributors, Ltd. v. Hogan,* 337 F. Supp. 1362 (S.D.N.Y. 1972). *Cf. P.A.J. Corp. v. Murphy,* 320 F. Supp. 704 (S.D.N.Y. 1970) (seizure of motion picture films and other property of theater owner). *See also Lido East Theatre Corp. v. Murphy,* 337 F. Supp. 1345

(S.D.N.Y. 1972) (motion granted to convene three-judge court to determine validity of New York's procedure for seizing allegedly obscene material without prior adversary hearing).

34. 438 F. Supp. 145 (S.D.N.Y. 1977).

35. *Id.*, 148.

36. Subsequently, Weinfeld also granted attorneys' fees to the plaintiffs. *See Boe v. Collelo*, 447 F. Supp. 607 (S.D.N.Y. 1978).

37. 319 F. Supp. 901 (S.D.N.Y. 1970). *Cf. Stinson v. Sheriff's Dept. of Sullivan County*, 499 F. Supp. 259 (S.D.N.Y. 1980) (refusing to grant summary judgment on behalf of jailers in case involving claims of alleged beatings and wrongful solitary confinement). *But cf. Segall v. Jacobson*, 295 F. Supp. 1121 (S.D.N.Y. 1969) (refusal to grant preliminary injunction, prior to trial, on merits and absent showing of irreparable injury, in matter involving student-written "rather puerile, name-calling article containing obscenities, among other vulgar matters"). Weinfeld often was quite sympathetic with the needs of prison officials to maintain order and administer prisons efficiently. *See Kivela v. United States Attorney General*, 523 F. Supp. 1321 (S.D.N.Y. 1981), *aff'd*, 688 F.2d 815 (2d Cir. 1982); *Merriweather v. Sherwood*, 518 F. Supp. 355 (S.D.N.Y. 1981); *United States v. Duke*, 458 F. Supp. 1188 (S.D.N.Y. 1978).

38. 361 F. Supp. 457 (S.D.N.Y. 1973), *aff'd*, 493 F.2d 1397 (2d Cir.), *cert. denied*, 419 U.S. 842 (1974).

39. 467 F. Supp. 803 (S.D.N.Y. 1979).

40. *Id.*, 816, 819.

41. 305 F. Supp. 1030 (S.D.N.Y. 1969).

42. *See* Janice Goodman, Rhonda Copelon Schoenbrod, and Nancy Stearns, "Doe and Roe: Where Do We Go from Here?" *Women's Rights Law Reporter* 1(4) (Spring 1973): 20, 22, 24. The protest consisted of a "substantial number of women" coming to court with "crying babies, and coat hangers. When they left, they took the babies with them but left the coat hangers scattered all over the courtroom." *Id.* at 24.

43. 305 F. Supp. at 1031–32.

44. *See* Nancy Stearns, "*Roe v. Wade*: Our Struggle Continues," *Berkeley Women's Law Journal* 4 (1988–89): 1, 3.

45. *Echevarria v. Carey*, 402 F. Supp. 183 (S.D.N.Y. 1975), *aff'd*, 538 F.2d 309 (2d Cir. 1976).

46. *Fhagen v. Miller*, 306 F. Supp. 634 (S.D.N.Y. 1969).

47. *Surmeli v. New York*, 412 F. Supp. 394 (S.D.N.Y.), *aff'd*, 556 F.2d 560 (2d Cir. 1976), *cert. denied*, 436 U.S. 903 (1978).

48. *Pabon v. Levine*, 70 F.R.D. 674 (S.D.N.Y. 1976).

49. *Brown v. Bronstein*, 389 F. Supp. 1328 (S.D.N.Y. 1975).

50. *Feld v. Berger*, 424 F. Supp. 1356 (S.D.N.Y. 1976).

51. *Id.*, 1357–58.

52. For a discussion of the many cases in which he so ruled, *see* Becker, "Weinfeld and Constitutional Law," 1052–59.

53. 604 F. Supp. 675 (S.D.N.Y. 1985).

54. 479 F. Supp. 207 (S.D.N.Y. 1979). *Cf. Thom v. New York Stock Exchange*, 306 F. Supp. 1002 (S.D.N.Y. 1969), *aff'd sub nom. Miller v. New York Stock Exchange*, 425 F.2d 1074 (2d Cir.), *cert. denied*, 398 U.S. 905 (1970) (upholding requirement that all employees of stock exchange be fingerprinted).

55. 482 F. Supp. 475 (S.D.N.Y. 1979).

56. 128 F. Supp. 617 (S.D.N.Y.), *aff'd*, 221 F.2d 760 (2d Cir. 1955), *aff'd*, 350 U.S. 422, *rehearing denied*, 351 U.S. 928 (1956).

57. 334 F. Supp. 84 (S.D.N.Y. 1971).

58. *Id.*, 87, 89.

59. *Hall v. Lefkowitz*, 305 F. Supp. 1030, 1031–32 (S.D.N.Y. 1969).

60. Author's conversations with Edward Weinfeld, 1965–1966.

61. The distinction also made sense for Cardozo, *see* Benhamin N. Cardozo, *The Nature of the Judicial Process* (New Haven, Conn.: Yale University Press, 1921), 110–13, even though he recognized it was "shadowy and evanescent." *Id.*, 110.

62. 410 U.S. 113 (1973).

63. 438 U.S. 265 (1978).

64. Conversation of author with Edward Weinfeld during hospital visit, mid-1980s.

65. *See* Judith R. Kramer, *The American Minority Community* (New York: Thomas Y. Crowell, 1970), 58–64.

66. *See generally* National Commission on Law Observance and Enforcement (Wickersham Commission), *Report on Lawlessness in Law Enforcement* (Washington, D.C.: Government Printing Office, 1931), 13–262.

67. Benjamin F. Wright ed., *The Federalist* No. 51 (Madison) (Cambridge, Mass.: Harvard University Press, 1961).

NOTES TO CHAPTER 10

1. Resume of Joseph David Tekulsky, Box 4, folder—Joseph D. Tekulsky, Weinfeld Papers.

2. Benjamin A. Hartstein to Edward Weinfeld, October 19, 1950, Box 4, folder—Joseph D. Tekulsky, Weinfeld Papers.

3. *See Martindale-Hubbell Law Directory*, vol. 2 (Summit, N.J.: Martindale Hubbell, 1950), 1217.

4. Sol Tekulsky to Eddie, October 13, 1950, Box 4, folder—Joseph D. Tekulsky, Weinfeld Papers.

5. Resume of Frederick B. Boyden, Box 4, folder—Frederick B. Boyden, Weinfeld Papers.

6. Affidavit of Edward Weinfeld, April 1, 1953, Box 4, folder—Frederick B. Boyden, Weinfeld Papers.

7. See "New Housing Bill Limits State Fund," *New York Times*, January 28, 1939, 3.

8. Biographical Data Sheet of Maurice N. Nessen, Box 4, folder—Maurice N. Nessen, Weinfeld Papers.

9. Author's telephone conversation with Maurice N. Nessen, June 7, 2000.

10. Biographical Data Sheet of Maurice N. Nessen, Box 4, folder—Maurice N. Nessen, Weinfeld Papers.

11. Author's telephone conversation with Maurice N. Nessen, June 7, 2000.

12. Author's telephone conversation with William N. Eskridge, July 21, 2000, reporting on his conversation of that date with Boris I. Bittker.

13. Affidavit of Edward Weinfeld, December 28, 1953, Box 4, folder—Maurice N. Nessen, Weinfeld Papers.

14. Edward Weinfeld to Paul D. Siegfried, March 9, 1983, Box 4, folder—Maurice N. Nessen, Weinfeld Papers.

15. *Martindale-Hubbell Law Directory*, vol. 11 (New Providence, N.J.: Martindale Hubbell, 1995), NYC669B.

16. *Martindale-Hubbell Law Directory*, vol. 4 (Summit, N.J.: Martindale Hubbell, 1975), 511B.

17. "NYLJ 100: Ranked by Size," *New York Law Journal*, December 13, 1999, 59.

18. See "Former Judge Moving Again," *New York Times*, February 20, 1983, sec. 1, 64.

19. Stephen Wise Tulin to Edward Weinfeld, February 25, 1954, Box 4, folder—Stephen Tulin, Weinfeld Papers.

20. Boris I. Bittker to Edward Weinfeld, February 26, 1954, Box 4, folder—Stephen Tulin, Weinfeld Papers.

21. Edward Weinfeld to Stephen Wise Tulin, June 23, 1986, Box 4, folder—Stephen Tulin, Weinfeld Papers.

22. Affidavit of Edward Weinfeld, September 14, 1954, Box 4, folder—Stephen Tulin, Weinfeld Papers.

23. Stephen Wise Tulin to Edward Weinfeld, July 2, 1976, Box 4, folder—Stephen Tulin, Weinfeld Papers.

24. "Shad Polier, Lawyer, Dead: Active in Civil Rights Cases," *New York Times*, July 1, 1976, 30.

25. Affidavit of Edward Weinfeld, September 14, 1954, Box 4, folder—Stephen Tulin, Weinfeld Papers.

26. Louis J. Naftalison to Edward Weinfeld, December 20, 1954, and Edward Weinfeld to Louis J. Naftalison, December 23, 1954, Box 4, folder—Barry H. Garfinkel, Weinfeld Papers.

27. Myres S. McDougall to Edward Weinfeld, December 17, 1954, Box 4, folder—Barry H. Garfinkel, Weinfeld Papers.

28. Fowler V. Harper to Edward Weinfeld, December 3, 1954, Box 4, folder—Barry H. Garfinkel, Weinfeld Papers.

29. Edward Weinfeld, Memorandum of Telephone Conversation with Professor Fowler Harper, March 1, 1955, Box 4, folder—Barry H. Garfinkel, Weinfeld Papers.

30. Edward Weinfeld, Memorandum of Telephone Conversation with Prof. Bittker at Yale, February 28, 1955, Box 4, folder—Barry H. Garfinkel, Weinfeld Papers.

31. Gloria to Judge & Lillian, undated, Box 4, folder—Barry H. Garfinkel, Weinfeld Papers.

32. Author's conversation with Barry Garfinkel May 7, folder 2004.

33. Edward Weinfeld to Barry Garfinkel, September 8, 1986, Box 4, folder—Barry H. Garfinkel, Weinfeld Papers.

34. Edward Weinfeld to Barry H. Garfinkel, August 21, 1978, Box 4, folder—Barry H. Garfinkel, Weinfeld Papers.

35. Erwin Cherovsky, *The Guide to New York Law Firms* (New York: St. Martin's Press, 1991), 188.

36. *See Martindale-Hubbell Law Directory*, vol. 2 (Summit, N.J.: Martindale Hubbell, 1958), 3050–51.

37. *See American Lawyer* (July 2002): 131.

38. Cherovsky, *New York Law Firms*, 188.

39. Louis J. Naftalison to Edward Weinfeld, December 20, 1954; Barry H. Garfinkel to Edward Weinfeld, February 13, 1955, both in Box 4, folder—Barry H. Garfinkel, Weinfeld Papers.

40. Edward Weinfeld, Memorandum of Telephone Conversation with Professor Fowler Harper, March 1, 1955, Box 4, folder—Barry H. Garfinkel, Weinfeld Papers.

41. Resume of Martin Lipton, Box 4, folder—Martin Lipton, Weinfeld Papers.

42. Charles Seligson to Edward Weinfeld, December 29, 1955, Box 4, folder—Martin Lipton, Weinfeld Papers.

43. Resume of Martin Lipton, Box 4, folder—Martin Lipton, Weinfeld Papers.

44. Harry W. Jones to Edward Weinfeld, January 9, 1956 (mistakenly dated 1955), Box 4, folder—Martin Lipton, Weinfeld Papers.

45. *Edward Weinfeld: A Judicious Life* (New York: Federal Bar Foundation, 1998), 91.

46. Edward Weinfeld's Notes for Speech at Annual Dinner Honoring Martin Lipton, November 18, 1975, Box 4, folder—Martin Lipton, Weinfeld Papers.

47. Martin Lipton to Edward Weinfeld, November 21, 1975, Box 4, folder—Martin Lipton, Weinfeld Papers.

48. Edward Weinfeld's Notes for Speech at Annual Dinner Honoring Martin Lipton, November 18, 1975, Box 4, folder—Martin Lipton, Weinfeld Papers.

49. Sheila Malkani and Michael Walsh eds., *The Insider's Guide to Law Firms, 1994* (Washington, D.C.: Mobius Press, 1994), 433.

50. See *American Lawyer* (July 2002): 134.

51. Cherovsky, *New York Law Firms*, 206.

52. "The Best Lawyers in New York," *New York Magazine*, March 20, 1995, 43, 45.

53. Judith T. Younger served as dean of Syracuse Law School from July 1, 1974 to June 30, 1975. She resigned in a dispute with the university's central administration over the law school's finances. *See* Judith T. Younger to Melvin A. Eggers, March 24, 1975, Box 4, folder—Judith T. Younger, Weinfeld Papers.

54. Weinfeld had a total of nine female law clerks, eight of whom served between 1975 and the judge's death in 1988. During the 1975–1988 period, 28 percent of Weinfeld's clerks were women.

55. In alphabetical order, the Weinfeld clerks who later went to the Supreme Court were Kevin T. Baine (Justice Marshall), Leonard H. Becker (Justice Stewart), Vicki Been (Justice Blackmun), Jeffrey Glekel (Justice White), John G. Koeltl (Justice Stewart), Daniel P. Levitt (Justices Goldberg and Fortas), Robert S. Litt (Justice Stewart), Eben Moglen (Justice Marshall), William E. Nelson (Justice White), Larry G. Simon (Chief Justice Warren), and Robert W. Werner (Justices Powell and Kennedy).

56. In alphabetical order, the eleven were T. Alexander Aleinikoff (Georgetown, Michigan), Vicki Been (New York University, Rutgers), William N. Eskridge (Georgetown, University of Virginia, Yale), Alan D. Freeman (Buffalo, Minnesota), Eben Moglen (Columbia), William E. Nelson (New York University, Pennsylvania, Yale), Victoria F. Nourse (Wisconsin), Mark F. Pomerantz (Columbia), Larry G. Simon (University of Southern California, Yale), Frank M. Tuerkheimer (Wisconsin), and Judith T. Younger (Cornell, Hofstra, Minnesota, New York University). The information in this footnote was compiled from various years of *The AALS Directory of Law Teachers*, which is distributed annually by West Group and Foundation Press.

57. *See* Edward Weinfeld to Frank M. Tuerkheimer, June 30, 1977, Box 4, folder—Frank M. Tuerkheimer, Weinfeld Papers (congratulating Tuerkheimer on his assumption of office).

58. *The AALS Directory of Law Teachers, 2002–2003* (distributed by West Group and Foundation Press), 236.

59. Edward Weinfeld to Mark F. Pomerantz, May 30, 1984, Box 4, folder—Mark F. Pomerantz, Weinfeld Papers.

60. Author's telephone interview with Mark F. Pomerantz, June 14, 2000.

61. Al Kamen, "Hocus Potus: Prague Falls to Shattuck," *Washington Post*, April 10, 1998, p. A21.

62. Author's telephone interview with Stephen J. Suffern, June 17, 2000.

63. Author's telephone interview with Irving Berger, June 14, 2000.

64. "Human Rights Watch Looks Within," *The New Yorker*, December 13, 1993, 53.

65. Author's telephone interview with Bruce Yannett, June 13, 2000.

66. Author's telephone interview with Robert W. Werner, June 14, 2000.

67. Announcement of the establishment of Forrester & Norall, November 1, 1981, Box 4, folder—Christopher Norall, Weinfeld Papers.

68. See *Martindale-Hubbell Law Directory*, vol. 11 (New Providence, N.J.: Martindale Hubbell, 2002), NYA180P.

69. See *Martindale-Hubbell Law Directory*, vol. 5 (New Providence, N.J.: Martindale Hubbell, 2003), FL642B.

70. Author's telephone interview with Robert L. Plotz, June 13, 2000.

71. Author's telephone interview with Nina Gillman, June 15, 2000; author's telephone interview with Philomena Burke, June 14, 2000.

72. Author's telephone interview with Janet Hurley, June 16, 2000.

73. In alphabetical order, the twenty-four are Kevin T. Baine (Williams & Connolly), Leonard H. Becker (Arnold & Porter), Laureen F. Bedell (Davis, Polk), Roger E. Berg (Kaye, Scholer), Thomas F. Connell (Wilmer, Cutler), Jeffrey Glekel (Skadden, Arps), Stuart Gold (Cravath, Swaine & Moore), Dori Ann Hanswirth (Squadron, Ellenoff), David Harms (Sullivan & Cromwell), Bert Robbins Kiessling (Cravath, Swaine & Moore), John G. Koeltl (Debevoise, Plimpton), Daniel P. Levitt (Kramer, Levin), Jerome Lipper (Tenzer, Greenblatt), Robert S. Litt (Williams & Connolly), Mitchell Lowenthal (Cleary, Gottlieb), Elizabeth A. Markowski (Shea & Gould), Charles W. Mulaney (Skadden, Arps), William B. Pennell (Shearman & Sterling), Steven A. Reisberg (Wilkie Farr), Ronald A. Sarachan (Ballard, Spahr), Jay T. Smith (Covington & Burling), Daniel S. Sternberg (Cleary, Gottlieb), Paul Vizcarrondo (Wachtell, Lipton), Bruce Yannett (Debevoise, Plimpton), and Alfred D. Youngwood (Paul, Weiss). Former Weinfeld clerks, that is, have become partners in the following nineteen firms: Arnold & Porter (Leonard H. Becker), Ballard, Spahr (Ronald A. Sarachan), Cleary, Gottlieb (Mitchell Lowenthal, Daniel S. Sternberg), Covington & Burling (Jay T. Smith), Cravath, Swaine & Moore (Stuart Gold, Bert Robbins Kiessling), Davis, Polk (Laureen F. Bedell), Debevoise, Plimpton (John G. Koeltl, Bruce Yannett), Kaye, Scholer (Roger E. Berg), Kramer, Levin (Daniel P. Levitt, Maurice N. Nessen), Paul, Weiss (Alfred D. Youngwood), Shea & Gould (Elizabeth A. Markowski), Skadden, Arps (Barry Garfinkel, Jeffrey Glekel, Charles W. Mulaney), Shearman & Sterling (William B. Pennell), Squadron, Ellenoff (Dori Ann Hanswirth), Sullivan & Cromwell (David Harms), Tenzer, Greenblatt (Jerome Lipper), Wachtell, Lipton (Martin Lipton, Paul Vizcar-

rondo), Wilkie Farr (Steven A. Reisberg), Williams & Connolly (Kevin T. Baine, Robert S. Litt), Wilmer, Cutler (Thomas F. Connell).

74. *See* 853 F. Supp. ix (S.D.N.Y. 1994).

75. The three were, in alphabetical order, Irving Berger, William E. Nelson, and Robert W. Werner.

76. The three were Alan D. Freeman, David Harms, and Martin Lipton.

77. Mark F. Pomerantz.

78. Although not political careers. Not a single one of Judge Weinfeld's former clerks has ever run for public office.

79. *A Judicious Life*, 96.

80. Alfred D. Youngwood to Edward Weinfeld, July 7, 1970, Box 4, folder—Alfred D. Youngwood, Weinfeld Papers.

81. *A Judicious Life*, 89.

82. Charles W. Mulaney, Jr., to Edward Weinfeld, August 7, 1975, Box 4, folder—Charles W. Mulaney, Jr., Weinfeld Papers.

83. Bruce Yannett to Edward Weinfeld, August 7, 1986, Box 50, folder—Bruce Yannett, Weinfeld Papers.

84. Vicki Been to Edward Weinfeld, August 14, 1984, Box 50, folder—Vicki Been, Weinfeld Papers.

85. Robert W. Werner to Edward Weinfeld, June 26, 1987, Box 50, folder—Robert W. Werner, Weinfeld Papers.

86. Thomas F. Connell to Edward Weinfeld, January 13, 1981, Box 50, folder—Thomas F. Connell, Weinfeld Papers.

87. John Shattuck to Edward Weinfeld, August 19, 1980, Box 4, folder—John Shattuck, Weinfeld Papers.

88. Eben Moglen to Edward Weinfeld, June 22, 1986, Box 50, folder—Eben Moglen, Weinfeld Papers.

89. *A Judicious Life*, 104.

90. *Id.*, 100 (Christopher Norall is misidentified in *A Judicious Life* as Christopher Sutton).

91. *Id.*, 100, 103, 114, 121.

92. 579 F. Supp. 652 (S.D.N.Y.), *aff'd sub nom. United States v. Perez*, 733 F.2d 1026 (2d Cir. 1984).

93. *A Judicious Life*, 118.

94. *Id.*, 118–19.

95. *A Judicious Life*, 118–19.

96. 579 F. Supp. at 657 n.11.

97. *A Judicious Life*, 119.

98. 733 F.2d at 1035.

99. *A Judicious Life*, 120.

100. Edward Weinfeld to Frank M. Tuerkheimer, November 17, 1971, Box 4, folder—Frank M. Tuerkheimer, Weinfeld Papers.

101. Daniel P. Levitt to Edward Weinfeld, May 2, 1966, Box 4, folder—Daniel P. Levitt, Weinfeld Papers.

102. *A Judicious Life*, 112–13.

103. *Id.*, 113.

104. The most thoughtful analysis of lawyers' use of narratives is contained in Anthony G. Amsterdam and Jerome Bruner, *Minding the Law* (Cambridge, Mass.: Harvard University Press, 2000).

105. 579 F. Supp. 652 (S.D.N.Y.), *aff'd sub nom. United States v. Perez*, 733 F.2d 1026 (2d Cir. 1984).

106. 733 F.2d at 1035.

107. *A Judicious Life*, 118.

108. "The Leaders' Remarks: Hopes for a Friendship, Even If Imperfect," *New York Times*, June 28, 1998, 9.

109. *See* "Chinese Officials Held in Campaign against Vast Sect," *New York Times*, July 27, 1999, A1; "China Steps Up Its Drive to Halt Dissident Sect," *New York Times*, July 23, 1999, A1; "Beijing Detains Leaders of Sect, Watchdog Says," *New York Times*, July 21, 1999, A1.

110. *A Judicious Life*, 103, 108, 116.

111. *Id.*, 111.

112. Robert S. Litt to Edward Weinfeld, undated, Box 4, folder—Robert S. Litt, Weinfeld Papers.

113. Steven H. Reisberg to Edward Weinfeld, November 8, 1982, Box 50, folder—Steven H. Reisberg, Weinfeld Papers.

114. *A Judicious Life*, 100, 102, 106.

115. Bruce Yannett to Edward Weinfeld, August 7, 1986, Box 50, folder—Bruce Yannett, Weinfeld Papers.

116. Robert W. Werner to Edward Weinfeld, June 26, 1987, Box 50, folder—Robert W. Werner, Weinfeld Papers.

117. Eben Moglen to Edward Weinfeld, June 22, 1986, Box 50, folder—Eben Moglen, Weinfeld Papers.

118. *A Judicious Life*, 96, 100, 114.

119. *Id.*, 96.

120. T. Alexander Aleinikoff to Edward Weinfeld, December 29, 1981, Box 4, folder—T. Alexander Aleinikoff, Weinfeld Papers.

121. Vicki Been to Edward Weinfeld, August 14, 1984, Box 50, folder—Vicki Been, Weinfeld Papers.

122. Eben Moglen to Edward Weinfeld, June 22, 1986, Box 50, folder—Eben Moglen, Weinfeld Papers.

123. Victoria F. Nourse to Edward Weinfeld, July 13, 1985, Box 50, folder—Victoria F. Nourse, Weinfeld Papers.

124. *United States v. Rubenstein*, 151 F.2d 915, 923 (2d Cir.), *cert. denied*, 66 S. Ct. 168 (1945) (Frank, J., dissenting).

125. Victoria F. Nourse to Edward Weinfeld, July 13, 1985, Box 50, folder—Victoria F. Nourse, Weinfeld Papers.

126. Author's telephone interview with Stephen J. Suffern, June 17, 2000.

127. *Id.* The author disagrees with Suffern's characterization of Weinfeld's sentencing practices. From my perspective in 1965–1966, Weinfeld gave much lighter sentences than most other judges, except in cases of white collar defendants, to whom he gave heavier sentences.

128. Fern W. Cohen, *Included Out (Excluded In) . . . Mostly about My Father, Tennis, Me, and Freud . . .* (ms. dated March 4, 2000 in possession of the author), 27, 35, 169.

129. Edward Weinfeld to Mrs. Harold Faber, February 10, 1971, Box 39, folder 12, Weinfeld Papers.

130. 548 F. Supp. 1390 (S.D.N.Y. 1982).

131. *A Judicious Life*, 84–85. Weinfeld granted the recusal motion only because the law demanded the appearance as well as the reality of a fair trial and impartiality and his relationship to Pomerantz made appearances somewhat questionable. *Id.*, 85–86.

132. Eben Moglen to Edward Weinfeld, June 22, 1986, Box 50, folder—Eben Moglen, Weinfeld Papers.

133. *Included Out*, 27, 169.

134. Victoria F. Nourse to Edward Weinfeld, July 13, 1985, Box 50, folder—Victoria F. Nourse, Weinfeld Papers.

135. *Included Out*, 129.

136. Victoria F. Nourse to Edward Weinfeld, July 13, 1985, Box 50, folder—Victoria F. Nourse, Weinfeld Papers.

137. Edward Weinfeld to Potter Stewart, December 9, 1965 (on behalf of William E. Nelson); Edward Weinfeld to Thurgood Marshall, October 14, 1969 (on behalf of William E. Nelson); Edward Weinfeld to Earl Warren, October 28, 1966 (on behalf of Larry G. Simon); Edward Weinfeld to Earl Warren, November 22, 1967 (on behalf of Alan D. Freeman); Edward Weinfeld to Earl Warren, October 14, 1968 (on behalf of Leonard H. Becker); Edward Weinfeld to Potter Stewart, October 16, 1972 (on behalf of Jeffrey Glekel); Edward Weinfeld to Harry A. Blackmun, December 5, 1978 (on behalf of William N. Eskridge), all in appropriate folders, Box 4, Weinfeld Papers; Harry A. Blackmun to Edward Weinfeld, February 22, 1984 (reporting "your warm support of Vicki in our telephone conversation a few days ago"); Edward Weinfeld to Harry A. Blackmun, November 14, 1985 (on behalf of Victoria Nourse); Edward Weinfeld to Warren E. Burger, September 18, 1985 (on behalf of Bruce Yannett); Edward Weinfeld to Harry A. Blackmun, December 15, 1986 (on behalf of Jay T. Smith), all in appropriate folders, Box 50, Weinfeld Papers.

138. Edward Weinfeld to Alison Reppy, July 21, 1958 (on behalf of Maurice N. Nessen); Edward Weinfeld to Malachy T. Mahon, April 2, 1969 (on behalf of

Judith T. Younger); Edward Weinfeld to Peter E. Herzog, November 13, 1973 (on behalf of Judith T. Younger's application for dean of Syracuse Law School); Edward Weinfeld to Joseph F. Mulligan, January 19, 1978 (on behalf of Judith T. Younger's application for vice chancellor of University of Maryland); G. W. Foster, Jr., to Edward Weinfeld, March 21, 1969 (thanking Weinfeld for his "reactions to Mr. Frank Tuerkheimer"); Edward Weinfeld to David J. McCarthy, Jr., December 20, 1973 (on behalf of Dan Levitt); Edward Weinfeld to W. D. Hawkland, September 30, 1968 (on behalf of William E. Nelson); Edward Weinfeld to Theodore J. St. Antoine, November 4, 1969 (on behalf of William E. Nelson); Edward Weinfeld to Roger C. Cramton, December 4, 1967 (on behalf of Larry G. Simon); Edward Weinfeld to Phil C. Neal, January 23, 1973 (on behalf of Leonard H. Becker); Edward Weinfeld to Anita Martin, December 24, 1973 (on behalf of Leonard H. Becker); Edmund W. Kitch to Edward Weinfeld, February 9, 1979 (reflecting phone call on behalf of Laureen F. Bedell); Bill Eskridge to Edward Weinfeld, September 8, 1982 (thanking Weinfeld for "warmly support[ing] my applications for teaching positions"), all in appropriate folders, Box 4, Weinfeld Papers; Edward Weinfeld to Merritt B. Fox, December 29, 1986 (on behalf of Kenneth Roth); Bruce J. Winick to Edward Weinfeld, March 12, 1987 ("appreciated speaking with you . . . concerning Ken Roth), all in appropriate folders, Box 50, Weinfeld Papers.

139. Edward Weinfeld to Paul D. Siegfried, March 9, 1983 (on behalf of Maurice N. Nessen), Box 4, folder—Maurice N. Nessen, Weinfeld Papers.

140. Edward Weinfeld to Griffin B. Bell, February 7, 1977 (on behalf of Frank Tuerkheimer's application to be United States attorney for the Western District of Wisconsin); Edward Weinfeld to William Leibovitz, December 15, 1986 (on behalf of Jerry Chasen's application "for appointment as a member of a commission or board of New York City"), both in appropriate folders, Box 4, Weinfeld Papers.

141. Edward Weinfeld to Sheldon Elsen, October 27, 1986 (recommending Jerome Lipper for Executive Committee of Association of the Bar of the City of New York); Edward Weinfeld to Norman Redlich, November 26, 1980 (recommending Jerome Lipper for Executive Committee of Alumni Association); Jerome Lipper to Edward Weinfeld, July 2, 1970 (thanking Weinfeld for his "successful efforts to effect my designation to the Grievance Committee"); Edward Weinfeld to David O'Hearne, November 17, 1970 (supporting "Dan Levitt's nomination to the Harvard Board of Overseers"), all in appropriate folders, Box 4, Weinfeld Papers.

142. Edward Weinfeld to Frederick B. Boyden, September 20, 1969 (congratulating Boyden on merger of his firm); Edward Weinfeld to Maurice N. Nessen, December 9, 1970 (congratulating Nessen on opening of new offices); Edward Weinfeld to Barry Garfinkel, August 21, 1978 (congratulating Garfinkel on growth of Skadden, Arps); Judith Younger to Edward Weinfeld, Friday (with en-

closures dated March 25, 1975 and March 24, 1975) (reporting on Younger's resignation as dean of Syracuse Law School); Edward Weinfeld to Jerome Lipper, March 23, 1987 (commenting on Lipper's Report, "The Adequacy of Legal Services: Is It Time for a Change?"); Edward Weinfeld to Jerome Lipper, November 4, 1970 (congratulating Lipper on partnership); Edward Weinfeld to Jerome Lipper, May 5, 1966 (congratulating Lipper on partnership); Edward Weinfeld to Alfred D. Youngwood, February 22, 1978 (congratulating Youngwood on "designation as Chairman of State Bar Association's Tax Section"); Edward Weinfeld to Alfred D. Youngwood, July 1, 1970 (congratulating Youngwood on partnership); Edward Weinfeld to Frank M. Tuerkheimer, November 5, 1985 (congratulating Tuerkheimer on becoming counsel to old LaFollette law firm in Wisconsin); Edward Weinfeld to Frank M. Tuerkheimer, June 30, 1977 (congratulating Tuerkheimer on assuming office as U.S. attorney for Western District of Wisconsin); Edward Weinfeld to Larry G. Simon, June 22, 1976 (discussing Simon's move from Yale to U.S.C. Law School); Edward Weinfeld to Larry G. Simon, September 20, 1968 (congratulating Simon on "start of your academic career"); Edward Weinfeld to Alan D. Freeman, November 12, 1971 (congratulating Freeman on beginning teaching career and talking about former clerks in teaching); Edward Weinfeld to Christopher Norall, November 9, 1981 (congratulating Norall on opening new firm); Edward Weinfeld to Christopher Norall, March 11, 1980 (congratulating Norall on becoming partner); Edward Weinfeld to John H. F. Shattuck, December 13, 1979 (commenting on a press interview of John Shattuck); Edward Weinfeld to John H. F. Shattuck, September 7, 1976 (commenting on a press profile of John Shattuck); Edward Weinfeld to Irving Berger, April 30, 1987 and August 17, 1987 (congratulating Berger on his move to Los Angeles); Edward Weinfeld to John G. Koeltl, January 2, 1979 (congratulating Koeltl on partnership); Edward Weinfeld to John G. Koeltl, February 23, 1979 (congratulating Koeltl on becoming executive editor of "Litigation"); Edward Weinfeld to Jeffrey Glekel, September 20, 1982 (congratulating Glekel on an article); Edward Weinfeld to Jeffrey Glekel, August 22, 1978 (congratulating Glekel on an article); Edward Weinfeld to Stuart Gold, January 17, 1985 (congratulating Gold on profile about him in New York Law Journal); Edward Weinfeld to Stuart Gold, June 6, 1980 (congratulating Gold on partnership); Edward Weinfeld to Kevin T. Baine, February 5, 1982 (congratulating Baine on partnership); Edward Weinfeld to Charles W. Mulaney, Jr., May 22, 1981 (congratulating Mulaney on partnership); Edward Weinfeld to Mark F. Pomerantz, May 30, 1984 (congratulating Pomerantz on partnership); Edward Weinfeld to B. Robbins Kiessling, June 2, 1983 (congratulating Kiessling on partnership); Edward Weinfeld to Robert S. Litt, December 11, 1980 (congratulating Litt on his appointment as deputy chief appellate attorney in U.S. attorney's office); Edward Weinfeld to T. Alexander Alkeinikoff, August 20, 1981 (congratulating Aleinikoff on his letter to editor in New York Times); Edward Weinfeld to Elizabeth M.

Markowski, May 8, 1986 (congratulating Markowski on partnership), all in appropriate folders, Box 4, Weinfeld Papers; Edward Weinfeld to Thomas F. Connell, January 16, 1987 (congratulating Connell on his partnership); Edward Weinfeld to Mitchell A. Lowenthal, June 12, 1984 (congratulating Lowenthal on appointment to State Bar Association committee); Edward Weinfeld to Steven Michaels, July 25, 1986 (congratulating Michaels on his litigation on behalf of state of Hawaii), all in appropriate folders, Box 50, Weinfeld Papers.

143. Edward Weinfeld to Barry H. Garfinkel, August 21, 1978 (recalling "discussion we had, now quite a few years ago, about what size firm with which you should cast your future"); Alfred D. Youngwood to Edward Weinfeld, February 2, 1964 (discussing conversation with Weinfeld about "possibilities available to me"); Leonard H. Becker to Edward Weinfeld, January 26, 1973 (following "telephone conversation" on Becker's "prospects"); Roger E. Berg to Edward Weinfeld, May 16, 1972 (thanking Weinfeld for discussing "my future plans"); William P. Casella, March 3, 1977 (thanking Weinfeld for help "in making a difficult decision"); Edward Weinfeld to Laureen F. Bedell, January 20, 1977 ("you definitely do belong in the law"), all in appropriate folders, Box 4, Weinfeld Papers.

144. Jerome Lipper to Edward Weinfeld, January 31, 1963 (reporting on Weinfeld's efforts to obtain apartment), Box 4, folder—Jerome Lipper, Weinfeld Papers.

145. Edward Weinfeld to Henry N. Ess, May 24, 1974, Box 4, folder—William E. Nelson, Weinfeld Papers.

146. Edward Weinfeld to Larry G. Simon, September 9, 1974, Box 4, folder—Larry G. Simon, Weinfeld Papers.

147. Julie Simon to Edward Weinfeld, July 24, 1967, Box 4, folder—Larry G. Simon, Weinfeld Papers.

148. *A Judicious Life*, 116.

149. 256 F. Supp. 244 (S.D.N.Y. 1966).

150. *See* William E. Nelson, "Judge Weinfeld and the Adjudicatory Process: A Law Finder in an Age of Judicial Lawmakers," *New York University Law Review* 50 (1975): 980, 989–93.

151. Edward Weinfeld to Paul D. Siegfried, March 9, 1983, Box 4, folder—Maurice N. Nessen, Weinfeld Papers.

152. *A Judicious Life*, 108.

153. Robert W. Werner to Edward Weinfeld, October 14, 1987; Edward Weinfeld to Robert W. Werner, October 19, 1987, both in Box 50, folder—Robert W. Werner, Weinfeld Papers.

154. *A Judicious Life*, 129

155. *Id.*, 127–29.

156. *Included Out*, 129.

NOTES TO CHAPTER 11

1. *See* 28 U.S.C. § 1407.

2. Earl Warren to Edward Weinfeld, May 16, 1968; Warren E. Burger to John M. Wisdom, November 29, 1976, both in Box 34, folder 1, Weinfeld Papers.

3. John M. Wisdom to All Members of the Multidistrict Litigation Panel, November 20, 1978, Box 34, folder 1, Weinfeld Papers.

4. *See In re IBM Peripheral EDP Devices Antitrust Litigation*, 407 F. Supp. 254 (Jud. Pan. Mult. Lit. 1976); *In re Professional Hockey Antitrust Litigation*, 369 F. Supp. 1119 (Jud. Pan. Mult. Lit. 1974). Both opinions are included in volumes of other Weinfeld opinions and thus appear to have been authored by the judge, even though they are official per curiam opinions. See also the cases cited in notes 14–16 below.

5. John Wisdom to Warren E. Burger, October 26, 1978, Box 34, folder 1, Weinfeld Papers.

6. *See* Earl Warren to Edward Weinfeld, May 16, 1968; Warren E. Berger to John M. Wisdom, November 29, 1976, both in Box 34, folder 1, Weinfeld Papers.

7. John Minor Wisdom to Warren E. Berger, December 8, 1976, Box 34, folder 1, Weinfeld Papers.

8. Warren E. Berger to John M. Wisdom, November 29, 1976, Box 34, folder 1, Weinfeld Papers.

9. John Wisdom to Tom C. Clark, February 28, 1977, Box 34, folder 1, Weinfeld Papers.

10. John Wisdom to Warren E. Berger, October 26, 1978, Box 34, folder 1, Weinfeld Papers.

11. Warren Berger to John Minor Wisdom, November 3, 1978, Box 34, folder 2, Weinfeld Papers.

12. Warren Berger to Edward Weinfeld, November 15, 1978; Edward Weinfeld to Warren E. Berger, November 17, 1978, both in Box 34, folder 2, Weinfeld Papers.

13. Edward Weinfeld to the Members of the Judicial Panel on Multidistrict Litigation, November 21, 1978, Box 34, folder 2, Weinfeld Papers.

14. *See In re Uranium Industry Antitrust Litigation*, 458 F. Supp. 1223, 1232 (Jud. Panel Mult. Lit. 1978); *In re Yarn Processing Patent Validity Litigation*, 341 F. Supp. 376, 384 (Jud. Pan. Mult. Lit. 1972).

15. See *In re Falstaff Brewing Corp. Antitrust Litigation*, 434 F. Supp. 1225, 1231 (Jud. Pan. Mult. Lit. 1977).

16. See *In re Petroleum Products Antitrust Litigation*, 407 F. Supp, 249, 252 (Jud. Pan. Mult. Lit. 1976); *In re Caesar's Palace Securities Litigation*, 385 F.

Supp. 1256, 1259 (Jud. Pan. Mult. Lit. 1974); *In re Republic National-Realty Equities Securities Litigation*, 382 F. Supp. 1403, 1407 (Jud. Pan. Mult. Lit. 1974); *In re Professional Hockey Antitrust Litigation*, 369 F. Supp. 1117, 1118 (Jud. Pan. Mult. Lit. 1974); *In re National Student Marketing Litigation*, 368 F. Supp. 1311, 1319 (Jud. Pan. Mult. Lit. 1973)

17. Edward Weinfeld to Edith Lehman, February 2, 1968, Box 27, folder 1, Weinfeld Papers.

18. *See* Minutes of Board of Trustees of Law Center Foundation, September 21, 1967, Office of the Dean, New York University School of Law, New York, N.Y.; Norman Redlich to Lillian Weinfeld, March 3, 1988, Box 37, Weinfeld Papers; Minutes of a Meeting of the Board of Trustees of New York University, November 17, 1975, 1, Box 48, Weinfeld Papers.

19. *See* Docket for the Meeting of the Board of Trustees of New York University, October 18, 1976, Box 48, Weinfeld Papers.

20. Norman Redlich to Lillian Weinfeld, March 3, 1988, Box 37, Weinfeld Papers.

21. *See* William E. Nelson to Edward Weinfeld, September 21, 1977, Box 4, folder—William E. Nelson.

22. Norman Redlich to Lillian Weinfeld, March 3, 1988, Box 37, Weinfeld Papers.

23. *Id.*

24. Author's telephone conversations with Norman Redlich, May 1 and May 2, 2001.

25. Norman Redlich to Lillian Weinfeld, March 3, 1988, Box 37, Weinfeld Papers.

26. Statement of Judge Edward Weinfeld on H.R. 8200 before the Subcommittee on Civil and Constitutional Rights, Committee on the Judiciary, House of Representatives, December 13, 1977, Box 21, Weinfeld Papers.

27. Statement of Edward Weinfeld, U.S. District Judge, Southern District of New York; Chairman, Committee on Bankruptcy Administration, Judicial Conference of the United States, on Senate Joint Resolution 100, July 16, 1968, Box 21, Weinfeld Papers.

28. *Id.*, 63.

29. *Id.*

30. *See* Joseph G. M. Browne, *Bankruptcy Law and Procedure* (Brooklyn, N.Y.: privately published, 1930), 36; Charles Warren, *Bankruptcy in United States History* (Cambridge, Mass.: Harvard University Press, 1935), 143.

31. Memorandum of the National Bankruptcy Conference re: Senate Bill 2266, November 28, 1977, 3, Box 21, Weinfeld Papers; Communication from the Executive Director, Commission on the Bankruptcy Laws of the United States, Transmitting a Report of the Commission on the Bankruptcy Laws of the United States, July 1973, part 2, 17, Box 21, Weinfeld Papers.

32. Marginal comments to Memorandum of the National Bankruptcy Conference re: Senate Bill 2266, November 28, 1977, 3, Box 21, Weinfeld Papers; Commission on the Bankruptcy Laws of the United States, Minutes of Meeting of May 17–19, 1973, 3, Box 21, Weinfeld Papers.

33. Separate Statement of Judge Edward Weinfeld, in Communication from the Executive Director, Commission on the Bankruptcy Laws of the United States, Transmitting a Report of the Commission on the Bankruptcy Laws of the United States, July 1973, part 1, 299, Box 21, Weinfeld Papers.

34. Wesley E. Brown, Legislation to Revise the Bankruptcy Laws, 2, in Judicial Conference ad Hoc Committee on Bankruptcy Legislation: Correspondence, Box 20, Weinfeld Papers; Ruggero J. Aldisert, Expanded Bankruptcy Court Jurisdiction and the Article III Solution, May 25, 1977, i, Box 21, Weinfeld Papers.

35. Memorandum of James L. Oakes to Irving R. Kaufman re: Bankruptcy Act Amendments, October 13, 1978, Box 20, Weinfeld Papers.

36. Memo of Chief Judge MacMahon to Judges Weinfeld, Motley, Pollack, and Lasker re: Bar Harbor Resolution, January 15, 1982; Memo of Judge Weinfeld to Chief Judge MacMahon re: Bar Harbor Resolution, January 21, 1982, both in Box 39, Folder 3, Weinfeld Papers.

37. Whitney North Seymour, Jr., to Edward Weinfeld, November 16, 1972, Box 41, folder 8, Weinfeld Papers; Pierre Leval to Edward Weinfeld, May 10, 1977, Box 40, folder 11, Weinfeld Papers.

38. *See* Leonard B. Sand, John S. Siffert, Walter P. Loughlin and Steven A. Reiss eds., *Modern Federal Jury Instructions*, vol. 1 (Newark, N.J.: Lexis Nexis, 2002), vii.

39. Steven Brill, "The Law: Benching Bad Judges, Should It Be Easier Than It Is to Remove Federal Judges?" *Esquire*, April 10, 1979, 20. *See* Irving Ben Cooper to Edward Weinfeld, March 27, 1979, Box 38, folder 2, Weinfeld Papers.

40. Samuel M. Rosenstein to Edward Weinfeld, May 29, 1980; Edward Weinfeld to Samuel M. Rosenstein, June 9, 1980, both in Box 38, folder 8, Weinfeld Papers.

41. Henry J. Friendly, "Edward Weinfeld: The Ideal Judge," *New York University Law Review* 50 (1975): 977.

42. Irving Mitchell Felt to Edward Weinfeld, May 22, [no year], Box 39, folder 12, Weinfeld Papers.

43. *See* Burton A. Zorn to Edward Weinfeld, May 4, 1966, Box 41, folder 18, Weinfeld Papers.

44. Lily Marcus to Edward Weinfeld, June 8, 1961, Box 40, folder 14, Weinfeld Papers.

45. Richard B. Menin to Edward Weinfeld, August 4, 1972, Box 40, folder 14, Weinfeld Papers.

46. *See* Geoffrey David Menin to Edward Weinfeld, August 21, 1972; Geoffrey David Menin to Edward Weinfeld, September 5, 1972, both in Box 40, folder 14, Weinfeld Papers.

47. *See* Howard Greenberger to Edward Weinfeld, July 22, 1968, Box 48, Weinfeld Papers.

48. *See*, e.g., Edward Weinfeld to Robert D. Childres, January 12, 1965, Box 41, folder 3, Weinfeld Papers (supporting admission of a nephew's son).

49. *Id.*

50. *See* John Lichtenberg to Edward Weinfeld, November 4, 1959; undated notes in Edward Weinfeld's handwriting, apparently of a telephone conversation, both in Box 40, folder 11, Weinfeld Papers.

51. Edward Weinfeld to John Lichtenberg, March 28, 1960, Box 40, folder 11, Weinfeld Papers.

52. Sidney Posner to Edward Weinfeld, July 23, 1975; Edward Weinfeld to Sidney Posner, July 28, 1975, both in Box 41, folder 3, Weinfeld Papers.

NOTE TO CHAPTER 12

1. Author's interview with Ann Schulman, May 21, 2003.

2. *See* Presidential Citation, 1965; certificate of Alumni Meritorious Service Award, 1966; Doctorate of Laws, 1969, all in Box 55, Weinfeld Papers; *New York University Law Review* 50 (1975): 975–1069; certificate of dedication of 1980 volume of *Annual Survey of American Law*; certificate re Judge Edward Weinfeld Professorship, 1983, both in Box 54, Weinfeld Papers; Program for Dedication of Edward Weinfeld Seminar Room, 1977, Box 16, Weinfeld Papers.

3. Certificate re Learned Hand Medal, 1973; certificate re Herbert Lincoln Harley Award, 1977; certificate re Samuel Gates Award, 1984; certificate re Fordham-Stein Award, 1984; certificate re Riot Relief Fund Medal, 1985; certificate of membership in Association of the Bar of the City of New York, 1985; certificate re Gold Medal Award, 1985, all in Box 22, Weinfeld Papers; LaGuardia Medal, 1987, Box 55, Weinfeld Papers.

4. "A Lifetime of Law and Quiet Diligence for Judge Weinfeld," *New York Times*, August 18, 1985, 38.

5. Edward Weinfeld to Mrs. Learned Hand, August 21, 1961; Thank You Card from Frances Hand to Edward Weinfeld, undated, both in Box 40, folder 2, Weinfeld Papers.

6. Edward Weinfeld to Joseph L. Eichler, October 16, 1961; Edward Weinfeld to Joseph L. Eichler, October 24, 1961; Edward Weinfeld to Joseph L. Eichler, November 6, 1961, all in Box 3, folder—Joseph L. Eichler, Weinfeld Papers.

7. Edward Weinfeld to Joseph L. Eichler, December 23, 1963, Box 3, folder—Joseph L. Eichler, Weinfeld Papers.

8. *See* "Lehman Mourners Led by President," *New York Herald Tribune,* December 9, 1963, 1.

9. Funeral Service for Hon. Herbert H. Lehman, December 8, 1963, 4, 7–8, Box 27, Weinfeld Papers.

10. Remarks of Judge Edward Weinfeld at services for Solomon I. Sklar, October 9, 1964, 1, 4, Box 25, folder 10, Weinfeld Papers.

11. Author's conversation with Ann Schulman, May 21, 2003.

12. Funeral service for Hilda Altschul Master delivered by Judge Edward Weinfeld, February 1, 1967, Box 25, folder 11, Weinfeld Papers.

13. Edward Weinfeld to Charles Poletti, February 29, 1968, Box 25, folder 1, Weinfeld Papers.

14. Fay Zorn to Edward Weinfeld, March 15, 1968; Eulogy Delivered by Edward Weinfeld for Burton A. Zorn, February 25, 1968, both in Box 25, folder 1, Weinfeld Papers.

15. Draft of Zorn Eulogy Marked "[Moscow]", Box 25, folder 1, Weinfeld Papers.

16. "In Memoriam: Honorable William B. Herlands," December 17, 1969, Box 25, folder 2, Weinfeld Papers.

17. Eulogy delivered by Edward Weinfeld for James Felt, March 7, 1971, 1–2, Box 25, folder 3, Weinfeld Papers.

18. Stephen Botein Memorial, November 9, 1986, 3, in Box 25, folder 4, Weinfeld Papers.

19. Amram Scheinfeld to Edward Weinfeld, February 11, 1974; Daniel P. Levitt to Edward Weinfeld, February 7, 1974; Benjamin S. Arnstein to Edward Weinfeld, February 7, 1974; Sidney Sugarman to Edward Weinfeld, February 5, 1974, all in Box 38, folder 1, Weinfeld Papers.

20. Botein Memorial, the Association of the Bar of the City of New York, May 6, 1974, 2, 17, 19, Box 38, folder 1, Weinfeld Papers.

21. Edward Weinfeld to Daniel P. Levitt, February 12, 1974; Edward Weinfeld to Amram Scheinfeld, February 14, 1974, both in Box 38, folder 1, Weinfeld Papers. *Accord,* Edward Weinfeld to Benjamin S. Arnstein, February 11, 1974; Edward Weinfeld to Harold J. Gallagher, May 9, 1974, both in Box 38, folder 1, Weinfeld Papers.

22. Robert B. McKay to Mrs. Bernard Botein, February 20, 1974; Michael Botein to Uncle Eddy, February 27, 1974, both in Box 38, folder 1, Weinfeld Papers.

23. Eulogy by the Honorable Edward Weinfeld on Behalf of Edith Altschul Lehman, March 10, 1976, 1, 2, 17, Box 26, Weinfeld Papers.

24. Richard Kaye Korn Eulogy, April 29, 1981, 1; Dr. Norman Simon Eulogy, March 26, 1985, 2; Justine Wise Polier Eulogy, November 11, 1987, 4; Draft of Tribute to Mike Greene, January 19, 1984; Proceedings *In Memoriam:*

Honorable Edward J. Dimock, September 9, 1986, 42, all in Box 25, folders 5–9, Weinfeld Papers.

25. Edward Weinfeld to Mrs. Walter R. Mansfield, January 7, 1987, Box 38, folder 5, Weinfeld Papers.

26. Bernard Friedman, M.D., to To Whom It May Concern, November 29, 1984, Box 2, Weinfeld Papers.

27. Author's telephone conversation with Ann Schulman, March 20, 2001.

28. Author's conversation with Ann Schulman, May 21, 2003.

29. Author's conversation with Edward Weinfeld, 1987.

30. Edward Weinfeld to Mrs. Herbert Pinsley, October 23, 1986, Box 38, folder 5, Weinfeld Papers.

31. Abraham Wolf to Edward Weinfeld, May 20, 1986, Box 38, folder 5, Weinfeld Papers.

32. Abraham Wolf to Edward Weinfeld, January 12, 1987, Box 41, folder 14, Weinfeld Papers.

33. *See* Sympathy Note from Edward Weinfeld to Mr. and Mrs. Len Wolf, August 31, 1987, Box 38, folder 5, Weinfeld Papers.

34. Stephen Botein Memorial, November 9, 1986, 5; Edward Weinfeld to Sheila Botein, November 18, 1986, both in Box 25, folder 4, Weinfeld Papers.

35. Edward Weinfeld to the Members of the Friendly Family, March 12, 1986, Box 38, folder 5, Weinfeld Papers.

36. Edward Weinfeld to Mrs. Paul Mogin, March 24, 1986, Box 10, Weinfeld Papers.

37. Author's conversation with Edward Weinfeld, 1986.

38. Joan Friendly Goodman to Paul Gewirtz, July 24, 1987 (correcting statements in Paul Gewirtz, "Commentary: A Lawyer's Death," *Harvard Law Review* 100 (1987): 2053) (letter in possession of author); author's telephone interview with Joan Goodman, June 26, 2003.

39. Pat Mogin to Edward Weinfeld, March 21, 1986, Box 10, Weinfeld Papers.

40. Author's conversation with Edward Weinfeld during hospital visit, December 1987.

41. Funeral Service for Hon. Herbert H. Lehman, December 8, 1963, 4, Box 27, folder 5, Weinfeld Papers.

42. *Edward Weinfeld: A Judicious Life* (New York: Federal Bar Foundation, 1998), 129.

43. The author was that former clerk.

44. *A Judicious Life,* 91.

45. *Id.,* 127.

NOTES TO CHAPTER 13

1. "1,800 Attend Funeral Service for Weinfeld," *New York Law Journal*, January 20, 1988, 1.

2. Remarks of Morris E. Lasker, Judge Edward Weinfeld, 1901–1988, Service at Temple Emanu-El, New York City on Tuesday, January 19, 1988, Box 25, Weinfeld Papers.

3. Remarks of Martin Lipton, Judge Edward Weinfeld, 1901–1988, Service at Temple Emanu-El, New York City on Tuesday, January 19, 1988, Box 25, Weinfeld Papers.

4. Remarks of Alvin H. Schulman, Judge Edward Weinfeld, 1901–1988, Service at Temple Emanu-El, New York City on Tuesday, January 19, 1988, Box 25, Weinfeld Papers.

5. Remarks of Amy W. Schulman, Judge Edward Weinfeld, 1901–1988, Service at Temple Emanu-El, New York City on Tuesday, January 19, 1988, Box 25, Weinfeld Papers.

6. "In Memoriam: Honorable Edward Weinfeld," 693 F. Supp. lxx, lxxii, lxxiv, lxxx (1988).

7. Remarks of Martin Lipton, Judge Edward Weinfeld, 1901–1988, Service at Temple Emanu-El, New York City on Tuesday, January 19, 1988, Box 25, Weinfeld Papers.

8. See John W. Dean, *The Rehnquist Choice: The Untold Story of the Nixon Appointment That Redefined the Supreme Court* (New York: Free Press, 2001), 1–28.

9. Paul Freund, "Proceedings in Memory of Mr. Justice Brandeis," 317 U.S. xxx (1942).

10. *See* Philippa Strum, *Louis D. Brandeis: Justice for the People* (Cambridge, Mass.: Harvard University Press, 1984), xii.

11. 208 U.S. 412 (1908).

12. *See generally* Gerald N. Rosenberg, *The Hollow Hope: Can Courts Bring About Social Change* (Chicago: University of Chicago Press, 1991).

13. *Edward Weinfeld: A Judicious Life* (New York: Federal Bar Foundation, 1998), 112–13.

14. *Id.*, 112–13.

15. Lon L. Fuller, "The Forms and Limits of Adjudication," *Harvard Law Review* 93 (1978): 353.

Index

Abortion rights, 165–66
Abrams, Charles, 91
Aleinikoff, T. Alexander, 181
American Law Institute, 178
Animal rights, 168–69
Anti-Semitism, 3, 10–11, 22, 171–72, 179
Antitrust, 142–43
Arraignment, of persons charged with crime, 87–88, 141–42, 185
Article III judge, 132, 173
Artloom Corp. v. Robbins Bros., Inc., 47–48
Assimilation, of Catholic and Jewish immigrants, 2–3, 18–19
Association of the Bar of the City of New York, honorary membership in, 208
Austrian v. Williams, 140–41, 149.

Baker, Newton D., 129
Bankruptcy, 52–43, 198–204
Bankruptcy Act of 1898, 200
Bankruptcy Administration Committee of the Judicial Conference, 194, 198–99
Bankruptcy judges, 201–3
Bankruptcy Laws, Commission on the, 199–204
Bankruptcy referees, 201–3
Berger, Irving, 181
Bernstein v. Fan & Bill's, Inc., 48–49
Bethlehem Steel Corp., United States v., 142–44

Bittker, Boris, 175–77
Black, Hugo, 131
Botein, Bernard, 98–100, 107, 213–14, 216
Botein, Stephen, 216–17
Boyden, Frederick B., 175
Bradley, Margaret, 18–20
Brandeis, Louis D., 130–31, 170, 224–25; appointment of, to Supreme Court, 22
Brennan, William J., 1, 4–5, 209
Bryant, William Cullen, 130
Burger, Warren, 195–97, 205
Burke, Philomena A., 182
Burlich, United States v., 160
Burton, Richard, 135
Business, nontreatment of law as, 33, 42
Butterick case, 55

Calamandrei, Piero, 127–28
Cancer, Weinfeld's bouts with, 193, 215, 218–20
Cardozo, Benjamin N., 128; Weinfeld compared to, 209, 221
Carribean, 71
Casella, William P., 182
Celler, Emanuel, 119–20
Chasen, Jerry S., 182
Chenkin v. Bellevue Hospital Center, New York City Health & Hospitals Corp., 167
Childhood, of Edward Weinfeld, 17–18

Churchill, Winston, 114
Clare, United States v., 160
Clayton Act, 142
Cohen, Al, 59
Cohen, Stanley, 149
Columbia Law School, 175, 178
Commonplace book, 123–31
Communism, 161–62
Compassion, on part of Weinfeld, 68, 173
Conflict, attitude toward, 74–75, 152, 173
Constitutional convention, of New York, in 1938, 83–90
Continental Bank & Trust Co. v. 150 Broadway Building Corp., 99
Cooper, Irving Ben, 204–4
Corporate litigation, 54–45
Cristoforo Colombo, 70
Crosby, Bing, 70

Death, Weinfeld's attitude toward, 210–20
Deference, to administrative agencies, 147–48
DeParias, United States v., 153
Deportation, 153
Deuteronomy, 126
Dewey, Thomas E., 91, 94–95, 118
DeWitt Clinton High School, 8, 23–24
Dignity, in Weinfeld's courtroom, 133–35
Dimock, Edward, 214
Diplomatic immunity, 149–40
Discretion, 151–44
District of Columbia Circuit Court of Appeals, Weinfeld's hesitancy to cite, 169
Divorce litigation, handled by Weinfeld as lawyer, 33–41
Dolen, Irving, 76
Dubin v. Shander, 52
Due process, 157–68
Dulles, John Foster, 118
Dying declaration, 44

Eichler, Joseph, 56, 59, 97–98
Eminent domain, 84
Entertaining, 62
Equality: in employment, 148–49; as goal of working-class New York, 8; between rich and poor in court, 126–27, 135–36; as value of Weinfeld, 4, 42, 157–48, 166, 170–71
Erie R.R. v. Tompkins, 141
Exclusionary rule, 88, 164

Factual analysis by Weinfeld: as judge, 139–41, 184–88, 225; as litigator, 32, 45, 225
Fairness, Weinfeld's quest for, 188–90
Fees, 47, 99. *See also* Income from law practice
Feinberg, Abe, 120–21
Feinberg, Wilfred, 120–21, 222–23
Felt, Irving, 106, 205
Felt, James, 212–13
Feminism, 4. *See also* Women
Ferguson, United States v., 137–39, 190–91
Field v. Rice, 54
First Amendment rights, 164–65
Fordham-Stein Award, 208
Forte di Marme, 71
Franke, Arthur, 77
Frankfurter, Felix, 129, 130
Franklin, Benjamin, 129
Freiwald, Belmont, 59
Freud, Sigmund, 74, 190–91
Friendly, Henry J., 109–10, 120, 147–48, 182, 205; death of, 217-19

Garfinkel, Barry, 177–78, 179
Gellert v. Gellert, 33–35
Gillman, Nina, 182
Giuliani, Rudolph, 141, 185
Goldberg, Arthur J., 119
Goldberg, People v., 44
Gorlice, 8–9, 11–12, 16
Grand jury, 160–61

Greater Blouse, Skirt & Neckwear
Contractors Assn., United States v.,
152–43
Greenberg, Sam, 59
Greene, Myron, 214
Gstaad, 70–71
Gurfein, Murray, 196–97

Hall v. Lefkowitz, 165–66
Hand, Augustus N., 127
Hand, Learned, 2, 4–4, 107–9, 127;
compared to Weinfeld, 209; death
of, 209–10
Handschu v. Special Services Division,
163–64
Harlan, John M., 108
Harper, Fowler V., 177
Hartstein, Ben, 24–25, 31, 175
Harvard Law School, 179
Henderson, Skitch, 135–36
Henry Friendly Medal, 178, 220
Henry Street Settlement, Lillian Wein-
feld's work in, 64
Herbert Lincoln Harley Award, 208
Herlands, William B., 212
Holmes, Oliver Wendell, 127
Holocaust, 88–89
Horn and Hardart Cafeteria, 14
Housing commissioner, 91–95
Housing policy, 85–86, 91
Hughes, Charles Evans, 127, 129
Human rights, 87–89
Human Rights Watch, 186–87
Hurley, Janet, 182

Illnesses, 207–8, 215, 218–20
Immigration and Naturalization Ser-
vice, 158–60, 167
Immigration law, 150, 158–60
Immunity from prosecution, 168
Impartiality, by Weinfeld, 136–38.
See also Fairness, Weinfeld's quest
for
Income from law practice, 53–46. See
also Fees
Indictments, multiple charges in, 163

Israel, 71
Ives, Irving, 117

Jewish Defense League, 149
Johnson, Lyndon, 119–20, 210
Joint Legislative Committee to Investi-
gate Bondholders and Shareholders
Committees, 78–83
Jones, Harry W., 178
J. Pratt Carroll, Inc. v. Murphy Fruit
Co., 31–32
Judicial style, of Edward Weinfeld,
4–4, 133–45, 169–73, 223–27
Jurors, in Weinfeld's courtroom,
133–34

Kahaner, Elliott, 135
Kaplan, United States v., 153–44
Kennedy, Robert F., 119–20
Keogh, James Vincent, 135
Koeltl, John G., 182
Korn, Richard, 214
Kraut, Alexander, 77–78
Kurland, Philip, 127

Labor, as commodity, 83
LaGuardia, Fiorello, 89
LaGuardia Medal, 208
Lamont, United States v., 161–62
Law firm partners, Weinfeld law
clerks as, 182, 187–88
Law professors, Weinfeld law clerks
as, 180
Learned Hand Medal, 208
Ledesma-Valdes v. Sava, 167
Lefkowitz, Louis, 100–101
Legal process school, 5
Legal realism, 156
Lehman, Edith A., 70, 102, 105–6,
119, 214
Lehman, Herbert H., 90–91, 93, 95,
102–7, 119, 121, 170; and ap-
pointment of Weinfeld to bench,
114–16, 122–23; death of, 210–11
Leik, People v., 46, 77
Lelesz, 8, 11, 16

Leval, Pierre, 106, 204
Leviticus, 126
Levitt, Daniel P., 179–80
Liberalism, of Weinfeld, 169–73
Lichtenberg, John, 106
Limitations, statute of, 140–41
Lipton, Martin, 178–79
Litigation strategy, 32, 39–41, 45–46
Loder v. Alexander Hamilton Institute, 53–44
London, 71
Longchamps, 14, 62
Long Island, 71
Lowenstein v. Lowenstein, 37–44
Lower East Side, 1, 7–12, 14–16, 18, 26, 59, 70; anti-Semitism on, 3,10–11; as home for Jewish immigrants, 11; Lillian Weinfeld's activities on, 62–65; poverty of, 3, 9–10
Lower East Side Neighborhoods Association, 64–65

MacMahon, Lloyd, 204
Mahler v. Oishei, 99
Manhattan. *See* Lower East Side
Manny Wolf's Restaurant, 14, 62
Mantle, Mickey, 69, 135
Manufacturers Trust Company, 80, 82
Marriage, to Lillian Stoll, 60
Marshall, John, 127
Marshall, Thurgood, 119
Master, Hilda Altschul, 211
McCarthy, Joseph, 161–62
McDougal, Myres S., 177
Michaels, Steven, 181
Mistakes, acknowledgment of, 57
Mosberg v. Trattner, 54
Moscow, Warren, 111
Moses, 126
Muller v. Oregon, 224
Multidistrict Litigation Panel, 194–97
Municipal Cafeteria, 14

Nachman, David, 73
National Football League, 69

National Hotel Management Corporation, 79–80
National Labor Relations Board, 160–61
Nessen, Maurice, 175–77
Neuwirth, Henry C., 23
Newark, 17, 20
New Deal, 4, 190
New York Giants, 69, 135
New York State Bar Association, 208
New York Times, article about Weinfeld's thirty-five years on bench, 209
New York University, awards from, 208; law clerks from, 178, 179; Weinfeld as student at, 25–28, 31; as trustee for, 197–98
Nixon, Richard, 223
Nolle prosequi, 152–53
Norall, Christopher, 182

Oakes, James L., 203
O'Dwyer, William, 95
Old Testament, 126, 224

Palm Beach, 71
Paris, 71
Peel v. Cohen, 78
Penn Central merger, 147–48
Pennell, William B., 179–80
Perfection, Weinfeld's quest for, 188, 221
Personal relationship with clients, 42–44, 46–47
Phi Sigma Delta, 26–28, 59
Plea bargaining, 144–47
Plotz, Robert L., 182
Poletti, Charles, 90–91, 101–2
Police misconduct, 163–64
Policy choice, Weinfeld's rejection of, 156–47
Polier, Justine Wise, 176, 214
Polier, Shad, 176
Pomerantz, Mark, 137–38, 181, 190–91

Pornography, 46, 150–41. *See also* First Amendment rights
Potocki, Genevieve, 77
Potofsky, Jacob, 70
Precedent, approach toward, as litigator, 32
Pretrial discovery, 47–49
Printz, People v., 44–45
Promptness, of Edward Weinfeld, 20
Proportional representation, 89–90, 121
P.S. 188, 18
Publicity, for litigation, 34–35, 44–45

Quinn, Vincent, 149

Reagan, Ronald, 169–70
Recusal, 137–39, 190–91
Red Cross, Lillian Weinfeld's work in, 62–64
Religion, inquiries about, 161
Roe v. Wade, 169
Roosevelt, Eleanor, 64
Roosevelt, Franklin D., 114
Roosevelt, Theodore, 19
Rosenstein, Samuel M., 205
Roth, Kenneth T., 181
Rothman, Bernard, 106

Sampson, Frank, 117
Samuel E. Gates Award, 208
Schulman, Amy, 73
Seabury Commission, 77
Searches and seizures, 88, 167
Securities regulation, 81–82
Selective Service System, 159–60
Seligson, Charles, 178
Sellman v. Baruch College of the City University of New York, 167–68
Senatorial courtesy, 115, 118–20, 122–23
Sex acts, unnatural, 40–41, 53–44
Shattuck, John H.F., 181
Shorthand, 114
Simon, Norman, 214

Skadden, Arps, Slate, Meagher & Flom, 177
Sklar, Sol, 211
Smith, Alfred E., 85
Social drinking: of Edward Weinfeld, 29–30; of Lillian Weinfeld, 73
Southern District of New York, 2
States Marine Lines, United States v., 168–69
Statutory interpretation, 149–41
Steingut, Irwin, 77–78
Stevenson, Adlai, Lillian Weinfeld's work in 1952 campaign of, 64
Stonehill Communications, Inc. v. Martuge, 150
Streit, Saul S., 78–81
Suffern, Stephen J., 181
Supreme Court clerks, Weinfeld law clerks as, 180

Taber, Janet, 182
Taft-Hartley Act, 160
Tammany Hall, 76–78, 83, 89–91, 115–17, 121
Taylor, Elizabeth, 135
Tekulsky, Joseph, 175
Temple Emanu-El, 1
Toney, United States v., 141–42, 184–85
Travel, 70–72
Truman, Harry S., 116, 122–24
Tuerkheimer, Frank, 12, 181
Tulin, Stephen Wise, 176–77

Udko v. Udko, 36–37
Ullman, In re, 168
Underdogs, representation of, 49–41
United Nations, 149–40
United States ex rel. Belfrage v. Shaughnessy, 162
United States ex rel. Casanova v. Fitzpatrick, 149–40
United States ex rel. Elksnis v. Gilligan, 144–47, 192
United States ex rel. Kusman v. District Director of Immigration and

United States ex rel. (Continued)
Naturalization at Port of New
York, 158–49
United States ex rel. Lee Till Seem v.
Shaughnessy, 158
University of California Regents v.
Bakke, 169
University of Pennsylvania School of
Law, 179

Vanderbilt, Arthur T., 128
Vollrath, Marie, 112
Vulcan Society v. Civil Service Com-
mission, 148

Wachtell, Lipton, Rosen & Katz,
179
Wagio Kong Tjauw Wong v.
Esperdy, 150
Wagner, Robert F., 90–91, 96,
115–18, 122
Wagner, Robert F., Jr., 91, 115–18
Waldman, Henry, 28, 106
Walking, by Weinfeld, 7–8, 12–14,
24
Warren, Earl, 195, 210
Warren, Edward H., 129
Warren Court, 4, 223.

Wechsler, Herbert, 91, 175
Weinfeld, Abraham, 3, 9, children
of, by first marriage, 9, death of,
60

Weinfeld, Ann, 60, 65–66, 118–19;
divorce, 67; indebtedness, 67; trip
to visit roommate, 68–69
Weinfeld, Bertha, 11, 60–61
Weinfeld, Fern, 60, 65–66, 68, 73–74;
boyfriends, 66; marriage, 66–67
Weinfeld, Isadore, 11, 23
Weinfeld, Fanny (née Singer), 11,
death of, 60
Weinfeld, Lillian (née Stoll), 58–74,
211, 218
Weinfeld, Morris, 11, 21; distance
from Edward, 19; partnership
with, 31, 33
Werner, Robert W., 181
Wilson, United States v., 163.
Wilson, Woodrow, 20–23, 121, 129,
170
Wisdom, John Minor, 196–97
Wise, Steven, 22–23, 176
Wolf, Abe, 216
Women: courtroom demonstration by,
165; representation of, 35, 42,
50–41
Work practices with law clerks, 192
Writing skills, of Edward Weinfeld,
19–20, 41, 139–47
Wyzanski, Charles, 113, 120

Yale Law School, 175–77, 205
Younger, Judith T., 179–80

Zorn, Burt, 106, 205, 212

About the Author

After graduating from New York University School of Law, William E. Nelson served as law clerk to Judge Edward Weinfeld during 1965–1966. He later was law clerk to Supreme Court Justice Byron R. White and received a Ph.D. in American history from Harvard University. He has taught at Harvard, the University of Pennsylvania, and Yale and is currently Edward Weinfeld Professor of Law at New York University.